The Face of the Crowd

THE FACE OF THE CROWD

Studies in Revolution, Ideology and Popular Protest

Selected Essays of George Rudé

Edited and Introduced by
Harvey J. Kaye

Humanities Press International, Inc.
Atlantic Highlands, NJ

First published in 1988 in the United States of America by
Humanities Press International, Inc.,
Atlantic Highlands, NJ 07716

Library of Congress Cataloging-in-Publication Data
Rudé, George E.F.
   The face of the crowd: studies in revolution, ideology and
popular protest: selected essays of George Rudé/ edited by Harvey
J. Kaye.
      p.   cm.
   ISBN 0-391-03589-4
   1. Crowds. 2. Ideology. 3. Revolutions. 4. Riots—History—19th
century. 5. Crime and criminals—History—19th century. 6. Social
movements—History—19th century. I. Kaye. Harvey J. II. Title.
HM 281.R78 1988
302.3'3—dc 19   88-13033
                                                                     CIP

Printed in Great Britain

For Doreen
Lorna, Rhiannon, and Fiona

Contents

Editor's Preface   ix
Acknowledgements   xi

Introduction: George Rudé, Social Historian (by Harvey J. Kaye)   1

Part I Studies in History and Revolution
1. Marxism and History   43
2. The Changing Face of the Crowd   56
3. The Study of Revolutions   72
4. Interpretations of the French Revolution   80
5. Georges Lefebvre as Historian of Popular
   Urban Protest in the French Revolution   107
6. Robespierre as seen by British Historians   115
7. "Feudalism" and the French Revolution   124
8. The French Revolution and "Participation"   135
9. Why was there no Revolution in England in 1830 or 1848?   148

Part II Popular Protest and Ideology
10. English Rural and Urban Disturbances on the
    Eve of the First Reform Bill, 1830–1831   167
11. Captain Swing and the Uprising of 1830   183
12. European Popular Protest and Ideology on the
    Eve of the French Revolution   189
13. Ideology and Popular Protest   197
14. The Germination of a Revolutionary Ideology
    among the Urban *menu peuple* of 1789   205

Part III Urbanization, Protest and Crime

15. The Growth of Cities and Popular Revolt,
    1750–1850: With Particular Reference to Paris   221
16. Crime, Criminals and Victims in Early
    Nineteenth-Century London   242

    Index   267

Editor's Preface

In October 1986 my family and I had the pleasure of hosting George and Doreen Rudé at our home on the occasion of their visit to the University of Wisconsin-Green Bay. They had flown down from Montreal for George to deliver a lecture on "Ideology and Popular Protest" sponsored by my department, Social Change and Development. The lecture was a tremendous success: George's ideas inspired those in attendance to think anew about the past, and in the discussions and gatherings which followed both he and Doreen charmed faculty and students alike with their wit, verve and imagination. At dinner that evening George explained that he was in the midst of writing a new book titled *The French Revolution after 200 Years* (London, 1988) and much to my surprise and thrill he asked if I would be interested in taking charge of a collection of his articles which he had hoped to see published in volume form but to which he had no time to attend. For his confidence in my ability properly to handle the project, and for providing me the opportunity to edit and introduce this selection of his writings, I thank him most warmly.

Of course, this is actually the second volume of George Rudé's collected essays, the first being *Paris and London in the Eighteenth Century* (1970). However, in contrast to the former book which consisted of articles organized around the single theme of the "pre-industrial" crowd and popular protest, and therefore representing a particular phase of his scholarly career, the present collection includes articles reflecting both the variety of his historical interests and the different phases of his scholarly labours. Thus, not only are there articles treating the eighteenth- and early-nineteenth century crowd and protest in France and England, but also essays dealing with Marxism and historical writing, the historiography of the French Revolution, urbanization and crime, and ideology and popular protest. A few of these essays have never before appeared in English (the translations were provided by George Rudé himself); others have been included in order to make them more accessible to students and scholars; and others were selected to enable the collection better to reflect the variety of George's writings. (It was decided at the outset not to reprint any of the pieces to be found in *Paris and London in the Eighteenth Century*.) It might be said that whereas the articles in parts II and III speak directly to current historical questions, those in part I are of more historiographical interest.

My Introduction to this volume is organized thematically rather than chronologically and, therefore, not all of Rudé's writings are treated equally. Although I refer to them in the notes below I would like to call attention here as well to the articles written by Fred Krantz and Hugh Stretton on George Rudé's scholarship, and life and thought, respectively, in introduction to the *Festschrift* in his honour (F. Krantz, ed., *History From Below*, Montreal: Concordia University Press edition, 1985). My own essay has benefited greatly from their surveys and reflections.

In the preparation of this volume I have been helped by a great many friends and colleagues. For their encouragement and advice I must thank Christopher Hill, Ellen Wood, Eric Hobsbawm, Victor Kiernan, Dorothy Thompson, Tony Galt, Craig Lockard, Ron Baba, Dave Jowett, Per Johnsen, Bill Sewell, and Ray Hutchison. But the most important contributions have been the enthusiasm and support provided by Doreen Rudé, my daughters Rhiannon and Fiona, and especially, my partner in all endeavours, Lorna Stewart Kaye.

HJK

Green Bay, WI
March 1988

Acknowledgements

The pieces collected in this volume, except for the Editor's Preface and Introduction, were originally published elsewhere. We are grateful for permission to include them in this collection.

"Marxism and History" appeared in *Marx: A Hundred Years On* (ed. B. Matthews, Lawrence and Wishart, 1983). "The Changing Face of the Crowd" was published in *The Historian's Workshop* (ed. L.P. Curtis, Jr., Alfred A. Knopf, 1970). "The Study of Revolutions" was included in *Historical Papers 1976* (Canadian Historical Association, 1976). "Interpretations of the French Revolution" was a Historical Association Pamphlet (1961; rev. ed. 1971). "Georges Lefebvre as Historian of Popular Urban Protest in the French Revolution" appeared in *Annales historiques de la Révolution Française*, no. 2, 1960. "Robespierre as seen by British Historians" was published in *Actes du Colloque Robespierre* (1965). "Feudalism and the French Revolution" appeared in *The Monash Historical Review*, 1965/66. "The French Revolution and 'Participation'" was a lecture reprinted in *A World in Revolution?: The University Lectures 1970* (ed. E. Kamenka, The Australian National University, 1970). "Why was there no Revolution in England in 1830 or 1848?" was published in *Studien Über Die Revolution* (ed. H.M. Kossok, Akademie-Verlag, Berlin, 1969). "English Rural and Urban Disturbances on the Eve of the First Reform Bill, 1830–1831" appeared in *Past & Present*, no. 37, 1967. "Captain Swing and the Uprising of 1830" was an article for *Tribune* reprinted in *People for the People* (ed. D. Rubinstein, Humanities Press, 1973). "European Popular Protest and Ideology on the Eve of the French Revolution" was published in *Vom Ancien Regime Zur Französischen Revolution* (eds E. Hinrichs, E. Schmitt, and R. Vierhaus, Vandenhoeck & Ruprecht, Gottingen, 1978). "Ideology and Popular Protest" was published in *Historical Reflections/Réflexions Historiques,* no. 3, 1976. "The Germination of a Revolutionary Ideology among the Urban *menu peuple* of 1789" appeared in *Die Französischen Revolution—Zufalliges oder notwendiges Ereignis?* (eds E. Schmitt and R. Riechardt, Oldenbourg Verlag, Munich, 1983). "The Growth of Cities and Popular Revolt, 1750–1850: with particular attention to Paris" was included in *French Government and Society, 1500–1800* (ed. J.F. Bosher, Athlone Press, 1973). And "Crime, Criminals and Victims in Early Nineteenth-Century London" is based on parts of G. Rudé, *Criminal and Victim* (Oxford University Press, 1985).

Introduction
George Rudé, Social Historian

George Rudé has been referred to as the "exiled doyen of our social historians".[1] "Exiled" denotes the fact that he spent almost his entire university teaching career not in Britain but in Australia and Canada. "Doyen" addresses his original and continuing contributions to the field of social history over three and a half decades and the influence which they have had on the development of the discipline. The contributions include: his pioneering researches into the history and sociology of the "pre-industrial crowd" which resulted in such innovative and renowned works as *The Crowd in the French Revolution, Wilkes and Liberty, The Crowd in History, 1730–1848,* and *Paris and London in the Eighteenth Century;*[2] his masterful syntheses of eighteenth-century history like *Revolutionary Europe, 1783–1815* and *Europe in the Eighteenth Century;*[3] and, through these and other books such as *Captain Swing* (co-authored with Eric Hobsbawm), *Protest and Punishment,* and *Criminal and Victim,*[4] his fundamental initiatives and regularly renewed efforts in the development of the approach to the study of the past known as "history from below" or "the bottom up".[5] Moreover, regarding the making of "history from below", not only did Rudé's work on the experience and struggles of the common people of eighteenth-century France and England serve as a model for social historians, but, as will be explained later, it provided an important link between two of the great historical traditions of this century, the "British Marxist historians" and the social historians of the French Revolution.

This essay is offered as an introduction to Rudé's work as a Marxist social historian. In all, he has written fourteen books, edited two others, and authored numerous articles, essays and reviews.[6] These many writings are quite varied (as *partially* indicated by the aforementioned

1

titles); nevertheless, in spite of the many historical subjects pursued, there are certain historical and theoretical concerns which have persisted through the course of Rudé's scholarly career. Thus, rather than attempt to survey his work in geographic, chronological, or subject-specific terms, the present chapter will consider it in terms of the three themes which have characterized and shaped it: identities, ideologies, and histories.[7] "Identities" refers to Rudé's pursuit of "the faces in the crowd" which can be seen as the central problematic not only of his early explorations of the so-called "mob" of the eighteenth century, but equally of his studies of the English agricultural labourers' struggles of the early 1830s and his later writings on crime, protest and punishment in the first half of the nineteenth century. "Ideologies" refers to his persistent endeavour to "put mind back into history" originating in his early writings as attempts to answer the question of the "motivation" of the eighteenth-century crowd but later shifting to a concern for the "ideology of popular protest". And "histories" treats his continuing interest in making sense of the "movement" of history in terms of both comprehending historical periods like "revolutionary Europe" and the "transitional", "pre-industrial" eighteenth century and understanding the role of human action in such, as in his book, *Robespierre*;[8] and it also refers to his own critical thinking about historical practice and its relations to both "politics" and "theory". Thus, following a brief biographical sketch this introductory essay is organized in terms of these three themes.

George Rudé

George Frederick Elliot Rudé[9] was born on February 8, 1910 in Oslo, Norway. His father, Jens, was an engineer and "inventor" and his mother, Amy, was the daughter of an English banker. They lived in Norway until 1919 when they moved to England. His father's work as an inventor produced little money but they did have a small income provided by his mother's family inheritance. Nevertheless, Rudé's education consisted of prep school in Kent, public school at Shrewsbury on a scholarship, and a degree in modern languages at Trinity College, Cambridge. Upon graduating in 1931 he took up a post as a modern languages master at Stow.

Rudé's upbringing and political education must be described as "conservative"; he was not a part of the generation of Cambridge Communists centred around Trinity in the 1930s.[10] However, in 1932, on a six-week vacation trip to the Soviet Union with a friend, Rudé was so impressed with what he found there that he returned to England a "committed communist and anti-fascist". During the next few years he immersed himself in the Marxist classics and in 1935 he joined the British Communist Party. He left Stow soon after and moved to London, intending to work in industry as an organizer for the Party; and though he did work actively with the Party through the 1930s, he did not end up in industry but, once again, in schoolteaching at St. Paul's in London. It was also in these years that he met Doreen de la Hoyde to whom he has been married ever since.

During the Second World War Rudé worked full-time for the London fire service and also remained extremely active with the Party. At the same time he began to study part-time for a first degree in history at the University of London. He has said that his interest in history was kindled by his readings of Marx and Lenin. His commitment to historical studies continued to intensify and grow, and upon receiving the B.A. he went on to complete a Ph.D. at London with a dissertation titled "The Parisian Wage-earning Population and the Insurrectionary Movements of 1789–1791" (1950). These were difficult times for George and Doreen Rudé for he had lost his teaching post in 1949 for politically-related reasons and the chill of the Cold War kept him out of university posts. Nevertheless, he persevered in his researches, first in Paris and later in London, and was eventually able to secure a full-time history post at a comprehensive school in north London.

Although financially difficult, these years were formative both for Rudé's scholarship and for the contributions he was to make to social historiography. Indeed, it is arguable that these were *the* formative years in the making—or *re*-making—of social history, and Rudé himself was a central participant in two of the "groups" fomenting this "from the bottom up". On one side of the English Channel were the "British Marxist historians" who during the years 1946–56 were joined together in the Communist Party Historians' Group of which Rudé was an active member; on the other side of the Channel were the "students" of the French Revolution working under the direction, or influence, of Georges Lefebvre.

Rudé's comrades in the Historians' Group included such scholars as Christopher Hill, Rodney Hilton, Eric Hobsbawm, Victor Kiernan, John Saville, and Dorothy and Edward Thompson. As I have argued in my book, *The British Marxist Historians,* each of these historians was to make outstanding individual contributions to his or her respective domains of historical study, but, also, as a group they were to make important collective contributions to the discipline of social history and historical-social theory more generally.[11] Framed by the historical problematic of the "transition from feudalism to capitalism", their studies—from the medieval to the modern—have been among the most important in the development of history from below. Recovering the history which was made by the lower classes but not written by them, they have approached the past through the grand hypothesis offered by Marx and Engels in *The Communist Manifesto* that "The history of all hitherto existing society is the history of class struggles", thereby developing Marxism as a theory of class determination.

Rudé's work has clearly been bound up with these initiatives and developments, but a few points should be noted here which will be considered further in the course of this essay. First, although "class-struggle analysis" has been a central feature of Rudé's readings and renditions of the historical record, it appears that he has been less willing than his fellow British Marxist historians to read "class" experience and formation in his subjects than they have in theirs. Second, although Rudé's view of the eighteenth century—in both England and France—is shaped by the question of the transition from feudalism to capitalism, and he has himself addressed it (for example, see "Feudalism and the French Revolution" in the present volume), his own work indicates reservations about extant formulations of that process and more often has been rendered in terms of the "ensuing" process of industrialization. Yet, if Rudé's writings evidence a certain reticence about both "class" and "the transition", they do not regarding the need to re-examine the past *from below* and in this effort he has been a foremost protagonist.

It is also noteworthy that Rudé himself made a unique and significant contribution to the historical explorations and deliberations carried out by the Historians' Group. Organized into "period sections", the Group's two major sections were those focussing on the 16th-17th Century and the 19th Century; however, there was a serious gap in the Group's coverage between the period of the English Revolution and that of the Industrial Revolution. As Eric Hobsbawm recalls: "[the eighteenth century was] a no man's land between the Group's two most flourishing sections, we simply had nobody who knew much about it, until George Rudé, a lone explorer, ventured into the period of John Wilkes".[12]

Although in my own work I have stressed and "celebrated" the contributions of the British Marxist historians to the making of history from below, Rudé's own experience reminds us that they were not alone in this effort. Pursuing his research on popular insurrections in Paris during the French Revolution brought Rudé into contact with Georges Lefebvre, who took a special interest in his work, and, also, with Albert Soboul and Richard Cobb. Soboul, Cobb, and Rudé became close friends and through shared archival adventures and labours contributed immensely to each other's scholarship (indeed, Lefebvre referred to them as the "three musketeers").[13] Their "mentor", Lefebvre, was, of course, the great historian of the French Revolution whose work on the peasantry and urban protests dramatically revised the form and content of the historiography of the Revolution of 1789[14] and laid the bases for the writings of Soboul on the Parisian *sans-culottes*,[15] by Cobb on the "revolutionary armies" and *sans-culottes* in the provinces,[16] and by Rudé on the "revolutionary crowds". Thus, scholarly and personal connections were established between the British Marxist historians and these social historians of the French Revolution which must surely have contributed to the development of both social history and history from below. (In fact, as Rudé regularly acknowledges in prefatory remarks to his major works, it was Lefebvre who originally proferred the term "history from below").[17]

Out of his researches in the 1950s, Rudé published a series of important articles on eighteenth-century protests in Paris and London, one of which, "The Gordon Riots: A Study of the Rioters and their Victims" (1956), was awarded the prestigious Alexander Prize.[18] However, he was still unable to secure a post at a British university. When, finally, he was offered such a position in 1960, it was not in Britain but at the University of Adelaide in Australia. Thus, at the age of fifty he commenced his university teaching career *and* his "exile" from England. His emigration to Australia also occasioned his departure from the Communist Party (for although he did not actually "resign" his British membership, neither did he join the Australian Party).[19] From 1960 to 1987 Rudé held professorships at the universities of Adelaide and Flinders in Australia and, for seventeen of those years, at Sir George Williams University in Montreal which in the 1970s was part of a merger creating Concordia University. Also, he has held Visiting Professorships at Columbia University in New York, Stirling University in Scotland (which offered him its foundations chair of history that, had he chosen to accept it, would have ended his "exile" in 1967), the University of Tokyo, and William and Mary in Virginia.

Rudé has been recognized as an outstanding lecturer and teacher, talents cultivated, no doubt, in his many years as a schoolteacher. His former students in Australia have honoured him by establishing the "George Rudé Seminar" held every two years in that country; and in Montreal Rudé was the founding director of the Inter-University Centre for European Studies/Centre Interuniversitaire d'Etudes Européenes, an enterprise established to foster historical and inter-disciplinary exchanges between the English and French branches of Canadian scholarship. Finally, it should be noted that Rudé, having reached the age of sixty-five, was actually a half-time professor at Concordia University from 1975 to 1987, spending more than half of each year back in England, in Sussex; and, as we know, he has continued to produce works of primary importance, like *Ideology and Popular Protest*.[20] His latest book, *The French Revolution after 200 years*,[21] will be published in late 1988. He says it is his last major work—but already he has begun to explore the subject of "terrorism" in historical perspective.

Identities: "The Faces in the Crowd"

In *Europe in the Eighteenth Century* (1972), Rudé observed that "whatever image the eighteenth century has projected, it has never been that of an age of the common man".[22] Indeed, that we are now beginning to comprehend that century in terms of the experience of the "common people" is due in good part to his own original research and writings on the crowds of revolutionary Paris and Hanoverian London. What he succeeded in doing was to reveal, as Asa Briggs phrased it, "the faces in the crowd" and thereby challenged the long-standing assumptions held and assertions made about it by writers on both the Right and Left. More specifically, his accomplishment was to restore to the eighteenth-century crowd—as an historically-specific mode of "popular" collective behaviour—its historical and "political" identity. Essentially, Rudé recognized that merely because the "*menu peuple*" of France and "lower orders" of England were excluded from their respective national political communities, did not mean that they were therefore without social and political interests, grievances, ideas, and aspirations—*or* the means of expressing them.

Rudé's original writings on "the faces in the crowd" include the articles published in the 1950s that were later collected in *Paris and London in the Eighteenth Century*, but his most significant primary works were *The Crowd in the French Revolution* and *Wilkes and Liberty*. Framed by narratives of the "larger" struggles, to which they were so central, these books offer analyses of the actions, social compositions, leaderships, motivations, and legacies of the crowds of Paris and London, respectively. From his very first studies of the French Revolution Rudé confronted the traditional conservative view, originally presented by Edmund Burke in his *Reflections on the Revolution in France* (1790), that the crowd was peopled by "the swinish multitude", an image later surpassed in colour by the French historian, Hippolyte Taine, when he described its participants as "dregs of society", "bandits", "thieves", "savages", "beggars", and "prostitutes".[23] Yet Rudé also had to deal with the picture advanced by the more liberal and "democratic" historians; for example, discussing the work of Jules Michelet, an upholder of the Republican tradition, he notes how he conjured up the revolutionary crowd as "the embodiment of all the popular and Republican virtues", equating it with the spirit of "*le peuple*".[24]

The problem, Rudé observes, is that conservatives and "Republicans" alike had projected their own political aspirations, fantasies and/or fears onto the crowd without having asked the basic historical questions. He attributes this practice not so much to scholarly laziness or lethargy but to the fact that regardless of the antagonistic character of their views they had been arrived at from a shared vantage point: "*from above*—that is, from the elevation of the committee room of the Committee of Public Safety, of the rostrum of the National Assembly or Jacobin Club, or of the columns of the revolutionary press".[25] When Rudé later extended his researches to Hanoverian London he found a distinct but similar set of notions prevailing as to the composition and character of the crowd. For example, Horace Walpole's original assessment of the Gordon rioters as being "chiefly apprentices, convicts, and all kinds of desperadoes" was echoed almost a century and a half later in the work of the historian, Dorothy George, upon which Rudé himself has often relied for historical detail of eighteenth-century London. Dr. George, Rudé states, "too readily assumed that the 'mobs' that rioted were . . . drawn from 'criminal elements', the slum population, or from 'the inhabitants of the dangerous districts . . . who were always ready for pillage'".[26]

His initial excursions into the archives of, first, revolutionary Paris and, later, Hanoverian London convinced Rudé that it was necessary to push further with his re-examinations of their respective crowds and to start by asking the primary questions: "What? Who? How? and Why?", especially "*Who?*" and "*Why?*"; indeed, as Rudé himself has admitted, "Who?" became his particular "obsession" in response to the continually "vague or prejudiced generalizations of historians".[27] In *The Crowd in History, 1730–1848*, a "synthetic" work written following the publication of his original studies of the eighteenth-century crowd, he proffered six questions to serve as guides for the study of the crowd in the "pre-industrial age":

> [1] What actually happened, both as to the event itself, and as to its origins and aftermath? . . . [2] How large was the crowd concerned, how did it act, who (if any) were its promoters, who composed it, and who led it? . . . [3] Who were the target or the victims of the crowd's activities? . . . [4] More specifically, what were the aims, motives, and ideas underlying these activities? . . . [5] How effective were the forces of law and order? . . . [6] Finally, what were the consequences of the event, and what has been its historical significance?[28]

Yet, as Rudé forewarns, to pose such questions is one thing, to be able to answer them is another, for it depends on the "availability of suitable records", by which he means not only the "historian's traditional sources: memoirs, correspondence, pamphlets, provincial and national newspapers, parliamentary reports and proceedings, the minutes and reports of local government and political organizations, and the previous findings of historians, chroniclers and antiquarians"; but, also, "police, prison, hospital, and judicial records; Home Office papers . . . tax rolls; poll books and petitions; notarial records; inventories; parish registers of births, deaths and marriages; public assistance records; tables of prices and wages; censuses; local directories and club membership lists; and lists of freeholders, jurymen, churchwardens, and justices of the peace". The necessity of the latter records is both pragmatic and "political" in nature. It is a practical issue because the traditional sources are not likely to provide the answers to the crucial questions "Who?" and "Why?", nor, for that matter, sufficient data to address the others adequately. It is a "political" issue because what the former sources are most likely to provide us with is the perspective "from above" since they are the records of the ruling and upper classes—"government, the official political opposition, the aristocracy, or the more prosperous middle class"; the participants in crowd actions like riots "rarely leave records of their own in the form of memoirs, pamphlets, or letters".[29]

He does not fully pursue the logic of his argument here, but it is clear from his own work and remarks elsewhere that even the latter sources ("police, prison, hospital and judicial records . . .") must be approached most critically *and* from the bottom up, for they too have been by and/or for the governors. As the historical sociologist, Barrington Moore, Jr., once put it: since "in any society the dominant groups are the ones with the most to hide about the way society works", to maximize objectivity and write critical history, "For all students of human society, sympathy with the victims of historical processes and skepticism about the victors' claims provide essential safeguards against being taken in by the dominant mythology. A scholar who tries to be objective needs those feelings as part of his ordinary equipment".[30] In "The Changing Face of the Crowd" (included in the present collection), Rudé reflects on his eighteenth-century studies and, revealing no surprises, speaks of his own particular sympathies: "I did not approach my subject without commitment . . . This does not mean I have ever felt *politically* involved with the wage-earners, craftsmen or rioters with whom I have largely been concerned, but that I have always felt a bond of sympathy with them, whether their activities have been peaceful or rebellious".

What answers did his questions garner in the "police records of the Archives Nationales and the Paris Préfecture de Police" and the various

"London and metropolitan records . . . [especially] judicial records"? In contrast to Taine's picture of the revolutionary crowd as having been made up of "dregs, criminals and bandits", Rudé found that "For all their diversity of scope, organization and design" there was "a certain uniformity of pattern in the social composition of these movements: . . . they were drawn in their overwhelming majority from the Parisian *sans-culottes*—from the workshop masters, craftsmen, wage-earners, shopkeepers, and petty traders of the capital".[31] Similarly, Rudé's labours in London revealed that neither could the Hanoverian crowd be so readily "fobbed off" as a "mob" recruited from amongst "slum dwellers" and/or "criminal elements". Fully acknowledging—as he also does in *The Crowd in the French Revolution*—that there were occupational and gender variations in the composition of the crowd depending on the "occasion" of its mobilization in strike, riot, or demonstration he states that it was, in fact, generally composed of "wage-earners, (journeymen, apprentices, labourers, and 'servants') . . . craftsmen, shopkeepers, and tradesmen".[32] At the same time, it should be noted that although his dramatically redrawn historical pictures of the Parisian and London crowds are filled with "working" people, Rudé is insistent—against various "socialist" renditions of the *sans-culottes* and lower orders—that these were not specifically "working-class" movements and, in fact, that there did not even yet exist specifically *class* formations in these "pre-industrial" social orders.[33] (This argument will be considered again in the last section of this Introduction in relation to his discussion of the "transitional" character of the eighteenth century and his understanding of "class" in that period.)

Uncovering the faces in the crowd was only a first step towards restoring its historical and political identity and those of its participants. The issues of the direction and purpose of crowd actions remained, for it might be argued that the composition of the crowd, or "mob", was not so significant if its participants were merely bribed and/or driven by a desire for loot, both of which also raised the spectre of hired gangs and conspiracies. But the questions of leadership and motivation were also addressed by Rudé. Regarding the former he did find that the crowds of both capital cities were more often led by those "from 'without' than from 'within'"and, moreover, that such leaders were usually from "higher" social strata[34] which could be read as supportive of the conservative view that the crowds were "mindless mobs" directed from above for purposes not all their own except in the most immediate sense of the assuagement of hunger (e.g., bread riots) or the expectation of lucre. *Or*, on the contrary, it might be taken as supportive of the liberal and Republican position that, for example, in the French Revolution the crowd—*"the people"* enjoined with its revolutionary bourgeois leaders—was indeed the embodiment of the "Republican spirit". In other words, "Who?" the leadership was is inadequate on its own; of crucial importance are the "autonomy" of the crowd and the "motivation" of its participants.

The next section of this Introduction will survey Rudé's persistent interest in the motivation and ideology of popular protest, and also note further his understanding of the legacies of such protest, but it should be stated here that his findings contradicted the contentions of both conservatives and liberals. That is, they reject both the view that the crowd was simply and "mindlessly" motivated by hunger and/or greed and that which reduces the crowd—in the name of "good *or* evil"—to having been merely an extension of the aspirations or conspiracies of its "leaders". It is true, as will be shown, that Rudé's discussions of the "social psychology" of the crowd provide a good deal of weight to "material" motivation—perhaps occasionally too mechanically as in his analyses of the revolutionary crowd's responsiveness to changes in "the price of bread"—and, also, that they do attribute the "political" development of the Parisian *menu peuple* and London "lower orders" in great part to the efforts of their "upper-class" leaders in what might be viewed as a "Leninist" fashion. However, he never treats the crowd and its participants in a one-dimensional way. for even his earliest studies reveal that the lower orders too had interests and aspirations which sometimes coincided with those from above and yet at other times did not.

The Crowd in History, 1730–1848 appeared in 1964. Limited to France and England, it drew on Rudé's previous studies and at the same time extended his explorations into the nineteenth century. The book also represented both a self-conscious effort on his part to respond somewhat to his critics and to develop a historical "model" of the "pre-industrial crowd" addressed not only to historians but, as well, to sociologists, who, Rudé found, had not advanced much beyond their historian colleagues on the subject. At the outset he offers a brief summary description of the "pre-industrial crowd" which, appearing in the "transitional period" before the full development of an industrial social order, was marked by historically antecedent modes of popular protest and yet was already beginning to evidence characteristics of industrial protest:

> In our transitional period the typical form of social protest is the food riot, not the strike of the future or the millenial movement or the peasant *jacquerie* of the past. Those engaging in popular disturbances are sometimes peasants (as in the past), but more often a mixed population of what in England were "lower orders" and in France *menu peuple* . . .; they appear frequently in itinerant bands, "captained" or

"generaled by men whose personality, style of dress or speech, and momentary assumption of authority mark them out as leaders; they are fired as much by memories of customary rights or a nostalgia for past utopias as by present grievances or hopes of material improvement; and they dispense a rough-and-ready kind of "natural justice" by breaking windows, wrecking machinery, storming markets, burning their enemies of the moment in effigy, firing hayricks, and pulling down houses, farms, fences, mills or pubs, but rarely by taking lives.[35]

In conclusion to the work Rudé wonders if "all the vigour, heroism and violence . . . led to any positive results? . . . what did the crowd achieve?" Though he exempts certain episodes from his generic assessment, his answer is that "In terms of immediate gains, it must be admitted that it achieved comparatively little". However, this does not mean that the "crowd"—as the most aggressive mode of popular protest and struggle—was historically inconsequential. Indeed, Rudé contends, both the crowds of the *menu peuple* and those of the "lower orders" contributed in dramatic ways to the making of eighteenth-century history. For example, on the crowds mobilized for "Wilkes and Liberty!" he writes: "The Wilkite disturbances in London not only achieved a remarkable series of personal victories for Wilkes himself but contributed substantially to the growth of a mass radical movement in England".[36] And, in a 1970 lecture on "The French Revolution and Participation" (included in the present volume) he says of the significance of the *sans-culottes'* initiatives that:

They certainly helped to push the Revolution leftwards: without their intervention the Jacobins could never have come into power; there would have been no "democratic dictatorship of the Year II"; and it is doubtful if the monarch would have been overthrown . . . They also won important concessions for themselves though they proved to be short-lived: the Maximum Laws, for example, with a ceiling placed on food prices; and the right to vote and to sit in local government.

Moreover, the legacies of the Hanoverian crowds—especially those of "Wilkes and Liberty!"—and the revolutionary crowds of Paris can be recognized, Rudé declares, in the Chartist movement of the 1830s and 40s and the revolutionary struggles of 1830 and 1848, respectively.

The Crowd in History not only offered a summary of his crowd studies, it also pointed ahead to his primary researches of the next twenty years, first, on "Captain Swing" and, then, on crime, protest and punishment during the Industrial Revolution. Although distinct in period and subject, these later writings continued to evidence Rudé's commitment to restoring the historical and political identities of the "lower orders".

Before proceeding, a problem regarding Rudé's crowd studies which is most evident in *The Crowd in History* should be registered. Although Rudé is eager to present the period 1730–1848 as "transitional", in order, no doubt, to formulate it in historically specific terms, he does not actually explore the relations between the developing modes of popular protest and "contention"[37] and changing relations of production and "class" experience. The historical sociologist, Charles Tilly, in his critically appreciative review of *The Crowd in History,* noted this to some extent when he wrote that Rudé's analysis does not adequately take up "underlying social changes".[38] This point will be returned to in the final section for it relates to Rudé's apparent reservations about treating the eighteenth century in terms of "class" and the "transition to capitalism". However, this was not to be a problem with his next book, *Captain Swing,* either because its subject, the English agricultural labourers' rising of 1830, occurred later in time and, thus, the structures of class were "clearer", or, possibly, because the work was co-authored with Eric Hobsbawm who, as something of an economic historian, had already written directly on the question of "the transition" and was much more attuned to the "political economy of class".

Bringing together in one project Hobsbawm's critical perceptions and knowledge of the development of capitalism, industrialization, "primitive rebellions" and "machine breakers",[39] and Rudé's intimate acquaintance with the "pre-industrial crowd" and passion and skills for archival labour and analysis, *Captain Swing* is a truly outstanding piece of historical scholarship. The particular skills of each historian are evident in the division of labour in the book: the introductory, background, developmental, and concluding chapters are by Hobsbawm; the chapters providing the details and "anatomy" of the rising are by Rudé (so also are the chapters on "Repression and Aftermath").[40] Nevertheless, as a collaborative work we find in the very opening lines a primary concern for the "identities" of the agricultural labourers which seems so characteristic of Rudé:

"Hodge"; "the secret people", "brother to the ox". Their own inarticulateness, our own ignorance, are symbolized by the very titles of the few books which have attempted to recreate the world of the English farm-labourer of the nineteenth century. *Who were they?* . . . Except for their gravestones and their children, they left nothing identifiable behind them for the marvellous surface of the British landscape, the work of their ploughs, spades and shears and the beasts they looked after, bears no signature or mark such as the masons left on cathedrals.

We know little about them, because they are remote from us in time. Their articulate contemporaries knew little more, partly because as townsmen they were ignorant about the country or cared nothing for it, partly because as rulers they were not allowed to enter the self-contained world of the subaltern orders, or because as rural middle class they despised it . . . The task of this book is therefore the difficult one, which nowadays—and rightly—tempts many social historians, of reconstructing the mental world of an anonymous and undocumented body of people in order to understand their movements, themselves only sketchily documented.[41]

Captain Swing is, of course, a study of the subject originally treated by the Hammonds in *The Village Labourer*.[42] Hobsbawm and Rudé wrote their own book, they said, not only because there was more to tell about the rising, but because there were "new *questions* to ask about the events: about their causes and motives, about their mode of social and political behaviour, the social composition of those who took part in them, their significance and consequences". They explain that, before 1830, the agricultural workers were no longer peasants but the social order in which they lived was still "traditional, hierarchical, paternalist, and in many respects still resistant to the full logic of the market". This was not a static situation, however, and in the decades leading up to 1830 this rural society experienced major changes brought about by "the extraordinary agricultural boom (and subsequent, though temporary, recessions)". The changes involved the alienation of the labourers' lands and the transformation of their hiring contracts, that is, the actual or further proletarianization of the labour force. Moreover, the reduction of the relationship between farmer and labourer to the "cash-nexus" stripped the labourer of "those modest customary rights as a man (though a subordinate one) to which he felt himself to have a claim". And yet, the agricultural workers were "proletarian only in the most general economic sense", for the nature of their labour and the social order in which they lived and starved inhibited the development of "those ideas and methods of collective self-defence which the townsmen were able to discover".

Nevertheless, (finally) instigated by the economic crisis of 1828–30 and stimulated by the French and Belgian Revolutions of 1830 and the contemporary British crisis, the agricultural workers expressed their demands by a variety of means: "arson, threatening letters, inflammatory handbills and posters . . . and [most significantly] the destruction of different types of machinery". Their demands—"to attain a minimum living wage and to end rural unemployment"— appear merely economic or "(though not formally) trade unionist". However, while the rising was never revolutionary (nor was there ever a call for land reform), Hobsbawm and Rudé's analysis shows that "there was a wider objective: the defence of the customary rights of the rural poor as freeborn Englishmen, and the restoration of the stable social order which had—at least it seemed in retrospect—guaranteed them".[43]

As Fred Krantz observes: "Rudé's hand is clearly present in the sections noted as primarily worked up by him" and his "method and technique" enable them to advance a "provisional profile of the village disposed to riot" based on village size, social structure, land tenure and type of agriculture predominating, prospensity to religious "independence" and proximity to "local communications centers, markets and fairs". Indeed, Krantz claims, comprehended in terms of national and local historical developments and particularities, Hobsbawm and Rudé essentially provide a "fully three-dimensional, empirically-grounded, analytic 'model'".[44] The chapter on "Who Was Swing?" is also impressive in its survey of the evidence on incendiaries, letter-writers, machine-breakers and wage-rioters, along with that for their leaders and allies. Observers were quick to recognize—for they often occurred in broad daylight—that wage riots, marches, ransomings, and machine-breaking were "perpetrated" by local labourers, but against contemporary opinion—for these were not "daylight" actions—Hobsbawm and Rudé's examination of the evidence shows that incendiaries and letter-writers too were locals. The "movement's" leaders and allies were often craftsmen and (even) farmers, the reasons for, and significance of which are discussed. In general, Rudé and Hobsbawm find that "The rioters were generally young men or men of early-middle age . . . overwhelmingly they were in their twenties or thirties" and, moreover, "the proportion of married men among the rioters was also high". In fact, the evidence "suggests a relatively high degree of stability and 'respectability' among the rioters as a whole". The conclusion to the chapter states:

> By and large, the labourers of 1830 fully deserved the good reputations that their employers gave them. They were not criminals: comparatively few had even the mildest form of prison record behind them. But they believed in "natural right"—the right to work and earn a living wage—and refused to accept that machines, which robbed them of this right, should receive the protection of the law. On occasion, they invoked the authority of the justice, or government—and even of the King and God himself—to justify their views and actions. For like most "primitive rebels", and like Sir John Hampden 200 years before, they were firmly convinced that justice—and even the law—was on their side.[45]

Captain Swing not only offered a re-interpretation of the origins of the agricultural workers' movement, as well as its practices and aims, it also offered a new view of its consequences. Hobsbawm and Rudé contend that the myths and ignorance about the movement being a failure were due in good part to the urban bias of the historians of social movements. For example, against the traditional view they reveal that "agrarian unrest continued well into the 1850s, and social incendiaries can be traced down to about 1860". Nevertheless, they acknowledge that the rising was a failure in that it neither succeeded in restoring the old social order, nor—except for a brief period—did it do much to improve the workers' standard of living. And yet in one important respect the agricultural workers' movement succeeded: "The threshing machines did not return on the old scale. Of all the machine-breaking movements of the nineteenth century that of the helpless and unorganized farm-labourers proved to be the most effective. The real name of King Ludd was Swing".[46]

The labourers may have believed that "the law was on their side". The judges who tried those caught believed otherwise. As Hobsbawm and Rudé note: "In all 1,976 prisoners were tried . . . 252 were sentenced to death (of these 233 were commuted, mainly to transportation, some to prison) . . . 505 were transported (of these 481 sailed) . . . From no other protest movement of the kind—from neither Luddites, nor Chartists, nor trade unionists—was such a bitter price exacted".[47] The chapters in *Captain Swing* on "Repression" and those transported to "Australia" inspired Rudé's next two primary studies: resident in Australia and then Canada, Rudé wrote *Protest and Punishment: The Story of the Social and Political Protesters Transported to Australia, 1788–1868* (which includes work on "protest and punishment" in Canada); and later, having returned to England in semi-retirement, *Criminal and Victim: Crime and Society in Early Nineteenth-Century England.* These two books are classic "Rudéan" works. Fred Krantz describes Rudé's writing style as "pointillist" and, I would add, none is perhaps more so than these, for Rudé's principal mode of presentation of his findings in both books is to lay out numerous cases, episodes, or micro-tales of crime, protest and punishment in order to introduce us directly to "the faces in the crowd" and the "experiences" which instigated their appearance in the courts or inclusion among those transported to Australia. In essence, in these works Rudé seeks to "redeem" those whose "crimes" were "protests" from the mass of those whose crimes were not. As he states at the outset of *Protest and Punishment,* in general we know a good deal about transportation and those who were transported from the writings of other historians; however, we do not know enough about those "whose crime was to have rebelled or protested against the social conditions or institutions of the country from which they came".[48]

The problem, Rudé explains, is "How do we make a distinction? How do we separate one type of convict—the protesting convict—from the rest? . . . How do we distinguish between 'protest' crime and crime in general?". Law-and-order conservatives, he complains, see all protest as a "crime against established society"; liberal writers have tended to comprehend all crimes as a form of protest; and yet others have proposed more "realistic" models, like Engels who tried to distinguish between "crimes against property and others". Rudé also notes, appreciatively but critically, the model advanced by Edward Thompson and his colleagues at the Centre for Social History at Warwick

University in the early 1970s, which distinguished between "*social* crime" and crime in general (a distinction which Hobsbawm and Rudé themselves offered in *Captain Swing*). For Rudé, however, these are all inadequate. Instead, he proposes "protest crimes", "marginal crimes", and "crimes in general" and he proceeds to explain his reasoning and method of reading the "cases". In brief, in comparison to the notion of "social" crime which may, nevertheless, be a "private act that has little to do with protest":

> Protest . . . is also a *collective* act though it may not always be carried out in the company of others. Such acts are fairly easy to recognize in the case of trade-union militants, machine-breakers, food-rioters, demolishers of turn-pikes, fences or workhouses, administers or receivers of unlawful oaths, treasonable or seditious persons, armed rebels and city rioters—all those, in fact, who generally protest within the context of a "popular movement" . . . But there are others: those whose activities belong to the shadowy realm between crime and protest where it is often no easy matter to tell the two apart. I refer to such types of law-breaking as rural incendiarism, poaching and smuggling, cattle-maiming, assaults on peace officers, and the sending of anonymous letters. These types of *marginal* protest . . . have to be judged, as it were, on their merits and treated with care and discrimination.[49]

Protest and Punishment is not merely a study of the British-Australian "experience" but includes those who were transported from Ireland and Canada as well. Reviewing the records of those who were transported, Rudé arrives at a total of 3,600 "protest criminals", that is "about one in forty-five of all transported convicts". Treating their experiences "from both ends: both in the Australian context and in that of the countries and counties in which the protests were made", Rudé reminds us that "Behind these figures are the faces of the men and women . . ."[50] And his two concluding chapters are characteristically Rudéan: "Who were the Convicts?" and "Who were the Protesters?". In the former he considers the historically changing view of the convicts from that of being "scum" to "heroes", and back again; and in the latter he compares the characteristics—age, literacy, marital status and criminal record—of the protesters in particular with the convicts in general. In the end he expresses concern that these protesters not be lost in the mass of those who were transported and—*especially,* I would add, in this year of the Australian Bicentennial (1988)—that the protesters who were transported be accorded the respect that is owed them: "the names of two dozen of such men, at most, appear in the *Australian Dictionary of Biography* and a few more in the *DNB;* so these will not be forgotten . . . But there are others no less worthy to be remembered . . . They, too, no longer deserve to be hidden in the shadows with all the other unsung heroes. Let them be allowed to emerge and bask a little in the approval that posterity has too long refused them".[51]

In *Criminal and Victim* Rudé's primary questions are "Who robbed whom?" and "Who were the victims as well as their assailants?" in England during the first half of the nineteenth century. To answer them he focusses on Sussex, Gloucestershire, and Middlesex because the first was rural, the second varied demographically and economically, and the last was urban and commercial. (The last article in this collection, "Crime, Criminals and Victims in Early Nineteenth-Century London" is in great part drawn from the book's material on Middlesex.) In a somewhat more developed fashion Rudé specifies the different "types" of crime: "(1) *acquisitive* crime, or crimes committed strictly in pursuit of material gain; (2) *survival* crime, in which the criminal's main concern has been to feed or clothe or shelter himself and his family at a time of unemployment or trade decline; and (3) *protest* crime, or crimes committed in attempting to redress injustice or social ills".[52]

Roughly summarized, Rudé's survey of the records of the three counties demonstrates that criminals were in the great majority of the labouring and working classes and victims "of the 'middling' or upper classes: most often shopkeepers, merchants, or householders and (in the rural counties) farmers, with a fair 'sprinkling of gentry . . .'". This leads him to ask two specifically "class" questions. First: "Does this tendency of criminals and victims to belong to different, if not opposing, classes in this confrontation mean that through crime and the combating of crime, they are engaged in a form of class war?" His answer to this is that although the innovations and changes of the time in England's criminal law and justice system were "a direct expression of a new class system and therefore an expression of class rule" and, also, their implementation and operation were characterized by "class bias", the prevalence of "acquisitive" crimes and "survival" crimes—as opposed to "protest" crimes—deny the description "class war".[53] The second question posed is: "Can one rightly speak of the existence of a 'criminal class', or of 'criminal classes'?" Allowing for the existence of a "minority of hardened criminals and isolated gangs of 'professionals'", he responds that these "were not in sufficient numbers to constitute a 'criminal class'", and the words he finds most appropriate to refer to accounts which suggest otherwise is "fantasies".[54]

Ideologies: "Putting Mind Back into History"

We have seen that along with confronting the "traditional" views of eighteenth-century Paris and London, Rudé also had to deal with the concomitant views of the direction and purpose of the crowds' actions. In "The Motives of Popular Insurrection" (1953) he notes that to Taine and many other historians "the revolutionary crowd is a conscienceless rabble, quite incapable of political thought, driven to rebel by the prospect of easy loot or by monetary inducements",[55] and, similarly, in "The London 'Mob'" (1959) that "While conceding that 'mobs' might be prompted by hunger, they [contemporaries] were even more ready to believe that the desire for loot or drink acted as the major factor in such disturbances; any sort of political awareness, however rudimentary, was not seriously considered. The 'mobbish sort' being notoriously venal, bribery [with its accompanying charge of "conspiracy"] by interested parties was deemed a sufficient stimulus to touch off riot or rebellion".[56] As was indicated in the previous section, although the leaders of the crowds were most often from "without" and "above" those who composed them, the *menu peuple* and "lower orders", Rudé's research revealed that the persistent "conservative" presumption as to the "motivation" of the Paris and London crowds were not substantiated by the evidence. Still, there remained the issue of the autonomy of the crowd and its participants: What were the motivations of the "common people" who took part in crowd actions? Were they their "own" or simply those of their higher strata leaders?

In his crowd studies of the 1950s and early 60s, Rudé repeatedly declares that along with recovering the "faces in the crowd" he is interested in the "motives" of those who took part in riots, demonstrations and rebellions and in exploring the "social psychology" of the eighteenth-century crowd. In this he was seeking to open up historical study to social science thinking; the study of collective behaviour has often been pursued—then, and now—in social-psychological terms and the study of "motivation" in particular has been associated with the discipline of social psychology. Thus, we find Rudé in his crowd studies using language like "the deeper urges and impulses of the 'mob'" and "entering into the minds of its participants".[57] Yet he was not only being influenced by contemporary social science practice, he was also following the lead of his mentor, Lefebvre, who had been extremely interested in developing *historical* social psychology and, as Rudé says, provided models for such in works like *The Great Fear of 1789: Rural Panic in Revolutionary France.*[58] In Lefebvre's own words: "Social history can therefore not be limited to describing the external aspects of antagonistic classes. It must also come to understand the mental outlook of each class".[59]

Rudé's own approach to the study of motives in his crowd writings is "materialist". Pointing out that crowd actions and "popular movements" antedated the specifically *political* struggles of the "revolutionary bourgeoisie" and "middle sort" of Paris and London, respectively, Rudé, early in his work, examined the possible links between economic hardship and popular disturbance (following, here, the lead of the French historian, C-E. Labrousse) and he found that popular protest was apparently quite responsive to price and wage fluctuations. This, he contended, illustrated that the motives of the crowds and their participants were not *simply* reflections of the aspirations of their "upper-class" leaders.[60]

Later, in his book-length studies of the eighteenth-century crowd, he continues to assert that the "most constant motive of popular insurrection during the Revolution, as in the eighteenth century as a whole, was the compelling need of the *menu peuple* for the possession of cheap and plentiful bread and other essentials . . ." (*The Crowd in the French Revolution*) and "Far more tangible [than other factors] is the evidence of a concordance between the movement of food-prices and certain phases of the 'Wilkes and Liberty' movement in the metropolis" (*Wilkes and Liberty*).[61]

On their own, such arguments seem to reduce the causes of crowd actions to economic determinism and, although Rudé recognized that this was a problem with Labrousse's work, his own analyses are, as I have stated, occasionally too mechanical. But Rudé does not treat the crowd one-dimensionally. His studies characteristically go on to consider the other, less immediately "material", motives which inspired crowd actions and popular protests. Indeed, both *The Crowd in the French Revolution* and *Wilkes and Liberty* are ultimately narratives of the "political education" and development of the crowds of Paris and London. As Rudé presents it, the political education of the revolutionary and Wilkite crowds involved the subscription or "absorption" of the ideas of the revolutionary bourgeoisie and politically-active "middle sort" by the *menu peuple* and "lower orders", respectively.

In a chapter of *The Crowd in the French Revolution* titled "The Generation of Revolutionary Activity", Rudé discusses the various ways in which the revolutionary slogans and ideas of "the rights of man" and "sovereignty of the people" were transmitted from "bourgeois" leaders to the *menu peuple*. For a start, although literacy was not common among the *sans-culottes* of Paris (and even less so in the villages) many could read. Those who could would read aloud at meetings of workers and others from the journals and pamphlets being produced by political writers which were often "addressed" directly to them. More "significant" and "systematic" was the "indoctrination of the *sans-culottes* with the ideas of the advanced political groups" which occurred by way of their "enrolment in the National Guard and, above all, in the clubs and societies and Sectional Committees". Finally, also important in "spreading ideas and moulding opinions", were the discussion and debates which transpired in "public meeting-places, workshops, wine-shops, markets, and food-shops".[62]

The revolutionary slogans and ideas, Rudé regularly reminds us, were not those of the *sans-culottes* themselves; and his use of such words as "indoctrination" to refer to the communication of those ideas by the revolutionary bourgeoisie to the *menu peuple* clearly evidences a Leninist conception of political education: the *sans-culottes* were on their own incapable of anything more than *economic* motivation ("trade union consciousness"), movement beyond that required the leadership and *political* ideas developed by bourgeois intellectuals. However, Rudé does evidence certain reservations about this formulation of the relationship. That is, the *sans-culottes* subscribed to the revolutionary ideas "because they appeared to correspond to their own interest in the fight to destroy the old régime and to safeguard the Republic", *but* they comprehended those ideas in their own terms—it was a process of "absorption" *and* "adaptation". Moreover, Rudé continues, because their own experience and interests were other than those of the revolutionary bourgeoisie, in time their different understandings of "rights of man" and "sovereignty of the people" strained the "alliance". Also, in a footnote Rudé does acknowledge that the *sans-culottes* likely had political ideas of their own, though he adds that "These can, however, have played no part in stimulating participation in revolutionary movements, except in that of 4-5 September 1793".[63]

More important were the efforts of the *menu peuple* to protect or restore their "traditional rights". In fact, Rudé proffers, against the views of both the conservatives *and* the writers and historians of the Republican tradition, that the crowds and their *sans-culottes* participants were hardly the "passive instruments" of their revolutionary bourgeois leaders, for had they been they would have been "imbued with a desire for 'total renovation' "—they would have actually sought to "turn the world upside down". Rather, he finds: "At every important stage of the Revolution the *sans-culottes* intervened, not to renovate society or to remodel it after a new pattern, but to reclaim traditional rights and to uphold standards which they believed to be imperilled by the innovations of ministers, capitalists, speculators, 'agricultural improvers' or city authorities".[64]

Thus, Rudé's Leninism is indicated by his apparent equation of *material* motivation with the *menu peuple* and the origination of "ideas" with the revolutionary bourgeois leadership, and yet we also see that his materialist conception of the necessarily "class-differential" comprehension of those ideas leads beyond a crude or simplistic Leninism.

In the same fashion that popular movements were already in motion prior to the French Revolution they were, too, in Hanoverian London prior to the campaigns for "Wilkes and Liberty!". Indeed, Rudé points out that eighteenth-century London was actually more turbulent than Paris up until the Revolution and, furthermore, that the "lower orders", or "inferior sorts of people", of London were actually characterized by a greater political awareness than the Parisian *menu peuple*. This, Rudé explains, was due in great part to the legacy of seventeenth-century struggles, but also because the London "middle sort" were closer to the "lower orders" than were their French counterparts to the *sans-culottes* and thus they were "more appropriate educators".[65] Although in general popular movements were imbued with a "sense of the seventeenth-century revolutionary tradition, the "*economically-motivated*" food riots and industrial disputes of Hanoverian London were not "political" movements, Rudé insists. The Wilkite movement, however, which Rudé sees as paralleling but not actually merging with the "industrial" struggles, had dramatic effects on the political development of the London crowd and the political education of the "lower orders".[66]

The question of motivation is considered at several levels in the book, *Wilkes and Liberty*. Again, Rudé grants that there was a significant relationship between the "material" motivation of the "inferior sort"—"rising food-prices . . . wage demands and industrial disputes"—and the Wilkite movements, but, he says, the former does not sufficiently explain the latter: "Beyond that, we must look to a complex of political, social and economic factors, in which the underlying social changes of the age, the political crisis of 1761, the traditional devotion to 'Revolution principles', and Wilkes's own astuteness, experiences and personality all played their part".[67] Especially we should note his discussion of Wilkes's "appeal" to the common people—both "middle" and "lower sort"—in his campaigns for "press freedom" and "political liberties". First, Wilkes's experience represented, or personified, the "political" experience and growing sense of injustice which had been accumulating: "Small wonder, then, that among such citizens and gentry, alarmed at the whole trend of events since the accession of George III, there should be many to whom Wilkes, who had been persecuted more relentlessly than any other by the new administration and returned blow for blow and insolence for insolence, might appear as an object of sympathy, respect or even of veneration".[68] Moreover, Wilkes's "image" was greatly enhanced by his own skilful and persistent espousal of the principles of "liberty" and "freedom" which harkened back to the "Revolution principles" and successfully harnessed and mobilized the common people's understandings of "the rights of the freeborn Englishman".

Wilkite crowd actions were, then, more "political" in character than those linked specifically to the price of bread or to wage and industrial disputes, but, like the economically – and socially – motivated popular movements, that for "Wilkes and Liberty" was also a "defensive" struggle asserting the *traditional* rights" of Englishmen against seemingly "new" oppressions. In other words, Rudé does not exaggerate the political development of the crowd and its participants: "It took time, of course, before such movements of the 'inferior set of people' became impregnated with a more solid body of political ideas and principles and before the notion of 'liberty' . . . began to clothe itself in the more tangible garbs of demands for annual Parliaments or an extension of the franchise—demands already voiced by tradesmen and freeholders [the "middle sort"] but not as yet by the smaller craftsmen, journeymen, and urban wage-earners". This further political development of the "lower orders" he attributes in good part to ideas from "without" and "above", in particular the French Revolution and the writings of the English democrats.[69]

Rudé does not fail to acknowledge the violence of crowd actions—in the case of "Wilkes and Liberty" as much as in the others. But, as he indicates, the very "culture" of Hanoverian London was violent and, he claims, "the violence of the poor was, in part at least, but a reflection of the violence of their rulers and social betters".[70] In fact, he declares, in contrast to the violence of the upper strata, that of crowd actions was characteristically against property not lives!

Indeed, Rudé's research reveals that even the most "reactionary" of crowd actions, that of the Gordon Riots which were directed against Roman Catholics, the violence was not directed against the Roman Catholic community as a whole, but rather against the propertied and wealthy. There was a distinctly "class" bias to the events. Rudé does not claim that "religion" was a "cloak" to the real motives but he does call for a recognition of the "social protest" dimension of the riots.[71]

In his laudatory review of *Wilkes and Liberty* in *The Guardian* (9 February 1962), A. J. P. Taylor wrote that Rudé had "put mind back into history and restored the dignity of man".[72] This was well-deserved praise for his crowd studies—both for *Wilkes and Liberty* and, I would add, *The Crowd in the French Revolution*. Yet, as I have shown, Rudé's study of motives suffered from a kind of "elitism" in that it tended, first, to attribute *material* motivation to the lower orders and the original possession of "ideas" to the higher, and, second, to portray the views of the former as "defensive" and "backward looking" and those of the latter as "forward looking". Thus, the political education of the lower orders is seen as depending on the propagation of the "progressive" ideas of the revolutionary bourgeoisie or middle sort among them. Rudé himself was to move towards this very conclusion. Writing in the Introduction to *Ideology and Popular Protest* (1980) he looked back and described how his treatment of the question "Why?" changed from focussing on the problem of "motivation" to focussing on "ideas or beliefs":

> concern with motivation led me to attempt to distinguish between the long and the short term and to draw a dividing line between "socio-economic" and "political" factors and to attempt to explain how the two became related and merged in such movements as that of the *sans-culottes* in the French Revolution or of the Londoners that shouted for Wilkes and burned down Roman Catholic chapels and schools in the riots of the 1760s to 1780.
>
> But, as I have come to realize, the study of *motives*—even when some attention is paid to such elusive concepts as N.J. Smelser's "generalized beliefs"—is an unsatisfactory one in itself, as it tends to present the problem in a piecemeal fashion and fails to do justice to the full range of ideas or beliefs that underlie social and political action, whether of old-style rulers, "rising" bourgeois or of "inferior" social groups.[73]

The change in Rudé's approach to the question "Why?" can be described as a shift from a concern with motives in the social-psychological sense—though it should be made clear that Rude's work never fell into "psychologism"—to an interest in the social history of ideas or "ideologies". This was signalled somewhat in *The Crowd in History* and *Captain Swing* and thus it might have been due to his having extended his scholarly efforts into the nineteenth century for in these later years the "emergent" ideas of the eighteenth century were adapted, revised, *and* more clearly articulated in the course of social change and the making of more specifically working-class movements. It was also due no doubt both to the changes taking place in the historical discipline to which he had himself contributed so much and to those occurring on the Left. In the late 1960s and early 70s, social history and "history from below" began to move to the forefront of the historical profession; at the same time—and to some extent fomenting the former development—the "New" Left's rebellion against the "orthodoxy" and "economism" of the "Old" had fostered a new interest in ideas and cultural questions and the "discovery" of a "Western Marxist" tradition including George Lukács, the theorists of the Frankfurt School, and Antonio Gramsci.[74]

The British Marxist historians themselves seem to bridge the Old and New Lefts. At one end of the group are the "senior" figures like Christopher Hill, Eric Hobsbawm, Victor Kiernan, and George Rudé, and, at the other, the (younger) E.P. Thompson, who was a central figure in the break with the Communist Party *and* the formation of the original British New Left. However, *as a group* the British Marxist historians were extremely influential in the development of the "new" history which emerged concurrently with the New Left and their own writings evidence strong sympathies with its aspirations. Rudé's work on the crowd was quite central to all this, but he was not himself of the

New Left. Consider his remark in the article, "Marxism and History", where he quotes Engels regarding the necessity of "authority and centralization" and how it ought to be kept in mind by "young 'revolutionaries' of our own time".[75] Nevertheless, Rudé's work did not remain stuck in its already-noted Leninist mould; indeed, his own writings of the 1970s and 80s were to be greatly influenced both by the studies of his fellow British Marxist historians and the younger historians who had themselves been inspired by his scholarship and by the contemporary theoretical and historical interest in the ideas of the Italian Marxist, Antonio Gramsci.[76]

In several essays written around 1970, Rudé expresses his new commitment "to trace the origins and course of the ideas that 'grip the masses' (to use Marx's phrase) and play so important a part in both the 'peaks' and 'troughs' of a popular movement", and in this same period he begins to formulate his new model for the study and comprehension of the ideology of popular protest.[77] It is this model that he proceeds to develop in historical terms in a series of marvellous articles published during the next ten years (three of them are included in the present collection[78]) which provided the basis for his book, *Ideology and Popular Protest* (in my mind, his best work for pedagogical purposes!).

The central question which Rudé addresses in this work is "Where did the ideas bound up with popular protest come from?". Though he does not express it in these words, it is evident that he was no longer satisfied with the "Leninist" model which had previously shaped his thinking—a model, as I have implied, which was reinforced by his concern for the social psychology of motivation—for he had come to see that he had underestimated the "ideas" and "beliefs" *of* the "lower orders" in the formation of the "ideology" of popular protest. However, as he tells it, his survey of the prevailing models to consider the ideas of popular struggle was not immediately rewarding. The Marxist tradition had attended overwhelmingly to the class structure and struggles of industrial capitalist society and had generally neglected the study of pre-capitalist social formations. Moreover, following the "orthodox" view derived from both Lenin and Lukács, the Marxist tradition had comprehended the development of class consciousness in the ahistorical and dichotomous terms of "false" and "true" consciousness.[79] Non-Marxist writers had more to say about pre-capitalist social orders and cultures but they regularly failed to perceive the "class"-differential and political nature of culture and ideas as is true, for example, in the *Annales'* concept of "mentalities".[80]

Yet there was an exception in the Marxist tradition, as Rudé discovered. In the writings of Antonio Gramsci, especially those of the *Prison Notebooks*,[81] Rudé found a Marxist thinker whose efforts and experience as a socialist activist in post-First World War Italy had led him to conceive of the problem of class *formation* in terms of the *making* of class consciousness and the place of ideology both in the process of domination *and* the struggles against it. Moreover, due to the particular circumstances which Gramsci confronted, he had concerned himself with the "consciousness" of both the industrial working class *and* the "popular classes"—peasants and artisans—with whom the working class would have to form an alliance in order to challenge effectively the "ruling bloc" of bourgeoisie and southern landowners (supported by the Catholic Church). Along with his absolute commitment to studying and conceiving these problems *historically,* and his attention to more than the so-called "fundamental classes" of bourgeois and worker, Gramsci's primary contribution has been his development of the theory of "hegemony and contradictory consciousness". "Hegemony" describes a historical situation in which the ongoing process of class struggle has been channelled, or contained, and "pacified" by the ruling class not merely through force and coercion, or the threat of such, but by ideological domination, suasion, compromise and, even, incorporation of selected "oppositional" ideas and aspirations.

"Contradictory consciousness" refers to the historically-evidenced fact that although the process of hegemony effectively contains class struggle, inhibiting the eruption of "class war", it cannot be "total", reducing the consciousness of the subordinated classes to "one-dimensionality" or "normative acceptance" of the social order, for the "material" experience of "class" exploitation and oppression continues to shape consciousness and "inspire" antagonisms. Also, Gramsci directs attention to "those less-structured forms of thought that circulate among the common people, often contradictory and confused and compounded of folklore, myth, and day-to-day popular experience".[82] Nevertheless, "contradictory" consciousness and "false" consciousness are not the same: in contrast to "false" consciousness, which is usually understood as awaiting the intervention from *without* and *above* of (socialist) intellectuals with *their* "ideas", Gramsci's contention is that within "contradictory" consciousness there exists the potential—indeed, bases—for class consciousness, the role of the (socialist) intellectual being in this case that of *developing* (socialist) consciousness in a dialectical relationship with the working class. For Gramsci, the working class and (socialist) intellectuals must establish an "organic" relationship.[83]

Rudé thus provided a Gramscian-inspired model, or theory, for the study of "popular" protest in "pre-industrial" societies—that is, societies in which we would not expect to find the specifically "class" formations and associated politics and ideologies characteristic of industrial capitalism:

Popular ideology in [pre-industrial society] is not a purely internal affair and the sole property of a single class or group . . . It is most often a mixture, a fusion of two elements, of which only one is the peculiar property of the "popular" classes and the other is superimposed by a process of transmission and adoption from outside. Of these, the first is what I call the "inherent", traditional element—a sort of "mother's milk" ideology, based on direct experience, oral tradition, or folk-memory and not learned by listening to sermons or speeches or reading books. In this fusion the second element is the stock of ideas and beliefs that one "derived" or borrowed from others, often taking the form of a more structured system of ideas, political or religious, such as the Rights of Man, Popular Sovereignty, *Laissez-faire* and the Sacred Rights of Property, Nationalism, Socialism, or the various versions of justification by Faith.

He makes sure to explain that there is "no Wall of Babylon" separating these two kinds of ideology. Indeed, Rudé explains, there is usually "a considerable overlap between them . . . among the 'inherent' beliefs of one generation, and forming part of its basic culture are many beliefs that were originally derived from outside by an earlier one".[84]

Rudé construes the "historical" perspectives offered by "inherent" and "derived" ideologies in the same fashion that he previously did the aspirations of the "lower orders" and "middle sort"; characteristically, "inherent" ideology is "backward-looking" and "derived" ideology is "forward-looking". "Inherent" ideology can engender a range of acts and struggles like "strikes, food riots, peasant rebellions, and even a state of awareness of the need for radical change"; moreover, significant "popular achievements" have been possible from struggles informed merely by "inherent" ideology. However, Rudé declares, for such struggles to posit "reform" rather than "restoration" and to move from resistance and rebellion to "revolution" requires the "inherent" ideology being "supplemented" by "derived" ideology—though he notes that this *too* may be conservative or reactionary and "backward-looking" as in the "Church and King" movements of French peasants in the Vendée after 1793. The actual process of merger between "inherent" and "derived" ideologies to form "popular" ideology, he observes, occurred "in stages and at different levels of sophistication". Insisting on the historicity of such processes he adds that "whether the resultant mixture took on a militant and revolutionary or a conservative and counter-revolutionary form depended less on the nature of the recipients or of the 'inherent' beliefs from which they started than on the nature of the 'derived' beliefs compounded by the circumstances then prevailing and what E.P. Thompson has called 'the sharp jostle of experience'". The "determining" force granted to the "derived" ideas should not be construed as the persistence of Leninism in Rudé's thought for, although there are certain residues, it is clear that "popular" ideology *is* conceived of as a "merger" even having original elements. Moreover, Rudé adds: "all 'derived' ideas in the course of transmission and adoption suffer a transformation or 'sea-change': its nature will depend on the social needs or the political aims of the classes that are ready to absorb them".[85]

His articles and the book, *Ideology and Popular Protest,* are not merely "theoretical" but predominantly "historical" in content. Drawing in particular on the historical studies of his fellow British Marxist historians and those of a younger generation of (predominantly American) social historians, as well as on his own scholarship on eighteenth- and nineteenth-century England and France, Rudé focussed on the ideology of popular protest characteristic of the transition from feudalism to capitalism. Thus, in the book there are chapters on: peasants in medieval Europe, under absolutism, and in Latin America; the English, American and French Revolutions (1789, 1830 and 1848); and England in the eighteenth- and nineteenth-century Industrial Revolution, along with a "Postscript" on industrial Britain. As indicated in the previous section, Rudé's crowd studies never failed to raise the question of the "legacy" of popular protest. In these writings on the ideology of popular protest he poses it most directly: "What happens to popular ideology once the rebellion or revolution is suppressed? Does it disappear so that it has to start all over again?". His reply—which is elaborated upon in the course of his book—is:

> No, obviously not . . . After the defeat of the English Levellers at Burford in 1649, of the Parisian *sans-culottes* in 1795, or for that matter the French *ouvriers* in June 1848 . . . the reaction might be real enough, as it was under the Cromwellian Protectorate and Restoration in England and the Napoleonic Empire and restoration in France. But what is also true is that the popular revolutionary tradition, having led an underground existence out of sight of the authorities, survived and re-emerged in new forms and under new historical conditions when the "people"—the recipients of the previous set of "derived" ideas—had also suffered a "sea-change".[86]

Histories: "All History Must Be Studied Afresh"

Rudé has not only been the author of a remarkable set of primary works, but along with the previously-considered *The Crowd in History* and *Ideology and Popular Protest,* he is the author of several masterful historical syntheses and a variety of critical writings on historiography (a selection of which is included in the first section of the present volume), the most important of the latter being his book, *Debate on Europe, 1815–1850.*[87] This section will look at Rudé's efforts to provide syntheses of the eighteenth and early nineteenth-century periods, the "classical" narratives of which his own original scholarship contributed so much to undermining. Although now subject to historical revision, I hope to show that these studies, along with Rudé's primary work, have themselves been influential in inspiring potentially more successful syntheses or narratives. First, however, we should note Rudé's own thinking about the writing of history.

Perhaps because so much of his work as a "pioneer" has entailed confrontations with the narratives and myths propagated by liberal and, especially, conservative writers about the eighteenth and nineteenth centuries, Rudé has regularly been invited to offer his reflections on the practice of history and other historians. His writings in this area are characteristically critical, but, at the same time, always appreciative of *good* historical study, whether from the Left or Right. His thoughts are well articulated in articles such as "Marxism and History", "Interpretations of the French Revolution", and "The Study of Revolutions",[88] among others, but are best represented in *Debate on Europe,* which Hugh Stretton describes as "both a novel history of ideas, and a model of the self-knowledge and understanding of the sources of historical disagreement which every working historian ought to have, and all too few do have".[89] The book provides a critical survey of historians' views and studies from contemporary times to the present (1970) of events and developments in European political, economic, cultural and social history from the end of the Napoleonic Wars to the revolts of 1848. The Introduction to the book is a marvellously crisp consideration of the variables or factors shaping historians' thoughts as they pursue, in the words of E.H. Carr, "the dialogue with the past" which is history and the intertwined debate with other historians past and present. In the light of the determining force of national, class, and "generational" origins, differential access and inclination to different kinds of evidence, and social, political, and religious views upon the interpretive act, Rudé insists that "there can be no single received or universal truth in [history] writing and that the 'varieties of history' (to use Fritz Stern's expression) must be largely attributed to factors such as these".[90] Moreover, we are reminded that however good the history, it is subject to revision because "although the past does not change the present does" and, therefore, the dialogue between past and present is transformed as our experience conjures up new questions, concerns and sympathies which we introduce into it. Yet, he adds, there are writers whose works, for various possible reasons, continue to speak to historical scholars even after generations, citing in particular the writings of Tocqueville, Marx and Engels.[91]

Not surprisingly, as a Marxist Rudé stresses the significance of "socio-political values" which divide scholars and he explains that in the course of the book he will be distinguishing historians in terms of three "camps" which he labels "Tory" or "conservative", "Whig" or "liberal", and "socialist" or "Marxist". (Giving each of these a broad definition, Rudé acknowledged that such "labels" are "of course, generalizations, which never exactly fit" and, thus, there are variations and degrees to which they do.) The question of values is *so* important, he contends, because values "affect not only the sort of books [historians] write and the judgements they make, but also the records they consult, the questions they ask and the methods they use to prepare and to present their answers". He finds—optimistically, perhaps—that the advent of the "new" social history has seemed to reduce the "polemic" for so long characteristic of historical thinking about the period 1815–50. However, he says, this does not mean that historical practice is any more "value-free" than previously, referring us, for example, to the debate underway at the time between liberals and Marxists on the consequences of the Industrial Revolution to working-class standards of living.[92] And yet he notes at several points in the text that the application of new methods and theoretical insights, along with the "opening up" of new archives, has allowed for real progress in the historical study of certain features of the past.[93] (The issues arising out of the years 1815–50 which have been a part of historical debate and are included in Rudé's survey are, of course, too numerous to indicate. But it should be stated that a reading of Rudé's discussion of the connections between the emergence of particular historical concerns and contemporary social issues—for example, the renewed historical interest in "nationalism" in the post-Second World War period instigated, it would appear, by the resurgence of Afro-Asian struggles for independence[94]—forces one to reflect on the relationship between present-day historical writings and current affairs and concerns.[95])

Rudé has always been a promoter of the idea that historians should make use of the methods and insights of the social sciences and, as we have seen, he himself drew upon such from sociology and social psychology. After almost thirty years, his "borrowings" from social sciences seem less radical now that historians have enmeshed themselves in everything from econometrics to semiotics. Yet whereas Rudé sought to "socialize" history without writing out "political" history, the same cannot be said of all the currents of "interdisciplinary" history which have emerged during the past generation; it should be registered that in contrast to a number of contemporary scholars who are inclined to merge history with the social sciences, Rudé has insisted on the essential autonomy of the historical discipline.[96] Indeed—perhaps even contradicting what I have said above—although he has always been ready and eager for a dialogue and exchange with the social sciences, Rudé has often been dissatisfied with the results (as we have noted). More significant than generically-constituted social-science thought has

been the influence of Marx and Engels on his historical scholarship. In
"The Changing Face of the Crowd" he commences his personal
reflections by declaring what he believes his work owes to a reading of
the founders of historical materialism:

> What I learned from Marx was not only that history tends to progress through a
> conflict of social classes . . . but that it has a discoverable pattern and moves forward
> (not backwards, in circles, or in inexplicable jerks) broadly from a lower to a higher
> phase of development. I learned also that the lives and actions of the common people
> are the very stuff of history, and though "material" rather than the institutional and
> ideological factors are primary, that ideas themselves become a "material force" when
> they pass into active consciousness of men. Moreover, I have also learned from Engels
> that, whatever the excellence of historical "systems" . . . "all history must be studied
> afresh".

For Rudé, then, a Marxist historian is one who sees history in terms of
"class struggle" not "a narrow economic determinism" and he believes
"conflict is both a normal and salutary means of achieving progress".
He has brought this to bear both in his primary work and in his
"synthetic" writings on eighteenth- and nineteenth-century Europe
including, in the latter instances, his books: *Revolutionary Europe,
1783–1815* (1964); *Robespierre* (1975); *Hanoverian London, 1714–1803*
(1971); and *Europe in the Eighteenth Century* (1972)—and we should note
here again his latest work, *The French Revolution After 200 Years.*[97]
Revolutionary Europe, the first, and probably the most important
considering the more than one hundred thousand students and others
(not including readers of the translated editions) who have been
introduced to the period through its pages!, is a splendidly written text
examining the French Revolution and its consequences in European
perspective and providing narrative and analysis along with clear
discussions of the many issues which have fascinated historians ever
since the fall of the Bastille. The particular "grand narrative" which
Rudé offers is expressive of his own scholarship but also incorporates
that advanced by his "colleagues", Lefebvre and Soboul, which they
had developed out of both the "Republican" and "Marxist" traditions.
In their works the Revolution is conceived of as a "merger of two
distinct movements—the bourgeois and the popular . . ."[98]

This class-structured rendition of the Revolution is also the
underlying narrative for *Robespierre,* a book which Rudé refers to as a
"political portrait rather than a personal biography". Robespierre is
portrayed extremely sympathetically by Rudé and one necessarily
imagines that Rudé's thoughts—as those of an admirer of the Soviet
Revolution—are related to his perceptions of Lenin; an idea which is
confirmed in the last pages of the volume where Rudé directly compares

and contrasts the leading figure of Jacobinism with that of the great Bolshevik revolutionary. In particular, Rudé's picture of Robespierre is that of a "revolutionary political democrat" persistently asserting the "sovereignty of the people" but, tragically, having to deal with the inherent contradictions of the revolutionary alliance between Jacobins and *sans-culottes*—and for Robespierre "the Revolution" was paramount in importance. Rudé also finds that although Robespierre "was not a socialist" he was, as Lefebvre had argued, a "social democrat" of sorts (though it should be pointed out that Rudé's definition of a "socialist" is rather "orthodox" for it requires "State ownership . . .")[99] At the end of the book Rudé offers an historical assessment of the place of the Revolution in history and, within it, Robespierre's particular contribution:

> The French Revolution was one of the great landmarks in modern history. No other single event did so much to destroy the aristocratic society and absolutist institutions of Old Europe and to lay the groundwork for the new societies—both bourgeois and socialist—that on every continent, have risen from their ashes since. To this transformation Robespierre made a signal contribution: not only as the Revolution's outstanding leader at every stage of its most vigorous and creative years; but also as the first great champion of democracy and people's rights. And this, essentially, is what establishes his claim to greatness.[100]

The subtitle of Rudé's book, *Europe in the Eighteenth Century: Aristocracy and the Bourgeois Challenge,* clearly signals his view of the class-structuring of the period. Introducing the volume, he refers to the "numerous pitfalls" one faces in writing the history of that "pre-revolutionary" century. Such difficulties include the danger of reducing all that transpired to being merely a "Preface" to the "Age of Revolution" (to use Eric Hobsbawm's term) and, also, the question of British "exceptionalism". Moreover, he observes, there is the general historiographical problem of "how to stress movement—which is the very stuff of history—as well as the conditions, 'structure' and 'continuity'". Admitting to having emphasized "internal conflicts" Rudé forewarns his readers "that a great deal of attention has been paid to social classes, to the institutions and ideas they generate and to the tensions and conflicts that arise between them. These in turn are presented as an important element in the historical process".[101] The book provides a comprehensive portrait of eighteenth-century Europe from population and social structure, to politics, government and ideas, to the struggles which shaped them.

Naturally, Rudé seeks to incorporate "history from below" and the popular classes into his narrative and analysis—though he was constrained by the paucity of such historical scholarship at the time.

Thus, the conflicts of the eighteenth century, upon which he primarily focusses are those between aristocracy and bourgeoisie, but, as he shows, the antagonisms and conflicts between the popular classes and the upper—both bourgeois and aristocrats—were also crucial determinants of the course of events. Indeed, Rudé contends, it was the fear of the middle class about the "inferior sort of people" which effectively inhibited them from mobilizing the common people against the aristocracy, the consequences of which were to the advantage of the Old Regime. (This fear was overcome in the Revolution of 1789!)[102] It must be said that what is actually most interesting about *Europe in the Eighteenth Century* is Rudé's not unsympathetic renderings of the rulers and dominant classes (for example, his discussion of "enlightened despots" and their efforts at reforms which were destined to failure—or, at best, limited success—"so long as the privileged orders were left in possession of their powers . . . to obstruct their operation".)[103]

Hanoverian London is an extremely detailed survey of urban life in the capital. Again, in characteristically Rudéan fashion it evidences his concern to integrate the "lower orders" into the historical picture. And yet, as in *Europe in the Eighteenth Century,* it is arguable that the most intriguing aspects of the work are Rudé's descriptions of the circumstances of the "propertied", aristocratic and bourgeois. Few historians denied the significance of inequalities of wealth and power in eighteenth-century England, but whereas classes and conflicts were not, perhaps, dramatic innovations in European studies, to insist on the centrality of these—especially conflict—in English life was to oppose the traditional view of the century as one of "consensus". Rudé, however, approaching London from the bottom up, and fully conscious of social and political protests "from below", insists that "class hostility" and "conflicts" were a central force in the eighteenth century. (I cannot help but remark that as much as Rudé is renowned for his attention to socio-political subjects in history, his insights into the class structuring of experience in *Hanoverian London* never fail to encompass culture and everyday life as well. For example, he writes of how "In the first half of the century there was a tidy class division in drinking: the poor drank gin or cheap brandy, 'the middle sort' drank porter or ale and the wealthier classes drank French or Portuguese wine".)[104]

Although Rudé's synthetic writings are framed by a "class-struggle and structured" mode of analysis, he remains as ambivalent in these works on the eighteenth century as he has been in his primary studies to present the historical experience of the time in *class*-specific terms. His reservations seem to be due to both an "orthodox" Marxist understanding of class *and* a commitment to comprehending the past in historically specific terms; that is, he is both unwilling to impose on, and unable to find in, the eighteenth century the model of *class* experience derived from the nineteenth (both in the sense of "in itself" and "for itself"). In this vein, Rudé has himself acknowledged the significance, and even correctness, of certain aspects of the "revisionist challenge" to the view of the French Revolution as a "bourgeois revolution" (a challenge originating with his own major professor at the University of London, Alfred Cobban).[105] For example, he has said that "terms like *aristocracy* and *bourgeoisie*... have developed a Marxist connotation from the nineteenth-century attempt to distinguish between major social groups according to their economic background or role... All this is useful, but obviously these modern connotations can be misleading in the context of the French Revolution in which words such as aristocrat or bourgeois tend to take on political connotations, and thus confusion arises among old and new meanings".[106] However, even though Rudé points to a source of the historiographical problem, he has not himself addressed it sufficiently to answer the revisionist critique which, although it has offered no better alternative, has greatly undermined the "bourgeois revolution" thesis. This is problematic: Rudé offers us a class-struggle analysis of the eighteenth century and French Revolution but, at the same time, he is unable to actually defend the class-based "bourgeois revolution" thesis.

Yet there has begun to emerge a Marxian effort to transcend the revisionist critique. Rudé's own student, George Comninel, stimulated in good part by insights found in Rudé's own writings, has begun to advance a new reading of the Revolution. In his book, *Rethinking the French Revolution,*[107] Comninel surveys the Marxist versus revisionist debate and shows how the Marxist tradition has consistently failed to consider critically the origins of its "class" model of the Revolution and the grounds upon which it has been based. He points out that Marx himself uncritically drew his version of the French Revolution from nineteenth-century "liberal" writers, never actually subjecting the origins, developments and events of the Revolution to a "historical materialist" analysis and, furthermore, that Marxists ever since have subscribed to—and sought to defend—the "bourgeois revolution" thesis, thereby reproducing Marx's originally-mistaken assumptions.

What Comninel calls for—and plans himself to pursue in a second volume—is the suspension, if not the disavowal, of the "bourgeois revolution" thesis in favour of a return to, and re-examination of, the *history* of the Revolution from a truly critical historical materialist perspective starting out from the historically specific relations of exploitation and appropriation of late eighteenth-century France and the class struggles to which they give rise. In fact, he provides a provisional rendition of such an analysis in the conclusion to *Rethinking the French Revolution* and, in its recognition of the significance of the popular struggles "without whose intervention the bourgeois and liberal-aristocratic revolutionaries could not have realized their goals",[108] it is evident that Comninel's efforts have been inspired by the scholarship of his mentor (as well as that of Lefebvre and Soboul). What we must now acknowledge is that although Rudé did not himself pursue it, his own works—by asserting and highlighting the centrality of the struggles from below—actually undermined the "bourgeois revolution" thesis and greatly contributed to the need for a fresh historical materialist analysis and, likely, a dramatically-revised grand narrative of the Revolution! Thus, Comninel's future work promises to be a major contribution to our understanding of eighteenth-century France and the Revolution of 1789, and to the further development of the class-struggle analysis of history,[109] not to mention representing a tribute to the work of Rudé.

Rudé himself provided the Foreword to Comninel's book and his appreciation and enthusiasm for its arguments are clearly expressed. He especially welcomes Comninel's insistence on both the necessity of rigorously applying the "principles of historical materialism" to the eighteenth century and, in the process, the need to reconsider the assumption that the decline of feudalism necessarily engendered the rise of capitalism in any direct or immediate fashion.[110] This, of course, reflects Rudé's own long-standing doubts and difficulties, noted earlier, about how to conceive the eighteenth century in terms of the transition from feudalism to capitalism and the development of "industrial" capitalism in both France and England. As indicated earlier, Rudé's problem on this score was due in part to his failure to examine or sufficiently consider the politico-economic processes and developments under way in the eighteenth century in England and France. Although the concept of "pre-industrial" society provided an extremely useful means by which to treat contemporary popular protests in England and France, the political economies and class structures of the two countries were quite different. At the same time, Rudé's persistent reference to the period as "transitional" and his insistence that it not be subsumed—in either the English or French case—under the "feudal" past or, too readily, under the "industrial-capitalist" future, because from his studies it was evident that the struggles of the age were historically unique, can be seen as inviting the pursuit of more rigorous politico-economic analyses of both Hanoverian England and pre-revolutionary and revolutionary France. Indeed, his repeated observation that the primary site of contention in the eighteenth century was "at the point of consumption rather than *production*", and that there was not yet a consciousness of class as in the nineteenth century, has remained an important question only now beginning to be properly addressed by social historians of a Marxist persuasion.[111]

This question posed by Rudé brings us to the work of his fellow British Marxist historian, E.P. Thompson (itself an influence on Comninel's ideas about the French Revolution), for it was Thompson who followed Rudé into eighteenth-century England and, in his own way, ran into the same problematic as his pioneering comrade: how to conceive of the popular struggles of the age? Thompson's answer, like Rudé's, was *"class struggle without class"*. But whereas Rudé did not pursue the self-contradictory implications of this phrase, Thompson has, and in so doing, he has explicitly reformulated the Marxian model of class formation. That is, Thompson eschewed the static and essentially ahistorical scheme of "class in itself—class for itself"—which Rudé too came to abandon in *Ideology and Popular Protest*—and, instead, offered a dynamic model posing the historically prior existence of class struggle/structure out of which "class", in the sense of a class-conscious formation, may potentially develop or, better, *be made*. Thompson himself explains that the possible attribution of "class" to eighteenth-century popular struggles requires, first, critical attention to the historically-specific social relations of exploitation and appropriation (which, it must be added, is—thus far at least—more often implied in his writings than explicity mapped out).[112] Thompson's work points the way towards a historical-materialist class-struggle analysis of eighteenth- and early nineteenth-century England in terms of the process of "primitive accumulation".[113] Having said this, it remains true that the work under way and to be done on the eighteenth century will have been constructed on the foundations laid out not only by Thompson who, as I have previously argued, has articulated in the clearest theoretical terms the class-struggle approach of the British Marxist historians, but also by Rudé who first advanced into the eighteenth century to recover the popular struggles of the time and thereby called up the "problematic" of "class struggle without class".

George Rudé's writings on eighteenth-century France, England and Europe, and his studies of the Age of Revolution reaching from Europe to North America and Australia, have influenced historical and social science scholarship around the globe. Although social historians in the 1980s have ventured down topical, methodological and theoretical paths which he himself would not have pursued, it is arguable that much of the social-history writing of the past generation, in its pursuit of history from below, was enabled by Rudé's own initiatives to mobilize the methodologies and theoretical insights of the social sciences and struggles to widen the social horizons of the past.

I have argued that the political project of the British Marxist historians as a group has been to contribute to the making of a democratic and socialist historical consciousness.[114] There can be no doubt that Rudé too, in spite of his "exile" from England to Australia and North America for so much of his university teaching career and, thus, geographically distant from his historian comrades, has been actively committed to that effort. Reading of the *sans-culottes'* mobilizations in the Revolution, of the movement for Wilkes and Liberty in Hanoverian London, of the struggles of the agricultural labourers in industrializing England and the transportation of so many of them to Australia, and of the aspirations and ideas of protests around the pre-industrial societies of the Atlantic World, one is necessarily reminded of the words offered by Antonio Gramsci to his son, written from a Fascist prison in 1937:

> I think you must like history, as I liked it when I was your age, because it deals with living men, and everything that concerns men, as many men as possible, all the men in the world in so far as they unite together in society, and work and struggle and make a bid for a better life. All that can't fail to please you more than anything else. Isn't that right?[115]

Historical scholarship continues to "progress" and Rudé's writings have, by their very instigation of new work, become subject to critical questioning by a younger generation of social historians.[116] Yet even if his studies of popular protest and his texts on eighteenth-century history come to be superceded by new researches and interpretations, or transcended by way of dramatic revisions to our grand narratives, Rudé's contributions will remain relevant as examples of pioneering and committed history writing. Moreover, so long as we continue to ask the central historical questions—"Who?" and "Why?"—we will continue to honour his work, for he would be the first to argue along the lines of the founders of historical materialism that "all history must be studied afresh".

Notes

1. Paul Preston, "A Review of *Criminal and Victim*", *British Book News*, Feb. 1986.
2. G. Rudé, *The Crowd in the French Revolution* (Oxford, 1959; rev. ed. 1967); *Wilkes and Liberty* (Oxford, 1962; rev. ed., London, 1983); *The Crowd in History, 1730–1848* (New York, 1964; rev. ed., London 1981); and *Paris and London in the Eighteenth Century* (London, 1970; US ed., 1971).
3. G. Rudé, *Revolutionary Europe, 1783–1815* (London, 1964; reprinted ed., 1967), and *Europe in the Eighteenth Century: Aristocracy and the Bourgeois Challenge* (London, 1972; paperback ed., 1974).

4. E.J. Hobsbawm and G. Rudé, *Captain Swing* (London, 1969; Penguin ed. 1973); and G. Rudé, *Protest and Punishment* (Oxford, 1978), and *Criminal and Victim* (Oxford, 1985).

5. On "history from below" or "the bottom up" see Harvey J. Kaye, *The British Marxist Historians* (Oxford, 1984), esp. pp. 222–32. I prefer the term "history from the bottom up"; George Rudé prefers "from below". In this instance, I defer to him and will most often use "history from below".

6. For a complete bibliography of Rudé's books and articles, see F. Krantz, ed., *History from Below: Studies in Popular Protest and Popular Ideology in Honour of George Rudé* (Montreal, Concordia University ed., 1985), pp. 35–40.

7. I must acknowledge the introductory articles to Rudé's *Festschrift*, *History from Below* (referred to in note 6,) in particular Frederick Krantz, "'Sans érudition, pas d'histoire': The Work of George Rudé" and Hugh Stretton, "George Rudé". Together those two essays provide the most comprehensive survey of Rudé's writings, life and thought and I have referred to them at a variety of points in the writing of my own essay.

8. G. Rudé, *Robespierre* (London, 1975). I did not have the space to treat this work adequately, but Fred Krantz provides a full and appreciative discussion of it in his essay referred to in note 7.

9. The family name was actually Rude, without the accent, but George changed it while at school in England. This biographical sketch is drawn from conversations with George Rudé in 1986–7 in Green Bay (Wisconsin), Rye (Sussex), and Montreal (Canada); but also draws heavily on the essay by Hugh Stretton referred to in note 6.

10. See V.G. Kiernan, "Herbert Norman's Cambridge", in *E.H. Norman: His Life and Scholarship*, ed. R. Bowen (Toronto, 1984), pp. 25–45; reprinted in H.J. Kaye, ed., *Poets, Politics and the People: Writings of V.G. Kiernan* [2] (London, forthcoming 1989).

11. See Kaye, *The British Marxist Historians* and Kaye's "Introduction: V.G. Kiernan, Seeing Things Historically", in *History, Classes and Nation-States: Selected Writings of V.G. Kiernan* (Oxford, 1988), pp. 1–28. For Rudé's comments on his fellow British Marxist historians, see "Marxism and History" in the present collection.

12. E.J. Hobsbawm, "The Historians' Group of the Communist Party", in *Rebels and Their Causes*, ed. M. Cornforth (London, 1978), p. 37.

13. See Rudé's recollections in "The Changing Face of the Crowd" (1970) in the present collection.

14. For Rudé on Lefebvre's work, see his essay "Georges Lefebvre as Historian of Popular Urban Protest in the French Revolution" (1960) in the present collection, and Rudé's "Introduction" to Lefebvre's classic work, *The Great Fear of 1789* (Paris, 1932; English trans. London, 1973). Also, see Lefebvre's *The Coming of the French Revolution* (Princeton, 1947) with a Preface by R. R. Palmer.

15. See Albert Soboul, *The Parisian Sans-Culottes and the French Revolution* (Paris, 1958; English trans. Oxford, 1964) and also his book, *The French Revolution, 1787–1799* (Paris, 1962; English trans. London, 1974).

16. See Richard Cobb, *The People's Armies* (1961; English trans. New Haven, Conn., 1987) and *Paris and Its Provinces* (Oxford, 1975). Cobb has been an extremely prolific scholar and writer; for a bibliography of his work, see the *Festschrift* in his honour, G. Lewis and C. Lucas, eds, *Beyond the Terror* (Cambridge, 1983).

17. For example, see Rudé's "Introduction" to *Paris and London in the Eighteenth Century*, p. 12.

18. G. Rudé, "The Gordon Riots: A Study of the Rioters and their Victims", is

reprinted in ibid., pp. 268–92.

19. See Stretton, "George Rudé", pp. 45–6. Also, on the crisis of 1956 and the reactions of the British Marxist historians, see Kaye, *The British Marxist Historians*, pp. 17–18.
20. G. Rudé, *Ideology and Popular Protest* (London, 1980).
21. G. Rudé, *The French Revolution after 200 Years* (London, 1988).
22. G. Rudé, *Europe in the Eighteenth Century*, p. 94.
23. G. Rudé, *The Crowd in the French Revolution*, p. 2, and *The Crowd in History*, p. 8.
24. G. Rudé, *The Crowd in the French Revolution*, p. 3, and *The Crowd in History*, p. 7.
25. G. Rudé, *The Crowd in the French Revolution*, p. 5 (my italics).
26. G. Rudé, *Paris and London*, p. 280, and *Wilkes and Liberty*, p. 15.
27. G. Rudé, *Paris and London*, p. 10.
28. G. Rudé, *The Crowd in History*, pp. 10–11.
29. Ibid., pp. 11–12. Rudé has always given primary importance to the archives, discussing them at the outset of his text, rather than in a footnote or appendix.
30. Barrington Moore, Jr., *Social Origins of Dictatorship and Democracy* (Boston, 1966), pp. 521–3.
31. G. Rudé, *The Crowd in the French Revolution*, p. 178.
32. G. Rudé, *Paris and London*, pp. 298–9.
33. Ibid., p. 129; *The Crowd in the French Revolution*, p. 181, and *Wilkes and Liberty*, p. 183.
34. G. Rudé, *Paris and London*, p. 19.
35. G. Rudé, *The Crowd in History*, pp. 5–6.
36. Ibid., pp. 259–60. This theme is further developed by E.P. Thompson in *The Making of the English Working Class* (London, 1963).
37. The term is taken from Charles Tillly, *The Contentious French* (Cambridge, Mass., 1986).
38. See Rudé's remarks in "The Changing Face of the Crowd" (in the present volume) where he also discusses other criticisms of his work.
39. See Hobsbawm's *Primitive Rebels* (1959; rev. ed. Manchester, 1971) and *Labouring Men* (London, 1968). On Hobsbawm's work, see Kaye, *The British Marxist Historians*, Chapter 5, pp. 131–76.
40. See Rudé's comments in "The Changing Face of the Crowd" (in the present volume).
41. E.J. Hobsbawm and G. Rudé, *Captain Swing*, pp. xvii–xviii.
42. On the Hammonds, see Hobsbawm's "Introduction" in J. Hammond and B. Hammond, *The Village Labourer* (New York, 1970) and G. Rudé's, "Introduction", in J. Hammond and B. Hammond, *The Skilled Labourer* (New York, 1970).
43. E.J. Hobsbawm and G. Rudé, *Captain Swing*, pp. xx–xxiii.
44. F. Krantz, "*Sans érudition, pas d'histoire*", p. 14.
45. E.J. Hobsbawm and G. Rudé, *Captain Swing*, pp. 201–11.
46. Ibid., pp. 242, 258. In the present volume, see Rudé's article "English Rural and Urban Disturbances on the Eve of the First Reform Bill, 1830–1831".
47. Ibid., pp. 224–5.
48. G. Rudé, *Protest and Punishment*, p. 1.
49. Ibid., pp. 2–4.
50. Ibid., p. 10.
51. Ibid., p. 247. Actually, on the comparison Rudé refers us for the most part to the tables in the Appendices to the book.
52. G. Rudé, *Criminal and Victim*, pp. 78–9; also see "Crime, Criminals and Victims in Early Nineteenth-Century London" in the present volume.

53. Ibid., pp. 117, 118–21.
54. Ibid., pp. 124–6.
55. G. Rudé, *Paris and London*, pp. 136–7.
56. Ibid., pp. 302–3.
57. Ibid., p. 304.
58. See footnote 14 above.
59. H. Lefebvre, "Revolutionary Crowds" in J. Kaplow, ed., *New Perspectives on the French Revolution* (New York), p. 175.
60. G. Rudé, *Paris and London*, esp. "Prices, Wages and Popular Movements in Paris during the French Revolution", pp. 163–77.
61. G. Rudé, *The Crowd in the French Revolution*, p. 200, and *Wilkes and Liberty*, p. 188.
62. G. Rudé, *The Crowd in the French Revolution*, pp. 210–19.
63. Ibid., pp. 199, 200 and note 3 on p. 200.
64. Ibid., p. 225.
65. G. Rudé, "Society and Conflict in London and Paris in the Eighteenth Century" (1969), in *Paris and London*, pp. 35–60.
66. G. Rudé, *Wilkes and Liberty*, Ch 6, pp. 90–104.
67. Ibid., p. 190.
68. Ibid., p. 187.
69. Ibid., p. 197.
70. Ibid., p. 12.
71. G. Rudé, *Paris and London*, pp. 289–90.
72. Noted by G. Rudé in "The Changing Face of the Crowd", in the present collection.
73. G. Rudé, *Ideology and Popular Protest*, p. 7.
74. The most comprehensive treatment of Western Marxism is offered in Martin Jay, *Marxism and Totality* (Oxford, 1985).
75. G. Rudé, "Marxism and History", in the present collection.
76. On Gramsci, see Joseph Femia, *Gramsci's Political Thought* (Oxford, 1981); and for a survey to 1981 of Gramsci Studies in English, see Harvey J. Kaye "Antonio Gramsci: An Annotated Bibliography of Studies in English", *Politics and Society*, 10 (1981), pp. 335–53, which is being updated by the Gramsci Study Circle (NYC) under the direction of Frank Rosengarten, *et al.*
77. G. Rudé, "The Changing Face of the Crowd" (in the present volume) and "The Pre-Industrial Crowd" (1969) in *Paris and London*, pp. 31–3.
78. See the articles in Section II of the present volume: "European Popular Protest and Ideology on the Eve of the French Revolution"; "The Germination of a Revolutionary Ideology among the Urban *menu peuple* of 1789"; and "Ideology and Popular Protest".
79. See Harvey J. Kaye, "Political Theory and History: Antonio Gramsci and the British Marxist Historians", *Italian Quarterly*, 97–8 (Summer-Fall 1984), pp. 145–66.
80. G. Rudé, *Ideology and Popular Protest*, pp. 15–25.
81. A. Gramsci, *Selections from the Prison Notebooks*, edited by Q. Hoare and G. Smith (London, 1971).
82. G. Rudé, *Ideology and Popular Protest*, pp. 20–4.
83. H.J. Kaye, "Political Theory and History", pp. 148–50, and Jerome Karabel, "Revolutionary Contradictions: Antonio Gramsci and the Problem of Intellectuals", *Politics and Society*, 6 (1976), pp. 123–72.
84. G. Rudé, *Ideology and Popular Protest*, p. 28.
85. Ibid., pp. 31–6.
86. Ibid., pp. 36–7.
87. G. Rudé, *Debate on Europe, 1815–1850* (New York, 1972).

88. These essays are included in the present volume.

89. H. Stretton, "George Rudé", p. 52.

90. G. Rudé, *Debate on Europe*, p. viii.

91. Ibid., pp. x, xiii.

92. Ibid., pp. xii, xv; and p. 69.

93. Ibid., pp. 179, 210–12.

94. Ibid., p. 102.

95. Consider the resurgence of "conservative" historiography and the political ascendance of the New Right in both Britain and the United States.

96. See his comments in "The Changing Face of the Crowd" in the present volume.

97. Time and distance have prevented me from having complete access to this manuscript (currently in press) and thus I have been unable to discuss it in this essay.

98. G. Rudé, *Revolutionary Europe*, p. 104.

99. G. Rudé, *Robespierre*, pp. 197–208, 151.

100. Ibid., p. 213. Also, see his essay "Robespierre as Seen by British Historians", in the present volume.

101. G. Rudé, *Europe in the Eighteenth Century*, pp. 11–14.

102. Ibid., p. 239.

103. Ibid., pp. 129–35, 140, 153–4, 305.

104. G. Rudé, *Hanoverian London*, p. 70.

105. For example, see Alfred Cobban's *The Social Interpretation of the French Revolution* (London, 1968). For Rudé's comments on the "revisionist challenge", see the concluding remarks to "Interpretations of the French Revolution", included in the present volume.

106. G. Rudé, "The French Revolution", in N. Cantor, ed., *Perspectives on the European Past* (New York, 1971), pp. 47–8.

107. G. Comninel, *Rethinking the French Revolution* (London, 1987).

108. G. Rudé, "Foreword" to ibid., p. x.

109. Comninel's work is also heavily influenced by the work of Robert Brenner in *The Brenner Debate* (Cambridge, 1985).

110. G. Rudé, "Foreword" to G. Comninel, *Rethinking the French Revolution*, p. xii. Also, see Rudé's thoughts on the "transition" in France in his essay, "Feudalism and the French Revolution", included in the present volume.

111. For example, see William Reddy, *Money and Liberty in Modern Europe* (Cambridge, 1987).

112. See E.P. Thompson, "Eighteenth-century English Society: class struggle without class?" *Social History*, 3 (May 1978), pp. 133–65, and, of course, his book, *The Making of the English Working Class*. On Thompson's work, see Harvey J. Kaye, *The British Marxist Historians*, Chapter 6, pp. 167–220. Also, see Hans Medick, "Plebeian Culture in the Transition to Capitalism", in R. Samuel and G. Stedman Jones, eds, *Culture, Ideology and Politics*, pp. 84–112.

113. Ellen Wood, "The Politics of Theory and the Concept of Class: E.P. Thompson and His Critics", *Studies in Political Economy*, 9 (Fall 1982), pp. 57–8.

114. H.J. Kaye, *The British Marxist Historians*, pp. 246–9.

115. For a selection of Gramsci's *Letters from Prison*, see the collection edited by Lynne Lawner (New York, 1973).

116. See J. Stevenson, "The 'Moral Economy' of the English Crowd: Myth and Reality", in A. Fletcher and J. Stevenson, eds, *Order and Disorder in Early Modern England* (Cambridge, 1985), pp. 218–38, and Tim Harris, *London Crowds in the Reign of Charles II* (Cambridge, 1987).

Part I
Studies in History and Revolution

1

Marxism and History

Marxist historiography naturally begins with Marx and Engels; and in its making they played a dual role. In the first place, they formulated the main principles of what became known as "historical materialism"; it was a long-drawn out process stretching over nearly half a century from the jointly written *Holy Family* (1845–6) to Engels's *Socialism Utopian and Scientific* (1890). But long before its completion they had begun to apply these principles in practice to the writing of works of history. It is with these historical works that this essay is primarily concerned, and also with the work of half a dozen recent Marxist historians in France and Britain.

Here Engels was the first in the field and, when only twenty-four years old, quite independently of Marx, he published *The Condition of the Working Class in England*. It was the first major attempt by either writer to apply the Marxist theory of history, which was only then beginning to mature in their minds, to a major study in social and political history. The book also had the great merit to be the first great historical study of the Industrial Revolution in action at a time when the very notion of an industrial "revolution" had only begun to exercise the minds and arouse the emotions of British writers and politicians. Its particular virtue perhaps was the author's capacity, after a short visit to England's industrial cities, to record clearly and comprehensively the industrial scene in Manchester, its slums and the lives and conditions of its working people, the first industrial proletariat in Europe. Engels also noted the doubtful benefits to the people of the rapid growth of cities that accompanied industrial advance: "The brutal indifference [he wrote], the unfeeling isolation of each in his private interests becomes the more repellent and offensive, the more these individuals are crowded together."

Other writers and chroniclers of the day—Disraeli, Kingsley and Mrs Gaskell—had also begun to describe and deplore the "condition of the people" and to call on authority to lighten their burden. But Engels went much further. Not content with merely "noting" and "deploring" and calling on the government to intervene, he realized, three years before it became a central point in the *Communist Manifesto,* that the overcrowding and industrialization did not merely brutalize men and increase their sufferings but, having reduced them to "machines pure and simple", also "(forced) them to think and demand a position worthy of men". So a central feature of the *Condition of the Working Class* is the description of the beginning of workers' resistance to exploitation, of their growing consciousness and will to struggle and their capacity, by organization and numbers, to hit back at the all-powerful employing class; and he even forecasts, within a brief span of years, the outbreak of a "revolution . . . with which none hitherto known can be compared".

Engels has, of course, been hammered by his critics for a tendency to idealize the "golden days" of England's pre-industrial past and, even more, for his apparently rash and lightly undertaken prophecy of revolution: a revolution, as is well known, that never came about. And he himself came to realize his mistake and, in 1892, in his Preface to the first English edition (the book first appeared in German), wrote that his "production bears the stamp of his youth, with its good and its faulty features, of neither of which he feels ashamed". Among these "faults" were his over-confidence in predicting a revolution; yet he very sensibly attributed this error to a number of factors, England's increasing industrial prosperity and the repeal of the Corn Laws among them.[1] He probably also had in mind the final passage in the book, in which he appears to be predicting that, in the last resort, avoidance of a bloody revolution would depend less on the objective social factors than on the possibility of reconciliation between the two contesting parties, that is, between "the better elements of the bourgeoisie on the one hand and the more educated workers [having become Communists] on the other".[2] It is hard to believe that such a conclusion would have been likely to commend itself to either Marx or Engels later; but, nonetheless, sandwiched between these lines is an important lesson in revolutionary strategy as valid today as when Engels penned it 150 years ago: that once the workers became organized and politically educated they would be less likely to engage in indiscriminate savagery and slaughter: "In proportion as the proletariat absorbs socialistic and communistic elements will the revolution diminish in bloodshed, revenge and savagery".[3] (It is curious that he puts the main emphasis on socialist ideas rather than on organization, or a combination of the two.)

Engels was also the author of the next historical work to be written by

Marx or himself under the influence of the new ideas. It once more bore witness to his versatility as now, six years later, he was turning his hand to a subject that was a far cry from the industrial England of the 1840s: to the peasants of southern Germany in the late Middle Ages. *The German Peasant War*, like much of Marx's and his own historical work, appeared first as a series of articles for the press; written in 1850, they were not published as a book until 1870. Engels had by this time had some experience of peasant protest through his recent active participation in the battles fought in revolutionary Baden in 1849. Like other authors of the event, in writing of the Peasant War, Engels had three main problems to face. They were the extreme complexity of German society in this transitional period, with the delicate balance that had to be struck between the burgher-led Free Cities, the feudal Princes on their lordly domains, and the peasants of the countryside; the role played by religion in a pre-industrial peasant struggle; and the diversities in the character, ideas and party attachments of the two principal leaders in the war, Martin Luther and Thomas Münzer. From this jigsaw Engels was able to establish that while the peasant masses, stimulated by their own basic grievances against feudal lord and unreformed Church, provided the shocktroops of revolution, it was the burghers, centred on the Free Cities and propelled by their own grievances against the restriction of feudal authority combined with the crusading spirit and slogans of Luther's Reformed Church, that provided the money and machinery of organization. It was religion, however, both of the Reformed and radical-revolutionary kind, that provided the rebellious peasants and their "plebeian" allies with an ideology of struggle.[4]

The author also showed considerable skill in presenting the character and behaviour of the two principal leaders and in describing how they reflected the composition and political attitudes of their respective parties. In this respect, he argued that Luther's "indecision and fear of the movement" and "his cowardly servility to the princes" faithfully mirrored "the hesitant and ambiguous policy" of the burghers; and he contrasts this with Münzer's "revolutionary energy and resolution", which in turn "was reproduced among the most advanced section of the plebeians and peasants". And he goes on to explain that whereas Luther "confined himself to expressing the conceptions and wishes of the majority of his class", Münzer, the revolutionary, "went far beyond the immediate ideas and demands of his peasant and plebeian supporters" and organized an "elitist group of the existing revolutionary elements" which was never more than "a small minority of the insurgent masses". This was a comparatively early attempt to apply the Marxist principle of the primacy of man's "material being" over his consciousness or, more specifically, to depict the behaviour and politics of leaders in terms of the struggle of contending social groups. However, as we shall see, this early attempt was soon far surpassed by Marx's more mature and more sophisticated portrayal of the Emperor Louis-Napoleon.

Both writers found themselves on more familiar ground when they wrote their articles (and subsequent books) on the revolutions of 1848 in France and Germany and on the Paris Commune of 1871. Their cooperation was so close at this time (in the early 1850s) that one might be excused for assigning a work to one writer when it should have been assigned to the other. Yet there were differences between them which are certainly more easily discernible today than they were to their contemporaries of the 1850s. Engels, for instance, appears to be more skilful in synthesis and in handling general history and in the narration of events (one might even say that he was the more accomplished historian of the two), whereas Marx is the great strategist of revolution and the master of satire and in handling the complex relations of classes and of political leaders and groups. But they were both faced by the problem of writing history almost as it passed before their eyes. The problem is really a twofold one. One aspect is the problem of changing perspectives determined by a sharp turn in events. An often quoted example is Marx's change of mind with regard to the seizure of power by the Commune. At first, as spokesman for the General Council of the First International meeting in London in September 1870, he warned the Parisians against "the desperate folly" of attempting another uprising; but when the uprising took place six months later and the Commune was installed, Marx, responding to an entirely new situation, praised the Parisians for "storming the heavens".

The other problem is that noted by Engels in his posthumous Introduction to Marx's earlier *Class Struggles in France* concerned with the French events of 1848–50, which he called "Marx's first attempt, with the aid of his materialist conception, to explain a phase of contemporary history from the given economic situation". But the problem, he noted (and he was writing forty years after the event), is that "a clear survey of the economic history of a given period is never contemporaneous; it can only be gained subsequently after collecting and sifting of the material has taken place".[5] He goes on to explain how far this affected Marx, who began his work at the end of 1849 and had completed his first three articles (or chapters) before he had occasion to appreciate the importance of the world trade crisis of 1847 as a precipitant of revolution in February and March 1848 and, later, of the renewed industrial prosperity of 1849–50 as a stimulus in turn to the revival of European reaction. So the forecast made late in 1848 of an imminent revival of revolutionary activity made in the first edition had to be discarded in the second.[6]

The *Eighteenth Brumaire of Louis Bonaparte,* which Marx began to write in the wake of the *coup d'état* of December 1851, had of course no such handicap as that mentioned above when it returned, briefly to the events of spring 1848 to Autumn 1850. But I shall confine myself here to a brief word on Marx's famous portrait of Louis Napoleon and on his reappraisal of the role of the peasantry after December 1848. Napoleon is presented in the magnificent opening pages, among the other mock-heroes of 1848, as the phantom of the great Napoleon. "From 1848 to 1851," he writes, "only the ghost of the old revolutionaries of 1789 walked about, from Marrast, the Republican in kid gloves, who disguised himself as the old Bailly, down to the adventurer who hides his commonplace repulsive features under the iron death mask of Napoleon".[7] This is Marx's withering political satire at its best.

To the French peasants of 1848, still a subject of bitter debate among historians, Marx in this volume makes partial amends for his sweeping denunciation of their role in *Class Struggles in France.* The "true peasant revolution" was then presented as the election of Louis Napoleon to the Presidency in December 1848, assured by a massive peasant vote. Now he conceded that, after the first *coup d'état,* a part of the peasantry were among the most vociferous to protest arms in hand against the outcome of their own vote of three years before. "The school they had gone through since 1848," he explains "sharpened their wits." Nevertheless, he insists that the peasantry as a whole continued for some time to supply a solid background of support for the Bonapartist dynasty. Yet as the Presidency passed into the Empire, the peasant freeholders (writes Marx) began to become persuaded that Louis Napoleon, for all his promises, was of no more use to them than the vote-seeking bourgeoisie. So, concludes Marx, "the interest of the peasants . . . are no longer, as under the first Napoleon, in accord with, but in opposition to, the interests of the bourgeoisie, or capital. Hence the peasants find their natural ally and leader in the *urban proletariat* whose task it is to overthrow the bourgeois order".[8] While this belief in a close worker-peasant alliance proved, as the events of March-May 1871 would show, to be over-optimistic, Marx, having adroitly considered all the other political and social groups that Louis Napoleon would be able to dupe in turn, ends his book with the remarkably accurate prophecy that "when the imperial mantle falls on the shoulders of Louis Bonaparte, the bronze statue of Napoleon will crash from the top of the Vendôme Column".[9]

While Marx was writing the *Eighteenth Brumaire,* Engels resumed his own historical work by writing a dozen pieces for the *New York Daily Tribune* which, forty years later (1891), became the book entitled *Germany: Revolution and Counter-Revolution* (it was originally attributed to Marx). The value of some chapters, such as those relating to the rise and fall of the national-revolutionary or conservative-national movements of Magyars, Czechs and Slavs within the old Hapsburg Empire, has probably proved ephemeral; but in handling the revolutions in Berlin and Vienna and peasant revolution in Austria he appears to have been on more familiar ground. His narrative and analysis of these events are of the highest quality throughout. His judgement on the peasant movement was that, in Austria at least, the peasants "have been the real gainers by the Revolution"; their successes, Marx and Engels both believed, brought the Austrian peasants into line with the French who had won their liberation in 1789. Perhaps his most notable passage, however is the one where he describes, and explains, the disintegration of the alliance of forces that brought down Metternich in Vienna.

> But [he writes] it is the fate of all revolutions that this union of different classes, which in some degree is always the necessary condition of any revolution, cannot subsist long. *No sooner is the victory gained against the common enemy than the victors become divided among themselves . . . and turn their weapons against each other. It is this* rapid and passionate development of class antagonism which, in old and complicated organisms, makes a revolution such a powerful agent of social and political progress; it is this incessantly quick upshooting of new parties succeeding each other in power which, during these violent commotions, makes a nation pass in five years over more ground than it would have done in a century under ordinary circumstances.[10]

As historians and political scientists (for in their case it is not possible to keep the two categories apart), it is Marx that is generally the more subtle, 'philosophical' and speculative of the two: it is difficult to imagine Engels penning Marx's portrayal of Louis Napoleon, cited just now. This is another way of saying, too, that Marx was the greater polemicist. This is particularly evident in the last of Marx's historical works, put together from the long Addresses to the General Council of the International on the Paris Commune and a number of "Fragments" and Appendices published in a single volume entitled *The Civil War in France* (1891). The book contains further pen-portraits in the *Eighteenth-Brumaire* manner, such as Ernest Picard, "the Joe Miller of the Government of National Defence"; Jules Ferry, "the penniless barrister" who, as Mayor of Paris during the siege, "contrived to job a fortune out of famine"; and above all, there is the central villain of the piece, Thiers, "that monstrous gnome" who, before he became a statesman, "had already proved his lying powers as an historian". But the satire is pushed aside in the magnificent final tribute:

Workingmen's Paris, with its Commune, will be forever celebrated as the glorious harbinger of a new society. Its martyrs are enshrined in the great heart of the working class. Its exterminators history has already nailed to that eternal pillory from which all the prayers of their priests will not avail to redeem them.[11]

Engels, for his part, is the more "political-theoretical" in that he is more inclined—sometimes to the indignation of present-day Marxist scholars or followers—to draw clearcut political conclusions regarding the need for authority in revolution. To take two examples, both concerning the Commune of 1871. One is the well-known, contentious, conclusion written twenty years after the event in his Introduction to Marx's *Civil War*. He is chiding the "Social Democratic philistines" of the day for recoiling in horror at the mention of the term "Dictatorship of the Proletariat"; and he adds, "Well and good, gentlemen, do you want to know what this dictatorship looks like? Look at the Paris Commune; that is the Dictatorship of the Proletariat." In a second passage, written in correspondence with an Italian socialist only eight months after the fall of the Commune, he is chiding rather than commending the Commune (as Marx did, too) for its "want of centralization and authority that cost it its life". And he adds (as if anticipating the views of some of the young "revolutionaries" of our time): "When I hear people speak of authority and centralization as of two things deserving condemnation, I feel that those who say this either have no idea of what a revolution is or are revolutionaries only in name".[12]

Later historians writing in the Marxist tradition have, of course, had the advantage (unless they have chosen to write of topical events) of not only learning important lessons from their forbears but also of seeing the whole history of which they are writing as *past* and not as "contemporaneous" events. They have therefore not had the same excuse, except where new facts or new collections of documents have come to light, to change their minds on important matters of interpretation almost as the ink dried on their original draft, as Marx and Engels were occasionally obliged to do in writing of historical events that they had first noted as eyewitnesses or observers. Moreover, they have had the further advantage of access to new sources and to the new fields in the social sciences that have been opened up in the last eighty years and were unknown to Marx and Engels, whose historical writing was, as we have seen, mainly focussed on the political and economic aspects of working-class movements and revolutions of the nineteenth century in Europe, the great exceptions being Engels's *Peasant War* and his sketch of man's pre-history (influenced by the American anthropologist, Lewis Morgan), the *Origin of the Family, Private Property and the State*.

But large regions of the world, such as Japan and the Pacific, Africa and Latin America (now being well trodden and explored by historians and anthropologists) were at that time virtually a closed book, as were the more recent vistas opened up by the behavioural sciences including modern social psychology. There were also other fields to which Marx and Engels made occasional reference, though they never had the opportunity to explore them adequately themselves; such were Marx's famous remark that religion was "the opium of the people" and his tentative reference to popular collective ideology when (in his Introduction to the *Critique of Hegel's Philosophy of Law*) he wrote that "theory becomes a material force when it grips the masses". Engels, too, in a letter to Joseph Bloch in 1890, allowed the ideological factor a part (though not "the decisive one") in shaping man's history; he instances in particular "the traditions which haunt men's minds".[13] So it would be reasonable to suppose that both writers would have shown some sympathy for the work done in the past half-century by Marxist (or near-Marxist) scholars to explore these questions more fully. Moreover, it was Engels, who of the two lived long enough to have time to relax and reflect on such matters, who all but said so when he wrote to Conrad Schmidt, another correspondent, in August 1890: "Our conception of history is above all a guide to history, not a lever for construction after the manner of the Hegelians. *All history must be studied afresh.*"[14]

It would be foolish to imagine that it is only Western historians raised in a Marxist tradition that have learned to apply these lessons to the writing of history; but space will only allow mention of such "fresh" thinking in the case of a half a dozen French and British historians who have been writing in the past fifty years. The first on my list is Georges Lefebvre, the great French historian of the Revolution of 1789; it was he who first called for a study of history "from below". His first important contribution was to "discover" the peasants who, though constituting four-fifths of the French population at the time, had been largely neglected up till then. Though Lefebvre chose as his principal focus the peasants of the Department of the Nord, his book, *Les paysans du Nord*, first published in 1924, was so detailed and raised so many questions of a more general validity that his conclusions have been taken to apply to the country as a whole. One of these was that it was not true—as it had been supposed—that the revolution of 1789 was essentially an urban one and that the peasant rebellion, in spite of the long-standing grievances of the rural population, was an offshoot of the Paris events of July 1789. On the contrary, argued Lefebvre, the peasants had a revolution of their own which they started in their own time. To quote from a paper he read in December 1932:

What I have tried to show is that there was a *peasant* revolution with its own autonomy
as regards its origins, its direction, its crises. We say autonomous as to its origins
because the peasant masses rebelled spontaneously under the impact of hunger and
the hopes raised by the summoning of the Estates General; and, quite independently
of the townspeople, the peasants conceived the notion of the "aristocratic plot"
without which the Great Fear [of 1789] would have been impossible to imagine.[15]

This "Great Fear" was an important element in the peasant
"revolution" of that summer, and Lefebvre became its historian; his
book, entitled *La Grande Peur,* was published in 1932 and was perhaps
the most original of all his works. He showed how the countryside in a
large part of northern and central France became gripped by an almost
universal panic, fed by the rumour of soldiers disbanded after the fall of
the Bastille who (it was believed) eager to avenge their humiliations on
the rebellious villages, were marching on the peasants' properties in the
shape of marauding "brigands".Even when the "brigands" turned out
to be nothing more than hungry villagers seeking food and shelter in the
farms and homesteads, the Fear continued, spreading from market to
market and village to village along the river valleys; so (wrote Lefebvre)
"fear bred fear", and fear also gave a great stimulus to the revolution in
the villages and market towns. And from all this bewildering confusion
of myth and rumour, defensive reaction and both orderly and disorderly
activity, Lefebvre drew the conclusion that the Great Fear was not just
an interesting psychological phenomenon, underlying the idiocy and
irrationality of human behaviour, but it had important positive
historical consequences as well.[16] It was Lefebvre, too, who, in the same
year, fired the first effective broadside at Gustave LeBon, the French
fascist "father" of crowd psychology, with his picture of the mindless
mob responding blindly to the call of any ambitious "leader".[17]

If Lefebvre and his pupil, Albert Soboul, the Marxist historian of the
Parisian "small people" or *sans-culottes,* have been the greatest
historians of revolution in France, in Britain that title should be given to
Christopher Hill, the author of numerous volumes on the English
revolution of the seventeenth century. In his earliest work, such as the
tricentenary volume of 1940, Hill made an honest attempt to give the
British reading public a Marxist synthesis of the revolution; but it was
not distinguished by subtle argument or original thought (qualities that
belonged rather to Maurice Dobb, the communist economist, whose
chapters on the English seventeenth century in *Studies in the
Development of Capitalism* were written shortly after [1946]). But the
difference was startling when Hill went on to deepen his study of
Puritanism and became (with A.L. Morton) probably the first Marxist
writer in the English language to explore some of those socio-political
aspects of religion that Marx had touched on a century before. He

carried the argument further when he went on, in *The World Turned Upside Down* (1972), to focus on the revolution "from below" both in its political and religious-ideological aspects. There were, writes Hill in his Introduction,

> two revolutions in mid-seventeenth-century England. The one which succeeded established the sacred rights of property (abolition of feudal tenures, no arbitrary taxation), gave political power to the propertied (sovereignty of Parliament and common law, abolition of prerogative courts), and removed all impediments to the triumph of the ideology of the men of property—the protestant ethic. There was, however, another revolution which never happened, though from time to time it threatened. This might have established communal property, a far wider democracy in political and legal institutions, and might have disestablished the state church and rejected the protestant ethic.[18]

A large part of the book is given over to the people who preached those radical ideas and those who received them; and the author has shown a unique ability to place the political and religious ideas of the common people side by side and to show how they merge in a common ideological context. On the one hand, there were the Levellers, apostles of a wider parliamentary democracy, and the Diggers who dug up the common land in search of the richer economic millenium with property held in common; and, on the other, there were the extreme religious sects, the Ranters, Seekers and socially radical Quakers, who preached free grace, denied sin and hell and preached sexual freedom and that "all comes by nature". But many men belonged to both: the Digger philosopher Winstanley was also close to the Ranters and Quakers; Milton, the Puritan poet and friend of Cromwell, has been called a "precursor to the Ranters"; and the Ranters themselves, according to their historian A.L. Morton, probably drew support from 'migrating craftsmen' or "masterless men". Hill argues that all these ideas were radical, though he does not claim that all were equally dangerous to the establishment. (It is significant perhaps that the Ranters and Seekers only began to flourish after the Levellers had been virtually silenced at Burford in May 1649.) The Army radicals—at least the Levellers and Diggers—left a tradition that refused to lie down; and Hill quotes a conservative opponent as writing long after the revolution:

> They have cast all the mysteries and secrets of government . . . before the vulgar . . . and have taught both the soldiery and people to look so into them as to ravel back all governments to first principles of nature . . . They have made the people thereby so curious and so arrogant that they will never find humility enough to submit to a civil rule.[19]

Eric Hobsbawm and Edward Thompson have been the main pioneers of the "new" labour history which began in England in the early 1960s.

There were two books, in particular, that announced its arrival: Thompson's *Making of the English Working Class* (1963) and Hobsbawm's *Labouring Men* (1964). In his Preface Hobsbawm described the "old" labour history, pioneered by the Webbs and G.D.H. Cole, as being a "straightforward chronological or narrative history of labour movements" and claimed that hitherto "there has been *comparatively little work about the working classes as such (as distinct from labour organizations and movements)* and about the economic and technical conditions which allowed labour movements to be effective, or prevented them from being effective".[20]

The greater contribution to this "new" history has no doubt been made by Edward Thompson, whose *The Making of the English Working Class* (first published in 1963) has probably been the most original and the most influential work in British labour and social history published since the last war. Thompson's concern for "people" as against "movements" or "institutions" is implicit in his choice of title and also in the definition of "class" that he gives in his preface: a "historical relationship" which is neither "structure" nor "category" and which "must always be embodied in real people in a real context". Moreover, he sees it as a "social and cultural formation", which can only be studied over a considerable span of time, in this instance over the half-century between 1780 and 1832, the time during which "most English people came to feel an identity against their rulers and employers". As he is concerned with development and therefore with *pre-industrial* and *industrial society* (here competely at variance with the Webbs and Coles), he is bound—and he does so with zest—to challenge the received wisdom of a number of orthodoxies. He lists them as, first, the Fabian orthodoxy, in which "the great majority of working people are seen as passive victims of *laissez-faire*"; secondly, the orthodoxy of the empirical economic historians, with their tendency to reduce workers to a "labour force" or "the raw material for statistical tables", and, finally, what he terms the "Pilgrim's Progress" orthodoxy, "in which the period is ransacked for forerunners—pioneers of the Welfare State, progenitors of a Socialist Commonwealth" and so on. His main quarrel with these orthodoxies is that they smother the workingman's own contribution to the "making" of his history and that, by putting a premium on success, expose the "losers" in the race—the Luddites, handloom weavers and their like—to "the enormous condescension of posterity".[21]

Hobsbawm has also paid attention to the "losers", most spectacularly in his *Primitive Rebels* (1959) a treatment of recent archaic and millenarian movements in Spain, Italy and Latin America which, in spite of their proximity to developing centres of population and industry, remain largely untouched by the values and ethos of contemporary capitalism. But he is less scornful of "movements" than Thompson and has cooperated with myself in writing *Captain Swing* (1969), a study of the English agricultural labourers' revolt of 1830—a revolt that, though the labourers have been generally written off as "losers", achieved some success in arresting the growth of threshing machines in England's southern counties.

Like Hill and unlike the earlier labour historians, all three of us have been concerned with the ideology of the common people as *history,* that is to attempt to trace the origins and development of the ideas that (in Marx's phrase) "grip the masses". Whereas the older labour historians ignored this element altogether or set its evolution in a narrow trade-union or "labour" mould, Thompson was prompted, by the very nature of his subject, to construct a picture of the developing ideology of the working class in all its aspects, social, political and religious. Thus Methodism, for all its dubious benefits, is revealed as playing in some respect a positive role in stimulating the workers' political activities. The Swing rioters of 1830 were also stimulated by a medley of political and religious ideas in which tradition played a major part. At the same time the July Revolution in France roused hopes of an early political reform; several of the Hampshire men were already involved in the Reform movement at home; and some of the Wiltshire men, like the Dorset labourers of 1834, were Methodist activists or preachers. Again, there was the underlying sense of "justice", probably more pervasive than the religious or political motivation that prompted the labourers to refuse to accept that machines, which robbed men of their "natural right" to work and enjoy a living wage, should receive the protection of the law. On occasion, they invoked the authority of the magistrates or government, including the king himself, to justify their actions. And, in September 1832, a Norfolk rioter claimed that "in destroying machinery, I am doing God a service".[22]

In this respect—along the lines of Engels's "traditions which haunt men's minds"—there is, of course, a great deal more to explore.

Notes

1. F. Engels, *The Condition of the Working Class in England* (London, 1981), p. 21. Moreover, to do Engels full justice, the "prophecy" was hedged about from the start with a number of qualifications.
2. Ibid., p. 324.
3. Ibid., p. 321.
4. For an appreciation of Engels's history by modern historians of the event, both Marxist and non-Marxist, see the Special Issue of the *Journal of Peasant Studies* devoted to "The German Peasant War of 1525", ed. Janos Bak, 3, 1 (Oct. 1975), pp. 89–135.

5. Engels, Introduction to Marx's *Class Struggles in France* (1895 edn) in Marx and Engels, *Selected Works in One Volume* (London, 1968), pp. 641–58.

6. There is a further problem here raised by Engels's stated contention that Marx was attempting to explain a phase of history "from a given economic situation". It sounds as if Engels was slipping (or that the translator was at fault?) in choosing such a "deterministic" formula when we consider that it was only two years before that he had assured Bloch that "the determining element is *ultimately* the production and reproduction in real life: more than this neither Marx nor I have ever asserted".

7. K. Marx, *Eighteenth Brumaire of Louis Bonaparte* (Moscow, 1977), pp. 10–12.

8. Ibid., pp. 107–10 (my italics).

9. Ibid., p. 116. In May 1871, the Vendôme Column, topped by a statue of Napoleon I, was destroyed by order of the Commune.

10. F. Engels, *Germany: Revolution and Counter-Revolution* (1969), p. 141 (my italics).

11. K. Marx, *Civil War in France* (London, 1933), pp. 23, 24, 63.

12. Draft of letter to Carlo Terzaghi, 14 Jan. 1872 (tr. from Italian), in *K. Marx and F. Engels on the Commune* (Moscow, 1971), p. 292.

13. Engels to Bloch, 21 Sept. 1890, in *Marx and Engels Correspondence 1846–1895* (London, 1934), p. 476.

14. Engels to Schmidt, 5 Aug. 1890, ibid., p. 473 (my italics).

15. G. Lefebvre, "La Révolution française et les paysans", *Etudes sur la Révolution française* (Paris, 1954), pp. 249–50.

16. G. Lefebvre, *The Great Fear of 1789. Rural Panic in Revolutionary France* (London, 1973), pp. xi–xiii.

17. G. LeBon, The Crowd (London, 1904); Lefebvre, "Foules révolutionnaires", in *Etudes sur la Révolution française*, pp. 271–87.

18. C. Hill, *The World Turned Upside Down* (London, 1972), p. 12.

19. Ibid., p. 58.

20. E.J. Hobsbawm, *Labouring Men. Studies in the History of Labour* (London, 1964), p. vii (my italics).

21. E.P. Thompson, *The Making of the English Working Class* (London, 1963), pp. 9–13.

22. E.J. Hobsbawm and G. Rudé, *Captain Swing* (London, 1969), p. 249.

2

The Changing Face of the Crowd

As an historian I was, by Anglo-Saxon standards at least, a late developer. My first published article was written at the age of forty-two; I took my first full-time history post (in a secondary school) at forty-four; my first book was published when I was forty-nine; and I was already fifty when I went to my first university post at Adelaide, in South Australia. Yet I am in no way suggesting that I was a boy from the bush who, in middling years, took to the pen or discovered he had literary or academic talents. Far from it. I had graduated at Cambridge with a modern languages degree when twenty-one, and for many years had taught French and German in a variety of secondary schools before deciding, shortly after World War II, to take another "first" degree in history at London. And, as it turned out, the study of languages proved to be of considerable advantage to me in the field of history that I later chose.

Moreover, I had further advantage, as it now seems to me, of having long been a Marxist, both in theory and in practice; it was, I believe, the reading of Marx, and probably of Lenin as well, that led me to history, Marx's historical ideas have been so long and so insistently misrepresented in certain countries that it may be a surprise to some that a professor of history should actually claim that a reading of Marx was of any solid advantage to him in his craft. What I learned from Marx was not only that history tends to progress through a conflict of social classes (a view, incidentally, that was held to be perfectly "respectable" a hundred years ago), but that it has a discoverable pattern and moved forward (not backward, in circles, or in inexplicable jerks) broadly from a lower to a higher phase of development. I learned also that the lives and actions of the common people are the very stuff of history, and though "material" rather than the institutional and ideological factors are primary, that ideas themselves become a "material force" when they

56

pass into the active consciousness of men. Moreover, I have also learned from Engels that, whatever the excellence of historical "systems" (like his own and Marx's, for example), "all history must be studied afresh." What I never at any time learned from either of them was that history should be interpreted in terms of a narrow economic determinism.

With such antecedents, it is perhaps not remarkable that I should have been drawn to the study of revolutions. But why to the French Revolution? Partly, I suppose, because I had acquired a good knowledge of French; partly because I soon discovered that the sort of problems I became interested in could best be studied in the French records of that period; and partly, too, because I had the good fortune to find in the late Alfred Cobban, who at that time directed research in French history at London, an excellent mentor and guide, tireless in the service of his students, and one who, while by no means sharing my own social-political views, actively encouraged me to find a Ph.D subject to my taste and to see it through to a reasonably rapid conclusion. My subject was the part played by the Paris wage-earners in the insurrections of the first two years of the French Revolution. While reading for my degree, I had been struck by the fact that no historian of the period (not even Mathiez whom, at this time, I had read more widely than Lefebvre) had seriously asked such questions as: who actually took the Bastille, stormed the Tuileries, expelled the Girondin leaders from the National Convention, or stood silently by as Robespierre was hustled to the scaffold? Not only who were they, but how did they get there? What were their motives and social aspirations, and by what means did they acquire them? I saw that historians friendly to the Revolution (at least from Michelet onward) had written about "the people" or, more specifically, about the *sans-culottes,* while others (beginning with Burke) had dismissed them as a "swinish multitude," a "rabble," a "mob," or a *"canaille."*

Although I distinctly preferred the "populists" to the "mobsters," I was not satisfied with either definition, as they both begged all the questions that I found to be of interest, and I began to think that a more precise analysis of "who", if it could be made, would throw a useful light not only on the activities, but on the outlook and motives of the common people who, as everyone conceded, had played an important part in the course and the outcome of the Revolution. I soon discovered, with Cobban's help, that it was not for lack of appropriate records that historians had dodged the issue: there was even a list in the Archives Nationales in Paris, fully described in Tuetey's sixty-year-old *Répertoire* of Parisian revolutionary manuscripts, that gave the names, addresses, ages, occupations, and militia units of every one of the 600-odd civilians who had been proved to have taken an active part in the siege of the

Bastille. For the rest, I had mainly to make do with the police records of the Paris Châtelet and Prefecture of Police, which I supplemented in later work with the official lists of those receiving awards, pensions and compensation, or jail sentences (according to the event) for the part they played in the great revolutionary *journées* of August 1792, June 1793, and May 1795. These proved to be a mine of information about those who had been arrested, killed or wounded, or against whom information had been laid; but, of course, they provided only a sample—and sometimes a rather fortuitous one at that—and had, in consequence, to be used with discretion and with ample reservations. Still, while conscious of its limitations, I have made this type of record a basic part of my research equipment ever since.

I must add here that I did not approach my subject without commitment, a fact that may cause no surprise after what I have said above. This does not means that I have ever felt *politically* involved with the wage earners, craftsmen or rioters with whom I have largely been concerned, but that I have always felt a bond of sympathy with them, whether their activities have been peaceful or rebellious. A recent reviewer, Edward T. Gargan in *The Nation* (February 13, 1967), wrote of my "nostalgia and affection for the class of artisan-craftsmen now vanished from our technological society"; and I would not wish to deny the charge. So although my work always had (to historians, at least) a sociological flavour, I have never felt in any way inclined to share the view of those American social scientists to whom riot and rebellion have appeared as an abnormal and distasteful deviation from "a stable, self-regulating state of perpetual equipoise." I believe, on the contrary, that conflict is both a normal and a salutary means of achieving social progress, and I have not hesitated in looking back on the past to identify myself more closely with some parties in the conflict than with others.

But I soon realized the limitations of my first subject of research. For one thing, it dealt only with the first two years of the revolution, from 1789 to 1791; and this, it did not take long to discover, in itself made it difficult to find a publisher. More serious was the fact that having chosen to study the part played by the wage-earners, my conclusions were bound to be a little negative. For, whatever the preconceptions with which I started, it gradually appeared that the wage-earners, while engaged in large numbers in these events, were not yet in a position to play an independent role or substantially influence the outcome. In fact, even the common people as a whole, the urban *sans-culottes*, who included workshop masters, independent craftsmen, and shopkeepers, as well as their employees, only developed a distinctive social-political movement of their own after the fall of the monarchy in 1792. So I decided both to broaden and to extend my field of research—to broaden it by embracing all those who took part in popular disturbances; to extend it by considering all revolutionary and eve-of-revolutionary events from 1787 to 1795, even looking back to the last of the great popular outbreaks of the Ancien Régime, the so-called *guerre des farines* (or "flour war") of 1775. So, with this end in view, I took occasional leave from my teaching post in London and returned to the Paris archives for a number of visits between 1951 and 1957.

It was through these return visits to Paris that I became closely connected with Georges Lefebvre and two of the most active of his associates, Albert Soboul and Richard Cobb. I had met Lefebvre, almost by chance, on the first day I set foot in the Archives Nationales in April 1949 and had, from the first and like so many others, been struck by his simplicity, modesty, his friendly though somewhat austere approach, and his complete and utter devotion to scholarship and research. He invited me to his house at Boulogne-sur-Seine, which was as austere and as redolent of all the Jacobin-Republican virtues as the master himself. From then on, we corresponded, regularly but infrequently, and I went to see him whenever I arrived in Paris, always before my departure, and perhaps once or twice in between; occasionally I saw him in the archives. So, over a period of some ten years, I doubt if I met him more than twenty times in all; yet I probably learned as much from him in these few encounters as I did from reading his books. Since the publication in 1924 of his great work on the peasants, *Les Paysans du Nord,* he had been the acknowledged master of the study of the Revolution "from below"; but how important this contribution was I discovered only as my own work proceeded. The part of his work that had the strongest influence on me was, I believe, his pioneering studies on the behaviour of revolutionary crowds and on the rumours and panics ("La Grande Peur") of 1789. Moreover, all who came under his spell took away with them valuable lessons on what he considered indispensable to "la bonne méthode" in all historical enquiry: *Sans érudition, pas d'histoire.* His mind remained extraordinarily vigorous and inventive until the day of his death in 1959. He was seventy-five when I first met him; in his eighty-sixth year, a few months before he died, he wrote me a letter expounding the benefits that the social historian, in particular, might derive from a closer association between history and the biological sciences.

I also greatly benefited from my friendship and collaboration with Soboul and Cobb. It was quite by chance, as far as I know, that we were all working, in no way prompted by Lefebvre, in complementary but distinctive fields within the French Revolution: Soboul on the Parisian sectional militants and *sans-culottes* of 1793–4, Cobb on the "revolutionary armies" and the *sans-culottes* in the provinces, and I on the Paris revolutionary "crowd." (Lefebvre once referred to us as *les trois mousquetaires.*) Soboul is, like myself, a Marxist and has something of the rigorous disciplinary approach to records of *le vieux maître* himself: his advice and guidance have always been invaluable to me in my work. Applied to Cobb, the term "discipline" does not perhaps appears to be the most appropriate; yet no man in France—or, I would suspect, at Oxford—has been so tireless and devoted a searcher after original sources as he. In fact, on one memorable occasion, when the Paris archives were officially closed and we had been given special dispensation to attend (as *étrangers de passage à Paris*), our zeal was so great that we were locked in at night and had to scale down a drainpipe to get out of the building! Moreover, Cobb's generosity is as boundless as his zeal, and I shudder to think how slim my own *dossiers* on Paris revolutionary committees and popular societies would have been without the numerous slips of information that he passed me from his own voluminous researches. So it was not by any means with tongue in cheek when I wrote in the Preface to my first book, *The Crowd in the French Revolution,* that with the help of friends such as these, it was, in a real sense, an expression of collective, rather than of purely individual enterprise.

It was Professor Cobban who suggested that I should make a book of the articles that I had by this time written on the "crowd" in the revolutionary period. The book was based, in part, on my original work on the wage earners of 1789–91, in part on my subsequent research and writing on the *sans-culottes* of 1789–93, with gaps filled in for the introductory and terminal periods of 1787–88 and 1794–5. The method was broadly similar to that which I had used in my thesis nearly ten years before. Yet the book, as it appeared to historians and to students outside France (where several of my earlier articles had been published), had a certain freshness and originality, both insofar as it was the first scholarly work to treat the revolutionary crowd as a composite theme over so long a period and because it used new records to answer new questions concerning the groups that composed it, their motives, and their modes of behaviour.

Reviewers treated the book kindly, though they tended to see it as just another book on the "mobs" and *journées* of the French Revolution, whereas I believed myself that it was the method used and the wider implications to which it pointed, rather than the historical framework itself, that were important. Some reviewers, therefore, though not ungenerous in their praise, seemed to me to have missed the point. Others, even when they were more critical, gave me greater satisfaction, as they appeared to see what the book was intended to be about. Among reviews that I particularly valued were those by Asa Briggs in *The Listener* (September 4, 1959), Eric Hobsbawm in the *New Statesman*

(March 28, 1959), Samuel Bernstein in *Science and Society* (fall 1959), Crane Brinton in *The American Historical Review* (July 1959), Georges Lefebvre in *Annales Historiques de la Révolution française* (April-June 1959), and Jacques Zacher and Sophie Lotte in the Soviet journal, *Voprosy Istorii* (1959).

Hobsbawm rightly saw that the essential point of the exercise had been to get down to such simple and basic, though hitherto neglected, questions as, "Who actually stormed the Bastille?" Briggs welcomed the book as the product of a new type of social history, already well established in France, which did not stop at the conventional frontiers and lines of demarcation of the political or social historian. But he rightly saw that I had not paid sufficient attention to the mechanism of insurrection, to the apparatus of law and order, and to the "psychology" of crowd behaviour in general and of violence in particular. Brinton, with equal justice, charged me with neglecting the irrational element in my analysis of motives. Lefebvre, on the other hand, commended my study of motives, in particular, and the methodology of my investigation; but, with characteristic modesty, he appeared to doubt if his own work had been of any value whatsoever to me. The Soviet reviewers subjected the book to a serious critical analysis; they praised the originality of its method and the "value" of its results, but they took me severely to task on a number of questions: in particular, they believed that I had failed to see that the eighteenth-century worker was just as interested in his wages as in the price of his daily bread; that I had underestimated the part played by the workers in the Réveillon riots of April 1789; that I had overestimated the influence of the middle classes on the political thinking of the *sans-culottes;* and that I had laid far too much emphasis on the role of tradition and "backward" thinking as a motive force in revolutionary events. The review provided an extremely useful forum for discussion and led, three years later, to an airing of views on these and related problems by my Soviet critics, Soboul, and myself in Armando Saitta's journal, the *Critica Storica.*[1] Unfortunately, the discussion petered out after this number, and we arrived at no agreed conclusions.

Meanwhile, I had become involved in the study of English popular movements of the eighteenth century, which I thought it might be useful to contrast with the French; here I attempted to apply the same methods as in my earlier researches. The results have not always been as fruitful as I had hoped, because the English judicial records before the later nineteenth century are, compared with the French, notoriously defective. But I had the good fortune to begin with the Gordon Riots of 1780, which I wanted to compare with the Réveillon riots of 1789, in which I saw a transition between the riots of the Ancien Régime and the

Revolution. I was fortunate because in this case the number of prisoners up for trial was relatively large, and the information about them in the *Proceedings* of the Old Bailey in London proved to be reasonably adequate. Moreover, having been struck by the difference in social status between the rioters and their victims (which, it seemed to me, provided a useful clue to the deeper causes of the outbreak), I chanced on the idea of using the taxation records (in the first place, the registers of the Riot Tax levied to compensate householders for damages suffered) as a means of determining the value of the victims' properties. From this emerged a paper on "The Gordon Riots: A Study of the Rioters and Their Victims," which won the Alexander Prize of the Royal Historical Society for 1955.[2]

It was in the course of this work that I first met Albert Hollaender, now Deputy Librarian at the Guildhall Library in London; I owe to him, far more than to anyone else, what I have learned of the use of London records. He has been a wise counsellor and a constant friend. He put me onto studying the "Gin" and the anti-Irish riots of 1736 and the "Wilkes and Liberty" disturbances of 1768–9; and at his prompting and under his direction I have contributed a number of papers to *The Guildhall Miscellany,* which he edits. He has been a severe taskmaster and is, above all, a stickler for footnotes, which, he insists, must be both numerous and accurate. On one occasion, he had me called to the telephone in the middle of a school history lesson to berate me unmercifully for having failed to match a note at the foot of the page with its equivalent in the text!

I had written a couple of articles on the Wilkite movements; the second of these, which appeared in *History Today,*[3] led to a publisher's invitation (it was not from the Clarendon Press) to write a book on John Wilkes. I decided to do so, but not along the lines suggested by the publisher in question. Wilkes himself was a fascinating character and an admirably suitable subject for a new biography. But biography was not in my line, and I was far more interested in doing a full-length study of the Wilkite movement or of Wilkes's supporters ("the Devil's disciples," as Asa Briggs called them) than of John Wilkes himself. Essentially, the method of approach was similar to the one I had used before, but both the subject and the records used (as usual, the one being largely determined by the other) were very different. For one thing, Wilkes's supporters among "the inferior set" (the social equivalent of the Parisian *sans-culottes* of 1789–95) provided only one element perhaps not the most important, among his followers; and the records, for reasons already noted, did not make it possible to explore this side of the question as deeply as I should have wished. So the claim made later by the *Punch* reviewer that I had "Namierized the Mob" was really quite misleading. Moreover, as the activities of City of London merchants, manufacturers, gentry, clergy, and, in particular, of Middlesex freeholders (who occupied properties valued at 40s. a year and above) played an important part in the proceedings, I had to have recourse to a wider range of records than I had used before. These included the records of London livery companies, rate books and land tax registers, city directories and lists of justices of the peace, and, above all, the Middlesex poll-books and (an invaluable find) the town and county petitions of 1769. Once more, what in my view was original about the book was not so much the subject or its conclusions as the method used to arrive at the results.

The book appeared in February 1962 (three years after my first), and received once more a friendly reception from the critics. In fact, A.J.P. Taylor's review in *The Guardian* (February 9, 1962) on the day of publication was so fulsome in its praise as to be almost embarrassing. I was surprised to learn that I had produced "an innocent stick of dynamite which levels the Namier view to the ground" and that I had "put mind back into history and restored the dignity of man." But in case I should have been tempted to take this praise to literally, I would have been brought sharply to earth by Hobsbawm's review in the *New Statesman* (February 16, 1962). Hobsbawm reminded me that, though I had established the sociology of the Wilkite movement and defined its boundaries, I had done little to answer the important question of why this development took place in England just at this time? In short, contrary to Taylor, he believed that my attention to the revival of popular radicalism, which had lain dormant for close on a hundred years, had not been sufficiently probing. This was constructive criticism, and I had to admit, tempting as it was to choose the more comfortable course of basking in the sunshine of Taylor's praise, that it was fundamentally just. Some critics were rather less constructive: the reviewer in *History* (October 1962) took much of the gilt off his qualified praise by methodically cataloguing what seemed to me an alarmingly long list of errors of fact; in the *Review Belge d'Histoire et de Philosophie* (1964), Jacques Godechot berated me for "playing down" the "revolutionary" potentialities of the English late eighteenth-century movements; and Brian Inglis, in *The Spectator* (February 9, 1962), thought I had written "the wrong book" and "should start again". And even though I received numerous and generally favourable reviews, it was evident that those critics who had reviewed both books—and I am thinking in particular of Hobsbawm and Briggs—thought the second a rather inferior successor to the first.

One reviewer, A.L. Morton, writing in *Marxism Today* (June 1962), had used the occasion to comment on my work as a whole and to establish the connection between my two books and the articles I had published on English eighteenth-century popular movements. I was anxious, when the opportunity arose, to write a synthesis of my studies on both England and France, supplemented by the similar work of others in the field. The opportunity was afforded by an invitation from Norman Cantor, then of Columbia University, to contribute a volume to a new series he was editing for Wiley in New York entitled "New Dimensions in History," in which comparative studies were to play a part. So I started work on *The Crowd in History: A Study of Popular Disturbances in France and England 1730–1848*, which was published at the end of 1964.

The book was intended to be more than just a synthesis of earlier work. For one thing, my own earlier published work had not gone beyond the eighteenth century, and it was necessary, in order to establish a reasonable claim to be dealing with the "pre-industrial" period in both countries, to extend my time span to 1848. This meant "filling in" with popular movements from the immediate post-Napoleonic era, from the 1830s, and from the transitional movements of 1848 in France and of Chartism in England. Here I was at the disadvantage of not being on such familiar ground, of only having done original preparatory work myself on patches of 1830 and 1848, and of finding myself compelled to fill in the missing pieces, where recent scholarly work was not available, by means of stop-gap measures either based on newspaper reports or on the (sometimes outdated) work of others. On the other hand, since my arrival in Australia in 1960, I had been building up from the convict records in Sydney and Hobart the case histories of transported Luddites, Chartists, Tolpuddle Martyrs, and machine-breaking labourers of 1830, and these served as useful additional materials for the English movements of the early nineteenth century. Moreover, I welcomed the opportunity the new book afforded of correcting some of the earlier omissions, misunderstandings, and mistakes that the more constructive of my critics had brought to light.

In particular, I wanted to lend more weight than I had done before to the irrational in human motivation, to the phenomenon of violence in crowd behaviour, to the forces of law and order, to the relations between leaders and followers in riots and revolutions, to the survival of archaic forms of thought and action carried over from an earlier age, to the role of religion and millenarian fantasies as adjuncts of disturbances, to the coexistence in popular movements of "backward-looking" and "forward-looking" concepts, to the special characteristics of counterrevolutionary (or "church and king") movements, and to the transformation of ideas in the process of assimilation and adaptation. I learned some lessons (though too few, as the book appeared when my own was almost completed) from Edward Thompson's *The Making of the English Working Class,* and more from Hobsbawm's *Primitive Rebels,* which had been published shortly after my first book in 1959. I also took an elementary reading course in sociology, reread Gustave LeBon (though without changing my views in his basic limitations), and derived considerable profit from reading Neil Smelser's *Collective Behavior,* which had appeared in the course of the previous year. So, although I added little original work of my own, the mixture was by no means the same as before.

The reception of *The Crowd in History* was not as generally favourable as had been that of my previous work. But more attention was paid to the book—and I looked on this as a distinctive "plus"—by sociologists and social psychologists. My first book had been reviewed by *The American Sociological Review* (February 1960) and the *British Journal of Sociology* (March 1960), but, as far as I know, by no other journals in this field. The third book, in addition to these, drew reviews (or at least a mention) from *The American Behavioral Scientist* (September 1965), *The Annals of the American Academy of Political and Social Science* (May 1965), *Sociology and Social Research* (April 1965), *Trans-Action* (September-October 1965), and *Social Forces* (September 1965), and there may have been others.

Some were friendly, others damned with faint praise, none were downright disparaging. Stephen Schafer, in *The Annals,* gave me a pat on the back for having "done so much work" and for presenting "so much substantial data," but thought the book rather an act of good will toward the importance of the crowd and the method of its study than a sociological analysis. D.C. Moore, on the other hand, in *Sociology and Social Research,* thought, somewhat charitably perhaps, that I was "well read in sociology and well aware of the relevance of [my] findings to social psychology and the theory of collective behavior." Even more laudatory were Herbert Blumer in *Trans-Action* and Charles Tilly in *The American Sociological Review* (August 1965). Blumer commended the virtues of my historical approach, though he pointed to the lack of an "analysis of the crowd as a generic group"; yet he was generous enough to blame this shortcoming not so much on me as on his fellow sociologists and social psychologists who had "done a rather miserable job in studying the crowd systematically." Charles Tilly, who is both a sociologist and a historian in France, recommended my "rich, solid work" to sociologists, but shrewdly pointed to certain drawbacks of my method and the sources on which it relies: "They concentrate on the event itself, leading to the construction of a typical natural history for each major class of events, while inhibiting analysis of negative cases, or of underlying social changes." This is a valid criticism; moreover, it is one that was also made, as will be seen, by the reviewer of *The Times Literary Supplement* in slightly different terms. Yet, by and large, as an intruder in the field of sociology, I suppose, I had come out of the encounter relatively unscathed.

Among historians I had a mixed reception. In England, I received favourable comments from Peter Laslett in *The Guardian* (May 7, 1965), James Joll in *The Observer* (May 9, 1965), and J.H. Plumb in *The Sunday Times* (June 20, 1965). In a special issue of *The Times Literary Supplement* (April 7, 1966) devoted to "New Ways in History," Edward Thompson, while generally well disposed toward the book, regretted that I had departed from my "own high standards" in producing inadequate, second-hand material on English grain riots of the eighteenth century as well as on Luddites and Chartists. Gwyn Williams, in *New Society* (August 1965), was far more critical, as was R.K. Webb in the *American Historical Review* (October 1965). Yet I received good points, in admirably lucid and intelligent prose from Edward Gargan in *The Nation* (February 13, 1967) and E.J. Hobsbawm in *The New York Review of Books* (April 22, 1965); and in a short article in the *William and Mary Quarterly* (October 1966), Gordon S. Wood raised doubts about the "uniqueness" of the American revolutionary crowd of the 1760s and 1770s and recommended that, in the light of my findings for France and England, it should be looked at once again.

It was left to the anonymous reviewer in *The Times Literary Supplement* (December 30, 1965) (who was, unmistakably, my old friend Richard Cobb) to mount the longest and most comprehensive indictment of the method and theme of my book; in doing so, he revealed the deep gulf that still separates historians and sociologists on problems of this kind and the difficulties besetting the historian (or the sociologist) who attempts to bridge it. He criticized my "arbitrary" choice of dates and my equally "arbitrary" choice of countries. "It is doubtful," he wrote, "if anyone can offer any valuable new interpretations, or propose any general laws governing collective behaviour, merely by stringing together, over a period of 118 years, a series of largely unconnected riots, divided into two main groups—urban and rural—in two European countries." He went on to question the value of drawing any general conclusions from a statistical analysis of rioters' occupations, for the man who describes himself as a wine merchant when caught in a riot may, at other times of the day, be a clerk, a brothel-keeper, or a riverside worker; "such people will not stand still and stay in a single occupation over several years to oblige historical arithmetic." And even if we knew all about his occupation(s), his age, name, and place of birth, we should still have to "follow him to his home," "get into his head," and find out whether he was a first child or a younger son—in short, to trace his case history from A to Z. And why should he riot one day rather than another and in this place rather than the next? And if a riot happens to follow in the wake of a labour dispute or an agitation over the price of bread, how do we know with any degree of certainty that the one event is related to the other? Moreover, "the study of the crowd is only the preliminary stage in the exploration of the popular movement," for "riots are only a series of peaks, sticking out above the waters of a submerged, but discoverable, history of the common people"; the historian is liable to have his vision clouded and his focus blurred if he attaches "undue importance to what may well have been, at the time, an isolated, accidental and semi-lunatic outbreak." What is the significance of riots, anyway? At this time in England (he claimed), "people *lived* with a certain amount of brawling and rioting, a national habit familiar enough to be given a place in *Jonathan Wild the Great.*" And finally, he chided me for a tendency to "intellectualize about collective motivation that must often defy analysis."

There was much in his review with which I found, after a preliminary bout of irritation, that I could readily agree. Of course, it would be better to study five or six countries rather than two. Of course, it would be preferable to take a longer time span (say 300 years) to study "pre-industrial" popular movements. Of course, we would have a more useful and valid picture of individual participants if we knew a great deal more about their case histories. Of course, one cannot be a hundred per cent sure about the relation of one event to another if one does not know all that happened in between. Of course, to understand riots one should know more about the places where riots did *not* happen as well as the places where they did. Of course, riots are "peaks," or exceptional events, and may therefore easily give one a distorted impression about the whole life span of a popular movement and about the everyday lives of the people who take part in them. Of course, some riots are more significant than others (even if the example of eighteenth century England is, *pace* Halévy, an extremely dubious one). And, of course, there is a great deal in the motivation of crowds, whether in their "collective mentality" or in that of the individuals that compose them, that defies the historian's or the social scientist's analysis.

But aren't these really counsels of perfection or, perhaps more properly, of despair? For even if we allow for the deficiencies in the book, which the reviewer had every right to criticize, is he not really saying that each historical event is unique and that it is useless, and even undesirable, to attempt to draw a causal link between one and another or to set them in a common conceptual framework, let alone (as in this particular case) to devise "general laws governing collective behaviour"?

Yet there is considerable truth in what the reviewer wrote. Above all, he put his finger on the dilemma of the historian who, while wishing to remain a historian, wants, in order to help him in his enquiry, to come to terms with the social sciences. Is he to abandon the safe haven of "the unique event" in order to devise general patterns and derive general conclusions from human conduct, which can never be fully documented or verified in strictly historical terms? It must be granted, for example, that it is far easier to document the "peaks" than the troughs of a popular movement and that there are therefore considerable dangers in attempting to mould them within a common framework of statistical analysis; granted, too, that my own particular mode of enquiry—*Rudéfication,* as the reviewer calls it—depends on adequate samples that are not always readily available. The more impressionistic method of building up a series of case histories or portraits is a tempting, and a safer, alternative; this becomes a possibility—and may even occasionally take care of the "troughs"—where the information is as rich as that provided by French police records of 1793–5, some English county prison registers of the nineteenth century, the Australian convict records of the mid-1820s to mid-1860s, or the present-day decennial census. But popular movements are not solely the expression of the individuals who compose them; they also have a collective identity, which it is equally necessary to attempt to measure and define. To do this, the historian must supplement the individual case history by such means as are available for determining the collective actions, moods, and motives of the "crowd." He must, in fact, look through his telescope at both ends.

To assemble his "case histories" and to get his closer and more personal vision, he may reasonably rely on the well-tried methods of historical research—provided he is willing and able to be flexible in his choice of questions and records. But to classify and correlate, and even to interpret, his findings, he may need (according to their nature and their volume) to have recourse to the computer and, more important, to lean heavily on the techniques and skills developed by the traditional social sciences. And here he is immediately confronted with a problem: Should he attempt to go forward alone, or should he draw not only on the experience but on the active cooperation of the anthropologist, the psychologist, the sociologist? In making his choice, he may do well to heed the warning voiced by Max Gluckman and his associates at Manchester in their book, *Closed Systems and Open Minds* (Edinburgh, 1964). All fields of enquiry in the social sciences (they tell us) are as open to the historians as to any other social scientist, whether they deal with societies, factory systems, urban development, human behaviour, or the advance of an undeveloped nation; so there is virtually no field into which the historian may not enter. Each discipline, however, has its own purpose, its own focus and points of emphasis, and its own means of exploration; yet each, in the course of the enquiry, will inevitably draw on the "assumptions" and experience of others. But there is a point, which the authors term the "limit of naîveté," beyond which it is wiser for the specialist in one discipline not to venture without the close cooperation of his colleagues in the others. In theory, the historian may, in the course of his researches, assume the mantle of the economist or social anthropologist; in practice, however, both his tools and his "assumptions" are different, and he may soon reach a point where a measure of teamwork may save him from embarrassment, if not, quite literally, from disaster. On looking back, I think that some such thoughts as these may have entered the minds (no doubt with ample justification) of certain of the social scientists who reviewed *The Crowd in History*.[4]

I have, therefore, been on safer ground in my more recent cooperation with Eric Hobsbawm in an essentially "historical" treatment of the English agricultural labourers' revolt of 1830.[5] As is well known, Hobsbawm is an economic historian of distinction (as I most certainly am not). He is also a labour historian who has worked on labour problems of both the nineteenth century and earlier times. And, in his *Primitive Rebels* (Manchester, 1959), he has studied the archaic and millenarian movements that, in the agricultural communities of certain industrial countries, have spilled over into the twentieth century. So it has been possible to give our joint book a wider frame of reference, and to raise new questions of which I should have been incapable on my own. In fact, our book is not merely a study of the villagers' revolt of 1830, but also a history of the English farm labourer—his outlook, working conditions, and way of life—during the first half of the nineteenth century. Moreover, this combined operation has made it possible, I believe, to meet some of the objections to my earlier work raised by a number of historians, including the "anonymous" reviewer of *The Times Literary Supplement*.

For one thing, the subject chosen is supported by a wealth of documentation—not only by the London and provincial press, the Home Office papers, the reports of Parliamentary committees, prison registers, the proceedings of assizes and quarter sessions, but also by local county records and the voluminous convict materials in Australia. These are far more varied, detailed, and also suited to the study of the "crowd" than the equivalent sources relating to the English eighteenth century. In consequence, it has been easier to present a living picture of both the riots and rioters and of the agricultural population out of which they grew. It has been possible, too, to trace the labourers' history over a longer period from "trough" to "peak" and back to "trough" in two directions: into the aftermath of rural incendiarism and union organization, and, for those transported, into their enforced exile in the Australian colonies. It has meant, further, that we have been able to consider a far larger sample than is common in such cases. Nearly 2,000 labourers and rural craftsmen were arrested, of whom about one quarter (the largest batch of convicts ever transported for the same "crime") were shipped to Tasmania and New South Wales. This, in turn, has provided the raw materials for a number of case histories, though these are still disappointingly few in number—not surprising, perhaps, in view of our subject and in the absence of the modern, fully detailed decennial census. So, on the score of the sample, the study in depth, and the relation of "peak" to "trough," I think this present work marks an appreciable advance on what I have been able to do, largely unaided and with other records, in the past.

Rather more important perhaps—and this is essentially a contribution of Hobsbawm's—has been the attempt not only to consider the villages that actually rioted, but to pose and answer the pertinent question: Why did *these* villages rebel while others (often their neighbours) did not? Was there anything in the riotous village's structure—its size, its type of agriculture and settlement, its social relationships, its landownership, its proximity to main lines of communication, its religious affiliations, its political leadership, its degree of literacy, pauperism or criminality—which made it more prone to riot than another? Or was it merely the fact of lying in the path of a movement that had already begun elsewhere? Even if the evidence suggested (as, in fact, it did), that a riot-prone village tended to be larger than the average; to contain a higher ratio of labourers to farmers; to have a larger proportion of craftsmen, small landholders, and shopkeepers; to have an "open" or "mixed" rather than a "close" landownership; to have a larger measure of religious independence; to be closer to markets and fairs; to have a longer history of local disputes; to have (on balance) a larger proportion of unemployed; and (more decidedly) to be engaged in tillage rather than pasture—all this could, on occasion, be made almost irrelevant by the simple fact of the powerful contagion that a concerted movement among its neighbours might exert on the most peaceful and least riot-prone village lying in its path. So the question might elicit no firm and conclusive answer. Yet the question was well worth asking; and to ask it was, at least, the beginning of a wisdom that I, for my part, had previously neglected.

Finally, I hope one day to fill another gap in my studies of the "crowd": to trace the origins and course of the ideas that "grip the masses" (to use Marx's phrase) and that play so important a part in both the "peaks" and the "troughs" of a popular movement. Whether pagan or religious, overt or submerged, such ideas are quite obviously a potent force in riots, rebellions, and revolutions. But it is useless to follow the traditional method of studying the ideas in their pristine, undiluted form without reference to the social context in which they germinate or the needs of the groups and classes that absorb them and the uses to which they put them. In this last book, we have tried to unravel some of the archaic and traditional notions underlying the labourers' movement. Yet a great deal more requires to be done, and over a far wider field. If the labour or social historian really wants to see "mind put back into history," this is one of the jobs he will have to undertake.

Notes

1. "I Sansculotti: una discussione tra storici marxisti", *Critica Storica*, I, 4 (July 1962), pp. 369–98.
2. *Transactions of the Royal Historical Society*, 5th series, vol. 6 (1956), pp. 93–114.
3. George Rudé, "Wilkes and Liberty", *History Today*, 7, 9 (Sept. 1957), pp. 571–9.
4. For a "historical" sociologist's statement of the problems involved in this type of interdisciplinary cooperation, see Charles Tilly, "Clio and Minerva", in John C. McKinney and E.A. Tiryakian, eds, *Theoretical Sociology: Perspectives and Developments* (New York, 1968).
5. E.J. Hobsbawm and George Rudé, *Captain Swing* (London, 1969).

3

The Study of Revolutions

There are three major, and quite distinctive, ways of studying revolutions. One is to study them in depth, each one in isolation as a unique event. This has now become thoroughly unfashionable, particularly among non-historians; and generally with justification. Yet to look at revolutions in this way has at least the merit of ensuring that those features of a revolution that distinguish it from any other—and there are such features—are not lost sight of.

A second method is to place all revolutions, or near-revolutions, arising within a given span of time within a common horizontal framework. In this way the English Revolution of the 1640's, the two Frondes and the Catalan revolt all become related in "the crisis of the seventeenth century."[1] Similarly, the American and French revolutions and all the subsequent late eighteenth-century revolutions and commotions that took place in Germany, Italy, Poland, Ireland, Holland, and Belgium are given the common label of a "democratic" or "Atlantic" revolution or of a "revolution of the West".[2] The French have an expression for this: it is *noyer le poisson;* and it is perhaps not surprising that to see their own revolution "drowned" in this manner has not aroused any great enthusiasm among the French.

However, it is the third way of looking at revolutions that more particularly concerns me in this chapter. It is that of placing all revolutions—and not only those falling within a comparatively limited time-span—within a common framework; this is, to relate all revolutions, regardless of time or place, to a single "revolutionary" model. To say "all" is, of course, to exaggerate—particularly as some historians or political scientists are more selective than others. Crane Brinton, the American historian, for example, if it can be said that he creates a "model" at all, creates a strictly vertical one into which he fits the four great classical revolutions of the West—the English, the American, the French and the Russian (the first edition of his book, *The Anatomy of Revolution,* goes back to 1938) into a single chronological pattern. So, having looked at each one of his four revolutions in turn, Brinton picks out half a dozen "pre-conditions" that, taken together, lead into the actual revolutionary outbreak or the point when (to quote his own words) "the fever of revolution has begun". These preliminary symptoms are as follows and appear roughly in the following order: an economically advancing society arrested by a sharp and sudden crisis; growing class and status antagonisms—not necessarily all from the side of the common people; the desertion of the intellectuals; a crisis within the ruling class; a crisis of leadership or of government; and, finally, a financial crisis that serves directly as a curtain-raiser to the explosion itself.[3] After the outbreak the fever-analogy is resumed; and the patient's condition works up "to a crisis, frequently accompanied by delirium, the rule of the most violent revolutionists, the Reign of Terror. After the crisis comes a period of convalescence, usually marked by a relapse or two. Finally, the fever is over, and the patient is himself again".[4]

Charles Tilly, the American sociologist and historian, who cites this passage in a recent paper, calls such a stage-by-stage presentation a "natural history of revolution". Its distinctive hall-mark, he argues, is that "it works backward from outcome to antecedent conditions" and thus, like a self-fulfilling prophesy, has the advantage of never being able to be proved entirely wrong.[5] Brinton's stage-by-stage model was the first of the kind to enter the field; but recently it has been joined by several others. Two of the best-known are Neil Smelser's theory of collective behaviour and Chalmers Johnson's study on *Revolutionary Change.* Smelser is not specifically concerned with revolutions but with all types of "non-normative" group behaviour; but, like Brinton, he has a set of six conditions that have to be fulfilled before it can be said that an act of "collective behaviour" has taken place. They are (1) the *structured conduciveness* of a given society to engage in a given form of collective behaviour; (2) *structural strain* within that society; (3) the growth and spread of a *generalized belief;* (4) *precipitating factors;* (5) the *mobilization* of participants for action; and (6) the operation of *social control* (which is a rather loose expression for anything like the army or police or the use of the media, that may check or delay the given act of behaviour).[6] Chalmers Johnson is both more simple and more complex than Brinton and Smelser: he also sees revolution as a kind of disease whose outbreak he explains in terms of three clusters of "disequilibrating" factors which, unfolding in succession, lead to the point of explosion.[7]

Apart from their evident bias in stressing revolution-as-aberration, all such all-embracing models (even one of a more limited and selective kind like Brinton's) have the evident disadvantage of leaving a whole number of "variable" factors out of account. They tend to overstress origins—the point at which the "pre-conditions" reach fruition—and pay far less attention to such important questions as how revolutions continue beyond a certain point in time and how and why they end. They give little thought to the typology of revolution: is the fact that one revolution may be "bourgeois" and another peasant or "proletarian" of little or no concern? Moreover, the human element itself is inclined to get left out: "Again," Tilly writes in his criticism of Smelser, "we face the Case of the Absconded Actor." And for "Actor" read not only the mass of the participants—say the workers or *sans-culottes* or peasants—but also their leaders and allies; not to mention what goes on in their heads.

Having noted some of these weaknesses in what he terms the "natural-history" model, Charles Tilly and his co-author James Rule, in investigating the origins and course of the French revolution of 1830, seek to correct them by setting up a model of their own. They call it a "political process" model because the outbreak of revolution is explained in almost exclusively political terms, in the struggle of rival "contenders", both incumbents and challengers, for control of the state. The new model has the undoubted virtue of simplicity and of keeping the reader's eye glued to the central problem of the seizure of power. It also presents challengers as acting in cooperation (thus not neglecting the important question of allies); moreover, it finds a far more plausible explanation of the tendency of revolutions to move leftwards than the hoary old Brintonian *cliché* of "the most violent revolutionists" coming out on top and instituting a Reign of Terror to keep themselves in power, by putting in its place the motion that what keeps the pot boiling—and most often drives the revolution leftwards in the process—is the multiplicity of contenders (deprived and lower-class groups included) that gradually enter the fray.[8]

All this (and quite apart from the wealth of new evidence that Tilly and his collaborators have unearthed in tracing the course of the revolution of 1830 from its earliest beginnings) is pure gain and should command the serious attention of all scholars in the field. But, alas, the Actor, except as a statistical phenomenon, still remains a remarkably elusive figure. It is not that Tilly has failed to draw up an almost endless series of personal case-histories: even the most diehard opponent of the computer-using historian could hardly expect that of him. But the question "who?"—admittedly something of an obsession of mine—plays all too small a part in his presentation as it does in those "natural-history" presentations whose shortcomings he so rightly condemns. And by "who" I mean, as I said before, both leaders and followers and something of their ideology or what went on in their heads.

As a counter-model to Tilly's and to those whom he rightly criticizes I wish to draw your attention to the model drafted by Lenin in 1915—which, therefore, was a clear two years before the October Revolution began.[9] (So there was no question of the supreme strategist of revolution merely being wise after the event.) Admittedly, Lenin is, in this case, only concerned with revolutionary situations and what he saw as the necessary requirement for them to move forward to the next and final stage—to the revolution itself. As is well known, Lenin's model has four points, but it is the fourth point that concerns me particularly here. The first three points cover ground that is similar to Brinton's (though, in his case, we can hardly say that he was indulging in a "natural-history" type of reconstruction as he was writing down pre-conditions for what had not yet taken place!). The three include (and I am not quoting textually) a crisis within the ruling class; an acute stage in the suffering and resentments of the common people; and increasing political activity of all dissident groups whether they belong to the ruling class or not. All this sounds familiar enough and it would not be difficult to read something of the kind in the situations in England in 1640, in France in 1789 and again in 1830 and 1848 (though clearly not in England in the 1830s and 1840s, Chartism notwithstanding, as there was no acute government or ruling class crisis at the time). But, Lenin tells us, according to his formula, there were also revolutionary situations in Germany in the 1860s and in Russia in 1859–61 and again in 1879 and 1880; and yet no revolution followed. (We might perhaps add from our own experience of more recent events that something similar happened, or failed to happen, in Italy in 1920 and in Germany in 1923 or 1931). Why was this? It was, says Lenin, because a fourth, and crucial, point in his model was missing: the "subjective" or human factor. This was (in his own words) "the ability of the revolutionary class to take revolutionary mass action, strong enough to break (or dislocate) the old government which never—not even in a period of crisis—falls if it is not toppled over." In short, what was missing was an alternative focus of leadership willing and able to take over, rather as Lenin declared that the Bolsheviks most confidently were in a famous scene at the First Congress of Soviets in Petersburg in June (?) 1917. This is the factor so often omitted in the models of the "dysfunctionists", the "break-down" theorists of revolution, and even by so acute an observer of revolutions as Ernest Labrousse who has been inclined to explain the point of explosion in purely "natural", rather than in "anthropomorphic", terms.[10]

And yet the lessons of history are there for all to read as to what happened in the case of revolutionary situations from which this fourth, human, factor was missing. In Russia, after the brave attempts of 1904 and 1905, a few concessions were won, but substantially the old autocratic-feudal system continued as before. In Spain, Italy and Germany in the 1920s and 1930s, for lack of this vital missing link, it was not only a matter of returning to the old pre-revolutionary situation with the old governments conducting their business as before, but something far worse—sometimes mistakenly called an alternative type of "revolution"—took its place.

Or, to approach the same question in a slightly different way, it is often taken for granted that, in the conditions of the spring and summer of 1789, the French bourgeoisie should have stepped into the breach and harnessed the energies of the masses—the peasants and *menu peuple* of the towns—to a common cause; as if, in fact, to form such an alliance of classes (or of "contenders" as Tilly would say) was as easy as eating pie. Yet it happened nowhere else in Europe, except briefly at Geneva in 1781 (and this is an important ingredient in the "uniqueness" of the revolution in France in that the notion of an Atlantic Revolution is pushed aside). As John Adams, the moderate American revolutionary, wrote of the Dutch Patriots who failed to mobilize popular resistance to the Prussians and English in the crisis of 1787, they were "too inattentive to the sense of the common people". There was no revolution at the time in Holland, and there would presumably not have been one in the 1790s without the active intervention of the French. But there *was* a revolution in France and one reason for it—an important one— was that the French bourgeoisie, after dragging its feet for so long and hesitating so long before taking over the national leadership from the privileged orders, when it came to the point, was both willing and able to give the lead that was wanted and bring the masses along in its train. Had they not been willing to do this (clearly a *human* choice) there would have been no revolution in France in 1789 "as sure as eggs is eggs" and as sure as there was no effective revolution in Germany after the autumn of 1848 because the Frankfurt Parliament (representing the German bourgeoisie) was unwilling to do what the French had done some sixty years before.

But, as I said earlier, the question "who" does not only relate to the leaders (important as these undoubtedly are) but to the masses or "followers" as well; and I have had more than once to complain that such a consideration rarely plays a part in the calculations of social scientists and other constructors of comprehensive models. It would be unfair to say that Charles Tilly is a conspicuous offender, particularly when he is so aware of the problem and so eloquently exposes the failing in others. But neither he nor those whose shortcomings he condemns is inclined to treat the participants *de base* in any but the most general terms. Least of all, as I said before, does he appear to take much interest in what goes on in their heads—in what I would term the popular ideology in revolution. The immediate—or even long-term—causes of popular participation in revolution is one thing; popular ideology that infuses that participation, and without which there can be no popular revolutionary activity at all, is something else. Elsewhere, I have tried to explain what distinguishes "popular" ideology from any other, how it is composed, how it takes shape and how it becomes transformed in the course of a revolutionary situation and beyond.[11] In more practical and more concrete terms the problem can be studied in Christopher Hill's *The World Turned Upside Down* and Albert Soboul's writings on the Parisian *sans-culottes*,[12] these are among the few historians of revolution who have given the phenomenon the attention it deserves; and, of course, it is one to which the computer, invaluable as are the other uses to which it may be put, can make only a minimal contribution. Here I certainly do not propose to explore the matter to any depth; but I should like to indicate how its study may perhaps be carried further by posing a number of questions relating to the origins of the popular revolution of 1789 and indicating how the answers may be found.

If we may assume that the popular radical ideology as it took shape before the end of 1793 owed something to the ideas directly propagated by the *philosophes* among a small group of devotees in the 1750s and 1760s and relayed to a far wider public through the remonstrances of the Parliaments in the 1760s to 1780s and the journals and pamphlets of the revolutionary bourgeoisie in the winter, spring and summer of 1788–9, we are nevertheless struck by the considerable transformation that these ideas suffered in the lengthy process of transmission. We can only guess what Voltaire or Holbach, or even Rousseau (the only real "populist" among them), would have thought of the uses to which their ideas were put by the common people of Paris a quarter of a century after they were penned; yet we have the earlier example of what Martin Luther thought of the German peasants who revolted in his name to give us a clue.

More important is the way in which we can observe how one set of ideas (say the "derived" notions of the Rights of Man and the Sovereignty of the People) becomes grafted onto the indigenous or "inherent" ideas of the common people just before or just after the revolution breaks out. There must, in fact, be some point of transition from an older to a newer stage of consciousness, or to that *mentalité révolutionnaire* of which M. Godechot speaks, that it would be of some interest to discover. In 1775, the last year of widespread popular disturbance of the Old Régime in France, there is no sign at all of any penetration of "philosophical" ideas among the poor: the documentation relating to the events of that year is rich enough to have told us if any had existed. Nor does it seem that the process had gone much further in country districts before the peasants began their own assault on the *châteaux* in the early months of 1789.

For the "small people" of the cities the case was different. For some years, particularly in Paris, a certain degree of "politization" of popular disturbance had been going on, mainly under the influence of the *Parlement*. But this politization was of a very elementary kind and was not accompanied, any more than among the small consumers of 1775, by any profound *crise de conscience* or awareness among the *menu peuple* of the need for social change. So, once more, as with the peasants, we must search for a point closer to the events of 1789; though, in this case we may stop a little earlier and look for our transition in the *révolte nobilaire* of 1787–8 (the period that M. Jean Egret more pertinently terms "pre-Revolution") rather than twelve or eighteen months later. This, I believe, is particularly true of those cities that became most directly involved in the events, such as Rennes, Dijon, Grenoble and Paris itself. In Dijon, for example, one may trace the development of such a *mentalité* through four stages (I am indebted for this suggestion to M. Daniel Ligou): First, a preliminary "inherent" stage in the bread riots of 1775, which, as I have already observed, were entirely innocent of any political intrusion from outside; next, a degree of elementary politization in the adoption (as in Paris) of the slogan "Vive le Parlement", that began around 1784 and continued into 1788; thirdly, in 1788, a closer identification with the *Parlement* in its challenge to royal "despotism", a growing *crise de conscience* and the first assimilation of "philosophical" ideas; and, lastly, a union of *peuple* and bourgeoisie against aristocracy and absolute monarchy (thus reversing the old aristocratic-popular partnership) in the summer of 1789. We may trace a similar development in other cities under the dual impact of the "aristocratic revolt" and the pamphlet campaign of the Third Estate in the early months of 1789—notably in Paris where one learns from the police archives that such phrases as *tiers d'état* had invaded popular speech by mid-April of that year. But this is only a preliminary essay; and far more scholarly work will have to be done before what is at present a tentative hypothesis may claim to become clothed in solid fact.

At this point you may well believe that what I am really saying is that all previous models should be scrapped—Mr Tilly's included—and that I want a fresh start to be made in order to remedy such shortcomings by constructing a brand-new model of my own. No, God forbid! Nor am I recommending a return to the old discarded method of treating each revolution in isolation as a thing-in-itself. This would be to throw out the baby with the bathwater with a vengeance, and I have no stomach for such games. Frankly, I want to have it both ways: to look at the general as well as the particular; to look at the general pattern of revolutions as well as the individual case-histories of those taking part. In short, I want to indulge in the luxury of looking through the telescope at both ends.

Notes

1. See T.H. Aston, ed., *Crisis in Europe 1560–1660* (London, 1965).
2. See, particularly, R.R. Palmer, *The Age of the Democratic Revolution,* 2 vols. (Princeton, 1959, 1964); J. Godechot, *Les révolutions,* and (by the same), *France and the Atlantic Revolution of the Eighteenth Century 1770–1799* (New York, 1965).
3. C. Brinton, *The Anatomy of Revolution* (New York, 1938, 1952).
4. Ibid., pp. 17–18 (1952 edn); cited by Rule and Tilly (see next note), p. 45.
5. J. Rule and C. Tilly, "Political Process in Revolutionary France 1830–1832", in *1830 in France,* ed. John M. Merriman (New York, 1975), pp. 41–85.
6. N. Smelser, *Theory of Collective Behaviour* (New York, 1963); cited by Rule and Tilly, pp. 51–3.
7. C. Johnson, *Revolutionary Change* (Boston, 1968).
8. Rule and Tilly, pp. 55–9.
9. V.I. Lenin, *Collected Works,* 45 vols. (Moscow, 1960–70), 21, pp. 213–14.
10. C.E. Labrousse, "1789–1830–1848. Comment naissent les révolutions", in *Actes du congrès historique du centenaire de la Révolution de 1848* (Paris, 1949), pp. 1–29.
11. G. Rudé, "Revolution and Popular Ideology", in *Revolutions in France and North America, 1760–1800* (Lafayette, Louisiana, 1974).
12. C. Hill, *The World Turned Upside Down* (London, 1972); and A. Soboul, *Les sans-culottes parisiens de l'An II* (Paris, 1958).

4
Interpretations of the French Revolution

No period of history has so frequently been re-written in the light of current preoccupations or been such a repeated battle-ground of conflicting ideologies as the French Revolution. Ever since Edmund Burke, 180 years ago, dipped his pen in vitriol to blast the Revolution in its infancy, generation after generation of Frenchmen, with occasional support from other countries, have joined in the fray and done their bit to disprove the validity of Ranke's contention that history is "what actually happened". The main events of the Revolution—the meetings of the Notables and of the States General, the Constitution of 1791, the fall of the monarchy, the execution of Robespierre, and the rise of Napoleon—have, it is true, been accepted as facts by even the most incredulous and disputatious; but precious little else. What sort of Revolution was it—one of "poverty" or "prosperity"? a *bourgeois* revolution that overthrew feudalism? a national struggle for liberty, democracy, or "eternal Justice"? or, again, a criminal conspiracy against the old social order? What did it achieve? What was its ultimate significance? What sort of men were its leaders, its supporters and its victims? What part was played in it by aristocracy, middle class, peasants, urban *sans-culottes*? When did it begin? When did it end? What were its most significant landmarks and turning-points? Was there one single French Revolution or were there several? Questions such as these have been asked and variously answered by succeeding generations and "schools" of historians. It is the purpose of this pamphlet to consider the main stages of this discussion and some of the changing views and interpretations that have arisen in the course of it.

The Restoration Period, 1815–30

After Burke's *Reflections* (1790) no really important contribution to the discussion appeared until the Restoration of 1815–30. It was a period admirably suited for the re-writing of history in political terms. Forty million pages of history, it has been said, were written in the year 1825 alone—a large part of them devoted to the Revolution.[1] Napoleon had been shipped to St. Helena to the general satisfaction of "respectable" society; Louis XVIII had returned with the *émigré* nobility and clergy; the Charter had been granted to appease liberal opinion and to ensure the restored monarchy of the general support of the "political nation". But memories of the momentous events of the past quarter-century died hard; and behind the façade of national unity conservative Legitimists and liberal Constitutionalists sharpened their pens (if not yet their knives) to settle old scores, and the stage was admirably set for a prolonged duel of words with the French Revolution as its major theme. "An opinion on historical fact," wrote the Liberal Berville, "cannot constitute an offence in the eyes of the law." Augustin Thierry was even more specific. "In 1817," he wrote, "preoccupied with a strong desire to contribute to the triumph of constitutional opinions, I began to look into the works of history for proofs and arguments which would support my political beliefs."[2]

It is hardly surprising, therefore, that under these circumstances the Liberals' thesis of the Revolution should take on a distinctly political complexion and should tell us almost as much about their own constitutional pretensions as about the Revolution itself. As supporters of limited monarchy and upholders of the Charter of 1814, the Liberals were anxious to prove that the Revolution was justified, that it had its roots in France's national past, and that the Charter itself, by the method of its granting, set an official seal of approval on the work of the "men of 1789". To Guizot the Revolution had its distant origins in the struggles of Gauls against Franks; in later history, the consecutive crimes of aristocracy, Church and Absolute Monarchy had all made its outbreak inevitable.[3] Madame de Staël considered it

one of the grand eras of social order . . . The same movement in the minds of men which brought about the revolution in England was the cause of that in France in 1789. Both belong to the third era in the progress of social order—the establishment of representative government.[4]

Though the constitution-makers of 1791 were not without their faults, the result of their work was to transform "the internal existence of the nation". For the abuses of the past, wrote Francois Mignet,

the Revolution substituted a system more conformable with justice and better suited
to our times. It substituted law in the place of arbitrary will, equality in that of
privilege; delivered men from the distinction of classes, the land from the barriers of
provinces, trade from the shackles of corporations and fellowships [sic!], agriculture
from feudal subjection and the aggression of tithes, property from the impediment of
entails, and brought everything to the condition of one state, one system of law, one
people.[5]

Of course, the Liberals were embarrassed by the "excesses" of the
Revolution and, in general, considered that it took a wrong turning after
1791. Being monarchists, they could hardly condone the execution of
Louis XVI; not being democrats, they found little to enthuse them in the
activities of the Parisian *sans-culottes*; and being Liberals, they detested
the "despotism" of the Committee of Public Safety and of Bonaparte.
With them, therefore, the Revolution tends to fall into two distinct
parts—the years 1789 to 1791, which are generally approved of; and the
years 1792 to 1794 (or 1799 or 1814) which are generally condemned.
There are, however, exceptions, Danton, for example, receives praise.
"Danton's mind," wrote Adolphe Thiers, "was uncultivated, but it was
noble, contemplative and, above all, possessed simplicity and
firmness",[6] and Mignet wrote of the death of Danton and Desmoulins:
"Thus perished the last defenders of humanity and moderation, the last
who sought to promote peace among the conquerors of the Revolution
and pity for the conquered."[7]

But the great exception to the general rule was the attitude of the
Liberal historians to the feats of arms performed by the soldiers of the
Republic and Empire: these, at all costs, must be rescued from oblivion
and seen as part of France's great heritage of military glory. "The
conduct of the French army during the period of Terror," wrote
Madame de Staël, "was truly patriotic . . . the soldiers belonged not to
any particular chief, but to France." And how, she asks, "was it possible
for the government of 1793 and 1794 to triumph over so many enemies?
This prodigy can be explained only by the devotion of the nation to its
cause. A million men took arms to repel the forces of the coalition; the
people were animated with a frenzy as fatal in the interior as invincible
without."[8] And even the "crimes" of the Convention and of the
Jacobins, though thoroughly reprehensible, were no worse, according
to the Abbé Mongaillard, than those perpetrated on St. Bartholomew's
Eve, at the time of the Fronde, and by Louis XIV.[9] In any case, the
aristocracy and higher clergy must bear their full share of responsibility
for the turn of events for, having joined with the rest of the nation in
promoting the Revolution, they deserted it after October 1789 and left
its direction in the wrong hands. "For the men of rank and property
offering no support to liberty," wrote Madame de Staël,

"democratic power necessarily acquired the ascendancy . . . In France, the nobility opposed these rights [i.e. the rights long enjoyed by the English Commons], but being too weak to struggle with the people, they quitted the country in a mass, and allied themselves with foreigners."[10]

Conservative writers, on the other hand, reflecting the views of the majority of returned *émigrés*, tended to view the Charter of 1814 with suspicion and to condemn the Revolution as a series of crimes against society, church, and state, leading by inevitable stages to regicide, terror and the dictatorship of the usurper Bonaparte.[11] None of these, however, if we except the Abbé Barruel's five volume polemic against Jacobinism written in exile, wrote a full-length history of the Revolution; but, though strongly divided amongst themselves on their attitude to the *parlements*, the nobility and the church (whether Gallican or Ultramontaine), they formed a more or less common front to press home the attack on the weaker points in the Liberals' arguments in a number of scattered pamphlets, political treatises and memoirs. The only one of them to have an influence comparable with that of the Liberal historians was Barruel, who first put forward the explanation that the Revolution was the outcome of a conspiracy hatched by Illuminati, Freemasons, *philosophes* and Jacobins.[12] This theory was to become part of the stock-in-trade of subsequent generations of conservative historians. In England, it found an early adherent in John Wilson Croker who, besides endowing the British Museum with his vast collection of Revolution tracts, drew heavily on royalist memoirs to refute the works of Thiers, and the "Jacobin historians" and to present the events of 1789 in terms of a conspiracy devised in the entourage of the Duke of Orleans.[13]

The July Monarchy, being fashioned in the image of the Liberals of the 1820s, added little that was new to their conception of the Revolution until it was in full decline. The Revolution of 1848, however, and the Second Empire that followed, raised new problems and produced another crop of historical writing on the subject. Jules Michelet began to work out his ideas on the Revolution as professor at the Collège de France in Louis-Philippe's reign; but his great seven volume *History* is impregnated with the spirit of the Republican democrats of 1848 and belongs essentially to that period.[14] Conservatives and Liberals of the Restoration, for all their differences and bitter mutual recriminations, were at least agreed in their contempt for the common people, or *sans-culottes*, of the Revolution. Thiers and Mignet both justified Bailly's proclamation of Martial Law against the Parisian petitioners of 17 July 1791, which led to the notorious "massacre" of the Champ de Mars; and Thiers liberally dubbed the rioters and insurgents of 1789 as "brigands."[15] Carlyle, writing in 1837, was more sympathetic: the poor workers and artisans of the Faubourg St. Antoine, who destroyed Réveillon's house in April 1789 and broke into his wine-cellars, were for him at least "poor lackels, all betoiled, besoiled, encrusted into dim effacement".[16] Michelet, however, viewed "the people" with more than pitying indulgence. They become the very life-blood, inspiration and driving force of the Revolution, whether in peace or war; and the leaders, in consequence, are reduced to playing the subordinate part of puppets that are brought to life, inflated or destroyed by the ebb and flow of the popular movement.

> L'acteur principal [he wrote in his preface of 1847] est le peuple. Pour le retrouver, celui-ci, pour le replacer dans son rôle, j'ai dû ramener à leurs proportions les ambitieuses marionnettes dont il a tiré les fils, et dans lesquelles jusqu'ici, on croyait voir, on cherchait le jeu secret de l'histoire.[17]

To Michelet the Revolution marked a regenerative upsurge of the whole French nation, born of the hunger, poverty and oppression of the masses and the lofty idealism and quest for "eternal Justice" of men of every social class; the Bastille surrendered to "the people" because "its conscience troubled it", and the revolutionary wars were fought with mystical fervour by the whole nation under arms. But, as a Republican democrat of 1848, he drew a distinction between the glories of 1789 to 1792—"l'époque sainte"—when the nation was united, and the "heroic" but "sombre" days of 1793–4—"l'époque des violences, l'époque des actes sanguinaires"—to which the Republic had been driven by dangers from within and without.[18] Concerned as he was to present the Revolution as a great popular movement, it is not surprising that Michelet's *History* should open with the events of the spring and summer of 1789 and close with Robespierre's overthrow in July 1794.

Michelet certainly broke new ground and his influence on subsequent generations has been profound; but, in several respects, Alexis de Tocqueville, whose *L'Ancien Régime et la Révolution* appeared a few years later, was a more original thinker. Like Michelet, Tocqueville was strongly influenced by his experiences of 1848, when he had served as a Minister, and perhaps even more by the Bonapartist *coup d'état* and Empire; but unlike Michelet he was a conservative Liberal, who shared none of his enthusiasm for democracy and was appalled rather than enthused by the part played by "the people"; in fact, he wrote that "this Revolution was prepared by the most civilized, but carried out by the most barbarous and the rudest classes of the nation".[19] However, far from presenting the Revolution as an unfortunate break with France's otherwise glorious past in the manner of the Restoration Conservatives, Tocqueville stressed the continuity of ideas and institutions linking the

Revolution and Empire with the Old Régime: in this he went considerably further than Guizot had done before him. "The French Revolution," he wrote, "will only be the darkness of night to those who merely regard itself; only the times which preceded it will give the light to illuminate it."[20] Certainly the Revolution saw a strengthening of the central administration in the authority conferred on the committees of government and their agents over both Assembly and local authorities—a process carried considerably further under the Consulate and Empire. But this, argued Toqueville, was merely the logical sequel to the "administrative revolution" that had already begun under Louis XVI; and he pointed to the extended powers of the Conseil du Roi, the all-pervading activities of the Intendants, the progressive reduction in the independence of *pays d'état* and local government, the growing integration of the Gallican church with the machinery of state, and the emergence of a whole new apparatus for the exercise of administrative justice. Such reforms were accompanied by a phenomenal increase in national prosperity: the commerce of Bordeaux, on the eve of the Revolution, outmatched that of Liverpool, and the French *bourgeoisie* could pride itself, as never before, on its wealth and economic power. The peasants, too, far from grovelling in abject poverty, backwardness and unrelieved squalor, were already the owners of half the land of France. Why then, he asks, was there a revolution in France and not in Austria, Prussia, Poland or Russia, where the people were far more impoverished and oppressed? It was precisely, he argued, because of the rapid pace of prosperity and enlightenment that the survivals of feudalism—in many ways actually intensified during these latter years of the old order—appeared all the more onerous and intolerable. Ministers and officials, whose job it should have been to administer and defend the existing system, were the first to be affected by the corrosive ideas of Encyclopaedists and *philosophes*; the *bourgeoisie*, by virtue of their growing wealth, resented all the more the exemptions and privileges of the other orders; and the peasants, having tasted of the sweets of personal freedom and ownership, were all the more exasperated by the surviving burden of feudal dues and obligations. Tocqueville sums up this part of his argument in a famous passage:

> It is not always by going from bad to worse that a society falls into revolution. It happens most often that a people, which has supported without complaint, as if they were not felt, the most oppressive laws, violently throws them off as soon as their weight is lightened. The social order destroyed by a revolution is almost always better than that which immediately preceded it, and experience shows that the most dangerous moment for a bad government is generally that in which it sets about reform . . . Feudalism at the height of its power had not inspired Frenchmen with so much hatred as it did on the eve of its disappearing. The slightests acts of

arbitrary power under Louis XVI seemed less easy to endure than all the despotism of Louis XIV.[21]

The Paris Commune and Taine

Among those whom the Revolution of 1848 had made enthusiastic for the popular cause was Hyppolite Taine. But the Liberal of 1848 became soured and disillusioned by his experience of the Commune of 1871 and, five years later, he published the most eloquent, bitter and scathing indictment of the great Revolution that had yet been penned.[22] But whereas earlier conservative historians had presented the Revolution as an unfortunate accident or the product of a conspiracy, Taine saw it as a logical outcome of the dissolution of government and of the old social order (which he, incidentally, condemned); thus anarchy—"spontaneous anarchy", as he calls it—was let loose and the "mob" took over. At one stage of his narrative, this appears to happen from the very start; elsewhere, he is more specific and dates the final surrender to anarchy and terror from the forcible return of the King to Paris from Versailles on 6 October 1789. "Cette fois on n'en peut plus douter; la Terreur est établie et a demeuré."[23] But he puts forward what was then a highly original explanation of the particular anger and violence of the popular outbreak: one factor was famine which, he claimed, had been chronic since January 1789 and was becoming progressively more severe; another was the high hopes aroused among the people ("la grande espérance") that, as the King himself had ordered the States General to meet and the *cahiers* to be drawn up, everything would be done to redress their wrongs. This, he believed, was as important as the economic crisis and the long-standing grievance against feudal exaction in prompting the peasants to take the law into their hands and to march on the mansions of their *seigneurs* to shouts of "Long live the King!"

But Taine, unlike Michelet, by no means identifies the insurgents with the French people as a whole: the provincial rioters of 1789 are presented as "contre-bandiers, faux-sauniers, braconniers, vagabonds, mendiants, repris de justice"; and the captors of the Bastille become "la lie de la société", "la dernière plèbe", "bandits" and "vagabonds"[24]—epithets that have served the conservative historians of the Revolution ever since. Taine goes further: the leaders, too, the Jacobins and other promoters of the concept of "popular sovereignty" are neither typical Frenchmen of their day nor normally balanced mortals: they tend, in fact, to be social failures and misfits, mainly of the lower midle class, men of unstable character, riddled with dogma and with an exaggerated sense of their own importance. 'Ce sont là nos Jacobins; ils naissent dans la décomposition sociale, ainsi que des champignons dans un terreau qui fermente.''[25] Taine's ideas were to have a great influence on later writers: not surprisingly, the destructive and unflattering picture that he painted of the Revolution appealed to extreme conservatives; but his social analysis proved of interest and value to a later school of radical historians as well.

The Third Republic and Aulard

As Michelet reflected the views of the Republican democrats of 1848 and Taine those of conservatives and ex-Liberals of the next generation, so Alphonse Aulard was a typical Radical of the Third Republic. Of a generation that had acclaimed Gambetta and seen the downfall of the Second Empire, he was the first occupant of the newly-created Chair of the French Revolution at the Sorbonne. His great four-volume *Political History* appeared at the turn of the century[26] and marks a sort of parting of the ways in the study of the Revolution. On the one hand, it ushered in a new era as being a work of exacting and scrupulous scholarship: Aulard was the first French historian to apply to a work of modern history the rigorously systematic and critical use of sources; here he took as his models Ranke and his school in Germany and French medievalists trained in the Ecole des Chartes. But Aulard's *History*, as its title suggests, still follows the nineteenth-century pattern of arguing about the Revolution in political and ideological terms, and the greater objectivity of the scholar has by no means eliminated the political bias of the citizen reared in the democratic-Republican tradition of Michelet. This bias and his general interpretation of the Revolution are evident in the preface to his first edition:

> I wish to write the political history of the Revolution from the point of view of the origin and the development of Democracy and Republicanism. Democracy is the logical consequence of the principle of equality. Republicanism is the logical consequence of the principle of national sovereignty. These two consequences did not ensue at once. In place of Democracy, the men of 1789 founded a middle-class government, a suffrage of property-owners. In place of the Republic, they organized a limited monarchy. Not until September 22nd did they abolish the Monarchy and create the Republic. The republican form of government lasted . . . until 1804 . . . when the government of the Republic was confined to an Emperor.

Equally significant of his conception of the Revolution is Aulard's

division of "the history of Democracy and the Republic" into four main
stages, which correspond to the divisions separating each one of his four
volumes—(i) 1789–92, "the period of the origins of Democracy and the
Republic"; (ii) 1792–5, "the period of the Democratic Republic"; (iii)
1795–9, "the period of the Bourgeois Republic" and (iv) 1799–1804,
"the period of the Plebiscitary Republic".[27] One suspects that had
Aulard been asked to choose one single decisive turning-point in the
course of the Revolution, he would have chosen October 1795 (the point
at which his second volume ends): not because it marked the end of the
"popular" Revolution with the defeat of the Parisian *san-culottes* in
Prairial (May 1795), but because it marked the adoption of the
Constitution of the Year III, whose essential characteristic he
considered to be "the suppression of the system of democracy
established on August 10, 1792".[28] In fact, a confirmed critic of the
Revolution like Cochin could justly tax Aulard with accepting the whole
period 1789 to 1795 as being all of a piece: Taine had done so, too, but in
order to damn it wholesale; not, as in Aulard's case, to present it as a
great and continuous struggle for the attainment of a highly desirable
objective. Even so, Aulard was by no means undiscriminating in his
admiration of the leaders of the Revolution. For him, as for many
radicals of his generation, Danton was the great man of the Republic, a
man cast in the heroic mould of a Mirabeau or a Gambetta, who,
although lacking a system and a programme, was a stranger to hatred
and vengeance and undeserving of the charges of cruelty and venality
that historians and contemporaries had heaped upon him. Robespierre,
on the other hand, for all his integrity and his outstanding services to the
Republic, was a meaner type of mortal: he did not hesitate to destroy the
Girondins in order to avenge an affront to his personal dignity and there
was some justification (Aulard felt) for considering him "a hypocritical
demagogue".[29]

Lord Acton, who was lecturing on the Revolution at Cambridge
during the years that Aulard was assembling the materials for his
Political History, greatly admired his scholarship and even thought that
the pending publication of the proceedings of the Jacobin Club, of the
Paris Commune and Electors, and other collections of documents would
soon make it possible to write the *definitive* history of the Revolution:
"in a few years all these publications will be completed, and all will be
known that ever can be known."[30] But, as a Whig, Acton stood far closer
to Tocqueville than he did to Aulard. "Tocqueville," he wrote, "was a
Liberal of the purest breed—a Liberal and nothing else"; and he clearly
shared his suspicion of democracy "and its kindred, equality,
centralization and utilitarianism". Like Tocqueville, too, he criticized
the French *philosophes* for their "disregard for liberty"—an influence,

he considered, that left its mark on the whole Revolution. But his outbursts of moral indignation are entirely his own, as, for example, his comment on the September Massacres: "We have touched low-water in the Revolution; and there is nothing worse than this to come. We are in the company of men fit for Tyburn." His judgement on Danton, completely at variance with that of Aulard, was in keeping: "With Danton and his following we reach the lowest stage of what can still be called the conflict of opinion, and come to bare cupidity and vengeance, to brutal instincts and hideous passion."[31] Even more significant of Acton's general attitude to the French Revolution was his assessment of the Constitution of the Year III which, for him, too, brought the revolutionary period to a close, though for reasons quite different from those of Aulard.

> The new Constitution (he wrote) afforded securities for order and liberty such as France had never enjoyed. The Revolution had begun with a Liberalism which was a passion more than a philosophy, and the first Assembly endeavoured to realize it by diminishing authority, weakening the executive and decentralizing power. In the hour of peril under the Girondins the policy failed, and the Jacobins governed on the principle that power, coming from the people, ought to be concentrated in the fewest possible hands and made absolutely irresistible. Equality became the substitute of liberty, and the danger arose that the most welcome form of equality would be the equal distribution of property . . . These schemes were at an end and the Constitution of the Year III closes the revolutionary period.[32]

A far more thoroughgoing critic of Aulard, and one who, in the tradition of Taine and the Restoration Conservatives, condemned all that the Revolution stood for, was Augustin Cochin. Cochin's particular contribution was to pick up the arguments first advanced by the Abbé Barruel, bring them up to date in the light of more recent research, and to present a fully renovated version of the "conspiracy" thesis as an explanation of the outbreak and further progress of the Revolution. A less gifted contemporary, Gustave Bord, had already made a rather crude attempt to present the Paris insurrection of July 1789 in terms of a masonic conspiracy.[33] Cochin was both more scholarly and more subtle and concentrated his attack more particularly on the events immediately preceding the Revolution in the two provinces of Burgundy and Brittany.[34] He argued that both masonic lodges and literary societies (he calls them "sociétés de pensée"), which existed in large numbers in French provincial towns towards the end of the century, were in reality political clubs, whose members, nourished on the ideas of the Enlightenment, planned and plotted the overthrow of the old social order. How was it possible, he asks, to organize a campaign to secure a double representation of the Third Estate in

January 1789, to elect similarly minded deputies to the meetings of local electors and to the States General at Versailles, to prepare *cahiers de doléances* of a common inspiration? "Il y a là un phénomène étrange qu'on n'a peut-être pas assez expliqué." The only reasonable explanation, he concludes, is that there was a plot—a plot that, in the first instance, was formed and directed by what he calls "la cabale des avocats", though he adds that, in Burgundy at least, it was composed equally of doctors, surgeons and notaries, "tous petits bourgeois obscurs, dont plusieurs se firent nommer députés aux Etats, dont aucun ne laissa un nom".[35]

A conservative historian of a very different outlook, and one whose influence in this country has been greater than that of either Taine or Cochin, was Louis Madelin, whose main work on the Revolution was published in 1911. Unlike most of the conservatives of the nineteenth century, Madelin condemned the anarchy of the Old Régime and approved of the aims of the men of 1789; he was also the first prominent historian of the Revolution to be a convinced Bonapartist. "The Revolution of 1789," he wrote,

> had been the work of the Nation. The "progress of knowledge" had opened the eyes of the upper classes to the abuses of inequality. The excess of the public suffering had driven the popular classes into rebellion. Their firm resolve to abolish the feudal system had stirred the peasants to revolt. The evident anarchy existing in the King's government had roused a general desire for a *Constitution*, but by the word Constitution ninetenths of the French nation understood nothing more than a charter which should reorganize the State. *Equality in matters of justice and taxation—the abolition of the feudal system—a methodical and orderly system of government—*these were what the Frenchmen of Janary 1789 sought to obtain.[36]

By August, argues Madelin, "almost all these things had been secured"; and for most Frenchmen, the peasantry in particular, the Revolution, having achieved its purpose, had come to an end. This, then, for Madelin is the real turning-point far more than Thermidor or the Constitution of the Year III; and after this, the Revolution is merely carried on for another ten years by its own impetus, the ambitions of political leaders, and the rapacity of the "mob" until, at long last, Bonaparte and his grenadiers came to clean up the mess, drive out the profiteers, demagogues and oligarchs on 18th–19th Brumaire, and to complete and consolidate the early achievements of the Revolution. "*Napoleon Bonaparte was to give France all that was expected of him.* And for that reason the Revolution did not come to an end on that evening of the 19th Brumaire, for it was to be written now in Codes, and Concordats, and Treaties."[37]

Madelin's contemporary, Hilaire Belloc, painted an entirely different picture of the Revolution. As a Roman Catholic, he considered the conflict between church and state in the Revolution to be of paramount importance, and he presents the events of 1789 to 1794 essentially as a battle of ideas. But, perhaps surprisingly, he shared Michelet's view of the Revolution as a great regenerative episode in the history of the French people; and even Robespierre comes in for praise. Danton, it is true, is his particular hero and is commended for his intelligence, courage, patriotism, eloquence and powers of leadership; yet Belloc is anxious to dispel the "legend" that Robespierre was "a man of blood": "He has left no monument; but from the intensity of his faith and from his practice of it, his name, though it will hardly increase, will certainly endure."[38]

Historians of the Twentieth Century

So far, the historians of the Revolution, for all the deep differences of social outlook, political affiliation or mere emphasis that divide them, have certain significant characteristics in common. For one thing, they all (even Michelet) see the Revolution "from above"—that is from the vantage-point of the King's Court at Versailles, the National Assembly, the Jacobin Club, the Committee of Public Safety, or the national press. The Revolution is presented as a battle of ideas or of rival political factions in which the main contenders for power are the King and the Court party, the *parlements* and aristocracy, and the Third Estate with their middle-class and liberal-aristocratic leaders. The peasantry hardly appears in the picture any more than the urban *sans-culottes*; and if they do, their thoughts and actions (where not merely blind outbursts of "mob" violence) are the reflections of those of the aristocracy, the revolutionary *bourgeoisie*, or the orators and journalists of the Tuileries and Palais Royal. This approach to the problems of the Revolution and their interpretation is as true of the Liberal and Radical historians as it is of the conservatives and royalists—as true of Thiers, Michelet and Aulard as it is of Taine, Cochin and Madelin; as true of those who saw the Revolution as a struggle for a Constitution (Thiers, Mignet, Madelin), for "eternal Justice" (Michelet), for Democracy and the Republic (Aulard), or for Liberty (Acton) as of those for whom it was an evil conspiracy designed to pull the old order out by the roots. Tocqueville, admittedly, does not quite fit in to this pattern, but he is altogether somewhat of a freak.

In the sixty years since Aulard wrote his *Political History*, the main school of historians of the Revolution has tended to shift its focus from the centre of events and from the classes that solely engaged the attention of their predecessors. Serious study has been made of economic and social questions, not merely to provide the political story with frills but to give new depths and a new perspective to the Revolution as a whole. The peasantry and urban *sans-culottes* (particularly in Paris, it is true) have been brought into the picture and studied "from below" as social classes and groups having their own identity, ideas, and aspirations, independent of those of the upper and middle *bourgeoisie* and the revolutionary politicians and journalists. Robespierre has been taken out of the Chamber of Horrors and put at the centre of the stage as the most consistent and important leader and spokesman of radical democracy. Finally, there has been a tendency to present the conflicts of the Revolution in terms of a struggle of classes rather than of ideas or ideologies. This reorientation of Revolutionary studies clearly owes a great deal to Marx and to the spread of socialist ideas in Europe during the past seventy-five years: to that extent it may be said to represent a new *socialist* interpretation of the Revolution. But it is not only that, since historians other than socialists have been affected by it; and, in that sense, it may be said to respond to the new problems and social developments of the twentieth century that have widened the horizons of historians generally—such developments as universal suffrage, market research, the Welfare State, mass trade unionism, the Russian Revolution, and the experiences of two World Wars. Partly, no doubt, too, historians of the Revolution have been influenced by historians in other fields, among whom Marc Bloch with his studies of medieval rural society has probably been the most eminent.

The first historian in France to give this new direction to Revolutionary studies was Jean Jaurès, secretary of the French Socialist Party and author of the *Histoire socialiste de la Révolution française*, published in 1901–4. In spite of its highly tendentious title, this was by no means a set party-piece or a political polemic, and it received the unstinting praise of Aulard. Jaurès accepted Michelet's and Aulard's general thesis that the Revolution was a struggle for the democratic Republic: to that extent he was no innovator and he claimed to owe his inspiration as much to the narrative vigour of Plutarch and the mysticism of Michelet as to the materialism of Marx. Besides, his four volumes are packed (in the manner of several of his predecessors) with lengthy passages from the speeches of Mirabeau, Vergniaud, Danton, Robespierre and Saint-Just, and from the writings of Brissot, Marat, Prudhomme, Desmoulins and Hébert. But, with all this, his *History* is essentially an economic and social interpretation of the Revolution. Aulard had previously discouraged such an attempt in view of the wide dispersal of documents; to which Jaurès replied that a history confined to the political issues was "a mere abstraction" and asked: "How can he (Aulard) fully understand the change that occurred during the Revolution from a bourgeois oligarchy to a democracy without conceiving of the social and political upheavals as intimately linked?"[39]

The presentation of the Revolution as a struggle of social classes was, of course, not a new one: Guizot, Thierry and Tocqueville had, with varying degrees of emphasis, suggested as much; Marx, Engels and Kautsky had treated it almost exclusively in such terms; and on the eve of the Revolution itself, Barnave had insisted that the conflict between the Third Estate and the privileged orders was essentially over property. But Jaurès was the first to write a full-length history of the Revolution with this as its central theme; besides, whereas Barnave had limited the conflict to two classes only and Tocqueville, Taine and others had confined their attention to the aristocracy, *bourgeoisie* and peasantry (and then only in the most general terms), he put on to his canvas, in addition to these classes, the *sans-culottes*—the workshop masters, small shopkeepers, journeymen and labourers—of the towns as well. In so doing, Jaurès probed far deeper than his predecessors into the evident divisions within the Third Estate—divisions that became more acute as the Revolution advanced, particularly after the summer of 1791. Again, although the peasantry and countryside continued to play a distinctly subordinate role, Jaurès on occasion shifted his focus from Paris and paid some attention to revolutionary developments in such cities as Lyons, Rheims, Rouen and Bordeaux. In one respect at least, he took after Tocqueville rather than Michelet. His study of the growing wealth and economic importance of the *bourgeoisie* on the eve of revolution led him to reject Michelet's thesis of a "révolution de la misère" and to stress the impetus given to its outbreak by the increasing irritation of the wealthy middle classes at their continued exclusion from privilege and political authority.

Not the least of Jaurès' achievements was the stimulus that he gave to the study of the economic aspects of the Revolution. In 1903, with Ministerial support and Aulard's cooperation, he founded the *Commission de Recherche et de Publication des Documents relatifs à la Vie économique de la Révolution*, whose purpose it was to collect and publish the most important economic documents relating to the Revolution. The venture was brilliantly successful and, by the time of Jaurès' assassination in 1914, 57 volumes had been published; to these were added, in the ten years following the First World War, a further 36 volumes—mainly of *cahiers de doléances* and of records of sales of *biens nationaux*. This work still goes on.

The most influential historian of the French Revolution, both in

France and abroad, in the years between the two World Wars was Albert
Mathiez. Mathiez was a great teacher and a persuasive writer, who
began his career at the end of the last century as a conventional historian
in the tradition of Michelet and Aulard: his early studies on the October
"days" and the church conflict in the Revolution bear the stamp of these
masters. But, having become a convinced admirer of Robespierre,
Mathiez broke with Aulard and, in 1908, founded the *Société des Etudes
Robespierristes*. Up to this time, Robespierre, unlike Danton, had
received little sympathy from historians and his importance had
generally been underestimated. To Thiers he had appeared to be "one of
the most odious beings that could have borne absolute rule over men";
Carlyle described him as "acrid, implacable-impotent, dull-drawling,
barren as the Harmatten wind"; to Madelin he was "the dismal lawyer
from Arras", and to Acton "the most hateful character in the forefront
of history since Machiavelli reduced to a code the wickedness of public
men"; while even Michelet charged him with dictatorial ambitions and
Aulard with hypocrisy.

In the numerous studies that Mathiez now began to devote to this
memory, Robespierre emerges not only as a man of incorruptible virtue
and unwavering principle, but as a great statesman of the Revolution
besides. In presenting this new image of Robiespierre, Mathiez was
influenced by Jaurès, who had criticized Danton's conduct in 1793–4
and, to that extent, had justified Robespierre's; but, more particularly,
he had been disillusioned by the record of the Radical governments of
1902 and 1906 and a series of financial scandals. In the light of these,
Danton became the typical Radical politician of the Third Republic,
opportunistic and venal, while Robespierre, in contrast, was a model of
revolutionary high-mindedness and incorruptibility. Mathiez'
experiences of the First World War completed the picture: added to his
other vices Danton now appeared as a "defeatist" moving in a circle of
shady "foreigners". The labels have stuck, though this "black-and-
white" portrayal of the Revolution's two outstanding leaders has been
considerably modified in the later work of Georges Lefebvre.[40]

In the course of his one-way duel with Aulard (for Aulard never
replied to his attacks), Mathiez had naturally been drawn into a study of
the Jacobin–Girondin dispute and had begun to look for social
differences underlying the political hostilities fought out between the
two parties in the Convention and Jacobin Club. This, together with a
deeper study of Jaurès, had aroused his curiosity concerning the social
and economic problems of the Revolution. This new interest had been
further stimulated by his reflections on the economic controls imposed
by the belligerents in the course of the First World War. He saw in these
a parallel with the Maximum laws enacted by the Convention under

pressure from the Paris Commune and *sans-culottes* in 1793. The result was his great monograph, *La vie chère et le mouvement social sous la Terreur* (1927), which was the first attempt to explain the origins and policies of the Revolutionary Government in terms of social conflicts and economic pressures. For the first time, too, a clear distinction was drawn between the *bourgeois* conception of "freedom" and that of the *sans-culottes*.

Meanwhile, Mathiez's most influential work, his synthesis of the whole Revolutionary period, *La Révolution française* (1922–27),[41] had taken shape. In outlining the causes of the Revolution, he repeated Jaurès' picture of the growing prosperity of the *bourgeoisie*; at the same time, he pointed to the "feudal reaction" that had set in during the latter years of the Old Régime, an observation that has already been made by Tocqueville. Again, he took over from Châteaubriand and some of the Restoration Liberals the idea that the real starting-point of the Revolution was not the meeting of the States General or the fall of the Bastille but the summoning of the Assembly of Notables in February 1787. It was this that provoked the "révolte nobiliaire" (as Mathiez called it) out of which the events of 1789 sprang: in Châteaubriand's words: "les patriciens commencèrent la révolution; les plébéins l'achevèrent."[42] So for Mathiez the Revolution falls into four distinctive, though interrelated, parts (and it is interesting to compare his divisions with those of Aulard): (*a*) the revolt of the nobility, 1787–88; (*b*) the *bourgeois* revolution, 1789–91; (*c*) the democratic and Republican revolution, 1792–93; and (*d*) the social revolution 1793–July 1794. It is hardly surprising that, with the view Mathiez held of Robespierre, the fall of the "Incorruptible" in Thermidor should bring the revolutionary era to an end; after that, "reaction" took over under the Thermidorians and the Directory.

Professor C.-E. Labrousse shares with Tocqueville the distinction of never having written the work on the Revolution that he intended and yet of having considerably influenced subsequent thinking on its origins by his work on the Old Régime. His studies on the movements of prices and incomes in the eighteenth century and on the eve of the Revolution have thrown new light on the crisis out of which the Revolution emerged.[43] Basing his conclusion on a wide range of statistical materials, Labrousse gives some support to Jaurès' and Tocqueville's views in stressing the general prosperity and economic expansion that marked a large part of the eighteenth century, though he shows that, even in these years, wages and smaller incomes tended to lag behind the prices of food and essential consumers' goods. After 1778, however, there was a recession as the result of which prices fell—gradually in most industrial and farm products, but reaching crisis proportions in wines and textiles.

During these years, the net profits of small tenant farmers, peasant proprietors, wine-growers and other *métayers* (share-croppers) tended, because of the heavy and sustained toll of tax, tithe and seigneurial exaction, to fall out of all proportion to the fall in prices, while large landed proprietors were cushioned against loss by means of their feudal revenues. On top of this cyclical depression came the sudden economic catastrophe of 1787–9, which took the form of bad harvests and shortage, with the price of wheat doubling within two years in the main productive regions in the north and reaching record levels in 27 out of 32 *généralités* in mid-summer 1789. This, in turn, was accompanied by a crisis in industry and large-scale unemployment in Paris and the textile centres; while wage-earners and other small consumers were compelled by the rise in prices to increase their expenditure on bread from one half to three quarters or four fifths of their earnings.[44] It was against this background of accumulated economic ills and social grievances, affecting the majority of social groups within the Third Estate, that the political crisis flared up at Versailles in May 1789.

One of the great merits of Labrousse's work has been to give solid substance to the generalizations and conjectures of earlier historians concerning the economic origins of the Revolution: in the light of the new evidence, for example, a new complexion is put on the old argument that has exercised historians since Michelet's day: was the Revolution the product of poverty or prosperity? Labrousse argues that, on the whole, it was neither the one nor the other, though he inclines towards Michelet's view rather than towards that of Tocqueville, Jaurès and Mathiez. At the same time, his analysis convincingly illustrates the nature of the grievances that brought these highly diverse elements within the Third Estate (the Abbé Sieyès' "nation") together in the spring and summer of 1789 in common opposition to landlords, tax-farmers, grain-speculators and tithe-extracting bishops. While this is by no means the whole story, it helps us to understand why the alliance within the Third Estate appeared to be so solid at this time and, by implication, why it tended to disintegrate as the Revolution advanced.

No recent historian of the Revolution, however, not even Mathiez himself, held an international reputation for scholarship equal to that of Georges Lefebvre, who died in Paris in 1959. Though born the same year as Mathiez and closely following him both at the Sorbonne and as editor of the *Annales historiques de la Révolution française*, he pursued a remarkably distinctive course. Lefebvre always acknowledged his debt to Jaurès, but it was he rather than Jaurès who was the real initiator of the attempt to study the Revolution "from below", or from the angle of the peasantry and urban *sans-culottes*. Perhaps the most striking of all the limitations of the nineteenth-century historians was their failure to take proper account of the part played in the Revolution by the peasants, who formed four-fifths of the population of France. The earliest pioneer in the field was the Russian Loutchisky who, before the turn of the century, began to make studies of peasant property in the Limousin and elsewhere.[45]

Loutchisky's researches were important in so far as they helped to answer the long-standing question as to the respective proportions of the land owned by peasants, clergy and nobility on the eve of the Revolution—a question that had, as we have seen, considerably interested Alexis de Tocqueville; but they had little to say about the social aspirations and attitudes of the rural population and were not in the least concerned with the part played by the peasants in the Revolution itself. After a preliminary study on the history of food supplies during the Revolution in the northern district of Bergues,[46] Lefebvre published his great pioneering work, *Les Paysans du Nord pendant la Révolution française*, in 1924. Here, for the first time, the peasants of the Revolution were presented not as a single undifferentiated mass, but as a conglomeration of widely varying social groups: for all their identity as a rural community which had made it possible for them to unite in a universal peasant rising in the summer of 1789, they were deeply divided by conflicting interests within the village, which ranged small proprietors against landlords and speculators and landless peasants against large tenant farmers and what Lefebvre called the *bourgeoisie rurale*.

These differences and conflicts were traced throughout the revolutionary years and measured in terms of social disorder, purchase of land, distribution of property, and relations with government representatives on mission and local authorities. But the Revolution, far from healing these differences by giving universal satisfaction, widened the breach and made the differences irreconcilable. For the "rural bourgeois", both old and new, derived substantial advantages by shedding the burden of tithe and seigneurial obligation and purchasing land at low prices; whereas the small and landless peasants, whose demands for controlled rents and the subdivision of farms went unheeded by successive governments, remained landless, poor and dissatisfied. This process and its results by no means corresponded to what took place in Paris and the provincial cities; and Lefebvre concluded that to the several minor revolutions of 1789–94 already noted by Mathiez must be added a specific "peasant revolution", obeying its own laws, distinctive and autonomous, with its own origins, course of development, crises and fluctuations.[47] Thus the French peasantry at long last was firmly placed on the revolutionary map and a new perspective given to the study of the Revolution as a whole.

A further new dimension was added to Revolutionary studies by Lefebvre's work on revolutionary crowds and on the rural disturbances of the spring and summer of 1789, known as "la Grande Peur".[48] Previous historians, whether sympathetically portraying the participants in revolutionary popular movements as "the people" (like Michelet) or unflatteringly labelling them as "rabble" or *canaille* (like Taine), had tended to treat them as disembodied abstractions and had failed to probe deeply into the motives that impelled them. Lefebvre insisted on the need to study these particular motives which, he maintained, were quite distinct from, and often at variance with, those of the revolutionary leaders. But he went on to argue that, in order to understand the causes and nature of these repeated popular explosions, it was not enough to determine the more or less rational impulses prompting individuals: account must be taken also of the "collective mentality" of the crowd. Thus the sociologist and the psychologist might be called in to aid the historian. His first exploration in this field of studies was his work on "la Grande Peur" of 1789, in which he portrayed the astonishing power of rumour and panic-fear to influence collective human conduct and to generate revolutionary activity. He went on to accept Taine's contention that the popular excitement of 1789 had in large measure been provoked by the "great hope" aroused by the royal promise of fundamental reform; but this, in turn, had further consequences. When these hopes appeared to be threatened by a series of real or imaginary "aristocratic plots", a defensive reaction set in, which Lefebvre termed the "volonté punitive", and which, he claims, lay at the base of all outbursts of mass vengeance from the murder of the governor of the Bastille to the September Massacres. It was, in fact, he argued, the fear of another outbreak of this kind that prompted Robespierre and his colleagues, in June 1794, to introduce the notorious law of the 22nd Prairial, which substituted the tempo and procedure of the court martial for the hitherto more leisurely methods of the Revolutionary Tribunal.

What Lefebvre had done for the revolutionary peasants, one of his closest associates, Albert Soboul, did, thirty-five years later for the Parisian *sans-culottes*.[49] No writer had doubted the importance of the part played by the Paris tradesmen, journeymen and sectional militants in the event of the Revolution; and, in the last sixty years, Mellié, Braesch, Mathiez and others have contributed solid work on their organizations and activities. But until Soboul's book appeared they had still lingered, somewhat unsubstantially, on the fringe of events, and there had been no fully documented study of their everyday activities, institutions, composition, social and political ideas and aspirations, and forms of behaviour. The result of his work has been both to give the *sans-culottes* a distinctive identity, to bring them to the front of the stage as a vital revolutionary force, and to illuminate the political history of the Revolution in one of its most critical phases. Historians had long debated the nature of the "de-Christianization" movement, the significance of the Laws of Ventôse, the respective rights and wrongs of Enragés, Hébertists, Dantonists and Indulgents, and the deeper causes of the tragedy of Thermidor. They will continue to be debated; but it was not until one of the essential elements in the story, the Paris *sans-culottes*, had been brought into perspective that the other pieces in the jig-saw could begin to fall into place without too heavy a reliance on conjecture, conspiracy-theories or moral judgements. Soboul now holds Aulard's, Mathiez' and Lefebvre's old Chair of the French Revolution at the University of Paris; and he has gone on to write a number of more general studies on the Revolutionary period, which have established him as the most prolific and most influential of the historians now writing in this field in the Republican-Marxist tradition.[50]

In British and American universities, thanks to a core of teachers devoted to the study of the Revolution, there has never been much time-lag in keeping up with such new developments; and scholars have not been slow to reflect in their published work the latest research carried out in this field in France and elsewhere. A school of Revolution studies was built up at Oxford by the late J. M. Thompson, whose *Robespierre* (two volumes, Oxford, 1935) and *The French Revolution* (1944) were both strongly influenced—though by no means exclusively—by Albert Mathiez. To the same tradition belong A. Goodwin's *The French Revolution* (1953) and Norman Hampson's *A Social History of the French Revolution* (1963); while George Rudé's *The Crowd in the French Revolution* (1959) and Barrington Moore Jnr's *Social Origins of Dictatorship and Democracy. Lord and Peasant in the Making of the Modern World* (1966) clearly owe more to Lefebvre than they do to Mathiez. On a larger scale altogether is Richard Cobb's monumental study, *Les Armées révolutionnaires: instrument de la Terreur dans les départements avril 1793—floréal an II* (2 vols., 1961, 1963), which for the first time puts the "revolutionary armies" of 1793 on the map. But it does more, it also throws a new and revealing light on the Revolution in the provinces, the "de-Christianization" campaign in large parts of France, the problems of requisitioning and feeding the cities during the Terror, and the disorganization of local government before the two ruling committees took things formally in hand in December 1793.

The new school of research may, then, claim to have opened up new vistas and to have shifted the focus to the social and economic aspects of the Revolution and to the hitherto largely "submerged" classes of the town and countryside; and, in so doing, it has perhaps tended to be less shrilly polemical and less blatantly partisan than its eminent predecessors of the last century. Inevitably, this has led to a certain disintegration of the traditional pattern of the Revolution: the Third Estate, for example, has become resolved into its component parts, and wage-earners, landless peasants, smallholders, and independent craftsmen are shown to have had their own distinctive ways of life and thought, social aims and forms of behaviour; the Revolution may even, as presented by Mathiez and Lefebvre, appear to resolve itself into a series of successive minor conflagrations. But does this mean, as Alfred Cobban has argued, that the Revolution has, by virtue of these developments, lost its old "indivisible unity" and that "the substitution of a capitalist-bourgeois order for feudalism is a myth"?[51] This, were it so, would, of course, denote a sharp departure from the traditional presentation of the Revolution by the Liberal Republican and radical historians of the past; yet it may seem to some a reasonable conclusion to draw from the writings of the new school of historians. The writers themselves, however, have strenuously denied any such drastic intention of recasting old values. Though Lefebvre consistently maintained that the Revolution was not made "for the sole advantage of the bourgeoisie" he equally insisted that it most decidedly "opened the way for capitalism",[52] and Soboul has stressed (and maybe here he is at variance with Mathiez) the essential unity of the Revolution—despite its growing complexity and the rich variety of its succeeding phases.[53]

Other Twentieth-Century Interpretations

It would, of course, be entirely misleading to suggest that the historians of the Jaurès-Mathiez-Lefebvre tradition, though they have been the most prolific and influential of recent years, have been the only ones to rewrite the history of the Revolution during the past half-century. On the one hand, they have found a critic on "the Left"—Daniel Guérin, whose two-volume work, *La Lutte de classes sous la première République: bourgeois et "bras-nus" (1793-1797)*, appeared in 1946. M. Guérin has put forward a Trotskyist interpretation of events, based on Trotsky's theory of "permanent revolution". The result has been to challenge the interpretations of all preceding writers, both critics and supporters of the Revolution, Radicals as well as Socialists and more orthodox Marxists. Radicals and Marxists have certainly differed as to the depths of the divisions that arose from 1789 onwards within the Third Estate and as to the degree of intensity of the conflict that divided Jacobins and *sans-culottes* in the crucial period of 1793–4; but they have generally agreed that, despite these divisions, both parties still had the common overriding objective of seeking to destroy the foreign enemy without and the remnants of feudalism and aristocracy within. The predominant social conflict has for them, therefore, not been at any stage one of *bourgeoisie* against *sans-culottes*, still less of Capital versus Labour. To Guérin, however, the *sans-culottes*, or "bras-nus" (a term borrowed from Michelet), constituted a preproletarian "vanguard" and the Revolution, from 1793 onwards, takes on the form of a proletarian revolution in embryo. In this context, Robespierre, as the leading spokesman of Jacobinism, is the villain of the piece and a reactionary who deliberately stems the revolutionary tide in the autumn of 1793: this, then, rather than Thermidor appears to Guérin to be the real turning-point of the Revolution. The Jacobin dictatorship and the Revolutionary Government of the Year II become, accordingly, a dictatorship of the *bourgeoisie* whose aim is to defeat the challenge of the resurgent "bras-nus" or *sans-culottes*. This new interpretation has stimulated a lively discussion but appears, up to the present, to have failed to gain many adherents among serious students of the Revolution.[54]

At the other end of the scale there are the outright opponents of the Revolution who, often drawing on new materials to support their arguments, have upheld the tradition of Taine or of the Restoration conservatives. Among these, Frantz Funck-Brentano seeks to discredit the Revolution by painting an idyllic picture of the Old Régime.[55] Like Tocqueville, he stresses the reforming zeal of the royal governments in its closing years. "The reign of Louis XVI," he writes, "was one of the greatest epochs in our history, a glorious twilight to the setting sun of old France." The reforms then undertaken, he insists, would, if continued, "have completely realized a peaceful revolution in the constitution of France". But "then came the Revolution, brutal, terrible, with the splendour of its pools of blood". And after it was all over, the twin-pillars of the Old Régime—the family-system and the old system of administration—had been destroyed; all a useless waste and to no purpose, for "had Louis XVI remained on the throne, he and his successors, his Ministers and their successors, in spite of themselves, would have been brought to realize them."[56] This is, of course, good old-fashioned stuff, hardly calculated to make the upholders of the radical tradition lose much sleep. Pierre Gaxotte, on the other hand, is very much a conservative of the twentieth century. Having been as horrified by the Russian Revolution as Taine had been by the Paris Commune, he engages in a polemic against the French Revolution, the Jacobins and the *sans-culottes*, whose violence and choice of colourful epithet would have done credit to the master. He falls back once more on the conspiracy-theory of the origins of the Revolution, drawing on the more

modern version elaborated by Cochin; but he equally uses the evidence
of Jaurès and Mathiez to give point to his contention that the eighteenth
century was an age of prosperity; the Revolution, therefore, was a crime
and in no sense a timely surgical operation.[57]

A more sophisticated critic is J. L. Talmon. His book, *The Origins of
Totalitarian Democracy*, is the first part of a trilogy whose aim it is to
trace the concept of "political Messianism" or "totalitarian democracy"
from its genesis in the ideas of Rousseau, Mably and Morelly via the
French Revolution to the Communist governments and People's
Democracies of the twentieth century. It is thus essentially a political-
philosophical treatise, whose starting-point lies in the ideological battles
of the present and in which the French Revolution serves as an
illustration to a theme rather than as an object of study. The Revolution
as a whole is condemned, not because it is seen as a criminal act or a
conspiracy (in the manner of the conservatives of the past), but as the
first episode in a historical sequence, mysteriously launched by a group
of eighteenth-century thinkers, which has tended to deny man his most
cherished possession, political freedom. "The most important lesson to
be drawn from this enquiry," the author concludes,

> is the incompatibility of the idea of an all-embracing and all-solving creed with liberty.
> The two ideals correspond to the two instincts most deeply imbedded in human
> nature, the yearning for salvation and the love of freedom. To attempt to satisfy both
> at the same time is bound to result, if not in unmitigated tyranny and serfdom, at least
> in the monumental hypocrisy and self-deception which are the concomitants of
> totalitarian democracy.

Another, very different, development has been the attempt to place
the Revolution in an "Atlantic" or "Western" context. The main
proponents of this view have been R. R. Palmer in the United States and
Jacques Godechot in France.[58] Their views are by no means identical;
but, in the work of both, the Western world on both sides of the Atlantic
is treated as a whole and a number of revolutions and radical movements
breaking out within this period in England, Ireland, Belgium, Holland,
Sweden, Switzerland, France and America are considered in the same
context; thus the French Revolution loses its particular identity and
becomes merely a phase in a wider and more general political cycle. The
idea is not entirely new, as it was by using similar arguments that
Madame de Staël and other Restoration Liberals attempted to make the
French Revolution more acceptable to their contemporaries. But
whereas the Liberals drew the line at 1791 because most of the rest of the
Revolution in France embarrassed them, there is no similar justification
today for omitting or ignoring the particular features of what Mathiez
termed the "democratic" and "social" revolutions of 1792–4, or even

the peculiarly French aspects of much that took place in 1789–91 as well. It has been objected, in fact, that it is only possible to conceive of a general "Western" or "World" revolution during this period in terms of a purely ideological-constitutional movement from which the *sans-culottes*, the *levée en masse*, the peasant risings, the food crisis, and even the constitutional experiments of 1792–4 are excluded or glossed over.[59]

Such debates, however, had been conducted in a relatively muted key and with a minimum of acrimonious name-calling on either side: Godechot and Soboul, for example, are both members of the editorial board of the *Annales historiques de la Révolution française* (and even Guérin, dropping his more rigorous Trotskyist stance, has offered an olive branch to some of his critics).[60] But, in the last half-dozen years, a new and sharper note has been struck and a number of broadsides have been levelled against the whole Republican-Marxist school of historians, and against the work of Soboul in particular. Where Guérin's earlier challenge came from the Left, a more recent challenge (though by no means a traditional-conservative one) has come from the Right; and it has taken the form not so much of advancing a new interpretation as of casting doubts on the interpretation of others. It began with Alfred Cobban's *The Social Interpretation of the French Revolution*, published in 1964. Cobban questioned the validity of "the social interpretation" that, he felt, had been the main direction given to Revolutionary studies over the past half-century or more. In so doing, he called for a more empirical approach to be given to the writing of social history and for the abandonment of such time-honoured concepts as the overthrow of "feudalism" or the triumph of a "bourgeois revolution". He believed, too, that the historical thinking of the "Lefebvre school"—particularly as reflected in Soboul's work—was strongly coloured by Marxist-Leninist political assumptions.

More recently, the challenge has been taken up, with a twist of their own, by a couple of young scholars of the Ecole Pratique des Hautes Etudes in Paris, F. Furet and D. Richet, authors of a two-volume history of the Revolution that appeared in 1965–6.[61] Here, as in Cobban's work, several of the underlying assumptions of the whole Republican school of historians since Aulard's day are called into question. This was only a beginning and Furet has resumed the attack with a new and more violent broadside levelled against the "revolutionary catechism" (the term is his) in an article published in the Annales in April 1971.[62] This time, the attack is made on a narrower front: it is no longer directed against the whole "Lefebvre school", still less against the Republican tradition in general; but, more specifically, against Soboul and Claude Mazauric, one of his closest supporters, who are presented as being not only Marxists but Marxists of a special stamp. So, ostensibly, it is no longer the Republican-Marxist tradition that is under fire, but only what Richet terms its "neo-Jacobin" (or Marxist-Leninist) component. Yet the same truths, dear to the Republican-Marxist historian but suspect to this Liberal-revisionist critic—the eighteenth-century "aristocratic reaction", the survivals of "feudalism" and "bourgeois revolution"—are again being questioned. So whether singled out for particular attention or not, the whole school of historians deriving from Jaurès via Mathiez to Lefebvre can hardly fail to recognise that a major assault is being mounted against positions that they all, whether Radicals or Marxists, have long held without serious challenge; and it will be surprising if they take it lying down and do not defend them with vigour.

So the chips are down again; and it looks as if the calm scholarly serenity with which the Revolution has been debated over the past thirty or forty years will give way to another round of polemical exchanges on ideological lines over what French historians (Soboul and Guérin among them) have called "notre mère a tous". Yet, seen in a wider perspective, this is only a phase in a duel that has extended over a century and a half; and, whether the outcome of the present exchange tilts the balance one way or the other, one can safely prophesy that Frenchmen will continue to brood, to speculate and to research further into the origins and outcome and ultimate significance of the French Revolution.

Notes

1. Stanley Mellon, *The Political Uses of History* (Stanford, Ca., 1958), p. 1.
2. Ibid., pp. 3–4, 5.
3. Ibid., pp. 12–14.
4. Germaine de Staël, *Considerations on the principal Events of the French Revolution*, 3 vols. (London, 1818), I, p. 14.
5. F.A.M. Mignet, *History of the French Revolution from 1789 to 1814* (London, 1915), p. 1.
6. A. Thiers, *The History of the French Revolution* (London, n.d.), p. 421.
7. Mignet, *History of the French Revolution*, p. 218.
8. De Staël, *Considerations on the principal Events of the French Revolution*, II, pp. 127, 131–2.
9. Mellon, *The Political Uses of History*, p. 27.
10. De Staël, *Considerations on the principal Events of the French Revolution*, I, p. 432.
11. Mellon, *The Political Uses of History*, pp. 58 ff.
12. Ibid., p. 72.
13. J.W. Croker, *Essays on the early Period of the French Revolution* (1857).
14. J. Michelet, *Histoire de la Révolution française*, 7 vols. (1847–53).
15. Thiers, *The History of the French Revolution*, pp. 9. 20, 29, 41, 44, 71; Mignet, *History of the French Revolution*, p. 96.

16. T. Carlyle, *The French Revolution* (1906), p. 120.
17. Michelet, *Histoire de la Révolution française*, 2 vols., (1940), I, p. 7.
18. Ibid., pp. 7–8.
19. A. de Tocqueville, *L'Ancien Régime* (Eng. trans. Oxford, 1937), p. 218.
20. Ibid., p. 220.
21. Ibid., p. 186.
22. H. Taine, *Les Origines de la France contemporaine. La Révolution*, 3 vols., (1876).
23. Ibid., I. p. 165.
24. Ibid., I. pp. 18, 53.
25. Taine, *La Conquête jacobine*, I, pp. 12–42. For a more serious investigation, see Crane Brinton, *The Jacobins* (New York, 1930).
26. F.V.A. Aulard, *Histoire politique de la Révolution française*, 4 vols., (1901). Eng. trans. *The French Revolution, a political History, 1789–1804*, 4 vols. (London, 1910).
27. Ibid., (English edn), pp. 9–10.
28. Ibid., III, p. 279.
29. Ibid., III, pp. 87–91.
30. Lord Acton, *Lectures on the French Revolution* (1910), p. 373.
31. Ibid., pp. 356–7, 21, 248, 226–7.
32. Ibid., pp. 342–3.
33. G. Bord, "La Conspiration maçonnique de 1789", *Le Correspondent*, 10 and 25 May 1906, pp. 521–44, 757–67. For a more balanced and thorough study, see Gaston Martin, *La Franc-maçonnerie française et la préparation de la Révolution française* (1926).
34. A. Cochin, *Les Sociétés de pensée et la démocratie* (1921); *Les Sociétés de pensée et la Révolution en Bretagne*, 2 vols. (1925). Both publications were posthumous: Cothin's studies date from 1904–14; he died in 1916.
35. Ibid., (first), pp. 235–82.
36. L. Madelin, *The French Revolution* (Eng. trans. London, 1916), pp. 625–6.
37. Ibid., p. 634.
38. H. Belloc, *The French Revolution* (1911), pp. 67–83.
39. J. Jaurès, Critical Introduction to the *Socialist History*, reproduced in F. Stern, *The Varieties of History* (1956), p. 160.
40. Thiers, *The History of the French Revolution*, p. 473; Carlyle, *The French Revolution*, p. 489; Madelin, *The French Revolution*, p. 116; Acton, *Lectures on the French Revolution*, p. 300; Michelet, *Histoire de la Révolution française*, II, p. 1017; Aulard, *The French Revolution*, III, p. 868. For a recent discussion of Robespierre as seen by historians in a number of countries (including France, England, Belgium, Spain, the USA, Hungary, Germany and Russia), see the report of the colloquium held during the Vienna International History Congress in August, 1965, entitled *Actes du Colloque Robespierre* (Paris, 1967), pp. 165–238.
41. Eng. trans. *The French Revolution* (New York, 1928).
42. Cited by G. Lefebvre, *Quatre-vingt-neuf* (1939), p. 7.
43. C.-E. Labrousse, *Esquisse du mouvement des prix et des revenus en France au XVIIIe siècle*, 2 vols. (1933); *La Crise de l'économie française à la fin de l'ancien régime et au début de la Révolution* (1944).
44. Ibid., (second), pp. ix-xii; *Esquisse*, II, pp. 640-1.
45. J. Loutchisky, *La Propriété paysanne en France à la veille de la Révolution, principalement au Limousin* (1912); *L'Etat des classes agricoles en France à la veille de la Révolution* (1911).
46. G. Lefebvre, *Documents relatifs à l'histoire des subsistances dans le district de Berques pendant la Révolution (1789–an V)*, 2 vols. (1914, 1921).

47. G. Lefebvre, "La Révolution française et les paysans", in *Etudes sur la Révolution française* (1954), p. 249.
48. *La Grande Peur de 1789* (1932); "Foules révolutionnaires", in *Etudes sur la Révolution française*, pp. 68–89.
49. A. Soboul, *Les Sans-culottes parisiens en l'an II: mouvement populaire et gouvernement révolutionnaire, 2 juin 1793–9 Thermidor an II* (1958). For a work directed by Soboul, see K. Tönnesson, *La défaite des sans-culottes* (1959).
50. See, e.g. his *Precis d'histoire de la Révolution française* (1962), and *La Civilisation et la Révolution française*, vol. I, *La crise de l'Ancien Régime* (1970).
51. A. Cobban, *Historians and the Causes of the French Revolution* (Hist. Assoc. pamphlet, 1958), pp. 38–9; *The Myth of the French Revolution* (1955), p. 20. See also *The Social Interpretations of the French Revolution* (1964), esp. pp. 25–35.
52. G. Lefebvre, "Le Mythe de la Révolution française" in *Annales hist. Rev. Franc.* (Oct.-Dec. 1956), p. 343.
53. A. Soboul, *The French Revolution 1787–1799*, trans. A. Forrest and C. Jones (London, 1974).
54. For criticisms of Guérin, see G. Lefebvre in *Revue historique*, 205 (1951), pp. 90–1; and A. Soboul, *Les Sans-culottes parisiens en l'an II* pp. 55–6.
55. F. Funck-Brentano, *L'Ancien régime* (1926); Eng. trans. *The Old Regime in France* (1929).
56. Ibid. (English), pp. 361–6.
57. P. Gaxotte, *La Révolution française* (1928); Eng. trans. *The French Revolution* (1932).
58. See, especially, R.R. Palmer, *The Age of the Democratic Revolution. A Political History of Europe and America, 1760–1820*, I, *The Challenge* (1959); II, *The Struggle* (1964); and J. Godechot, *France and the Atlantic Revolution of the Eighteenth Century, 1770–1799* (1965).
59. For criticisms of Palmer's first volume, see M. Reinhard's review in *Ann. hist. Rév. franç.* (April–June 1960), pp. 20–3. For Palmer's reply see his "The Age of the Democratic Revolution" in L.P. Curtis, Jr.,'s *The Historian's Workshop. Original Essays by Sixteen Historians* (1970), pp. 169–86.
60. D. Guérin, *Jeunesse au socialisme libertain* (1959), pp. 133–67;
61. F. Furet and D. Richet, *La Révolution française*, 2 vols., (1956–6).
62. F. Furet, "Le Cathechisme revolutionnaire", *Annales*, 26 (March–April 1971), 2, pp. 255–89.

5

Georges Lefebvre as Historian of Popular Urban Protest in the French Revolution

The great historians of the nineteenth century, being preoccupied with the ideological and constitutional struggles of the French Revolution, paid scant attention to its social and economic aspects. They understood well enough that the popular element—the "people" or "rabble" (according to the writer's fancy) had, by the force of its intervention, given these events a new dimension; but, in their opinion, whether as "people" or "rabble" the masses engaged in revolution had no particular interests of their own: they were simply acting out a role assigned to them by the bourgeoisie or responding to the intrigues of conspirators, Freemasons or men of money anxious to settle accounts with the Old Regime.

Such writers, therefore, had no interest in studying the composition or the motives of those taking part, at the grass-roots level, in the great demonstrations or *journées* of the Revolution; yet they still felt it necessary to give them a label. To Burke, the apostle of a counter-revolution, the participants of the October "days" of 1789 were "a band of rogues and cruel assassins reeking of blood".[1] To Taine the captors of the Bastille were "a social scum that floated to the surface", whilst "the capital seemed to have been handed over to bandits and to the dregs of the populace". The women and other participants in the October events that followed were "the street-walkers of the Palais Royal, accompanied by seamstresses, beggars, women without shoes, fishwives recruited for gold for the past week, to say nothing of down-and-outs, street-prowlers, brigands and thieves . . ." The Paris *sectionnaires* and federal volunteers of August 1792 were, in turn, "almost all drawn from the lowest social dregs or engaged in a variety of infamous crafts, 'chuckers-out' from brothels and the like, all exercised in spilling blood".[2] Michelet, on the other hand, for whom the Revolution was "the dawn of justice", saw these participants in quite a different light, especially (it should be noted) when their activities did not run counter to the interests of the revolutionary middle class. The captors of the Bastille he simply termed "the people"—*le peuple tout entier*; and to underline the part played by the women in October 1789, Michelet spells it out: "for that part of the people which is the most truly *popular*, I mean the most instinctive and the most inspired, must surely be the women."[3]

It is evident that Michelet's views and those of the Republican historians that followed are far removed from those expressed by Taine and his school; yet they had one thing in common. It is that whether they saw the revolutionary crowds as "the people" or as "the rabble" or "dregs of society", they were both inclined to see them as abstractions rather than as creatures of flesh and blood. Progress in this respect came only in part with social evolution and in part through the impact of Marx's ideas in the early years of the twentieth century. Georges Lefebvre describes the process as follows:

> The triumph of capitalism and the trade-union and socialist reaction which followed forced one to recognize that the Third Estate was not homogeneous and that peasants and workers had to be distinguished from the bourgeoisie. So historians began to explore the antecedents of this conflict and to see if the same classes at the time of the Revolution were not motivated by similar concerns for unemployment, shortage of bread, and unequal land distribution, in short by the material conditions in which they lived.[4]

More specifically, with the appearance of Jean Jaurès', great study, *The Socialist History of the French Revolution* (1901–4), historians began to devote themselves in a scholarly and serious manner—and without the injection of such evident bias—to the study of revolutionary crowds and the social elements that composed them.

Although Jaurès himself only touched on the particular problems of the peasants and urban *sans-culottes*, it was he who, in the opening years of the century, gave the stimulus to the new direction in revolutionary studies that characterized the work of Albert Mathiez and Georges Lefebvre. Mathiez, it is true, was for long preoccupied by the more distinctly political struggles within the Convention and its governing Committees; but he was also the author of one of the first great books in the social history of the Revolution, *La vie chère et le mouvement social sous la Terreur* (1927), in which the popular movement (to borrow Lefebvre's phrase) was studied "from below". It was Mathiez, too, who gave the first treatment in depth to several of the popular *journées* of the Revolution in Paris, including those of October 1789, July 1791, August 1792 and 25 February 1793.[5]

Lefebvre also paid serious attention to the popular *journées*, though he was at first mainly concerned with those involving the peasants, whose revolutionary role had been largely neglected up to this time. In this respect we must mention above all *Les paysans du Nord* (1924) and *La Grande Peur de 1789* (1932). In the second he traces the origins, development and interdependence of a long succession of popular movements arising in different parts of France with a precision and a clarity of perception unmatched before or since and using a method of investigation that has served as a model for later historians.[6]

So it is probably in the field of peasants in revolution that Lefebvre made his most enduring and most significant mark. But he was also a great innovator in the study of the motives and mentality of the revolutionary masses as a whole. Once the facts had been unearthed it remained to explain them. Why did the masses become involved? "The political motives for popular intervention", he writes, "are undeniable: the desire to abolish privilege and the hierarchic structure of society, to establish equality of rights, to smash the aristocratic plot and to overthrow the monarchy which had become its accomplice."[7] But it is false (he continues) to represent this popular intervention, in the manner of Republican historians from Michelet to Aulard, as though it had similar objectives to those of the bourgeoisie. "The bourgeoisie", he explains, "merely wished to strip the aristocracy of the privileges that distinguished it from themselves, whereas the people wished to strike at the social roots of aristocratic power ... The crowd had its own particular motives for intervening as it did."[8] And of these "particular motives"—leaving aside for the moment the more strictly *political* considerations—nothing was more pressing and nothing more conducive to stir and to mobilize the masses at moments of revolutionary crisis than shortage, unemployment and the high cost of food.

Such motives were not well understood by the revolutionary leaders: "The men of 14 July", declared Gonchon of the Faubourg Saint-Antoine in January 1792, "do not fight over sweets"; and, in February 1793 (at the time of the grocery riots), Robespierre in similar vein proclaimed that it was proper to fight to secure the Revolution but not to riot over "paltry merchandise".[9] But while despising such motives, the party leaders tried nonetheless to turn them to their own advantage. "However", Lefebvre explains, "in the development of popular participation there was always an element that eluded them. Below the surface of the political crises which they understood well enough, there were economic crises that gave their own impetus to the popular revolutionary movement and invested it with that mysterious quality that contemporaries attributed to conspiracy when their own interests appeared to be threatened and that Romantic writers would later look on as acts of Providence."[10]

But, of course, to explain popular participation in such events it is not enough simply to seek motives, whether social, economic or political:

the deeper springs of action of those taking part will still elude us. We need to go further by attempting to enter into the minds of the participants, both individually and collectively, as they gather at bakers' shops and at market gates and in the course of riots and demonstrations. It was a question that deeply concerned Lefebvre, and with good reason. He first discussed it in an early work, *L'histoire des subsistances dans le district de Bergues* (1914); he returned to the subject in *Les paysans du Nord* (1924) and, notably, in two works that appeared in 1932: *La Grande Peur de 1789* and a paper read to the Centre de Synthèse under the title of "Foules révolutionnaires".[11]

Earlier historians had tended to present the revolutionary crowd either as a criminal band (like Taine) or as an aggregate of individuals impelled by more or less identical motives or ideas. In neither case did there appear to be any problem of complexity; for, even if the crowd were an aggregate, its collective mentality remained to all intents and purposes the same as that of the individuals composing it. Such a presentation, simplistic as it sounds, might serve well enough to convey the mentality of those taking part in public demonstrations convoked by known leaders with defined objectives, as on the occasion of the Festival of the Federation of 14 July or of that of the Supreme Being staged by Robespierre on 6 June 1794. It might also explain to some degree the state of mind of the participants in the great military or political *journées* organized by the National Guard or the Paris Commune.[12]

But it is evident that such an explanation would be less than adequate to take proper account of the mentality of revolutionary crowds that gathered more or less spontaneously at the entrance to markets or at the doors of bakers' and grocers' shops: as in the case of the popular demonstrations of 1789 or of the food riots of February 1792 and 1793, or again of the *journées* of Germinal-Prairial of the Year III; nor can it explain phenomena like the Great Fear or the September Massacres. Here it is no longer a case of individuals forming a collective whose mentality corresponds almost exactly to that with which they started; but rather of a radical "mutation", whereby a simple aggregate of individuals becomes transformed into a "revolutionary crowd" with a mentality newly formed. Such a "mutation" is characteristic of the first great *journées* of 1789. Thus on 12 July of that year, we see how strollers in the Palais Royal, on hearing the news of Necker's dismissal, become transformed into revolutionary bands that become engaged in a whole series of activities which it would have been quite impossible to foresee or to concert in advance: such as the burning of the customs posts surrounding the city, the assult on the *couvent* Saint-Lazare, the search for arms at gunsmiths' and in the Hotel des Invalides, culminating in the massive assault on the Bastille (partly planned in advance, it is true) and the murder of its governor. On 5 October, the women first assembled to search for bread; and "it was only later", writes Lefebvre, "that the crowd was abruptly transformed into a column that marched on Versailles".[13]

But how account for these transformations? It is a question that should be of some concern to the historian and sociologist as well as to the specialists in crowd psychology. But even the *social* historian, for all his attention to the externals of social relations, has rarely ventured onto this domain;[14] and the sociologist has done little better. So the field has been left clear to specialists, or persons claiming to be such, like Gustave LeBon. But LeBon, never having made a scientific (that is, an *inductive*) study of a revolutionary crowd and being ignorant of social history, represented such crowds as others had done before him: that is purely and simply as abstractions. In addition, as the author had been nourished on the prejudiced accounts of Taine, the crowds became in his hands little more than bands of criminals and degenerates, responding blindly to the summons of hired and corrupted leaders. Moreover, according to LeBon, even educated persons who join a crowd thereby lose their critical faculties and become reduced to a common level of animality.[15]

Lefebvre, on the other hand, realized that the revolutionary crowd was a social and historical phenomenon that had to be studied like any other. He therefore differs both from those who have seen the crowd as nothing but an aggregate of autonomous individuals and from those, like LeBon, who have seen in it no more than a manifestation of animal behaviour. According to Lefebvre, what distinguishes this type of crowd from the individuals who compose it is the development of a "collective mentality" which expresses itself in a wide variety of activities, often of a violent kind, in which the participants had they remained individuals would not have become engaged. To Taine, the violence of the crowd merely reflects the violence of the individuals that compose it; and LeBon, despite his "psycho-analytical" pretensions, arrives at broadly similar conclusions. But as Lefebvre has argued:

> The crowd intervened with all its force; but there do not have to be criminals in its ranks for it to treat aristocrats with physical violence. It is natural for the crowd to generate a nervous state of excitement, so that excesses of this kind may be committed by normally respectable persons.[16]

In addition, Lefebvre understood well enough that this "collective mentality" was not solely the product of the situation in which these individuals found themselves at the point of forming a crowd. It is true enough that the news of Necker's dismissal or the realization that the "brigands" at the time of the rural panic were a myth may have served as a catalyst that transforms a meeting of individuals into a crowd with objectives of its own. But this change is not solely due to the impact of an unexpected development; for one can hardly claim that another crowd, formed in a different *historical* situation, would react in a similar way. Georges Lefebvre explains the matter thus: "When individuals form a crowd the elements of an earlier mentality are simply pushed to the back of their consciousness; but the intrusion of an outside event may be enough to return them to the fore"; and in this way the participants become once more acutely conscious of their former solidarity. This sudden awakening of group consciousness, provoked by a violent emotion, gives the collective body a new dimension which may be called (rather clumsily perhaps) a "state of crowd".[17]

Among these "outside events" Lefebvre notes in particular fear, propagated by rumour and spread, in rural districts, from one market to the next. This is the central theme of *The Great Fear of 1789* which brought a new dimension to the study of the social history of the French Revolution. It was during these months that fear was seen to develop and spread within the villages and market towns with quite astonishing and unforeseen results. But not only in the villages; for, in Paris, too, fear contributed substantially to political ferment, as it did in the popular outbreaks of July 1789, in August-September 1792, and again in Vendémiaire of the Year IV (October 1795), when the Paris sections sprang to arms to oppose the so-called *buveurs de sang* and crush a rumoured conspiracy (provoked, ironically enough, by the prisoners' own fear of a repetition of the notorious September Massacres of 1792!)[18]

Several problems, of course, still remain to be resolved and several questions must be asked. How, for example, were the slogans of the leaders and their lieutenants transmitted to the demonstrators and insurgents? How and to what extent did the masses, having imbibed the democrats' revolutionary slogans and ideas, absorb them and adapt them to serve their own political ends? How far is the violence generated by the crowd—what Lefebvre called the "punitive will" of the people[19]—also due, as Babeuf believed, to the bad example set by the Old Regime? Or should it be ascribed, in part at least, to the incitement to violence of leaders like Marat, Hébert or Fournier *dit l'Américain?* A further, profounder, problem exercised Lefebvre during his later years: the importance of biological factors in stimulating human activity. In a letter addressed to me on this subject in March 1959, he wrote:

> Hunger . . . engenders anxiety, fear and violence. To which I would add: between the hunger and these behavioral manifestations there appears an intermediary: that is the change that undernourishment effects in the human anatomy: the digestive system, the blood, the nerves, and eventually, the brain itself—or, at least, in its

physiological functions. This intermediary is a biological one. The existence of the biological factor is undeniable; and it is a problem whose solution will naturally depend on the active participation of biologists, but one that historians must not neglect when they attempt to probe more deeply into the springs of human behavior.[20]

But so far, at least, historians of the Revolution have given it only scant attention. Louis Chevalier, it is true, who is a demographer turned literary historian, has touched on the problem in a book concerning "the industrious and dangerous classes in early 19th-century Paris".[21] Historians must return to it, as to so many other of Georges Lefebvre's ideas that have enriched the study of the French Revolution.[22]

Notes

1. E. Burke, *Reflections on the Revolution in France* (London, 1951), p. 66.
2. H. Taine, *Les origines de la France contemporaine. La Révolution* (3 vols., Paris, 1876), I, pp. 18, 53-4, 130, 272. Translation from the French, here as elsewhere, is by the present author.
3. J. Michelet, *La Révolution française* (9 vols., Paris, 1868-1900), I, pp. 377-9.
4. G. Lefebvre, *La Révolution française. La Révolution de 1789* (C.D.U., Paris, n.d.), p. 3.
5. See A. Mathiez, "Étude critique sur les journées des 5 et 6 octobre 1789", *Revue historique*, 67 (1898), pp. 241-81; 68 (1899), pp. 258-94; 69 (1900), pp. 41-66; *Le Dix Août* (Paris, 1931); *Les grandes journées de la Constituante, 1789-91* (Paris, 1913); *Le Club des Cordeliers pendant la crise de Varennes et le massacre du Champ de Mars* (Paris, 1913); *La vie chère . . .*, pp. 139-61.
6. See, for example, M. Vovelle, "Les taxations populaires de febrier-mars et novembre-décembre 1792 dans la Beauce et sur ses confins", *Memoires et documents*, 13 (Paris, 1958); and G. Rudé, "La taxation populaire de mai 1775 à Paris et dans la region parisienne", *Annales historiques de la Révolution française*, [*A.H.R.F.*] April-June, 1956.
7. *A.H.R.F.*, 133 (Oct.-Dec. 1953), p. 290.
8. *La Révolution de 1789*, pp. 141-2.
9. Mathiez, *La vie chère*, pp. 46-9, 151-7.
10. See note 7.
11. *A.H.R.F.* 11 (1934); reprinted in *Etudes sur la Révolution française* (Paris, 1954), pp. 271-87. See also "Sur la loi du 22 prairial an II", *A.H.R.F.* (1951), and *Etudes*, pp. 68-9.
12. "Foules révolutionnaires", *Etudes*, p. 272.
13. Ibid.
14. See, for example, P. Caron, *Les massacres de septembre* (Paris, 1935), p. vi.
15. G. LeBon, *La Révolution française et la psychologie des révolutions* (Paris, 1912), pp. 55-61; see also his *Psychologie des foules* (Paris, 1895).
16. *La Révolution de 1789*, p. 141.
17. *Etudes*, p. 271.
18. Ibid.

19. "Sur la loi du 22 prairial an II", *Etudes*, p. 83.
20. Private letter of 23 March 1959.
21. L. Chevalier, *Classes laborieuses et classes dangereuses à Paris pendant la première moitié du XIXe siècle* (Paris, 1958; Eng. edn. New York, 1973). The book was reviewed by Lefebvre in *A.H.R.F.*, 156, 1959.
22. A conference was in fact held on the subject, after Lefebvre's death, in Paris in the autumn of 1965, attended by Albert Soboul and presided over by L. Chevalier. Its proceedings, however, do not appear to have been published.

6
Robespierre as seen by British historians

In tracing the development of the thinking of British historians on the subject of Robespierre account must be taken of four factors: of the period in which the historian was writing; of the sources available to him at the time; of the author's social and political prejudices; and of the political traditions of the United Kingdom as the "mother of Parliaments" and as the nation considered less devoted than others to its own revolutionary past. It may be useful, too, to divide the subject into five main periods: that of the 1790s to 1820, combining both the full flood of Jacobinism and of its antithesis of counterrevolution; the period of revolutionary resurgence and birth of a labour movement of the 1830s and 1840s; the great "Whig" or "liberal" period of the 1850s to 1880s; the period of the 1890s to the outbreak of the First World War; and, finally, the inter-war period of the 1920s and 1930s.

During the first period the counterrevolutionaries among commentators and historians had the field all to themselves. Burke's *Reflections* still dominated middle-class opinion; writers took their information from the memoirs of monarchists and "Thermidorians"; Robespierre thus invariably appeared as a "tyrant" or "man of blood". On 30 August 1794 there was published in London an anonymous pamphlet entitled *The History of Robespierre, Political and Personal* accompanied by a "Short Sketch of the Person, the Life and Designs of Robespierre". This was a crude portrait of the "blood-thirsty monster", "the promoter of rape and massacre", but it was a portrait that owed its inspiration less to reality than to the author's febrile imagination. Among other remarkable "facts" with which it regaled its readers was its insistence that Robespierre was the nephew of Damiens, "assassin" of Louis XV; that he had been a shop assistant in Dublin before becoming a lawyer in Paris; that he had been the "prime minister" of

Philippe-Egalité in whose service he had poisoned the Prince de Lambesc and forged his will; and other fantasies in a similar vein.[1]

In 1795, also in London, there followed the *Memories of the Reign of Robespierre* by an English lady of Girondin persuasion, Helen Maria Williams. The work covered the period from 31 May 1793 to 10 Thermidor (28 July 1794); and in it Robespierre is quite simply treated as a "tyrant", a "malevolent genius" and "a great conspirator against the liberties of France".[2]

The first British historian to comment on the life and career of Robespierre was John Adolphus, the Tory author of a short history of England running from 1763 to 1783. In 1799 he went on to publish his *Biographical Memoirs of the French Revolution*,[3] in which he devoted an eighty-page chapter to "the Incorruptible", largely based on Montjoie's *Memoirs* and an anonymous *History of Maximilien Robespierre's Conspiracy* of Thermidorian inspiration. In the author's view the Committee of Public Safety was an "atrocious body" and the local Revolutionary Committees were composed of "an abominable horde of spies and robbers". Robespierre was no better: in short he was a "blood-sated tyrant", an "execrable monster"; in addition he attached to him epithets like "thankless", "envious", "cowardly", "vain", "treacherous", "perjured" and "depraved"; and, for good measure, he added: "A smile of approval never passed his lips which were always contorted by a sour grimace of envy." So historians and memorialists at this time continued to repeat the same tendentious, hostile and contemptuous slanders in which serious historical assessment played no part at all.

In fact, it is not until the second period, that of the 1830s and 1840s, that we find the beginnings of any attempt to present Robespierre's character and career in a historical context. Thiers's and Mignet's liberal *Histories* of the Revolution had already appeared in the 1820s and a further important development in Revolutionary studies, of significance to both French and English scholars, took place with the publication in 1834 to 1838 of Buchez and Roux's *Histoire parlementaire de la Révolution française*. Yet it is true enough that the two first works to appear in England at this time, those of Sir Archibald Alison and William Smythe, were little better as essays in historical criticism than those of their forebears; nevertheless, one can already detect a certain advance towards a more subtle and balanced analysis. Alison's *History*, published in two volumes in 1833,[4] is dull and pedantic, heavily laced with marginal notes, but uncritical of its sources which include the Memoirs of Chateaubriand and Lacretelle and the anonymous *Mémoires Révolutionnaires*, the latter distinguished by its attribution of appropriately selected bloodthirsty phrases to Collot d'Herbois and

Saint-Just and to Robespierre the dictum: "A nation can only be regenerated under a mountain of corpses." But to the hoary old image of the man of blood Alison adds that of the "fanatic" besotted with "virtue". "His troubled rule", he writes, "is not lacking in heroic examples of virtue"; and if Robespierre and his "decimivirs" massacred their opponents, it was done "in the name of public safety".[5] William Smythe, also, while calling "the Incorruptible" "atrocious" and applying him other epithets borrowed from Freron, at least endows him with one good quality, his "austere virtue, which [he claims] endeared him to the populace".[6]

From Smythe and Alison we come to a far more renowned and more influential writer, Thomas Carlyle, the "Chelsea sage" and (in Taine's opinion), the "English Michelet". (One might add that he was also something of a Taine, the recorder of the anarchy and social upheaval engendered by revolution.) Carlyle had read the official *Moniteur*, Buchez and Roux's *Parliamentary History* and various Memoirs—these above all: his work is shot through with portraits faithfully drawn from personal accounts of the Revolution's events. As an admirer of Germany and the German Romantic movement, he heartily disapproved of France. It was a *moral* antipathy and he saw the Revolution—rather in the manner of Michelet—as a punishment for the sins of the Old Regime. Besides, Carlyle had experienced, and he feared, the upsurge of the masses and the "dangerous classes" in the England of the 1830s: it is in fact significant that he gave his book, *The French Revolution,* the sub-title of *A History of Sans-culottism.* Indeed, for him the Revolution represented a state of chaos in which the *sans-culottes* reigned supreme under the aegis of its apostle, the "great pontiff" Robespierre, whom he also designates as the "Dalai Lama of the Patriots", the "Jesuit doctor", "Mahomet-Robespierre" and (most characteristically) as "the sea-green Incorruptible". According to this portrait he was the "eternally incorruptible . . . *acrid, implacable-impotent, dull-drawling, barren as the Harmatten wind*"; and he thus describes his meeting with Danton in the autumn of 1793: "With that terror of feminine hatred the poor sea-green Formula looked at the monstrous colossal Reality and grew greener to behold him . . . a poor spasmodic incorruptible pedant, with a logic-formula instead of a heart, of Jesuit and Methodist-Parson nature, full of sincere cant, incorruptibility, poltroonery, barren as the east wind."[7] As an admirer of great men in history—Frederick II was his favourite—Carlyle found only two men in the French Revolution to his taste: Mirabeau, "royal Mirabeau, a man, a reality"; and Danton: "With all dross, he was a Man, fiery-real, from the great firebosom of Nature herself."[8] Compared with these two "men", Robespierre presented a poorly image indeed, prone to inspire pity or contempt rather than hatred or admiration. In fact, Hilaire Belloc, who wrote a commentary on Carlyle as well as biographies of both Robespierre and Danton, reproached him for his lack of realism in portraying "the Incorruptible" as more of a man of wax than as a creature of flesh and blood.[9]

In sharp contrast to the romantic and quasi-prophetic style of Carlyle was the dry and sober style of his contemporary John Wilson Croker. Croker was a great collector of revolutionary pamphlets, of which 48,000 are housed in the British Library in London. His *Essays* were published in a single volume in 1857, but they had previously appeared as articles in the conservative *Quarterly Review* in the course of the 1830s; among them was a 130-page essay on Maximilien Robespierre.[10]

Croker was a deeply conservative man who admired Burke whose views he shared on the origins and meaning of the French Revolution. Like Burke he saw the Revolution as the product of a conspiracy in which the Duke of Orleans played a major role; and for him, as for Burke, the Revolution marked a long Reign of Terror from beginning to end.[11] He was therefore bitterly critical of the "liberal" views of Mignet and Thiers; he detested Danton and Desmoulins as the henchmen of Phillippe-Egalité; he utterly despised the Girondins and the Thermidorians, too, whom he saw as "terrorists" devoid of principle and solely motivated by fear, hatred and ambition.[12] It is all the more remarkable, therefore, that Croker should have conceived a certain degree of sympathy for Robespierre and that he should have been the first historian writing in English to have presented of him a portrait which, though critical, was both sensitively sketched and historically conceived.

Croker traced Robespierre's career step by step from the first sessions of the National Assembly in the summer of 1789; he sees him already then as the foremost leader of the Jacobin party and, by 1791, he describes him as "one of the most eminent orators of the Constituent Assembly". The author goes on to analyse more precisely Robespierre's attitude to the events of 20 June and 10 August 1792; and he blames the Girondins (notably Louvet) for the deep discords that divided the National Convention after September of that year. Later, he attempts to unravel the mystery of the famous note on the "single will" that Robespierre wrote in June 1793; and at every phase of the Jacobin domination that followed he conscientiously discusses the problems that the ruling party, and notably Robespierre, had to face.

But why did Robespierre and his principal associates fall in Thermidor? Croker rejects the explanation offered by the "men of Thermidor" themselves, which had been accepted by other British historians up till then, preferring to it Napoleon's "scape-goat" version whereby the "Incorruptible's" downfall had been due to his attempt to dismantle rather than to intensify the Terror. And he concludes: "Mysterious and inexplicable as Robespierre's later conduct must appear, we tend to believe that the principal cause of his fall was that he was suspected of having wished to return to the path of decency, clemency and religion."[13]

Yet, at this time, in England it was only with the Chartists that Robespierre found defenders and apologists that were unreservedly and unequivocally devoted to his cause; notably in James Bronterre O'Brien, the well-known translator of Buonarroti's *Conspiracy of the Equals*, which was published in London in 1836. In the following year, O'Brien published the first (and only) volume of his *Life and Character of Maximilien Robespierre*. It is a book conceived in the Babouvist tradition and piously dedicated to the memory of a man whom the author, in a later work (dating from 1859) terms "the greatest reformer and law-giver that the world has ever known" and whose birth "more than any other event has honoured the name of France".[14] In relation to Robespierre, O'Brien adopts a blatantly class position: the more his memory has been blackened by the bourgeois and ruling classes, the more does this prove that he was the best and the most virtuous of men. "The better I succeed", he writes, "in showing that Robespierre's conduct was magnanimous and divine, all the more will his memory be detested by the respectable and middle classes."[15] It will be noted that there is no sign of that bitter criticism that Robespierre aroused during the nineteenth century among certain groups of the Left in France, in Tridon and Blanoui for example. It is also noteworthy that O'Brien, unlike the socialists of a later generation, condemned the Terror and refused to believe that Robespierre had any part in it.

Unfortunately, O'Brien ends his history with 1791, and he never returned to it; thus, as a life of Robespierre, it loses a great deal of its value. But, when all is said and done, is this a *history* at all? It is, to say the least, a debatable point. A pious panegyric has a certain place in historiography, it is true, and may not be devoid of interest, but as a portrait of Robespierre I doubt if this one has the value of (let us say) Carlyle's.

To complete the period of the 1830s and 1840s we still have to consider *The Life of Maximilien Robespierre* (1849) by George Henry Lewes, which has the merit of being the first full-length biographical study of the subject in English. The author had been strongly influenced by the events of 1848 in France and in addition to the royalist memorialists and the *Memories of Charlotte Robespierre concerning her Two Brothers,* he had read the works of Lamartine, Michelet and Louis Blanc; and from the latter he had drawn on letters by Robespierre that had remained unpublished until then. Yet there is little new in the book.

According to Lewes three great men emerged from the Revolution: Mirabeau "the genius of the Revolution"; Napoleon, "the soldier of the Revolution" who "with his despotism brought it to a close"; and "Robespierre, who tried to be its king" and "to rule it by metaphysical philosophy". He portrays Robespierre, somewhat in the manner of Archibald Alison, as a fanatic; it is a balanced portrait but one that would be of little interest to present-day readers.[16]

We may pass quickly over the third period, that of the 1850s to 1880s, because in England little that was new appeared on Robespierre or the Revolution at this time: with the exception of a short portrait of Robespierre published in his *Critical Miscellanies* by John Morley, a Liberal, in 1877. So I come to the centenary of the Revolution, a period marked in France by a long series of publications, including the *Procesverbaux* of the Jacobin Society and the Proceedings of the Committee of Public Safety, both edited by Aulard and both having a considerable influence on Revolutionary studies on both sides of the Channel. For it was under that stimulus, no doubt, that there followed in rapid succession the works of Henry Morse Stephens (1891–2),[17] Hilaire Belloc,[18] and, notably, of Lord Acton, whose courses on the French Revolution given at Cambridge from 1895 to 1899 were published in 1910 under the title of *Lectures on the French Revolution*.

Acton, a liberal Catholic with "Whiggish" leanings and a great admirer of Tocqueville, thought Robespierre "the most detestable person that held the centre of the historical stage since Machiavelli first codified the wickedness of public men".[19] The dictum has become famous; yet it does not faithfully reflect the author's feelings. Like Carlyle, Acton was a moralist turned historian. As a Whig he detested the Terror and the Revolutionary Government; like Tocqueville, he recoiled before the social and political consequences of equality. For him Robespierre was evidently the incarnation of Terror and equality combined; therefore he was a person both redoubtable and hateful. But as a moralist, Acton, like Croker, had a certain sympathy for the "Incorruptible" which he did not extend to his enemies. Among these none, in his view, sank so low as Danton and his coterie, men propelled by ambition, greed and the vilest instincts; whereas Robespierre, for all his faults, acted "on behalf of some kind of democratic system".[20] Like Croker, he poses the problem of the "mystery" surrounding the fall and death of Robespierre, and he repeats the expression that Cambaceres used to describe the Thermidorian drama to Napoleon: "It was a cause that was judged but never pleaded."[21]

The last phase in this historiographical survey falls in the period immediately following the First World War and the Russian Revolution of 1917. It was the period, too, when the experiments conducted by

Sigmund Freud had a certain influence on literature and social science. So it is not surprising that among historians some were found who dabbled in psychoanalysis. There was, for example, Reginald Somerset Ward whose work, *Maximilien Robespierre. A Study in Deterioration*, appeared in 1934. According to this author, Robespierre fell into the temptation of stoking up popular passions. In fanning the flames of disorder (he argued) Robespierre betrayed what the author believed to be "the spiritual side" of his profession as a man of law. Hence the "deterioration" that he traces from 1789 on, but above all from 1793.[22] In fact, behind the façade of pseudo-science the writer betrays on every page his anti-popular prejudices, and, like those of a century or more before, his work tells us far more about the author himself than he tells us about his subject.

Finally we come to the British historian who has done far more than any other to make the story of Robespierre intelligible to the English reader. I refer to J.M. Thompson, the greater "popularizer" of the French Revolution, whose lectures at Oxford were attended by successive generations of students. In 1929 Thompson published his *Leaders of the French Revolution*, containing a portrait of Robespierre; in 1935 there followed his *Robespierre*, a biography in two volumes and, in 1943, *The French Revolution*, a general study of the Revolution from 1789 to Thermidor.[23]

A radical Liberal in politics, Thompson was strongly influenced by Mathiez without, however, being completely convinced by his portrait of Robespierre. I would say rather that his own portrait owes as much to Croker as it does to Mathiez. In brief, to Thompson Robespierre was by far the most important figure in the Revolution, the undisputed leader of the Left in the Assembly after the death of Mirabeau in April 1791 and the consistent champion of social democracy. At every phase of the Revolution he saw him as the incarnation of the spirit of the vanguard party: the liberal spirit of 1789, the democratic spirit of 1792 to 1793 and what he called the "regimented deception" of 1794. Yet, like Croker, Thompson does not hide his preference for the Robespierre of 1789 to June 1793 to the man of the Republic of Virtue of the Year II; he sees in fact a sharp break between the liberal of 1789 to 1792 and the authoritarian spokesman for the Committee of Public Safety after July 1793. Thompson attempts to explain this difference; but as he seeks an explanation in personal factors without paying serious attention to social pressures, to the war, to the needs of France under foreign invasion and the rifts that were weakening the Jacobin-popular alliance, he failed to find one. So for him as for Croker and Acton, there always remained an element defying analysis, the "mystery" of Robespierre.[24]

The case of Thompson illustrates both the strength and the weakness of British historical writing on the subject of Robespierre. On the one hand, one sees in these examples—among those written from the 1830s at least—the attempt made by honest historians to trace a picture at once intelligible, sympathetic and critical, of a man carried to power and to the leadership of a nation under arms at a critical moment in its history. But this man, though a liberal in 1789, becomes the head of a "revolutionary" (therefore unconstitutional and authoritarian) government four years later; the democratic Constitution of 1793 is set aside and Terror and regimentation follow. Was this the personal choice of a man suffering from the delusion that he alone was fit to govern? Was it done to realize an ideologue's dream; or was it largely the outcome of circumstance (or what Saint-Just called "la force des choses")? That was the "mystery" that had to be resolved. But English political experience had since 1649 been so different from the French; and certainly no English statesman or politician since Cromwell had been confronted by the same choices as Robespierre and his colleagues were in 1793 and 1794. That the Jacobin leaders, in order to save both the nation and the Revolution, felt obliged to choose the path of dictatorship and a directed economy, that is what British historians, reared in the British parliamentary tradition, have found difficult to understand. That is why an adequate history of Robespierre in the English language still remains perhaps to be written.

Notes

1. *The History of Robespierre, Political and Personal, containing his Principles, Actions and Designs in the Jacobin Club, Commune of Paris, and the Convention* (London, 1794).
2. Helen Maria Williams, *Memories of the Reign of Robespierre* (3 vols., London, 1795). A second edition appeared in 1 volume in 1929 with a foreword by F. Funck-Brentano.
3. John Adolphus, *Biographical Memoirs of the French Revolution* (2 vols., London, 1799), II, pp. 365, 391, 407, 415, 423, 425, 433, 443.
4. Sir Archibald Alison, *History of Europe during the French Revolution* (2 vols., London, 1833).
5. Ibid., II, pp. 304–6.
6. William Smyth, *Lectures on the History of the French Revolution* (2nd edn, 2 vols., London, 1855), II, p. 352. These lectures, given at Cambridge in 1820–30, appeared in a first 3-volume edition in 1840 under the title of *Lectures on History. On the French revolution.*
7. Thomas Carlyle, *The French Revolution* (2 vols., London, 1955), II, pp. 79, 334.
8. Cit. A. Cobban, "Carlyle's French Revolution", *History*, 48 (1963), p. 311. See also H. Ben-Israel, "Carlyle and the French Revolution", *The Historical Journal*, I, 2 (1958), pp. 115–35,
9. Carlyle, *The French Revolution* (2 vols., London, 1906), I, p. xi.

10. John Wilson Croker, *Essays on the Early Period of the French Revolution* (London, 1857), pp. 299–430.
11. Ibid., pp. v–vii.
12. Ibid., pp. 39–71.
13. Ibid., p. 420.
14. James Bronterre O'Brien, *A Dissertation and Elegy on the Life and Death of Maximilien Robespierre* (London, 1859), pp. 31–2.
15. O'Brien, *The Life and Character of Maximilien Robespierre* (London, 1837), p. 15.
16. George Henry Lewes, *The Life of Maximilien Robespierre, with Extracts from Unpublished Correspondence* (London, 1849).
17. Henry Morse Stephens, *A History of the French Revolution* (2 vols., London, 1886, 1891): *Orators of the French Revolution* (2 vols., London, 1892).
18. Hilaire Belloc, *Robespierre. A Study* (London, 1901); *The French Revolution* (London, 1911).
19. Lord Acton, *Lectures on the French Revolution* (London, 1910), p. 300.
20. Ibid., pp. 226–7, 284.
21. Ibid., p. 299.
22. Reginald Somerset Ward, *Maximilien Robespierre. A Study in Deterioration* (London, 1934), pp. 4, 91, 232.
23. J.M. Thompson, *Leaders of the French Revolution* (Oxford, 1929); *Robespierre* (2 vols., Oxford, 1935); *The French Revolution* (Oxford, 1943).
24. *Leaders of the French Revolution*, pp. 215, 219; *Robespierre*, II, pp. 277–80.

7

"Feudalism" and the French Revolution

What was it that the French Revolution destroyed? The Constituent Assembly itself claimed, in August 1789, that it had abolished "the feudal regime"; and, in a broader sense, Professor Fanshof is no doubt right in stating that, during the Revolution, "feudalism" (*la féodalité*) was "virtually adopted as a generic description covering the many abuses of the *Ancien Regime*".[1] This elastic use of the term has certainly done service in the writing of many historians since the event; yet Professor Reinhard, among others, now insists that it was "seigniorial" rather than "feudal" rights that were at stake;[2] and Professor Alfred Cobban, who often seems to take a delight in throwing out the baby with the bathwater, appears to doubt if it was even this.[3]

What then is "feudalism"? Is it (to use it in its narrower "institutional" sense) a system whose sole sheet anchor is the military fief, or (following Marc Bloch and others) is it more sensible to talk of a "feudal society" in which the manorial system, military fiefs, vassalage, serfdom, and divided political authority all have their part to play? Professor Ganshof, who is certainly not prepared to bandy the term about loosely, admits that both are legitimate uses;[4] thus encouraged, I propose to build my own working "model". I am starting with the assumption that "feudalism" or "feudal society" has social, economic and political aspects. *Socially,* I see it as a pyramid or hierarchy of interconnected social relationships, bound together by contract and custom and a network of personal services and obligations—a system in which every man has his Lord and every lord (up to the king) his overlord, and in which the peasant-serf alone (at the base of the pyramid) is unfree. *Economically,* according to my model, feudalism rests on an agrarian economy whose unit is the manor, or (in France) the *seigneurie:* "nulle terre sans seigneur". *Politically,* my model may take one of two forms: it may be "centripetal", as in England under William I; or "centrifugal", as in France up to the fifteenth century or in England under Stephen and in the days of "Bastard" Feudalism. It all depends on the extent to which the King is "first" among his "equals". In the latter case, the *seigneur*, rather than the king, is really lord of his own domain. And it might be added that in either case the king's effective primacy was limited by the claims of the Church, which was a local branch of the Universal Church at Rome.

But, in practice, feudalism never corresponded exactly to any such abstract model. There was always a residue of free peasants (in France, land held in *franc alleu*). William I short-circuited the system of vassalage in its purest form by imposing his Oath of Salisbury on tenants as well as on tenants-in-chief. Almost from the start, the King began to recruit and consult "new men" as professional advisers. He raised professional armies, and the levying of scutage in England under Henry I was a sign that the system of military tenures was already being dented. In France, *bourgeois* began to purchase fiefs in the thirteenth century, and the King (to raise money or to protect his military tenures) imposed the *franc-fief* as a fine on those who bought them. Moreover, feudal economy was never entirely manorial. Urban crafts and trade, as exceptions to the "model", had to be provided for. Thus gradually there was built up a system of exemptions from the operation of vassalage and feudal obligation. Guilds and chartered towns came into being under royal protection. Similar "liberties" and exemptions from old feudal claims were extended to the lay barons, who formed themselves into privileged corporations or *corps de noblesses*, and to the Church which, in France at least, emerged as a corporate body privileged to tax itself—a sort of state within the State. In brief, feudalism was never from start to finish simon-pure and it tended, progressively, to "bastardize" itself and to create its own off-shoots.

What happened, more precisely, to feudalism in France? It was undermined (as, for that matter, elsewhere) by a dual process. In the first place, it was corroded by the more or less blind forces of social and economic change. Thus (to cite the most typical) the unfree peasants' labour service was gradually commuted for a monetary payment; and *bourgeois* gradually extended their purchase of the barons' old domains, thus partly destroying the old system and partly becoming absorbed by it (or something closely related to it). More systematically and deliberately, the old system was progressively disrupted by the conscious action of kings and royal governments. From Louis XI in the fifteenth century to Louis XIV in the seventeenth, the centripetal authority of the monarchy was gradually built up. Broadly, it was done in three ways: first, by the extension of royal justice and tax-collection at the expense of the *seigneuries;* secondly, by the promotion of "new men," accompanied by the sale of offices, to replace the old; and, thirdly, by such blatantly deliberate devices as appointing Intendants in the provinces, removing nobles and Princes of the Blood from political office and provincial governorships, and bringing the wealthier aristocracy to dance attendance on the King at Court. Thus *political* feudalism was, to all intents and purposes, already dead by the time Louis XIV began to move his court from Paris to Versailles in the 1670s.

Socially, feudalism had also been undermined, both by the invasion of *bourgeois* office-holders and purchasers of land and by the insidious extension of the royal writ. As all Frenchmen in practice as well as in theory became subjects of the king, nothing but the occasional shadow remained of the older system of overlordship, local allegiance and vassalage. Moreover, in one respect at least, the nobility had invaded the old preserve of the *bourgeoisie* (far less, it is true, than in England but far more than in Poland or Hungary.) Not all trades were closed to the *corps de noblesses* and noblemen could sell grain, as they could engage in overseas trade and even in some of the more lucrative urban crafts. But, in one important regard, the old system retained its substance as well as its shadow. The manorial system was, as we shall see, far from dead; in fact, it had acquired a new lease of life.

What then remained of "feudalism" in France by the eighteenth century and on the eve of the Revolution? In its original simon-pure sense obviously very little; but of its "bastards" or off-shoots a considerable amount. These survivals include such royal adaptations of old feudal practices as the *franc-fief,* the peasants' obligation to do forced work on roads (the *corvée des routes*), and the *droit de triage,* devised by Louis XIV, in 1669, to allow the *seigneur* to transfer to his own estate a third of the commons in the case of enclosure. There were the old "feudal" enclaves within France, such as those held by the Imperial Princes in Alsace and in the Comtat of Avignon by the Pope. War had not finally ceased to be seen by the king as an extension of the royal domain. Added to these were such offshoots as the guilds (mauled by Turgot in 1776, but surviving in substance none the less); the compensatory "liberties" and "immunities" of aristocracy and chartered towns: and the rights of the Church to tax itself by the *don gratuit* and to levy tithe—nominally for the maintenance of churches and clergy, but in large part diverted to strictly secular proprietary uses. Moreover, the extension of royal jurisdiction at the expense of the old baronial courts had, in a sense, defeated its original intention and created a new social caste subversive of the royal and centripetal authority. For the Parlements, though nominally royal courts of justice, had through the sale of public offices become the preserve of a new exclusive and hereditary caste which, far from expediting the demise of the remnants of feudalism, was inclined, when the opportunity offered, to perpetuate them in the name of "property" and "traditional liberties."

But, above all, there remained the substance of the old manorial system, in many respects buttressed rather than weakened by the accession of fresh blood. Personal bondage, or serfdom, however, had, as we noted already, largely disappeared: from Normandy already in the thirteenth century and, on the royal domain as recently as 1779. There were survivals of it in the *bordelage* of the Bourbonnais and the *Quevaise* of Brittany; but, substantially, it was now confined to Franche Comté and the Nivernais, where perhaps half-a-million peasants[5] were still subject to various forms of *mainmorte*. The *mainmorte* most frequently imposed on the peasant tenant (including nominal "freeholder") the duty to reside on the lord's estate; it restricted his right to bequeath land and to marry, it enforced oaths of allegiance, tallage at will and levies for the right of residence. Yet, by now it rarely exacted the old forms of compulsory labour service on the lord's domain.

More onerous by far in their total incidence were the payments in service or in kind that the peasant was obliged to pay his manorial lord. These might take the form of either regular or "casual" payments. Regular payments, originally incurred as a commutation of the old labour service, might include the *cens* (fixed charges in cash) or the *champart* (or *terrage* or *soyeté*) which, being a levy in kind on the peasant's crop, was by far the more vexatious of the two.[6] In addition, there still survived (in Auvergne, Champagne, Artois and Lorraine) the seigniorial *corvée*, or labour service, compelling the peasant to work 12–15 days a year on the lord's land, at harvest and at other times. The most common of the *droits casuels* were the payment to the lord of a tax, amounting to a fixed proportion (varying according to district between $1/_{13}$ and as much as ½) of the purchase price in the case of a transfer of property; and the *aveu*, the statement of his obligations to his lord made by the new tenant on entering into possession: this could be a costly legal business.

The lord might have other lucrative rights as well. The so-called "monopolies" or *banalités* entitled him to compel the peasant to bring his grain to be ground at his mill, his flour to be baked at his bake-house, and his grapes (or olives or apples) to be pressed at his wine (or olives or cider) press. This system, in particular, lent itself to the most flagrant abuses: Cobban calls it not "feudal" but "a commercial racket"[7] (but could it not be a mixture of both?) In addition, there were the monopolies of hunting and fishing, which entitled the *seigneur* to the exclusive use of the pigeon-cotes, to deny the peasants the right of access to the river, and to ride roughshod over his fields in pursuit of game. There were the rights to levy tolls on roads, canals and bridges (*péages*) and to compel the peasant to bring his civil suits into the lord's own court of justice. The sum total of these obligations might be extremely onerous, or they might be comparatively light: it depended on the district, the province, local custom, the nature of the peasant's status or contract, and (an important factor) the yield of the annual harvest. Taine estimated the contribution made by the peasant by such obligations as amounting to an average of 14 per cent of his total income; Marion suggests 11–12 per cent for the Bordelais; and some peasant *cahiers de doléances* of 1789 raised the proportion to even a quarter or a third.[8] However, the variations were probably too great to make much sense of any overall calculation. What is more important is that these burdens on the land were universally resented by the peasants, already subjected to the *taille* and tithe; and they appeared all the more vexatious in years of bad harvests and economic depression such as those that ushered in the Revolution of 1789.

And, to add to peasant resentment, there was the further irritation of the so-called "feudal reaction" of the latter half of the century. Was this "reaction" a legend or a reality; and was it "feudal" or something else? Historians have argued the point, and remain divided.[9] Certainly contemporaries—landowners as well as peasants—both believed in the reality of the "reaction" and were agreed on its nature. The belief is to be found in the peasant *cahiers* and in Boncerf's pamphlet of 1776, in which it is baldly stated that "feudal tyranny awakes furious after a century of slumber and silence."[10] Was such a view justified? Once more, it is partly a matter of vocabulary and the precise meaning we are prepared to extend to similar terms. In a wider sense, there can be little doubt that the period saw an "aristocratic" resurgence or reaction, even more striking in France than in Poland, Sweden, Hungary and Britain.[11] It was a time when the Parlements and aristocracy, incited by the weakness and fumbling "despotism" of royal government, were resuming their age-old battle with the Crown—a challenge that reached its culminating point in the "aristocratic revolt" of 1787–8. It was also a time when the avenues to high office and social preferment were being progressively closed to the richer middle classes: so much so that by the 1780s several Parlements were closing their ranks against them, all 135 Bishops were recruited from the nobility, and a law of 1781 made it almost impossible for a commoner to rise to commissioned rank in the army.

But, of course, to the peasants as to Boncerf it was not these developments that were of prime concern, but the alleged intensification of "feudalism" on the land. In one respect at least, there was progress rather than "reaction": as we have noted, an edict of 1779 abolished the final vestiges of serfdom on the royal domain (an example, incidentally, that other lords of unfree tenants were remarkably hesitant to follow). But, generally, the movement took a contrary course. Not that there was by any means a reversal to earlier more restricted forms of cultivation. Far from it: it was a period of rising corn prices when landowners were eager to extend their acreage and increase the rents on farms. To do so, in many cases, "feudal" practice was adapted to new uses; and feudal revival, *bourgeois* enterprise and new methods of surveying went hand in hand. There is therefore more than a grain of good sense in Professor Cobban's contention that "it is possible to describe the so-called 'feudal reaction' as less a reversion to the past than the application to old relationships of new business techniques."[12]

I should prefer to call it another instance of "bastard" feudalism. For the newly awakened commercial instincts of the landowners led them in many cases to renew their manorial registers (*terriers*) and to make fresh and systematic surveys (*cadastres*) of their holdings and seigniorial rights. This was done with the three-fold object of reviving such ancient dues and rights as had fallen into disuse; to increase the incidence of existing obligations; and even to invent or discover new ones; and fleets of tax collectors, lawyers and archivists (*feudistes*) were hired to do the job. In some places, neighbouring *seigneuries,* with their attendant rights and obligations, were amalgamated for more efficient exploitation. Elsewhere, old seigniorial rights were farmed out to go-ahead farmers and agents, new men whose more efficient and businesslike methods of operation often estranged and alarmed the peasants, many of whom (if we are to trust their *cahiers*) even began to regret the good old days of the former *seigneur*! Complaints were soon rife about increases in the *champart,* the doubling of the *cens,* or a tightening of the screws in the case of *banalités* and "casual rights." And, not to be outdone, the administrators of the royal domain followed suit; for this was equally a period when royal toll charges were increased, fines for trespassing on royal forests were revived or more rigorously exacted, and more onerous game laws were decreed.

Besides, there were other, more "forward-looking" types of innovation. The same motives that prompted the *seigneur* (whether a nobleman or a commoner) to exact a larger tribute from his peasants also prompted him to enlarge his holdings and improve the value of his land for grain or pasture by enclosing the common fields and usurping the ancient communal rights of gleaning and of gathering firewood. As in England, the years 1767–71 in France saw a spate of enclosure edicts for the benefits of the landlords, who could expect to reap the lion's share in such transactions from the highly profitable *droit de triage.* But, equally, common lands were leased out to "improving" *fermiers;* in Lorraine, privileged rights of grazing (the *droit de troupeau à part*) were farmed out to enterprising tenants; and forests were leased to owners of iron works and forges. Such practices can only in exceptional cases be termed "feudal"; but it is hardly surprising that the harassed peasant proprietor and small freeholder, looking back on them when drafting their grievances in 1789, should have included both innovations and reversions to ancient usage under the common label of "feudalism."[13]

We should note, too, the shrewdness of Tocqueville's remark that "at the height of its power feudalism did not inspire so much hatred as it did on the eve of its eclipse."[14] This "hatred" was to become far more evident in the course of 1789; and, on the eve of revolution, it was far from being universal even among the non-privileged Third Estate. Among the best-known *philosophes*, the only specific and consistent opponent of "feudalism" was Voltaire, who fought the Parlements year in and year out and campaigned for the freedom of the serfs of Franche Comté. Rousseau's teaching was implicitly rather than explicitly anti-feudal and Montesquieu, being more concerned to fight "despotism" than "privilege," provided some comfort for the proponents of an "aristocratic" (if not a strictly "feudal") revival. The *bourgeoisie* could, equally, not be expected to be thoroughly wholehearted in their hostility to "feudalism." They were certainly opposed to many of its off-shoots, such as aristocratic privilege and exemption from the payment of taxes, and the increasing monopolization of offices by the more recently enobled *noblesse de robe*. Tithe seemed to many an obnoxious anomaly; for most the guilds were a hindrance rather than an aid to trade and industry; and *bourgeois* purchasers of seigniorial estates had long established the obligation to pay the *franc-fief* and *lods et ventes*. Moreover, the sum total of seigniorial obligations could not fail to be seen as a fetter on capitalist rural development. But, while this was so, many *bourgeois*, being holders of ex-noble fiefs, were liable to see the dues and services that they brought with them as legitimate rights of property. In consequence, *bourgeois* proprietors were more inclined to criticize "abuses" than to condemn the "feudal régime" entirely; and, in 1789, we shall find remarkably few main *cahiers* of the Third Estate (as that of the *baillage* of Autun) that call for its total suppression—but never without adequate compensation to landlords.[15]

Naturally, the peasants saw the problem in a somewhat different light. Not that they were united, when it came to draft their *cahiers*, on what should be done about it. Much would depend on the particular abuses and vexations from which they suffered, as much would depend on the wealth and status of the different types of peasant. As they were divided over such questions as enclosure and the sales of common lands, so they were divided over tithe, the communication of the *corvée*, and over the exchange of seigniorial for royal justice (would the second prove, in fact, to be the cheaper?) But they were most certainly united on the necessity to abolish not only the "abuses" but some or other of the fundamental aspects of the *régime féodal*. Their *cahiers* tell us so quite clearly (though some favour a degree of compensation to the landlords and others unconditional confiscation).[16] It is evident, too, in the peasant litigation in the months preceding and following the outbreak of the Revolution.

These outbreaks started, in the manner of nearly all peasant disturbances of the eighteenth century, as food riots.[17] This was in December, 1788, at a time of steeply rising prices and general economic crisis.[18] But, very soon after, we read of peasant atacks on royal and aristocratic forests in the Paris region; and, in the following February, there were reports of risings against the payment of the *champart* (or *soyeté*) in Artois and against seigniorial title-deeds in Dauphiné. These scattered insurrections developed in late July and early August into a vast national conflagration against the *régime féodal* as a whole and, in particular, against the manorial registers housed by the landlords in the *châteaux*, monasteries or abbeys.[19] A great impetus was given to this movement by the fall of the Bastille and the subsequent rumours of marauding "brigands"; but it had started long before. In Franche Comté (to cite a typical example) attacks were made on 23–24 July on the abbey of Cherlieu, where monks and prior were forced to kneel and make public renunciation of all their feudal and associated rights: *mainmorte, lods et ventes*, tithes, *banalités*, rights of hunting and keeping pigeon-cotes, the *corvée*, and all earlier title-deeds were signed away.[20] All over France such incidents took place and showed, in the destructive violence that they left behind them, that the peasants' attitude towards their seigniorial obligations had, under the impact of economic and political crisis, considerably hardened since drafting their *cahiers* in the spring of 1789.

The newly created National Assembly met on 3rd August and was faced with a difficult problem: should the deputies attempt to crush the peasant risings, fully meet their demands, or find a compromise solution? After an initial display of oratorical self-sacrifice they decided on the latter course. In the most famous of its decrees of 4–11 August, the National Assembly

> abolishes the feudal régime entirely, and decrees that both feudal and *censuel* rights and dues deriving from real or personal *mainmorte* and personal servitude, and those representative thereof, are abolished without indemnity, and all others declared redeemable; and that the price and manner of redemption shall be established by the National Assembly. Those of the said dues which are not suppressed by the present decree, however, shall continue to be collected until reimbursement has been made.[21]

The Assembly went on to abolish without compensation rights of hunting, seigniorial courts and tithes for the upkeep of the clergy; but other tithes and "perpetual ground-rents"—the *cens* and the *champarts*—were declared to be redeemable. Thus already a distinction was being made between one type of "feudal" privilege and another—the first to be suppressed forthwith and the other to be redeemed as a legitimate marketable property right. A further point to note was the close association made by the Assembly between what it called the "feudal régime" on the land and all other privileges, immunities and exemptions, whether aristocratic or not. For it abolished in the same decrees the fiscal exemptions of the aristocracy, the privileges of chartered towns, annates and Peter's Pence (payments made to Rome), and plural benefices above 3,000 livres; declared justice and public offices to be open to all on equal terms; and suppressed venal offices in return for compensation.

Yet the law remained vague and subject to different interpretations. Above all, the apparently sweeping nature of the first decree alarmed the king, who held up his sanction for several months; and it raised the peasants' hopes of a more thoroughgoing reform. So the Assembly and its Feudal Committee decided to give the new law a closer definition. In February 1790, under the guidance of a "feudal" lawyer, Merlin of Douai, the deputies attempted to draw a clear distinction between "legitimate" property rights and those "usurped" or established by "violence." The latter alone should, properly speaking, be termed "feudal." They included manorial courts, *corvées* and *mainmorte*, exclusive rights to hunt and fish; rights to maintain pigeon-cotes, to collect tolls and market fines and to levy personal taxes; and the obnoxious *franc-fief* and *droit de triage*. For these no compensation should be paid. But others were considered to be equivalent to "simple rents and charges upon the land" and, as legitimate property rights, should become redeemable by monetary compensation. They included the great bulk of the dues paid by the peasants in respect of the holding or transfer of land: such dues as the *cens*, the *champart, lods et ventes* and other *droit casuels*. In addition, the peasant was required to prove the "illegitimacy" of the right from whose obligation he claimed exemption. Moreover, redemption would prove a heavy burden, the purchase price being fixed at twenty times the annual payment in cash or twenty-five times the annual payment in kind—or the equivalent of one third the annual yield of 7–8 consecutive harvests. Merlin, in summing up the debate, claimed that

> in destroying the feudal régime, you did not mean to despoil the legitimate proprietors of fiefs of their possessions, but you changed the nature of these properties. Freed henceforth from the laws of feudalism, they remain subject to those of landed estate; in a word, they have ceased to be fiefs and have become true freeholds

(*alleux*). . . There are no more fiefs; hence all the actual dues (*droits utiles*) with which the formerly feudal property is burdened should no longer be considered as anything but purely property rights."[22]

But the peasants, to whom all seigniorial dues and exactions were "feudal" and equally undesirable, failed to appreciate the nicety of Merlin's distinctions. So the revolution in the villages simmered on, occasionally breaking out in such violent eruptions as that which convulsed the South-West in 1790.[23] But, generally, it took the more peaceful forms of endless litigation and the obstinate refusal to pay any further dues or compensation. Either way, it proved remarkably successful. On 24th August, 1792, the Legislative Assembly declared that all landed property was free of "feudal" claims unless the owner could prove that they originated in a lawful purchase of transfer. Thus the onus was removed from the peasants and placed squarely on the shoulders of the former *seigneurs*. Yet all "legitimate" rights that could be substantiated by the display of a valid title remained redeemable; and the peasants remained unsatisfied. It was the Jacobins who completed the burial of the *régime féodal* begun in August 1789. A law of 17th July, 1793, ordered the destruction of all "feudal" title-deeds regardless of their origin; and all "feudal" dues were declared to be abolished without compensation, whether supported by a "legitimate" title of ownership or not. Finally, on 25th February, 1794, the National Convention ruled that all former seigniorial obligations were null and void wherever the contracts involved were "originally sullied by the slightest mark of feudalism."[24] So the peasants had won their point; and this remained the law of the land under Napoleon and the Restoration, and remains so to the present day.

Earlier, the Constituent Assembly had abolished all types of privileged "corporation" (Gallican Church, *corps de noblesse*, guilds, chartered towns, and even workers' "coalitions", Parlements, titles of nobility and the old royal courts of justice). Thus feudal remnants, their "bastard" off-shoots, the instruments of absolute monarchy, and the old "aristocratic" society had perished all together. In this wider holocaust the *bourgeois* and liberal aristocratic revolutionaries had played the major part. But in the destruction of the *régime féodal*—the most obnoxious of the feudal remnants—the *bourgeoisie* had most decidedly dragged its feet, and the prime movers and final victors had been peasants.

Notes

1. F.L. Ganshof, *Feudalism* (London, 1952), p. xv.
2. M. Reinhard, "Sur l'histoire de la Révolution française", *Annales (Economies-Sociétés-Civilisation)*, (1959), p. 557.
3. Alfred Cobban, *The Social Interpretation of the French Revolution* (London, 1964), pp. 25–53.
4. Ganshof, *Feudalism*, p. xvi.
5. Calculations vary between 300,000 and 1,500,000 (Sydney Herbert, *The Fall of Feudalism in France* (London, 1921), pp. 6–7.
6. For these and other peasant obligations to the *seigneur*, see Herbert, ibid., pp. 3–52.
7. Cobban, *The Social Interpretation of the French Revolution*, p. 51.
8. Herbert, *The Fall of Feudalism in France*, pp. 36–8.
9. Alun Davies, "The Origins of the French Peasant Revolution of 1789", *History*, 49, 35 (1954); Herbert, *The Fall of Feudalism in France*, pp. 42–5.
10. Herbert, ibid., pp. 41–2; Davies, ibid., p. 35, notes 31–2.
11. R.R. Palmer, *The Age of the Democratic Revolution*, vol. I: *The Challenge* (Princeton, 1959), pp. 23, 285–465.
12. Cobban, *The Social Interpretation of the French Revolution*, p. 47.
13. See Herbert, *The Fall of Feudalism in France*, pp. 43–52; Davies, "The Origins of the French Peasant Revolution of 1789", pp. 35–7.
14. A. de Tocqueville, *The Old Regime and the French Revolution* (New York, 1955), p. 177.
15. Cobban, *The Social Interpretation of the French Revolution*, pp. 37–8; G. Lefebvre, *Etudes sur la Révolution française* (Paris, 1954), pp. 249, 258–9.
16. Herbert, *The Fall of Feudalism in France*, pp. 75–88.
17. See G. Rudé, "The Outbreak of the French Revolution", *Past & Present*, 8 (Nov. 1955), pp. 28–42.
18. C.-E. Labrousse, *La crise de l'économie française à la fin de l'ancien régime et au début de la Révolution française* (Paris, 1944), pp. ix–xli.
19. See G. Lefebvre, *Etudes sur la Révolution française*, pp. 249–50; and (in far greater detail) *La Grande Peur de 1789* (Paris, 1932).
20. Herbert, *The Fall of Feudalism in France*, pp. 95–6.
21. J. Hall Stewart, *A Documentary Survey of the French Revolution* (New York, 1951), p. 107.
22. Cited by Cobban, *The Social Interpretation of the French Revolution*, p. 42.
23. Herbert, *The Fall of Feudalism in France*, pp. 165–8.
24. Ibid., pp. 188–98; N. Hampson, *A Social History of the French Revolution* (London, 1963), pp. 185–6.

8

The French Revolution and "Participation"

Every revolution casts its shadow before it and leaves its legacy of legends, traditions and more tangible achievements. I am speaking, of course, of the completed revolutions and, therefore, not so much of the Russian, the Chinese or the south-east Asian. And of these completed revolutions none left so rich a crop of legend and reality as the French.

The traditions left by revolutions may be a help to succeeding generations of revolutionaries; or, on the contrary, they may prove a millstone or a liability. Régis Debray, the young Frenchman who won his spurs in the Bolivian jungle, may have been thinking of something of the kind when he wrote in his revolutionaries' manual, *Revolution in the Revolution?*:

> We are never completely contemporaneous in our present. History advances in disguise: it appears on the stage wearing the mask of the preceding scene and we think to lose the meaning of the play. We see the past superimposed on the present, even when the present is a revolution.

Such a "superimposition" may be unfortunate, as Marx noted of the French revolution of 1848, "[when] only the ghost of the old revolution walked about—from Marrast, the Republican in kid gloves, who disguised himself as the old Bailly [the first revolutionary mayor of Paris], down to the adventurer who hides his commonplace repulsive features under the iron death mask of Napoleon".

More solidly and positively, the first French Revolution also left its legacy of watch-words, or (as the French would say) *idées-force;* and, in particular, the famous trinity of Liberty, Fraternity and Equality. But to know something of their real significance, we have to look a little more closely at each in turn. Liberty; but liberty for what and for whom? In

135

the first place, of course, freedom from absolutism; freedom of worship, assembly, writing and the press, the freedoms that are solemnly enshrined in the Constitutions of 1791 and 1793. The same freedoms also inspired the Spanish liberals of 1812, 1820 and 1836; Poles and Belgians in the 1830s; and Italians, Germans, Swiss and Hungarians in 1848; as they no doubt still inspire some Asians and Africans of the present day. But there are also the other—the economic—freedoms, such as the freedom to buy and sell, to trade and to hire and fire. They involve such rights as the "sacred" right of property, the freedom of the market and the end of monopolies and controls. But to whose advantage? That's the rub; for while everyone might be with you when you spoke of the freedom to meet, to organise or to think as you pleased, it was not quite the same when you spoke of the freedom of supply and demand, of the capitalist freedom to buy cheap and sell dear; and this, as we shall see, was a matter of some importance for the "small people" the *menu peuple,* or the *sans-culottes* of the French Revolution.

The second watch-word is that of Fraternity: not only the fraternity of Frenchmen, but of the people of the whole world, including (for the first time in history) the fraternity—and freedom—of the negro slaves. The Revolution, in fact, was seen by many not only as a French event, but an international event as well. Christopher Hill, the English historian, reminds us that this was, itself, not entirely new. He tells us of an English revolutionary of the 1640s who thought that the Long Parliament would "lay the cornerstone of the world's happiness"; and, even before 1640, he tells us also of a certain George Hakewell who described himself as a "citizen of the world"; and that was a full century and a half before the famous Anarcharsis Cloots of the French Revolution did so in the 1790s! But a great deal of this lay in the realm of speculation and aspiration rather than in that of reality. The negro slaves, however, were freed by the Jacobins in 1794; yet their freedom was, at this stage, short-lived, for Napoleon restored them to servitude a few years later. More durable were the practical consequences flowing from the Revolution's proclamation of "popular sovereignty" and the nation state. Popular sovereignty meant France for the French, and no nonsense about the Dutch, the Germans or the Pope having the right to continue to maintain their old feudal or dynastic enclaves on the soil of France! And if it meant this for the French, why not for the other peoples of Europe as well? To quote the late Alfred Cobban: "It was through the combination of the revolutionary idea of democratic sovereignty with the new importance attached to national differences that the Nation State ceased to be a simple historical fact and became the subject of a theory". And theories, once they reach a certain degree of maturity, can be most explosive historical phenomena, as Napoleon later discovered in Italy and Spain and Metternich and the Congress statesmen discovered after 1815. So we find Greeks, Serbs, Roumanians, Poles, Latin Americans, Italians and Germans turning theory into reality and proclaiming their nationhood in the course of the century that followed.

Yet an even more original and more distinctive feature of the French Revolution was the emphasis it placed on equality. This, writes the great French historian Georges Lefebvre, "was the real mission of the revolution. [For] while in England and America the alliance of aristocracy and upper middle class had precluded a stress on civil equality, in France the bourgeoisie had been compelled to stress it by the unbending attitude of the nobility". For in the early stages of the revolution in France the French nobility refused to follow the example set by the English nobility 150 years before: to come to terms with the up-and-coming middle class (or, as in the English example, with the gentry who, in a sense, belonged to both). Specifically in France, the aristocracy refused to surrender their privileges and exemptions from paying taxes. At this point, the monarch might (in theory, at least) have sided with the commons against the lords; but when it really came to a showdown, the King threw in his lot with the "privileged orders"; and this no doubt helps to explain why, in France, aristocracy and monarchy went down together and why no English-style compromise emerged.

So the stage was set for a thoroughgoing sweeping-away of privilege and its substitution by equality. Fiscal immunity was done away with and all were declared equal before the law and equally eligible to hold posts in local government and administration. But *political* equality—democracy—by no means followed automatically. The famous Declaration of Rights of 1789 admittedly declared (as Rousseau had done before) that all men should have a share in legislation. But when it came to the point of framing the new Constitution and when principle had to be spelled out in practice, citizens (all adult males) were divided into "actives" who had the vote and "passives" who did not: it all depended on whether one had enough property to pay the required amount in taxes. In much the same way, the English Levellers of the seventeenth century, though they demanded the vote for all "freeborn Englishmen", would have denied it to working men, or "servants". Yet the French revolutionaries went much further once the monarchy had been overthrown and the Republic had been proclaimed in September 1792. They extended the franchise to all Frenchmen of 21 and over, a reform that first received official legislative sanction in the Jacobin Constitution of 1793. But, like the liberation of the negro slaves, it was a short-lived experiment, for it was withdrawn by the Jacobins' successors in 1795. And after this the new "revolutionary" Constitutions in Europe, often imposed by the French, were based on the French

Constitution of 1795 and those that followed later; which meant that they, too, only gave the vote to property-owners, though sometimes on a fairly extensive franchise. But the democratic tradition, first launched in Paris, persisted. Even after the fall of the Jacobins, we find the Genevans still practising a democratic constitution in 1795 and, later still, the Piedmontese staged a radical rebellion against the French in which they demanded a democratic constitution four years after the French themselves had given theirs up. Such demands did not have much chance of realisation under Napoleon, and they were frowned on equally severely by the Allied victors after the Napoleonic Wars; but they reappeared, with varying degrees of success, in the revolutions of 1830 and 1848. So the democratic tradition, too, left some tangible results.

Socialism also stemmed, in part—as a kind of by-product—from the French Revolution. I say "by-product", because even the most extreme democrats of the Revolution, such as Robespierre, Saint-Just, Marat and Hébert, and even Jacques Roux, the "Red Priest", and the so-called *Enragés,* were not socialists at all; and the idea of dividing up property by a "loi agraire" or Agrarian Law, was denounced by every political group. Yet the germ of the idea could be found in Rousseau's *Social Contract* and, more specifically, in the writings of two other *philosophes,* Mably and Morelly, all of which had appeared before the Revolution itself and carried some influence at the time. However, the only revolutionary to attempt to formulate a political system and programme from such "collectivist" ideas was Babeuf, who, late in the Revolution—in 1796—launched his "Conspiracy of the Equals", which was intended to establish a collectivist society based on communist principles. But Babeuf's "conspiracy" was hatched at a time when the insurrectionary ardour of the *sans-culottes* (or poorer classes) was already a spent force, and it proved to be still-born. However, it also proved to be a "delayed-action" bomb; for 35 years later, under the very different industrial conditions of the early 1830s, Babeuf's ideas, relayed to the Parisian workers by Babeuf's old associate and disciple, Filippo Buonarotti, played an important part in the revolutionary and conspiratorial movements that came to a head in February 1848. So the French Revolution, irrespective of the intentions of all the main political groups ranging from moderate to extreme Left, served, in this indirect fashion, as a spawning ground for socialism—or, more correctly, for an important element in socialism—as well.

So we see that the Revolution left a number of legacies and *idées-force,* the liberal, the nationalist, the egalitarian, the democratic, and the socialist among them. But it left another tradition besides, and one that is my particular concern in this chapter. That is the tradition of radical popular democracy and direct popular participation in the conduct of affairs, which is probably the most original and the most unique of all the legacies the Revolution left to later generations. For while the ideas, even the most radical of them, generally emanated "from above" and were only assimilated by the people at a later stage, popular democracy was a contribution that the people made themselves. The French Revolution may with some justice be called a "bourgeois" revolution in the sense that the people who led it were, most typically, "bourgeois" and that what came out of it was more to the advantage of the middle classes than to any other social groups; but it was also a revolution in which the *menu peuple,* or lower classes—the peasants and urban *sans-culottes*—played a quite distinctive role, a role of the very first importance and one that left a deep impression on both the course and the outcome of events. This "popular" element in the French Revolution—this degree of popular participation—distinguished it from nearly every other. It was something that had not been seen in either the English or American revolutions that came before it; nor would it be seen, to anything like the same degree, in the revolutions of 1848, and it would have no parallel at all in the so-called "Meiji Restoration" in Japan a few years later. In fact, it is not merely the greater thoroughness of the French Revolution that marks it out, but this element of a "revolution within the revolution" makes it quite distinctive and unique among the "bourgeois", or even "bourgeois-democratic", revolutions of the past.

It is the failure to recognise this fact, I believe, which is the basic fallacy in Professors Palmer and Godechot's theory of an "Atlantic Revolution". Professor Godechot writes:

> The French Revolution was only one aspect of a Western, or more exactly an Atlantic, Revolution which began in the English colonies of America a little after 1763, was carried forward by the revolutions in Switzerland, the Netherlands and Ireland, before reaching France between 1787 and 1789. From France it spread again to the Netherlands and reached into the Rhineland, Switzerland and Italy.

So according to this view, the revolution in France was merely one of several late eighteenth-century revolutions bearing a common label as "revolutions of the West". There is some truth in all this; but, as I see it, the fallacy is even greater. For to place the French Revolution under this *omnibus*-label is to blanket its peculiar quality—not shared by those other revolutions—as a revolution in which there was quite a remarkable degree of participation of the people "from below".

So we come to the theme of participation, involving the people at large. But who, first of all were "the people"? The Abbé Sieyès, who was a great constitution-maker, both under the Revolution and Napoleon, had his own views about it. In 1789, when he was a radical spokesman for the *bourgeoisie* (or Third Estate), he asked an important question: "What is the Third Estate?"; and he answered: "C'est la nation". But by "Third Estate", as he made amply evident later, Sieyès did not mean the people as a whole, but the property-owners or *bourgeoisie*, who alone should participate directly in the process of law-making while the population at large should be satisfied with allowing others to vote and legislate on their behalf. At the time, the Constituent Assembly adopted Sieyès' plan of separating the "active" from the "passive" citizens; but the distinction did not remain to everybody's liking for long. Fashions changed; and, four years later, we find a Paris Section adopting a formula that was quite contrary to that of Sieyès: "La Nation, ce sont les *sans-culottes*"—in other words, it was no longer the *bourgeoisie* but the *sans-culottes*—the small people—who had become the nation and should, therefore, call the tune. And who exactly were the *sans-culottes*? In the first place, they were the small craftsmen, tradespeople and wage-earners of Paris and the other cities. But they might also be said to include the "middling" and lower peasantry, that is to say those peasants who were not large proprietors or belonged, more properly, to a sort of rural *bourgeoisie*. Now what did these people, who, combined, formed the great majority of the nation at large, expect to get out of the Revolution?

First let us see what they wanted at its outbreak, in 1789; and then let us see what they expected from it four years later. This will tell us something of the way the Revolution, having satisfied certain popular demands, whetted the appetite for more.

We begin, then, with 1789 and with the largest group, the peasants, both rich, "middling" and small proprietors, and poor. The rich peasants wanted more land; they wanted better prices for their grain; they wanted to pay lower wages and lower taxes. On the whole, they did not want enclosure as they used the commons for pasture; however, they wanted to end the ancient communal right of gleaning and pasture for the village poor, as this took up land that they wanted for themselves. The small and "middling" peasants wanted more land; they wanted to retain communal rights, and they might want enclosure wherever it could be used to extend their own holdings. Lastly, there were the poor, or landless, peasants. They certainly wanted land, if necessary by breaking up the commons; they also wanted higher wages and, being small consumers and not producers for the market, cheaper bread as well. So there were evidently considerable differences of interest between one type of peasant and the next; but they all had one interest in common. This was to end what was called "feudalism" on the land, and in particular the old traditional dues and obligations that they owed to the landlord. If they could end those, they would all appear to benefit;

and, to achieve this, they joined forces once the Revolution began, against a single common enemy: the landed proprietor, whether he was a noble or a *bourgeois*.

The *sans-culottes*, the small people in the towns, were also divided. As I have said, they included shopkeepers and master craftsmen as well as wage-earners. The small proprietors, whether shop-keepers or others, were naturally interested in higher profits and lower wages; and the wage-earners, not surprisingly, had an interest in seeing that their wages did not fall. But, in the conditions of the time, when the cost of bread accounted for something like half, or more, of the poor man's budget, the overriding interest of both workers and small employers was that bread should be both cheap and in plentiful supply. So the *sans-culottes*, too, like the peasants, had an important interest in common; and where the peasant saw his main enemy in the rich landowner, the *sans-culottes* saw his in the speculator, wholesaler, large merchant or monopolist. But gradually, as the Revolution developed, both public enemies—both the landlord and the speculator—appeared to assume a common identity under the common political label of "aristocrat"; and, for practical purposes, it did not much matter whether people so labelled were really aristocrats (or former aristocrats) or not. So the term "aristocrat" became a generic term, embracing all enemies of the people, whether landlords, large merchants, speculators or any other real or apparent stumbling blocks to the realisation of popular demands. The emergence of a common public enemy of this kind served also to cement the unity of the peasants and the *sans-culottes* for a number of years. Some writers have held that this city-country alliance ended with the end of the "peasant revolution" in 1793; Mr Barrington Moore, however, has argued that it survived for another year: till the summer of 1794.

How, then, had the situation changed by 1793, which has generally been seen as the year in which the Revolution reached its high-point? By this time, all except the poorest peasants had attained all that they could hope to achieve through revolution: in short, the "peasant revolution" was virtually completed. But there still remained the poorer townsmen, or *sans-culottes*. They were no longer the same as they had been in 1789. In purely social terms, of course, they were still the same *menu peuple* of small tradesmen, craftsmen and wage-earners. They still tended to live in the same sort of dwellings, to wear the same sorts of clothes, to speak the same sort of language, and to share the same kind of social attitudes and entertainments. Richard Cobb gives us a graphic picture of these common bonds in his portrait of the typical *sans-culotte* of 1793. But they had taken on a new, more self-conscious identity as well: this is already evident in the now general use of the term *sans-culottes* itself, at first applied as a pejorative label by conservatives and now proudly accepted by the *menu peuple* itself as a common badge of identification. The price of food and bread still remained, as it would throughout the revolutionary years, the basic and prime concern. But the demand for bread was more closely allied to the political means to ensure it. There was more emphasis placed on a more thorough system of controls, a demand that was received by even the Jacobins with evident expressions of dismay. But one of their own spokesmen, the *Enragé* leader Jacques Roux, drew a clear enough distinction between the notion of liberty as conceived by the *sans-culottes* and that of their critics, when he told the National Convention in June 1793: "Liberty is a hollow sham if one class can deprive another of food with impunity. Liberty is meaningless where the rich may exercise the power of life and death over their fellows with impunity." The *sans-culottes*—or at least a considerable number of them—gave practical expression to this distinction in participating in the two food riots that broke out at the doors of grocers' shops in January 1792 and February 1793. The last of these, in particular, involved districts scattered over the length and breadth of Paris and were loudly condemned by the leaders of the political parties, by both Girondins and Jacobins. However, the *sans-culottes*, though they failed to win any positive results on these two occasions, realised a considerable part of their aims in the fresh riot, or insurrection, of September 1793. It began with a demand for cheaper bread and escalated into a political demonstration, with the support of the Paris Commune, within the Convention itself. Its outcome was the enactment, three weeks later, of the General Maximum law, which imposed a ceiling on the prices of nearly all the necessities of life—and also (and this was not quite so much to the taste of some of the *sans-culottes*) on the price of labour as well.

But the social demands of the *sans-culottes* went much further than merely the assurance of the minimum necessities of life. They were also concerned with another aspect of social equality: with what the Jacobin leader, Lepeletier, in a speech delivered in August 1793, called *l'égalité des jouissances*, which means roughly the equality of social benefits. In order to ensure this, the *sans-culottes* demanded the right to work or to public relief, education for all, and the progressive taxation of the rich. But they considered their aims to be incompatible with the existence of capitalism or commercialism; so *sans-culotte* thinking at this time is both anti-feudal and anti-capitalist, and so feudalism and capitalism, both being related as public enemies, were inclined to become confused. How then could this ambivalent attitude to property be resolved? By a general attack on property and an equal distribution of goods by something like the old Agrarian Law, or *loi agraire*, put forward by the brothers Gracchus in Ancient Rome? By no means. The most typical of the *sans-culottes* and certainly their spokesmen in the Paris Sections, were small proprietors—master craftsmen and shopkeepers—rather than wage-earners; and they had no desire to see their properties abolished. But what they did want was a limitation of property in order to get nearer to their ideal—the ideal first formulated by Rousseau—of a Republic of small proprietors. They wanted to spread property more widely, not abolish it; and, like the Russian peasants of 1917, they wanted to increase not the size of properties but the number of small proprietors. The classic formulation of this petty-proprietorial view was that made, early in September of that year, by the Paris *Section des Sans-culottes*, which demanded that no man should have more than one workshop, one farm, one plough or one store. I am not suggesting, of course, that all the *sans-culottes* held similar views, but it is of interest to note that such a policy was put forward at this time by a typical meeting of small craftsmen and tradesmen in Paris. This has nothing whatever to do with socialism; but it is the extreme limit of what we may call egalitarian individualism; and it is no coincidence that it should have been expressed at this particular stage of the Revolution—neither earlier nor later—when these same petty proprietors were at the height of their influence and power. We should note, too, that such views were not particularly to the liking of the Jacobin leaders, who, although they had a deep regard for Rousseau, were equally concerned to prosecute the war to a successful conclusion with the aid of other classes beside the *sans-culottes*.

By 1793, the *sans-culottes* had more specific political aims as well. By this time, they had come to dominate the Paris Sections and the Commune, or municipal authority, besides; so they were a political force to be reckoned with. Here, too, their aims and demands were becoming a source of some embarrassment to their Jacobin allies. Having seized control of the Sections in the course of a series of stormy sessions in August and September, they insisted that they should be fully autonomous, without government supervision or control, and that they should remain *en permanence*, that is in permanent session, instead of being restricted to twice-weekly meetings as the Convention had prescribed. The Parisian *sans-culottes* went considerably further. They claimed the right, through their primary assemblies (which, in Paris, were the forty-eight Sections), to have a preliminary say in all legislative measures, to brief their elected representatives by an "imperative mandate", and to recall, at short notice, any deputies who ignored the instructions of their constituents. They claimed further powers as well; for if the Convention, or parliament, behaved unjustly or ignored the people's wishes (or, more precisely, the wishes of the people of Paris) they would have not only the right, but the "sacred" obligation, to stage an insurrection and overthrow the government and Assembly by force.

This theory of "direct democracy", which played so important a role in the political thinking of the Parisian *sans-culottes,* was of course absolute anathema to the man in authority in the Committees of government, the Jacobin Club and the Convention, including even the more advanced of the democrats such as Robespierre and Saint-Just.

It is perhaps of some interest to consider briefly where these ideas came from. Broadly speaking, they came, on the one hand, from "philosophers" such as Rousseau and those who repeated their teachings; and, on the other, from the direct experience of war and revolution of the *sans-culottes* themselves. It took time, of course, for such a comparatively sophisticated body of ideas as those of Mably, Morelly, Montesquieu and Rousseau to percolate through to the people in the streets and workshops, of whom a considerable proportion (though the exact proportion can only be guessed at) were unable to read or write. The first steps to indoctrination were probably those taken by the Parlements, who, in the years before the Revolution, were engaged in a prolonged duel with the king and his ministers and, to further their cause, printed their protests or Remonstrances, which were widely read and distributed. With the Revolution, the role of indoctrinator was taken over by the spokesmen and journalists of the Third Estate, such as the Abbé Sieyès with his famous pamphlet on the Third Estate that I mentioned before. So we find such phrases as "tiers état", "nation", "citoyen", "social contract" and the "rights of man" being used for the first time in the speech of the common people of Paris in the spring and summer of 1789. Two years later, at the time of the Champ de Mars "Massacre" of July 1791, we find cooks and journeymen tradesmen reading or subscribing to the revolutionary press, while others are attending public readings in some of the new clubs and societies, of which many have reduced their subscriptions to a few *sous* a year so that even wage-earners can afford to belong. Meanwhile, the National Guard was opening its doors to those previously excluded and, after August 1792, the Sections were open to all and most working men acquired the vote. So the process of indoctrination in the ideology of revolution went on apace, and naturally reached an even higher stage when the *sans-culottes* took over the control of most of the Sections after the summer of 1793.

But, of course, the ideas that the *sans-culottes* inherited from others and that they took such a time to assimilate, were no longer quite the same as those penned by Montesquieu or Rousseau or relayed by the pamphlets of the Parlements or in the speeches of the *bourgeois* of the Third Estate, the Jacobin Club or Convention. Like the ideas of Martin Luther, when assimilated and adapted by the German peasants of the 1520s, they suffered a "sea-change". As Engels wrote to Kautsky in the centenary year of the French Revolution, "the plebs gave a meaning to the revolutionary demands of the bourgeoisie that they did not possess before". So we find the Réveillon rioters of April 1789 already giving a meaning to the term "tiers état" that was not at all the one intended by the Abbé Sieyès. Very soon after, it became fashionable to believe that the "rights of man" should include the rights of every one, not only of "active" citizens, to have a say in legislation. "Liberty" also, in popular usage, became re-defined: in particular, it was considered intolerable that a wealthy merchant or speculator should have the "liberty" to force up prices and leave the poorer citizens short of bread. As for "popular sovereignty", it was not enough to see it in terms of an occasional right to vote; it must be something far more active and dynamic; and so it came, by the autumn of 1793, to mean nothing less than the direct and fully "participatory" democracy of the Paris Sections.

Naturally, the *sans-culottes'* direct experience and their participation in revolutionary events helped them to arrive at these conclusions; it was not just a matter of assimilating the ideas of others. This experience and participation might take any one, or more, of three forms. First, there was the experience of shortage and rising living costs, the realization of which was simple enough without any "philosophical" elucidations! Then there was the matter of directly participating in the work of revolution, either by taking part in riots or demonstrations or (at a later stage) "militating" in the Sections or serving on local committees. The long succession of revolutionary events, or *journées*, such as the assault on the Bastille, the capture of the Tuileries or the expulsion of the Gironde from the Assembly, not to mention such food riots as those of February and September 1793, provided in themselves a rich fund of experience. Just as important, no doubt, was the day-to-day participation in the work of Sectional committees, anti-hoarding committees, *comités révolutionnaires*, Popular Societies, battalions of the National Guard, and even in the policy-making sessions of the Paris Commune which, slowly after August 1792 and swiftly after July 1793, became a regular feature of the political life of the Parisian *sans-culottes*. So, out of this experience and this participation in events there began to emerge new leaders and spokesmen for the *sans-culotte* point of view. But they remained confined to the lower organs of revolutionary government. In the National Convention itself, there were never more than a handful of *sans-culottes;* and not one of these was from the capital itself.

But, in spite of their exclusion from the higher ranks of government and legislation, the *sans-culottes,* in their heyday—roughly from July to December 1793—wielded a considerable influence and exercised a substantial degree of authority. From this pinnacle of power their decline took place in three main stages. In the first place, they were "demoted" by their own partners in revolutionary activity, the Jacobins themselves. In December 1793, the Convention passed the Law of 14th Frimaire, which, by establishing a strongly centralised "revolutionary" government, whittled down considerably the powers of the Parisian *sans-culottes*. The revolutionary committees of the Sections (their particular strongholds) were made responsible to the Committee of General Security at the centre; and, soon after, many of the popular societies were closed down, and Hébert and the "Hébertists", who had been among their most articulate spokesmen, were arrested and guillotined in Robespierre's struggle with "the factions". The Commune, for long a centre of "Hébertism" and "sans-culottism" was purged and the empty places filled up with men who could be relied upon for their loyalty to the main Jacobin group. From now on, local initiative was killed and the Sections ceased to be much more than rubber-stamps for the government's decision; and, as Saint-Just lamented, "la révolution est glacée" (which means, roughly, that the Revolution had become ossified). An even more decisive step in stripping the *sans-culottes* of all influence on events was taken after the fall of Robespierre and his group in the blood-bath of Thermidor (July 1794). Robespierre's successors not only closed the Jacobin Club and dismantled the Terror, but they set out to eradicate all survivors of "sans-culottism" as well. The Sections were purged of all such elements, the revolutionary committees and remaining popular societies were disbanded, and the Paris Commune was closed down altogether. Finally, in the spring of 1795, the *sans-culottes* reacted and made a last desperate attempt to stage a come-back in the massive rebellions (which were food riots and political protests combined) of Germinal and Prairial. They received only half-hearted support from their old allies, the Jacobin remnants within the Convention. So they were defeated and crushed, their leaders were executed, they were arrested in their hundreds and disarmed in their thousands. It was the final flicker of independent *sans-culotte* activity; and there was no popular political revival again until the next French revolution in July 1830.

What did the *sans-culottes* achieve by their participation in the revolution of 1789? They certainly helped to push the Revolution leftwards: without their intervention the Jacobins could never have come into power; there would have been no "democratic dictatorship of the Year II"; and it is doubtful if the monarch would have been overthrown or if the Austrians and Prussians would have been driven from French soil. They also won important concessions for themselves—though they proved to be short-lived: the Maximum Laws, for example, with a ceiling placed on food prices; and the right to vote and to sit in local government. More permanent were the gains of the peasants, which were also won by popular participation; such as the abolition of the old "feudal" dues on the land and the eventual annulment of all payments to be made *in lieu;* and such gains were respected by all subsequent governments in France, even by Napoleon and the restored monarchs of 1815. Mr Barrington Moore carries this argument even further and claims that the destruction of the old feudal, or semi-feudal, landlord class, which was one of the most signal of the Revolution's achievements, proved to be vital for the whole subsequent history of French democracy.

Like the "bourgeois" revolution, the popular revolution also left its legacy and its traditions; and popular radical democracy revived, though sometimes under new guises, in the French revolutions of 1830, 1848 and 1871. There were echoes of it, too, in the Left alliance and Popular Front of 1936–39 and in the local "patriot" committees set up to expel the Germans and punish the collaborators at the end of the last war. Most recently, memories of 1793 have been recalled in the street-fighting and behind the barricades of the student rebellion (or "revolution") of May–June 1968. But, before I finish, perhaps I should strike a cautionary note. There are no exact historical parallels, for history never quite repeats itself in the same way; and as Marx showed in the case of the two Napoleons, which I cited earlier, history plays strange tricks when it repeats itself in a new guise. Torn from its former historical moorings, the mixture is never the same as before. To adapt political ideas to suit a particular interest is a game that conservatives as well as revolutionaries can play. The French colonels who staged a colonialist *coup,* in the name of General de Gaulle, in Algeria in May 1958, set up what they called a Committee of Public Safety in imitation of the Jacobins of 1793. The descendants of the Parisian *sans-culottes* can, in new historical conditions and with remarkably little change of style, appear just as easily in the guise of M. Poujade's right-wing anti-tax protesters of the 1850s as in that of the socialist workers of 1936 or the radical students of 1968. In the same way, the arguments used by the American rebels against George III are repeated, almost word for word, by Mr Ian Smith and his "white-supremacists" in Rhodesia today; and Mr Barry Goldwater and the John Birch Society drew heavily on the political armoury of Jefferson and the Jacksonian democrats in the USA.

So I'll leave you with a conundrum; or is it just a simple paradox? Old wine may, as in such cases, taste sour in new bottles; but I'm afraid it's no good trying to pour it back into the old.

9

Why was there no Revolution in England in 1830 or 1848?

In the 1830s and 1840s, England, like her Continental neighbours, suffered a series of social and political crises, and, at various times, contemporaries believed that she, like them, was heading for a revolution. In the middle of the Reform Bill crisis in the early 1830s, Charles Greville, the memorialist, reported that his friends in the Athenaeum Club were "convinced that a revolution in this country was inevitable".[1] In 1845, Engels made his well-known prophecy of a pending revolution,[2] and, writing later of this period, Charles Kingsley, the novelist, recorded that "young men believed (and not so wrongly) that the masses were their natural enemies, and that they might have to fight, any year or any day, for the safety of their property and the honour of their sisters".[3] And every High School history textbook tells of the extraordinary siege-like measures adopted by Lord John Russell and his colleagues to disperse the great Chartist meeting on Kennington Oval in April 1848.[4]

Historians, looking back on these events, have been inclined, and probably with justice, to attribute greater revolutionary potentialities to the events of 1830–2 than to those of the 1840s, even of the last great Chartist challenge of 1848. Professor Rostow selected these years to mark the high point of his "social tension chart" of 1790 to 1850; G.M. Young, the chronicler of Victorian England, wrote of them as being of "a sustained intensity of excitement unknown since 1641"; G.M. Trevelyan believed that it was only the passage of the Reform Bill that saved "the cultivated upper classes" from "violent revolution"; and, even more emphatically, Cole and Postgate claimed that "never since 1688 had Great Britain been so near actual revolution as in 1831; never in all the troubles of the next two decades would she come so near to it again".[5]

148

What was there, then, so remarkable about these years? Have the retrospective judgements of historians been justified? And why, in spite of all that happened, were the prophecies of contemporaries not realized?

First, let us consider the critical situation that unfolded between 1830 and 1832. At the centre of the crisis lay the battle over the Reform Bill, first presented to Parliament by Lord Grey's Whig Ministry in March 1831. Yet the reform of Parliament, though the most explosive and the most important, was only one of several issues that divided Britain at this time.

Broadly speaking, they all had a common origin in the social transformation, uprooting and upheaval that had been taking place in Britain since the American war of the 1770s and 1780s, and more particularly since the end of the wars with France in 1815. The Industrial Revolution, whatever its ultimate benefits, had left a trail of grievances and nostalgic yearnings. For some, the French wars brought a temporary reprieve: farmers and handloom weavers, for example, knew prosperity and even the village labourers' wages were protected. But, with the end of the war, the bubble burst: corn prices fell, land went out of cultivation, farmers' profits shrank, labourers were thrown on poor relief; even the landlords, temporarily at least, shared in the general agricultural crisis. The village became the battleground of conflicting interests in which the farmer, ranged against the landlord over rent and the parson over tithe, took it out on the labourer by reducing his wages or turning him over to the overseer. In the manufacturing districts, the wages of domestic and handloom workers, which had been buttressed by the war, entered on a new and disastrous downward spiral, while factory workers' wages were depressed by the progressive reduction of piece rates and the massive influx of Irish poor. Even the manufacturer saw his prospects of a rosy future blighted by Corn Laws, trade restrictions, the squalor, ill-heath and misgovernment of the boroughs and expanding cities, and the obstructions of the old unreformed and landlord dominated Parliament at Westminster. So he took to Free Trade and Radical Reform. Meanwhile, across St. George's Channel, the land-hunger of the Irish peasants and the broken promises of the Act of Union of 1801 had sown the seeds of a new rebellion.

And to these longer-term grievances and tension we must add two more immediate "precipitating" factors. One was the high price of corn: for twenty-one consecutive months from January 1830, the quarter of wheat in the London Corn Exchange never fell below 70s. (Its average over the previous seventeen years had been 59s.) The other was the outbreak of revolution in France and Belgium in the summer of 1830, which, even if its influence may have been exaggerated, brought new colourful banners and slogans to Irish rebels and English reformers.

So, by the end of 1830, there were four distinctive movements in being, which, though they ran separate and largely independent courses, had an accumulated effect that caused the Government considerable concern.

First, there was the massive outbreak of the English agricultural labourers, described by the Hammonds as the "last peasants' revolt",[6] whose origins went back to the depression and rural distress which followed the Napoleonic wars. The labourer, as the principal victim in the three-cornered struggle between farmer, squire and parson, had his wage reduced and his allowance cut when he was thrown on the parish. It was not so much (as both contemporaries and historians have argued) that the labourer resented the degradation of being paid from the rates. If the parish had paid him a living wage, he might have cheerfully stomached the insult. But it had become customary to stand him down in the winter months and leave him to subsist on a reduced allowance. Moreover, threshing machines had recently been introduced to displace his labour in districts where they had not been used before—notably, in 1830, around Canterbury in Kent.

So the movement started in Kent, a county of relatively high wages, in the summer of 1830; it took various forms: arson, threatening letters, wages riots and a general assault on threshing machines. From Kent it spread westwards into Sussex, Hampshire, Wiltshire, Gloucester, Worcester and Somerset and reached into Devon and Cornwall. A second wave began in Berkshire and travelled east and north into Oxfordshire, Buckingham and Northampton; and a third wave, starting in Norfolk, travelled south through Suffolk and Essex, and from there north through Cambridge and Lincoln, touching the Yorkshire Ridings and leaving its mark as far north as Carlisle. It was virtually all over by December 1830; but there were new outbreaks in Kent and Norfolk in 1831, and there was a last isolated incident of threshing-machine breaking in a Cambridgeshire village in September 1832. Meanwhile, the movement had left a heavy toll of repression: nineteen men had been hanged, 644 had been jailed and 481 (including two women) had been sent in irons to New South Wales and Tasmania.[7]

Secondly, there were the industrial movements in the manufacturing districts and coalfields, variously composed of factory workers, miners, handloom weavers, and skilled craftsmen like the nail-makers of Birmingham. The handloom weavers had, like the nail-makers, been chronically depressed since the end of the wars,[8] while the factory workers were suffering from the recent general trade recession and unemployment of 1829–30. In addition to their economic hardships, they had been touched by the political Reform arguments of the

Radicals and the new socialist and cooperative ideas of Robert Owen. Many factory workers, in particular the spinners around Manchester and Blackburn, had joined John Doherty's National Association for the Protection of the Working Classes, which, by 1831, claimed 100,000 members and, by this time, also included Yorkshire powerloom weavers, Midlands hosiery and lace workers, Staffordshire potters and miners from the Yorkshire, Lancashire, Midlands and Welsh coalfields. The spinners were less violent in their activities than the miners, weavers and hosiery workers, who were more inclined to turn strikes into attacks on machinery. But, owing to the spinners' militancy and their higher degree of organisation and political attachment, it was their strikes and meetings that caused the Government the greatest concern and, in the summer of 1830, troops were sent as a first priority into the Manchester factory area and Doherty's public meetings were the subject of alarmed reports to the Home Office. And when Henry Hunt, the Radical leader, was elected to Parliament at Preston in December, a correspondent wrote that "the town was filled with some hundreds of the very lowest dregs of the factories", carrying tricolour flags and banners inscribed "Bread or Blood" and "Liberty or Death".[9]

The third ingredient was provided by the Irish who, in the autumn of 1830, goaded by hunger, economic hardship and political frustration, broke into open rebellion. In September, Daniel O'Connell, the nationalist leader, launched a campaign to dissolve the Union with Britain, and toasts were drunk in Dublin to the cause of the Belgians who had recently rebelled against the Dutch, "and may others [it was added] imitate their bright example." There were food riots in Limerick and Roscommon, and the land-hunger and tithe-war in the south and west were in the winter of 1831, attended by the nightly assaults and depredations of Whiteboys, Ribbonmen and the elusive followers of "Captain Rock". Once more, as with the English labourers, the outbreak was followed by another massive wave of transportation to Australia.[10]

The fourth ingredient was, of course, the English movement for parliamentary Reform and the bitter hostility this encountered among the old landed aristocracy and properties classes. The movement had a long history, having been successively nourished by eighteenth-century London Radicalism, the agitation of Wilkes and the Yorkshire freeholders, and a succession of Radical writers and agitators from Cartwright and Paine to Cobbett and Francis Place. Its most constant theme had been the need for a reform of Parliament—whether by more frequent elections, an extension of the suffrage, the abolition of sinecures and "pocket" boroughs, or the secret ballot; though it had also concerned itself with demands for lower taxes, reduced tithes and pensions, cuts in government expenditure, and an end to "Old Corruption" and to the privileges of city corporations.

The issues were to become more closely defined with the return of Lord Grey's Whig Ministry, pledged to reform, in November 1830 and by the presentation to Parliament, after intensive negotiations within Cabinet, of the first draft of the First Reform Bill in March 1831; the Bill included the provisions that the vote be given to the £10 householder in the boroughs and that a large number of "rotten" and "pocket" boroughs should be disfranchised. But even before that, the Reform movement had received a fresh stimulus from the Paris revolution of July 1830; and, in August, enthusiastic meetings were being held to toast the French in every great city in the Kingdom.[11]

At this time, the main centres of the Radical and Reform movement were Birmingham and London. Birmingham held pride of place, as it was here that the first Political Union, the parent of the most influential of the Reform associations that sprang up on the eve of the Reform Bill, was founded in December 1829; its founder, Thomas Attwood, the banker and currency reformer, was considered by Francis Place to be "the most influential man in England".[12] Unions spread to other cities, and Home Office reports note their appearance at Worcester, Kidderminster, Evesham, Blackburn, Carlisle, Manchester, Aylesbury and High Wycombe before the end of 1830. The Unions were designed to unite the middle and lower classes in combined action for parliamentary reform. This was, in fact, easier to realise in some cities than in others. At Birmingham, owing to the continued prevalence of the small workshop and to the common experience of a trade depression, there was considerable cooperation between the classes. At Bristol, the Reform movement was supported by the craft unions. In country towns, the workers' role tended to be nominal rather than real. In large manufacturing towns like Manchester and Leeds, the division between capital and labour had already reached a point where any form of durable cooperation was almost impossible to achieve.[13]

In London, too, organisation tended to divide on the basis of class; and London became the centre of the more extreme, or working-class, Radicalism. The National Union of the Working Classes, which made a class appeal that the Political Unions lacked, had its headquarters at the Rotunda in Blackfriars Road; and here hundreds (or even thousands) came weekly to listen to the popular Radical orators of the day: Henry Hunt, William Cobbett and Richard Carlile. Tricolour flags were borne; and, in November, such tension was aroused by a proposed visit to the City of the Duke of Wellington, who was escorting the King to the Lord Mayor's Banquet, that the royal visit had to be cancelled.[14]

London Radicalism radiated outwards into Kent, Sussex and the

West. Maidstone was said to be "infested with radicals", and Rye had been the scene of violent anti-Tory disturbances in April and May. Cobbett lectured at Maidstone and Battle at the height of the rural riots in October; and, in November, a former "new" policeman was arrested at Battle, charged with wearing a cap with tricoloured ribbons and with saying that "if they were of his mind, there would be a revolution here". Horsham, in Sussex, was another "hot-bed of sedition". Radical handbills had been distributed there before the labourers entered the town in November, and a public meeting to demand Reform and a lowering of tithes and taxes was billed to take place there a few days later.[15]

The Wellington Ministry resigned in November 1830; the elections that followed were attended, in various towns, by clashes between Tories and reformers. Soon after, the Reform Bill was drafted, and congratulatory messages came in from county meetings all over the country. But after a successful second reading in the Commons, the Bill was defeated in committee, and Parliament was dissolved at the end of April. The general election was accompanied by another round of riots: incidents were reported from Wigan, Boston, Banbury, Rye, Horsham and Whitehaven, in Cumberland. At Boston, the tricolour was unfurled, and the mayor of Rye wrote of "scenes of revolutionary terror".[16]

But far worse was to come when the Lords rejected Grey's second Bill on 8 October. That evening riots broke out at Derby, and at Nottingham two days later. At Derby, the City gaol was attacked and prisoners were released; rioters marching on the County gaol were shot down by troops; several were killed and wounded; but there were no arrests even after the promise of a pardon and rewards of £50 and £100. At Nottingham, following a Reform meeting in the Market Square, the Castle, the property of the Duke of Newcastle, was burned down and Colwick Hall (the seat of John Musters) was broken into, ransacked and fired. On the second day, William Lowe's silk mill at Beeston was demolished, Lord Middleton's estate of Woollaton Park was attacked, and the mayor ordered victuallers and publicans to close their doors and imposed a general curfew. Seventy one persons, including lace-workers and framework knitters, were committed, of whom twenty-four were brought to trial, nine of them being sentenced to death.[17] One of the prisoners, Thomas Smith, a framesmith, who owned his shop in Prospect Place, at Radford, gave the court an eyewitness account of what took place:

I was at work [he said] at that shop last Monday but one (the day the meeting was held in Nottingham Market) from 7 o'clock till between 10 and ½ past in the morning.

Some papers came round on Sunday with Bills for all people to go to the meeting, I did not see one, but I heard talk of them & somebody told me what was in them, and it was agreed for all the people at Prospect Place to go to the meeting and take a flag with them. It was a white lace flag trimmed with black crape and with black bunches . . . there was a flag in the Mob with the words "The Bill and no Lords" on it . . . I left Prospect Place on the Monday morning a little before 11 to come to the Meeting and the whole inhabitants of Prospect Place came along with me. The flag was with us. We came direct to the Market Place and then we stood and heard what the speakers said. I stopped till the Meeting was over, and then I went home and got my dinner and went to work at my own shop . . . I went to work between 1 and 2 and worked till a little after 5. Several of the Prospect Place people had then got together about having had their flag taken from them, and I went to them; they stood out of doors. I stopped about quarter of an hour with them and then went to Mr. Bird's at Prospect Place and stopped there about 5 or 10 minutes. From there I went to the Tom and Jerry public house, the sign of the Pheasant, at Prospect Place and got half a pint of ale . . . As I came out there I met with 4 men . . . and they told me the Mob had pulled a Mill down in the Forest and the soldiers had been there; and they said they were going to see and asked if I would go with them. I agreed to go and we all 5 of us went to the Forest . . . It was then about 6 o'clock. We all came away together to go and look at the windows the Mob had broken . . . and then we went into the Plough and Harrow . . . and drank ½ a pint of ale each . . . and then we came out and went down Clumber Street, and just as we got to the bottom of Clumber Street we saw a man come upon the full gallop to the Police Office for the soldiers, and the people said Colwick Hall was on fire and the Mob was pulling it down. And when we three walked up and down the streets for some time and then we all went into Clarke's at the Bell . . . We had drunk 2 pints and were on with the third when the news came in that the Castle was on fire. We immediately drunk up our ale and went to look at it . . . We were about 50 or 60 yards from the place where the wall was pulled down to get in the Castle yard; we were never nearer than that . . . We were there about ½ an hour and then we all 3 went home together . . . It was about half past 9 when we got home . . . I went in and went to bed and never was out till 7 the next morning; nobody was in my house with me but my wife and four small children . . . When I got up on the next morning Tuesday I went to work about 7 o'clock and worked till near 9 o'clock, and then I went to my breakfast . . . and then back to my shop and worked till nearly one . . . I got my dinner and then started to come up to New Radford . . . As soon as I got into the close against Old Radford Church I saw a fir-coloured flag on Mr. Foot's factory . . . and met a man named Joseph Bostock . . . Bostock said to me Beester Mill is on fire; would I go and look at it? . . . I saw the smoke and then I and Bostock started to go; and when I got to Mr. George Harrison, the miller of Radford, I saw him with his uncle in the yard and Mr. Harrison gave me a paper . . . and told me he wanted me to show the Mob that paper as he understood they meant to pay him a visit; the paper was to say that Mr. Harrison did not sign the anti-Reform Petition . . . We went down to Lenton on the road Beeston Mill. When we got to Lenton the Mob was there. I then went on the bridge against Lord Middleton's Lodge and I read Mr. Harrison's paper there; and then went on again towards Beeston . . . I read the paper again . . . and when I got near to Lord Middleton's gates at Beeston Lane End, I saw a cavalry man that I knew . . . and then I went on to the said gates . . . and then I went on in company with Bostock to Beeston Mill to look at it and stopped looking at it with him about a quarter of an hour or more, and then came away and as I was coming away with Bostock I met 3 men . . . and they asked me if I would go back with them to look at the Mill, and I agreed to go back with them and left Bostock . . . After we had looked at the Mill we

went and had some ale and tobacco at the Dog in Beeston and then we came home; but
I went to Mr. Harrison's and got some beef and ale, and then went home and went to
bed[18]

Other disturbances followed. At Chatham, in Kent, 4,000 people
attended a Reform meeting on 12 October; at Coventry, handbills were
given out attacking the Bishops, who had shown themselves the most
bitter enemies of Reform; there were minor skirmishes in Leicester and
Loughborough and more considerable riots at Tiverton and Yeovil, in
Somerset, and Blandford and Sherborne, in Dorset.[19]

But by far the biggest outbreak came at Bristol on 29 October. Rioters
held the streets for three days and did almost as much damage as the
Gordon rioters in London fifty years before. Converging on Queen
Square in the centre of the town, they demolished the Mansion House,
Lawford's Gate, the Bishop's Palace, Canons' Marsh, the Customs
House, the Excise House, and toll-houses all over the city; they broke
into the Bridewell, the Gloucester County Prison and New Gaol and
released prisoners; and destroyed forty-two offices, warehouses and
dwellings. A dozen rioters were killed, nearly 100 were wounded, and
180 persons were committed to prison, fifty on capital charges. Of 129
prisoners brought to trial, 4 were hanged, 37 were jailed and 54 were
transported to Australia.[20] It was the last great urban riot in British
history.

Bristol was followed by something of an anti-climax. There was an
attempt made at Bath to stop the Yeomanry from going to Bristol;
crowds assembled at Worcester; there were rumours or fears of riots at
Wells and Chard, at Bognor, Salisbury, Exeter, Chelmsford and
Blackburn; but they came to nothing. The Political Unions of
Bridgewater and Chard appealed for peace and quiet and a "respect for
private property". Even the National Union of the Working Classes
agreed (though reluctantly) to call off a mass rally planned to take place
in London on 7 November.[21]

Yet it needed another six months of party negotiations, parliamentary
"lobbying" and public agitation before William IV, and subsequently
the Lords, accepted the Reform Bill and allowed it to become law. What
happened in between? At first, after Bristol, there was a lull; but when,
after winning another general election, the Whigs were once more
defeated in the Lords, Grey resigned in May and the king invited the
Duke of Wellington, the bitter old enemy of Reform, to form a Ministry.
As Wellington looked round for supporters, the agitation, led by the
Political Unions in Birmingham and London, broke out afresh. Bells
were rung in churches, protesting petitions poured into Westminster,
the king was besieged in his coach, there were calls for a taxpayers strike

and a run on the banks ("To stop the Duke, go for Gold!"); in London and Birmingham, there was talk of barricades and pikes; there was a riot in York (but nowhere else) and Francis Place, to underline the gravity of the crisis, wrote to his friend and fellow-conspirator, John Cam Hobhouse: "If the Duke comes into power, we shall be unable longer to 'hold to the laws'—break them we must, be the consequences whatever they may, we know that all must join us, to save their property, no matter what may be their private opinions. Towns will be barricaded—new municipal arrangements will be formed by the inhabitants, and the first town which is barricaded shuts up all banks."[22]

Three days later, the opposition to reform collapsed, Wellington gave up the attempt to form a Ministry, and Grey was back in office. The Whigs' Bill, with minor amendments, passed through the Commons and, after the king had agreed to coerce the Lords by threatening to create a number of reforming peers, through the Upper House as well. So the compromise solution of the aristocratic Whigs and middle-class Radicals—to enfranchise the £10 householder and to disfranchise the more "rotten" of the "rotten" boroughs—became law, and all further opposition by the Bill's opponents, whether by anti-Reform Lords or working-class Radicals, virtually ceased.

So there was no revolution in 1832, as there had been none in 1831. But was it because Wellington saw the red light and yielded to the Radicals' threats? Was it for some other reason? Or was the threat a bluff, and was there never any real danger of revolution at all? Some historians—G.M. Trevelyan and J.R.M. Butler in particular—have taken Francis Place and the Philosophical Radicals at their word and have believed, or assumed, that had it not been for Wellington's timely surrender, England would have been plunged into revolution on behalf of Reform.[23] Others have taken a longer view and attributed the Englishman's failure to engage in revolution, not only in 1832 or 1831 but over the whole period from 1815 to 1848, to some particular element in the English way of life, such as practical common sense or the restraining influence of religion. Elie Halévy, for example, has insisted that "the *élite* of the working class, the hard-working and capable bourgeois, had been imbued by the evangelical movement with a spirit from which the established order had nothing to fear".[24]

Of course, it is quite impossible to demonstrate to everyone's satisfaction whether such a view is justified or is quite erroneous. All we know for certain is that many people believed, at some point in 1831 or 1832 (as they believed again in the 1840s), that a revolution was near at hand, and that in fact such a revolution never came about. And to me, at least, the explanations given by Halévy or Trevelyan and Butler for this non-occurrence are superficial and unconvincing. The view that it was

Wellington's surrender to the Political Unions that averted a revolution is based on the assumption that there was in England at this time a revolutionary situation and that it needed but a spark to set it off. Equally, the suggestion that England was saved from revolution by the restraining hand of Methodism or Non-Conformity (even if it can be shown that the English were as deeply imbued with the evangelical spirit as Halévy and others have claimed[25]) attributes to this single factor of religion an altogether exaggerated role. Above all, these historians appear to believe that a revolution can be switched on, or can spontaneously erupt, almost regardless of the social and political realities of the day.

For the important questions that need to be asked are: was there in those years at any time a combination of factors that made for a "revolutionary situation"? Is it conceivable that the various movements that have been described could, either singly or in unison, have provoked a revolutionary explosion? If so, what sort of revolution, and on whose behalf would it have been carried through? It may perhaps be instructive here to draw a comparison between England and France.

In France, there was widespread dissatisfaction with the government of Charles X and his Ministers in 1830 and, in July, there took place that convergence of material and political factors that made for a revolutionary situation. The French middle classes—all but the most wealthy and those connected with the aristocracy and the Court—were being progressively robbed of the benefits of the Charter, adopted by Louis XVIII after Napoleon's abdication, which had guaranteed a large part of the social gains and liberties of 1789. Lands forfeited during the Revolution were being returned to émigré nobles, new privileges were being given to the Church and, as a final provocation, Polignac's Five Ordinances of St. Cloud muzzled the press, dissolved the Chamber and further restricted the already narrowly limited right to vote. So, behind the confusion of contending party interests, the central political issue was clear: to defeat the "feudal reaction" and restore, or to enlarge, the liberties conceded in the Charter.

Moreover, the mass of the people—particularly the workers in the towns and in industry—were hungry and discontented; there had been two successive harvest failures, and the price of bread had, in 1829, risen to an unprecedented height. Yet socialist ideas were in their infancy and played no part in the event, any more than the radical clubs which sprang up in the following months; so the workers, not being strong enough to voice a political programme of their own, enrolled under the banners and slogans of the liberal bourgeoisie. So the shock-troops of rebellion were ready to hand, armed with a clear purpose and with a common cause to fight for.

Meanwhile the government, deserted by even its own pensioners and allies, was in a state of crisis. Having sought to temporise under Villêle, it now tried "the heavy hand" under Polignac. Neither course worked, and the army, once it came to a showdown, could no more be relied upon than the bourgeois National Guard which it had disbanded (while leaving them their arms) in 1827. So, in July 1830, France found itself faced with Lenin's four prerequisites for a revolutionary situation: widespread hardship and dissatisfaction, embracing both middle and lower classes; unwillingness of the people and inability of its rulers to carry on in the old way; and an alternative focus of leadership willing and able to replace the old, to seize power and to create a new system of government.[26]

What was the situation in Britain in 1830 to 1832? There was certainly dissatisfaction among the lower classes. We have observed the conflicts in the manufacturing districts and the desperate revolt of the labourers in the southern and Midlands counties. In Ireland, a rebellion was developing in which peasants, urban poor and middle-class nationalists made common cause against alien British rule. In England, there was an economic crisis in 1829–30 and the price of bread, as we have noted, was exceptionally high throughout 1830 and the greater part of 1831. Middle-class and working-class Radicals worked side by side, against aristocrats and Tories, for parliamentary Reform; there was considerable class hostility against the privileges and sinecures of Lords and Bishops; and the Political Unions, in particular, were able, over a period of months, to harness the various discontents in cities and country towns against the common enemy in the Commons and the House of Lords. In some cities, the Unions commanded a large measure of common allegiance; they had the power to arouse a "great hope" (without which no revolution is possible): the hope of filling empty bellies and of redressing manifold grievances by a reform of Parliament; and they had the power to inspire, even if they did not deliberately provoke, great urban riots in the old chartered cities of Nottingham, Derby and Bristol.

And so, it is probably no exaggeration to say with Cole and Postgate that England stood *nearer* to revolution at this time than at any other time since 1688, even nearer than she stood at the height of the Chartist movement in the 1840s. Yet, even so, it does not appear that, as in France, these explosive ingredients were sufficient to make for a revolutionary situation. It is always easy to be wise after the event; but the missing ingredients should be evident to any serious student of revolutions. Perhaps the workers on the farms and in the factories and towns *were* united enough and angry enough (the "restraining hand" of Methodism notwithstanding!) to have made a revolution if they had been called upon to do so and if the political crisis of October 1831 or May 1832 had been even more acute. Yet it is doubtful, as (if we except the Reform movement) the protest movements of 1830–31 ran separate courses, were conducted for different ends, were engaged in by different sorts of people, and were separated in both time and place. There was, it is true, a certain overlap between the activities of the rebellious country labourers, the striking handloom weavers and the rioting townsmen; but these were marginal, as was the impact of political ideas on the labourers and weavers.[27] And the Irish rebellion, for all its intensity and violence, found little echo in England and could be safely swept, after a moment's consternation at Westminster, under the political mat.

Even more important, the English middle classes were in no such situation as the French: for them the basic "principles of 1789" had been fought for, and largely won, in earlier battles. They were, it is true, concerned about parliamentary representation and the government of towns; they were opposed to landlords and clergy over rents and tithes; they had become converted to Free Trade; they resented the privileges and pretensions of Lords and Bishops. In brief, they wanted the vote, more efficient and cheaper government, and a reduction in tithes, rents and taxes. But they wanted reform for themselves and not for the urban and industrial workers; and, with few exceptions, they gave little support to the more extreme Radical demand for Manhood Suffrage. Nor were they willing to press their own demands to the point of summoning the "lower orders", like their counterparts in France, to man the barricades and overthrow the existing rulers; and they were all the more loth to do this as the English workers had already begun (as the French would do at Lyons in 1831) to form their own industrial and political organizations to promote their own particular claims.

If this analysis is correct, the outbreak at Bristol may be seen as a danger signal not only to the aristocratic opponents of Reform but to the middle-class radicals and reformers as well. It is certainly a remarkable fact that, during the six months separating the Bristol riots from the ultimate crisis in May 1832, there was no further significant disturbance (except the single incident at York), no further public agitation in the streets. If Francis Place and his friends had seriously intended to prepare for a revolution, would they so ostentatiously have cold-shouldered the National Union of the Working Classes in London, discouraged public demonstrations, and privately expressed their fears of what a "revolution" might bring in its train?[28] In fact they appear to have quite deliberately accepted a compromise Reform Bill rather than attempt to drive a harder bargain with the active support of the urban workers.

Moreover, there was at no time a real crisis of government or of ruling circles as there was in France. The Irish troubles, like the labourers' revolt, took place far from the seat of government and caused hardly a ripple of political excitement at Westminster. The industrial strikes and the October city riots caused the authorities considerable alarm, but they were easily settled with the deployment of a few companies of troops; and, these, unlike the army in France, remained steadfastly loyal. Even in May 1832, when the country was for a few days without an officially sworn Ministry as Wellington cast around for supporters, there was no real crisis of authority, no desertion of the ranks among the governors,[29] and there is little doubt that the old rulers could, with minor adjustments in personnel, continue to govern "in the old way". This is not to say that the Reform Bill was of no importance, but it was a compromise solution which, by giving the middle classes the vote and the prospect of an eventual share in government, at most speeded the pace of normal constitutional development.

In short, there was no revolution in 1832 not so much because the Tories or the Lords surrendered to the threats of Whigs or Radicals, as because nobody of importance wanted one and because that combination of political and material factors that alone would have made one possible was conspicuously lacking.

By 1848, certain of these factors had matured. Since the late 1830s, there had been three periods of recession when food had been scarce and prices high: in 1838, 1842, and 1846–47; and the whole period 1838–45, in particular (with a high point in 1842), had been one of considerable hardship for the workers, above all for the chronically depressed handloom weavers; but also for factory workers, miners, potters and the craftsmen in the cities. After the destruction and collapse of the great "National" unions in 1834, trade union organization had been built again, on a more solid basis, in the "sacred months" and "turn-outs" of 1839 and 1842. In the campaign for the People's Charter, launched in 1838, there appeared for the first time in England an independent political movement of the working class and the rudiments of a workers' political party in the National Charter Association. So the workers were moving forward from the stage of the sporadic outbursts of the "pre-industrial" period, as typified by Luddite outbreaks against machinery and the labourers' revolt of 1830, to a higher stage of industrial and political organization in which they put forward a clear-cut programme of their own. Moreover, their determination to achieve a radical reform of Parliament was infinitely greater and more widespread than it had been in 1830 or 1832.

But, equally, the demand for a People's Parliament—that is, a Parliament largely composed of working-class Members controlled by working-class voters—was a far more radical challenge to the established order than that made by the Reform Bill in 1831; and, in the social and political context of the times, it could only have been achieved by means of a revolution. But who would carry such a revolution through? Evidently, not the workers alone: the whole history of Chartism (and this is hardly surprising) emphatically reveals that they were quite unprepared to do so. It could, in fact, only be accomplished with the aid of a substantial part of the middle class. And such aid was far less easy to come by than it had been in the crisis of 1830. The reasons are not hard to find. In the intervening years, the middle class had won the vote, a substantial share in local government, the New Poor Law (with its saving on the rates), the payment of tithe in cash, the first State aid for education, a series of Free-Trade budgets, a new field of investment in the railways, and, in 1846, the repeal of the hated Corn Laws. And it is highly significant that the last of these was won, almost deliberately, with the minimum of Chartist or working-class support. For, during these years, the cleavage between capital and labour had become markedly greater, and it had become evident to even the most radical of the middle-class reformers that to toy with revolution or to stoke up rebellion in city streets or in manufacturing districts might have far more serious social consequences in the 1840s than a dozen years before.

In consequence, to win their Charter, the organized workers would have had to rely almost entirely on their own resources; and these, even in 1842, the year of the second and sharpest Chartist challenge, were quite inadequate to do the job. After this, the movement lost momentum; its leaders were divided and supporters fell away; and the last great Chartist rally, that of April 1848, was something of an anti-climax, artificially stimulated by political events in Europe rather than by the situation within Britain itself. Besides, "better times" appeared to be on the way; the crisis of 1846–7 was all but over; the first instalment of the Ten-Hour Day had been won; and factory reform, scarcely begun in 1830, was, temporarily at least, blunting the sharp edge of the industrial conflict.

So perhaps the question "Why no revolution in *1848?*" as an addendum to the title of this paper can be so easily disposed of as to seem hardly worth the asking!

Notes

1. Quoted by W.H. Maehl (ed.) *The Reform Bill of 1832. Why not Revolution?* (European Problem Studies, New York, 1967), p. 1.
2. F. Engels, *The Condition of the Working Class in England* (London, 1920).
3. Quoted by F.C. Mather, *Public Order in the Age of the Chartists* (Manchester, 1959), p. 1.
4. Ibid., p. 163.

5. W.W. Rostow, *British Economy of the Nineteenth Century* (Oxford, 1948), p, 124; G.M. Young, *Victorian England, Portrait of an Age* (London, 1961), p. 27; (for Trevelyan) Maehl, *The Reform Bill of 1832*, p. 2; G.D.H. Cole and R. Postgate, *The Common People 1746–1938* (London, 1945), p. 248.

6. J.L. & B. Hammond, *The Village Labourer* (London, 1911).

7. For a fuller account, see E.J. Hobsbawm and G. Rudé, *Captain Swing* (London, 1969).

8. For Birmingham during this period, see A. Briggs, "Thomas Attwood and the Economic Background of the Birmingham Political Union", *Cambridge Historical Journal,* 11, 2 (1947), pp. 190–216.

9. For details, see G. Rudé, "English Rural and Urban Disturbances on the Eve of the First Reform Bill, 1830–1831", in the present collection.

10. *Gentleman's Magazine*, vols. 50 and 51 (1830–31), passim.

11. Ibid., 50, p. 171. See also N. Gash, "English Reform and French Revolution in the General Election of 1830", in *Essays presented to Sir Lewis Namier,* eds R. Pares and A.J.P. Taylor (London, 1956), pp. 258–88.

12. A. Briggs, "Thomas Attwood", p. 190.

13. Public Record Office, Home Office 52/8, 52/11, 52/12, 52/13; A. Briggs, "The Background of the Parliamentary Reform Movement in Three English Cities (1830–32)", *Cambridge Historical Journal,* 10, (1952), pp. 293–317.

14. *Gentleman's Magazine,* 50, 2, pp. 559–60; E, Halévy, *The Triumph of Reform 1830–1841* (London, 1950), pp. 11–12, 44–5.

15. P.R.O., Treasury Solicitor's Papers, 11/4051.

16. *The Times*, 20 Nov. 1830; *Gentleman's Magazine,* 51, 1, pp. 179, 362; H.O. 52/8, 9, 12, 14, 15.

17. *Gentleman's Magazine,* 51, 21, p. 363; H.O. 52/12, 15; Treas. Sol. Papers, 11/1116/5736.

18. T.S. 11/1116/5736.

19. H.O. 52/12, 13, 15.

20. *Bristol Mercury,* 1 Nov. 1831; H.O. 27/43, 40/28, 52/12; T.S. 11/405/1250.

21. *Gentleman's Magazine,* 51, 2, p. 460; H.O. 52/12, 13, 15.

22. For these events, see Halévy, *The Triumph of Reform 1830–1841*, pp. 47–59; A. Briggs, *The Age of Improvement* (London, 1959), pp. 242–8; *Life and Struggles of William Lovett,* 2 vols. (London, 1920), I, pp. 77–9; G. Wallas, *The Life of Francis Place 1771–1854* (London, 1918), pp. 278, 289–323; J.R.M. Butler, *The Passing of the Great Reform Bill* (London, 1914), pp. 377–426 (esp. pp. 410–11; quoted by Maehl, *The Reform Bill of 1832*, p. 72).

23. Maehl, ibid., pp. 2, 71–6.

24. Ibid., p. 87.

25. For views opposed to Halévy's on this point, see E.J. Hobsbawm, *Labouring Men* (London, 1964), Chapter 3; K.S. Inglis, *Churches and the Working Classes in Victorian England* (London, 1963, esp. Chapter 1); and (with some reservations) E.P. Thompson, *The Making of the English Working Class* (London, 1963), Chapter 11.

26. M. Girard, "Etude comparée des mouvements révolutionnaires en France en 1830, 1848 et 1870–71" (Les Cours de Sorbonne, Paris, n.d.), esp. pp. 48–59, 69, 71–2; D.H. Pinkney, "The Crowd in the French Revolution of 1830", *American Historical Review,* (Oct. 1964), pp. 1–17. See also S. Charlety, *La Restauration (1815–1830)* (vol. 4 of E. Lavisse, ed., *Histoire de France contemporaine depuis la Révolution jusqu'à la paix de 1919,* [Paris, 1921]), pp. 329–93.

27. See G. Rudé, "English Rural and Urban Disturbances . . . 1830–1831".

28. G. Wallas, *The Life of Francis Place*, pp. 279–323.
29. See E.L. Woodward, *The Age of Reform 1815–1870* (London, 1941), pp. 82 bis 83.

Part II
Popular Protest and Ideology

10

English Rural and Urban Disturbances on the Eve of the First Reform Bill, 1830–1831

Historians have noted the revolutionary potentialities of the disturbances that broke out in English towns and country districts between 1830 and 1832. They mark the high point in Professor Rostow's "social tension chart" of 1790 to 1850; G.M. Young writes of these years being of "a sustained intensity of excitement unknown since 1641"; and Cole and Postgate state even more emphatically that "never since 1688 had Great Britain been so near actual revolution as in 1831; never in all troubles of the next two decades was she to come so near to it again".[1]

Broadly speaking, all the disturbances of the time had a common origin in the social transformation that had been taking place in English towns and villages since the American war—or more particularly since the end of the wars with France. Whatever the Industrial Revolution did for the standard of living, it certainly left a trail of grievances and nostalgic yearnings. For every person who saw an endless vista of rising profits, "utility" and "improvement", there must have been ten who saw the change as a mixed blessing, regretted the shattering of old values, or looked to the future with gloom and foreboding. For some, the French wars brought a temporary reprieve: farmers and handloom weavers, for example, knew prosperity and even the village labourers' earnings were protected. But, with the end of the war, the bubble burst: corn prices fell, land went out of cultivation, farmers' profits shrank, labourers were thrown on poor relief; even the landlords, temporarily at least, shared in the general agricultural crisis. The village became a battleground of conflicting interests in which the farmer, ranged against the landlord over rent and the parson over tithe, took it out on the labourer by reducing his wages or turning him over to the overseer. In the manufacturing districts, the wages of domestic and handloom workers, which had been buttressed by the war, entered on a new and disastrous downward spiral, while factory workers' wages were depressed by the progressive reduction of piece rates and the massive influx of Irish poor. Even the manufacturer saw his prospects of a rosy future blighted by Corn Laws, trade restrictions, the squalor, ill-health and misgovernment of the boroughs and expanding cities, and the obstructions of the old unreformed and landlord-dominated Parliament at Westminster. So he took to Free Trade and Radical Reform. And such, broadly, had been the situation for the past fifteen years.

But to these longer-term grievances and tensions we must add two more immediate "precipitating" factors. One was the high price of corn: for twenty-one consecutive months from January 1830, the quarter of wheat in the London Corn Exchange never fell below 70s. (its average over the previous seventeen years had been 59s., [and, curiously, this was the figure to which it fell just a week before the Bristol riots]).[2] The other was the outbreak of revolution in France and Belgium in the summer of 1830, which brought new colourful banners and slogans to the English Reform movement.

So there were considerable and varied discontents in England in 1830. But we must not assume from this that these discontents were of equal political significance, nor that the movements that gave them expression were necessarily closely related, or presented an equal danger to the existing order. It will be the purpose of this chapter to discuss the nature of these movements and how and why they contributed, or failed to contribute, to a potentially revolutionary situation.

Broadly, they are of three distinctive types—distinctive not only as to their immediate causes and the issues that they raised, but distinctive also as to their forms of action, their aims and ideology, their geographical location, the nature of their participants, their period of maximum concentration, and their consequences or measurable results. First, there was the agricultural labourers' movement, largely centred in the southern counties and mainly confined to the autumn of 1830. Secondly, there was the movement of industrial workers in the manufacturing districts of the Midlands, the North and the West, which began in 1830 but did not reach its high point until 1834. And, thirdly, there was the political Reform movement, based on the cities and boroughs, also starting in 1830 and attaining its climax, before the passage of the First Reform Bill, at the end of 1831.

Of course, if we were to look beyond England, we should add a fourth movement which, by its intensity and violence, eclipsed all others. I refer to the contemporary rebellion in Ireland which was variously compounded of Daniel O'Connell's political movement to dissolve the Union, the food riots in Limerick and Roscommon, and the land-hunger and tithe war in the south and the west, which, in turn, was attended by the nightly assaults and depredations of Whiteboys and Ribbonmen and the elusive followers of Captain Rock. But this falls outside my present subject; not only because I am solely concerned with England, but also because it is at least doubtful if the Irish movement, for all its scope and violence, made any appreciable impression on the English.

To begin with the English labourers of 1830. Their movement, described by the Hammonds as "the last peasants' revolt",[3] had its origins in the depression and rural distress following the Napoleonic wars. The labourer, as the principal victim in the three-cornered struggle between farmer, squire and parson, had his wages reduced or his allowance cut when he was thrown on the parish. It was not so much (as *The Times*, Gibbon Wakefield and several historians have argued) that the labourer resented the degradation of being paid from the rates. If the parish had paid him a living wage, he might have cheerfully stomached the insult. But the point is that it had become customary to stand him down in the winter months and leave him to subsist on a reduced allowance. Moreover, threshing machines had recently been introduced to displace his labour in districts where they had not been in use before—notably, in 1830, around Canterbury in Kent.

So the movement started in Kent, a county of relatively high wages, in the summer of 1830—at first with arson and threatening letters, but gradually developing into wages riots and a general assault on threshing machines. By early November, it had spread into the Sussex Weald; and from there it continued westwards, by a "contagious" process, into West Sussex, Hampshire, Wiltshire, Gloucester, Worcester, Dorset, Devon and Cornwall; its furthest western outposts were Hereford and Monmouthshire, where farmers' properties were threatened (though not destroyed). Meanwhile, a new focus of disturbance had appeared in Berkshire, whence it travelled eastwards and northwards into Oxfordshire, Buckingham, Bedford, Huntingdon and Northampton. A third wave started, late in November, in the north-east corner of Norfolk and travelled south through Suffolk and Essex; then up through Cambridgeshire, Leicester and Lincoln, touching the Yorkshire Ridings and leaving its mark as far north as Carlisle. It was virtually all over by December 1830; but there were renewed outbreaks in Kent and Norfolk in 1831, and there was a last isolated incident of threshing-machine breaking in a Cambridgeshire village in September 1832.

In several counties—and notably in Wiltshire, Hampshire, Gloucester, and in parts of Dorset, Kent and Norfolk—the distinctive hall-mark of the labourers' movement was the breaking of agricultural machinery, and in some districts, machine-breaking was extended to the foundries and workshops where the machines were manufactured: such was the case at Andover, Hungerford, Fordingbridge and Wantage; and, at High Wycombe, the main activity was the destruction of the machinery in the paper mills. But it assumed other forms as well: the dispatch of threatening letters (often signed "Swing"); wages movements; forced collections of money; assaults on overseers and parsons; tithe riots; attacks on workhouses. There were a handful of enclosure riots: two in Oxfordshire and one in the Forest of Dean; there were a couple of food riots (both in Cornwall); and in every one of the twenty-five and more counties affected—but principally on the Kent-Surrey border, in West Norfolk, Cambridgeshire, Hertfordshire and Lincoln—there was rick-burning and the firing of farms, barns and country mansions. In short, the methods used were the traditional "direct-action" methods of "pre-industrial" England.

The rioters were overwhelmingly country labourers, but there was a leavening of village craftsmen (about one in seven of all those among the 2,000 arrested whose occupations are given), and even occasional small-holders and farmers—though these more often incited the labourers against parsons or landlords while playing no further active part. Their ideology, too, was that of the old English village: the insistence on a "fair wage" and a "just price" against the new-fangled notions of the "open market" and competitive bargaining between workers and employers. To them it seemed common justice to destroy machines that threatened their livelihood, and at times they invoked the authority of justices, farmers, the king, or even God himself, for acting as they did. They clung stubbornly to the ancient rights and traditions of the village, and one Norfolk Chairman of Quarter Sessions felt compelled to warn his prisoners that "it is a mistaken dream that a third of the tithe belongs to the church, a third to the poor and a third to the rector".[4]

And the consequences of the riots? First, there was the solemn act of retributive justice, whereby nineteen men were hanged (all but three of them for arson), 644 were jailed, and 481 (including two women) were transported to Hobart and Sydney. There was a short-lived increase in wages and allowances, which reverted to "normal" once the panic was over; in some districts, the broken threshing machines were not replaced; and it may be that in the old "Speenhamland" counties, at least, the new "Bastilles" of 1834 did something to raise earnings: they had at least the merit of drawing a clear distinction between wages and parish "hand-outs". But the political effects were virtually nil. At most, there were a few tears shed for the labourers in high places; there was a number of heated exchanges between the Government and Radical M.P.s in Parliament; and the bulk of the transported rioters were granted the cold comfort of a Free Pardon after five years in Australia. But the incident was soon forgotten; and it could, like the plight of the

Irish peasants, be conveniently swept, after a decent interval, under the political carpet.

I come next to the movements in the industrial and manufacturing districts. They had their more recent origins in the trade depression and unemployment of 1829–30; but they were given a particular stimulus by such factors as reductions in piece-rates, the use of new machinery, the growth of trade unions and the agitation of Owenites and Radicals.

I say "movements" because it is necessary, I believe, to draw a broad line of distinction between those engaged in by factory workers; by craftsmen of traditional craft centres such as London and Birmingham; by handloom weavers, framework knitters and the like; and by such intermediate groups as miners, iron and pottery workers. Of these, the old craftsmen alone were comparatively little touched, during these years, by economic or wage issues, though they were more likely than others to respond to the political-Reform arguments of leaders like Francis Place in London and Thomas Attwood in Birmingham.

The factory workers, particularly the spinners around Manchester and Blackburn, were more susceptible to Owenite ideas and more inclined than others to enrol under the trade union banner of John Doherty. Doherty's National Association for the Protection of the Working Classes was founded in June 1830. Every trade society was invited to join; and Doherty extended his operations beyond the spinners, who formed the initial and permanent core of his society, to obtain a more precarious hold on Yorkshire powerloom weavers, Midlands hosiery and lace workers, Staffordshire potters and miners from the Yorkshire, Lancashire, Midland and Welsh coalfields; by 1831, he could claim a combined membership of 100,000.[5] The aims of the Association were forward-looking: to protect labour and improve wages in the new developing industrial society. The leaders, being Owenites, tended to indulge in the millenarian fantasy of rapidly transforming society into a cooperative commonwealth through labour and combination; but they looked to the future and theirs (to adapt Edward Thompson's phrase[6]) was a "chiliasm of hope", not of despair; and they believed in peaceful agitation and generally (though not always) abjured the old methods of violent assault on machinery or property.

Yet the spread of Doherty's movement in the manufacturing districts alarmed the authorities; and, in the summer of 1830, troops were sent as a first priority into the Manchester area. On 24 August, the officer in charge of the Manchester force warned his commanding officer of a pending "turn-out" of the spinners at Hyde, Stalybridge and Ashton-under-Lyne in protest against a reduction in piece-rates. He was impressed by the workers' unity and militancy and added anxiously that

"The excitement caused by the Revolution in France is greater than I should have anticipated: they talk a great deal of their power of putting down the military & constables."

His senior, in turn, in forwarding the report to Peel, expressed concern at "the power of the leaders of the working classes". In October, further alarm was expressed at the "serious danger" of a general combination of colliers and spinners under Doherty's direction in Lancashire.[7] In early November, copies of the National Association's Address were being distributed in Leicester, where Doherty was billed, six weeks later, to speak at a general meeting of trades.[8] Two weeks before, he had addressed a gathering of 15-20,000 spinners at Duckinfield, near Manchester. The workers arrived in procession, "headed [runs a report] by bands of music & carrying tricoloured flags before them"—a fact that so much alarmed "respectable persons" that they thought it wiser not to enrol as "specials".[9] But some employers, at least, were grateful that the new methods of agitation were not the same as the old. None more so than the woollen merchants and manufacturers of Bradford and Huddersfield, who had been among the principal victims of the "Luddite" outbreaks of 1812 and 1826; and who, in meeting at Bradford in December 1830, were able to report that, during the past month, there had only been one single threat to damage property or machinery.[10]

Yet the old "Luddite" methods of bargaining still lingered on in the coalfields, in the hosiery centres of the Midlands and among weavers in East Anglia and the West. In February and March 1830, there were miners' wages riots at Wynnstay in Wales and at Coalbrookdale in Shropshire. On 24 December, 1,000 pitmen assembled at the Waldridge colliery in Durham, "stopped the Engine necessarily kept going in order to pump out the Water, and then threw large Iron Tubs, Wooden Cisterns, Corves, and other Articles, down the Shaft." The next year, there were colliers' riots in Derbyshire and at Bilston, in Staffordshire; in Northumberland, the miners' conduct was said to be "outrageous"; and, in June, there were bloody riots of iron workers at Merthyr Tydvil, in Glamorgan, who, in striking for a regular wage and an end of "truck", disarmed the military sent to suppress them, and stormed and destroyed the manorial Court of Requests.[11]

The weavers and hosiery workers were even more liable to turn strike into riot. On 2 June 1830, unemployed stockingers attacked the workhouse at Hinckley, in Leicestershire. In August, weavers rioted at Kidderminster over piece-rates and broke the windows of a master tailor. Further energies were released by the agricultural labourers' example. During the disturbances in Norfolk, two silk mills were damaged by weavers at Norwich; while, in Wiltshire, clothing machinery was destroyed at Figheldean, a cloth manufactory at Wilton, a silk mill at Barford St. Martin, and a sacking manufactory at Fordingbridge across the Hampshire border. Sawmills were destroyed at Southampton (in this case by fire) and at Catton in Norfolk. Threats were made (though never carried out) to attack foundries at Salisbury, paper mills in Hertfordshire, and carpet-weaving machinery at Burton, in Northamptonshire, and the officer commanding the army in the West warned of the grim possibility of a general assault on the clothing mills of Westbury, Trowbridge, and Bradford-on-Avon in the manufacturing district of Wiltshire.[12]

In the wake of the labourers' movement, there was a cotton spinners' strike and riot at Glossop, in Derbyshire; needle-workers destroyed presses at Redditch, in Worcestershire; and in a "tumult" of stockingers at Loughborough, a master weaver's house was partially "pulled down". The hosiery workers, however, were not always violent in their methods, any more than they had been in the peaceful phase preceeding the great Luddite movement in Derby, Leicester and Nottingham in 1811–12; and, a week after the Loughborough riot, we read of a meeting of delegates of the two-needle framework knitters of the three hosiery counties at Nottingham, where they issued "a respectful appeal" to the employers to increase their wages.[13]

There was far less industrial rioting and machine-breaking in 1831; but two incidents are perhaps worth a mention. One was the four-weeks' strike at J. Heathcoat's lace factory at Tiverton, in Devon, which started with a peaceful claim for the restoration of the old rates of wages and developed into a "riotous assemblage" with attacks on property. The other was the destruction by weavers of Beck's steam factory at Coventry in November. It is of some interest—both because it is one of the last recorded examples of industrial "Luddism" in England; and because it resulted in the transportation to Australia of Thomas Burbury, described as a cattle doctor and the not unworthy ancestor of one of the leading citizens of present-day Tasmania.[14]

Equally spectacular, and certainly more fruitful, was the political Reform movement that was largely centred in the cities and reached its climax in the urban riots of 1831. It had a long history, having been successively nourished by eighteenth-century London Radicalism, the agitation of Wilkes and the Yorkshire freeholders, the Middlesex and Westminster elections, Hampden Clubs and a procession of Radical writers and agitators from Cartwright and Paine to Cobbett and Francis Place; Its most constant theme had been the need for a reform of Parliament—whether by more frequent elections, an extension of the suffrage, the abolition of sinecures and "pocket" boroughs, or the secret ballot; though it had also concerned itself with demands for lower taxes, reduced tithes and pensions, cuts in government expenditure, and an end to "Old Corruption" and to the privileges of city corporations. A Radical handbill of December 1830, entitled *Englishmen Read! A Letter to the King from the People of England,* which circulated in the northern counties, accompanied its call for a reform of Parliament with a general complaint that

> the whole of the laws passed within the last forty years, especially within the last twenty years, present one unbroken series of endeavours to enrich and to augment the power of the aristocracy, and to impoverish and depress the middle and labouring part of the people.[15]

The issues were to become more closely defined with the return of Lord Grey's Whig Ministry, pledged to reform, in November 1830 and by the presentation to Parliament, after intensive negotiation within Cabinet, of the first draft of the First Reform Bill in March 1831. But, even before that, it had received a fresh stimulus from the Paris revolution of July 1830; and, in August, enthusiastic meetings were being held to hail the French by reformers in London, Edinburgh, Liverpool, Birmingham and other cities.[16]

At this time, the centres of the Radical and Reform movement were Birmingham and London. The Birmingham Political Union, the parent of by far the most influential of the Reform associations that burgeoned on the eve of the Reform Bill, was founded (or, more accurately, revived) by Thomas Attwood in early 1830. Unions spread to other cities, and Home Office reports note their appearance at Worcester, Kidderminster, Evesham, Blackburn and Carlisle by late November, and at Aylesbury and High Wycombe a few weeks later. The Unions were designed to unite the middle and lower classes in combined action for parliamentary reform. To quote the Address of the Kidderminster Political Council on launching a Union in November 1830: "The objects are to unite the middle and the lower classes of the People and to obtain by every just, legal and constitutional and peaceful means, an effectual and Radical Reform in the Commons House of Parliament."

Leaders were predominantly middle class, but among the rank and file the balance between the classes varied widely: in country towns, workers might play a purely nominal role; at Birmingham, there was a fair balance between classes; at Bristol, there was considerable support from the craft unions; while in the manufacturing cities of the North, where the interests of workers and employers were harder to reconcile, it was complained that the Unions were "almost without exception composed of men of the lowest description".[17]

And it was centres like these that at first caused the authorities the greatest concern. Home Office reports describe great radical meetings at Middleton and Blackburn in October, and at Carlisle in October and December. At Blackburn, tricolour flags were carried together with banners inscribed "Unity is Strength" and "Liberty & Fraternity". At Carlisle (described as "the main centre of Radicalism"), hay-ricks were fired, threatening letters were received, and the Union was accused (quite unjustly) of planning to win reform by violence and by " a general rising of the working classes".[18]

But the real centre of the more extreme, or working-class, Radicalism was London. The National Union of the Working Classes, which made a class-appeal that the Political Unions lacked, had its headquarters at the Rotunda in Blackfriars Road; and here hundreds (or even thousands) came weekly to listen to the popular Radical orators of the day: Henry Hunt, William Cobbett and Richard Carlile. Tricolour flags were borne; and, in November, there was such tension and panic engendered by a proposed visit to the City of the Duke of Wellington, who was escorting the King to the Lord Mayor's Banquet, that the royal visit had to be cancelled.[19]

London Radicalism radiated outwards into Kent, Sussex and the West. Maidstone was said to be "infested with radicals", and Rye had been the scene of violent anti-Tory disturbances in April and May. Cobbett lectured at Maidstone and Battle at the height of the rural riots in October; and, in November, a former "new" policeman, Charles Inskipp, was arrested at Battle, charged with wearing a cap with tricoloured ribbons and displaying other French revolutionary trophies, and with saying that "if they were of his mind, there would be a revolution here".[20] Horsham was another "hot-bed of sedition". Radical handbills had been distributed there before the labourers entered the town in mid-November, and a public meeting to demand Reform and a lowering of tithes and taxes was billed to take place there a few days later.[21]

The Wellington Ministry resigned in November 1830, and the elections that followed were attended by clashes between Tories and reformers. We read of such incidents at Northampton and Banbury in November, and at Norwich and Preston in December. At Preston, where Henry Hunt was returned, the town was filled (a correspondent wrote) with "some hundreds of the very lowest dregs of the factories", carrying tricolour flags and banners inscribed with "Bread or Blood" and "Liberty or Death". "I hope [this correspondent added] the advocates of Universal Suffrage will take warning—if their System is adopted, none but the Hunts & Cobbetts of the Kingdom will be returned to Parliament".[22]

As the Reform Bill was being drafted, congratulatory messages came in from county meetings in Bedfordshire, Berkshire, Middlesex and Cornwall; and bonfires were lit and processions held all over Scotland. But after a successful reading in the Commons, the Bill was defeated in committee, and Parliament was dissolved at the end of April. The general election was accompanied by another round of riots. This time, incidents were reported from Wigan, Boston, Banbury, Rye, Horsham and Whitehaven, in Cumberland. At Boston, the tricolour was unfurled on the market place, and the mayor of Rye wrote of "scenes of revolutionary terror".[23]

But far worse was to come when the Lords rejected Grey's second Bill on 8 October. That evening riots broke out at Derby, and at Nottingham two days later. At Derby, the City gaol was attacked and prisoners were released; rioters marching on the County gaol were shot down by troops; several were killed and wounded; but there were no arrests even after the promise of a pardon and rewards of £50 and £100. At Nottingham, following a Reform meeting in the Market Square, the Castle, the property of the Duke of Newcastle, was burned down and Colwick Hall (the seat of John Musters) was broken into, ransacked and fired. On the second day, William Lowe's silk mill at Beeston was demolished, Lord Middleston's estate of Woollaton Park was attacked, and the mayor ordered victuallers and publicans to close their doors and imposed a general curfew. Seventy-one persons, including lace-workers and framework knitters, were committed, of whom twenty-four were brought to trial. At Chatham, in Kent, 4,000 people attended a Reform meeting on 12 October; handbills against bishops, the main opponents of Reform, were distributed at Coventry; there were minor disturbances at Leicester and Loughborough and more considerable riots at Tiverton and Yeovil, in Somerset, and Blandford and Sherborne in Dorset.[24]

But by far the biggest outbreak came at Bristol on 29 October. Rioters held the streets for three days and did almost as much damage as the Gordon rioters in London fifty years before. They demolished the Mansion House, Lawford's Gate, the Bishop's Palace, Canons' Marsh, the Customs House, the Excise Office, and toll-houses all over the city; they broke into the Bridewell, the Gloucester County Prison and New Gaol and released prisoners; and destroyed forty-two offices, warehouses and dwellings. A dozen rioters were killed, nearly 100 were wounded, and 180 persons were committed to prison, fifty on capital charges.[25] It was the last great urban riot in English history.

It alarmed those in authority, and probably the great majority of middle-class reformers as much. So what followed was something of an anti-climax. There was an attempt made at Bath to stop the Yeomanry from going to Bristol; crowds assembled at Worcester; there were rumours or fears of riots at Wells and Chard, at Bognor, Salisbury,

Exeter, Chelmsford and Blackburn; but they came to nothing. The National Unions of Bridgewater and Chard appealed for peace and quiet and a "respect for private property". The Chard Union insisted: "We want no *Revolution* but the just *Restoration* [the word is significant] of our rights. *Revolution* is the last desperate act of an oppressed nation—of an insulted People. *Restoration* will prevent *Revolution* in England".

Even the National Union of the Working Classes agreed (though with considerable reluctance) to call off a mass rally planned for 7 November in London, its place being taken a few days later by a far smaller and more "respectable" meeting of Political Unionists addressed by Sir Francis Burdett.[26] And it is a remarkable fact that, though it was nearly another six months before the Reform Bill was finally carried, after another general election, the resignation of the Whigs and a threat to swamp the Lords with reforming peers, there were virtually no further popular disturbances. When, in May 1832, Grey, after a second defeat in the Lords, resigned and Wellington attempted to form a Ministry, there was a revival of public agitation: bells were rung in churches, protesting petitions poured into Westminster, the king was besieged in his coach, there were calls for a taxpayer's strike and a run on the banks; and, in London and Birmingham, there was even talk of barricades and pikes. But the focus of agitation had moved, significantly, from the streets. It was now confidently directed by the Political Unions, and the later fate and shape of the Reform Bill were decided by the manoeuvres and negotiations of political parties and groups (both within and outside Parliament) rather than by the intervention of the lower classes in the towns. In short, it would appear that, since Bristol, the major parties to the dispute had seen the red light.[27]

To return to my three movements. What links were there between them? To those in authority there appeared to be plenty and they were inclined to ascribe them (rather as Sir Robert Walpole had done, under similar circumstances, a hundred years before) to a common conspiracy. When the first ricks were burned and the first threshing machines destroyed in Kent and tricolour flags were paraded in the North so soon after the revolution in Paris, the air became thick with rumours that "itinerant Radicals", Popish or Methodist preachers, Frenchmen or agents of O'Connell, were travelling round the countryside inciting the workers to burn and to riot. A favourite tale was that "strangers" in "green gigs" had been seen lurking round barns with combustible materials. From Egham, Surrey, came numerous addresses, warning against "the artful and wicked designs of foreigners and strangers". One read:

Awake from your trance! The enemies of England are at work actively to ruin us.

Hordes of Frenchmen are employed doing the deeds of incendiaries . . . Shall the conquerors of the Nile, of Trafalgar, and Waterloo be tricked by the arts and deceits of Frenchmen, or of base Englishmen, corrupt and infidel?[28]

From Kent, Lord Camden, the Lord Lieutenant, warned Peel that the fires were caused "By those who wish Revolution in England"; and he believed that "the main directors" (presumably Cobbett and Carlile) resided in London.[29] Cobbett's lectures in Kent and Sussex could hardly fail to arouse suspicion; and Henry Hunt, who, in November, went on a business trip to the south, visiting seventy villages in the riot-torn areas (and stopping once to address a meeting of farmers and labourers), was readily believed to be up to no good; and his election at Preston in December, supported by factory workers carrying banners with blood-chilling slogans, was hardly calculated to remove the impression. Equally, the military commanders in the counties, whose job it was to police the various areas of disturbance and to drive a wedge between the different groups of rioters, were naturally inclined to see them all in a common context.

Yet these fears and "cloak-and-dagger" explanations, excusable as they might be in the circumstances at hand, were greatly exaggerated and betrayed a lack of understanding. Essentially, these were separate movements with their own distinctive aims and modes of conduct. There was certainly some overlap, some interaction between them; particularly between the labourers and weavers (not to mention the paper-workers at High Wycombe). It may even be argued that the renewed outbreak of "Luddism" among weavers, after lying dormant for the past four years, was provoked by the "contagion" and example of the villagers: we have noted instances of this in Leicester, Norfolk and Wiltshire. There was also, no doubt, an ideological bond, if no actual physical contact, between the labourers and the Bristol and Derby rioters; and, at Nottingham, laceworkers played a prominent part. But there was no contact whatever between the labourers and the factory workers in the north, and it is remarkable that even in Wiltshire, where the riots assumed greater dimensions than in any other county, they stopped short of the manufacturing districts in the west.

Yet there was considerable interplay between labourers and townsmen, particularly in the smaller county capitals and market towns. The labourers entered town to hold wages meetings, sometimes with the connivance of the locals: as at Horsham, and perhaps at Andover, Hungerford and Chichester. Threatening letters, signed "Swing" (the trade mark of the labourers' movement), appeared in Cambridge, Carlisle and other towns. In Cambridge, one letter, received by the Provost of King's, was couched as follows:

Revd Sir,
Thou wilt soon her that I have not forgot thee, nor the College that thou belongist too.
Thou shalt hear further from *me* when King's College is in flames.
(Signed) Swing Head Quarters.[30]

In Carlisle, their purpose was more directly political and they had nothing to do with the riots in the south. One, dated 5 December 1830, ran:

Dear friends Take notice if you do not attend the meeting of the rannegal [= general?] reform we will boe your shops up to the hair, for we are determined to carry the battle [on], but we are determined to release these three men that is in the gale. you must attend the meeting persisely at 6 a clock on Monday evening. I remain your loving friend

Sargin Swing[31]

More significant, no doubt, was the penetration of the labourers' and factory workers' movements by the Radical and Reform agitation of the towns. We have noted the parading of tricolour flags by factory workers at Blackburn, Middleton and Preston; and, in December 1830, we read of nightly readings from Cobbett's works before 8,000 ironworkers in Glamorgan.[32] The labourers' movement was touched (though not necessarily provoked) by Radical propaganda at Maidstone, Battle, Horsham, Banbury, Ipswich, and villages around Andover in Hampshire. Two of the rioters' leaders in this district, Joseph and Robert Mason, were convinced Radicals; another arrested rioter, William Winkworth, a shoemaker of Micheldever, was a subscriber to Cobbett's *Register;* and no less than seventeen villagers arrested in these parts had previously signed a Reform petition at the Swan Inn, at Sutton Scotney.[33] These men, who injected Radical ideas into the labourers' movement, were generally village craftsmen more literate than the rest—men like Philip Green, a chimney sweep of Banbury, said to be "a great admirer of Cobbett", and John Adams, a cobbler, who, in leading the rioters around Maidstone, told Sir John Filmer of East Sutton Park that "there were many sinecures" and that "the expenses of Government should be reduced".[34] Yet these contacts were only marginal to the general labourers' movement. To the factory workers they meant much more; but their movement lay in temporary abeyance after 1830 and they contributed comparatively little to the Reform movement of 1831.

Finally, why did the revolution, to which England has been said to have been so near, not come about? Mainly because the middle classes, who called the tune, had no need of one. Neither the village labourers nor the handloom weavers, for all their anger and destructive violence, wanted a revolution: their concern was simply to restore, by traditional means, their traditional livelihood which they rightly believed to be endangered. Occasionally, the labourers may have had more far-reaching aims: as, for example, at Peterborough, where a farmer wrote that the labourers had threatened that, once the threshing machines were broken, "if grievances were not redressed . . . by the House of Commons . . . they would then attack the landlords"; but this was only one incident in a thousand.[35] But, in any case, they were largely on their own and lacked solid middle-class support. The factory workers, as we have seen, had more forward-looking aims; they were a growing and not a declining force, and were susceptible to both Owenite and Radical ideas. But they only stood at the threshold of a self-conscious working-class movement, and were not yet ready to play an independent political rôle.

So it was only the Reform movement that had any sort of revolutionary potential. It had a clear programme of demands; it had an easily identifiable enemy; it had numbers, and the organization of the Political Unions; it could command the loyalty of both middle and lower classes; it had the power to arouse a "great hope" (without which no revolution is possible): the hope of filling empty bellies and of redressing manifold grievances by parliamentary reform; it could even tap briefly the political resources offered by high food prices, unemployment and an uncertain economic future. The middle-class leaders, and certain of the liberal aristocrats as well, were not averse, in order to win their Bill, to playing with fire or even toying with revolution. But the Bristol events, after those at Derby and Nottingham, had a sobering effect on both sides. On the one hand, they chastened the aristocratic and Tory opposition, making it more amenable to relinquishing entrenched positions. On the other hand, they discouraged all but the most radical of the Reform leaders from making any attempt to drive a harder bargain with the support of the streets.[36] To many, after Bristol, Manhood Suffrage no longer seemed so alluring a proposition. So, once they had the assurance that the Bill's main proposals, to enfranchise the £10 householder in the towns and to disfranchise the more "rotten" of the nomination boroughs, would go through without further obstruction from the Lords, they decided to call it a day.

Notes

1. W.W. Rostow, *British Economy of the Nineteenth Century* (Oxford, 1948), p. 124;

G.M. Young, *Victorian England, Portrait of an Age* (London, 1961), p. 27; G.D.H. Cole and R. Postgate, *The Common People 1746–1938* (London, 1945), p. 248. See also E.L. Woodward, *The Age of Reform 1815–1870* (Oxford, 1949), pp. 82–3.

2. *Gentleman's Magazine*, vols. 50 and 51 (1830–31).

3. J.L. and B. Hammond, *The Village Labourer* (London, 1911). A more comprehensive study of the movement is contained in E.J. Hobsbawm and G. Rudé, *Captain Swing: A Study of the Labourers' Revolt of 1830* (London, 1969).

4. *East Anglian*, 18 Jan. 1831.

5. Cole and Postgate, *The Common People*, pp. 231–2; N.J. Smelser, *Social Change in the Industrial Revolution* (London, 1959), pp. 262–3.

6. E.P. Thompson, *The Making of the English Working Class* (London, 1863), p. 375.

7. H[ome] O[ffice papers] 40/26, pp. 55–74, 156–61.

8. H.O. 40/27, p. 29.

9. H.O. 40/26, pp. 324–31.

10. H.O. 40/26, pp. 501–10.

11. H.O. 52/9 (Monmouth), 52/11 (Wales), 52/15 (Salop), 52/12 (Durham, Derby), 52/15 (Staffs), 52/14 (Northumberland), 52/15 (Wales); *Gentleman's Magazine*, 51, 2, p. 553.

12. H.O. 52/8 (Leicester), 52/11 (Worcester); Worcester Rec. Off., Epiphany Q.S., 1831; 52/9 (Norfold); Wilts Rec. Off., Account Books, 1830–1; *Times*, 219 Nov. 1830; H.O. 50/27, p. 459.

13. H.O. 52/12 (Derby); Worcester Herald, 8 Jan. 1831; H.O. 52/8 (Leicester); Leicester Rec. Off., Q.S. 31/1/3; H.O. 52/8 (Notts).

14. H.O. 52/12 (Devon), 52/15 (Warwicks); *Australian Dictionary of Biography*, 1 (1788–1830, A-H), pp. 178–9.

15. H.O. 50/26, pp. 340–1.

16. *Gentleman's Magazine*, 50, 2, p. 171. See also Norman Gash, "English Reform and French Revolution in the General Election of 1830", in *Essays presented to Sir Lewis Namier*, eds R. Pares and A.J.P. Taylor (London, 1956), pp. 258–88.

17. H.O. 52/11 (Worcester), 52/8 (Lancs), 52/12 (Cumberland), 40/27, pp. 505–6, 52/11 (Worcester), 52/13 (Lancs).

18. H.O. 40/27, pp. 536–42; Cumberland Rec. Off., Carlisle City Corp., Correspondence, 1830–1.

19. *Gentleman's Magazine*, 50, 2, pp. 459–60; E. Halévy, *The Triumph of Reform 1830–1841* (London, 1950), pp. 11–12, 44–5.

20. [P.R.O.;] T[reasury] S[olicitor's Papers], 11/4051.

21. H.O. 52/10 (Surrey), 52/15 (Sussex).

22. *Times*, 29 Nov. 1830; H.O. 52/9 (Oxon), 52/12 (Norfolk), 52/8 (Lancs).

23. *Gentleman's Magazine*, 51, 1, pp. 179, 362; H.O. 52/14 (Lincoln), 52/15 (Oxon, Sussex), 52/12 (Cumberland).

24. H.O. 52/12 (Derby), 52/15 (Notts); T.S. 11/1116; H.O. 52/13 (Kent), 52/15 (Warwicks, Somerset), 52/12 (Dorset.

25. H.O. 52/12 (Glos); 40/28, pp. 117–60; T.S. 11/405; *Gentleman's Magazine*, 51, 2, pp. 459–60; *Bristol Mercury*, 1 Nov. 1831. I am indebted to Mr. J.M. Main, of Flinders University, Adelaide, for allowing me to consult his paper, "The Bristol Riots and the Reform Crisis, 1831", also read at Melbourne on 19 Jan. 1967.

26. *Gentleman's Magazine*, 51, 2, p. 460; H.O. 52/15 (Somerset), 52/12 (Dorset), 52/13 (Sussex), 52/15 (Wilts), 52/12 (Devon, Essex), 52/13 (Lancs), 52/12 (Dorset), 52/14 (London); *Gentleman's Magazine*, 51, 2, p. 461; *Life and Struggles of William Lovett*, 2 vols. (London, 1920), 1, p. 77-9.

27. For useful accounts of this extremely complicated chain of events, see Halévy, *The*

Triumph of Reform, pp. 47–59, and Asa Briggs, *The Age of Improvement* (London, 1959), pp. 252–8.

28. *Times,* 29 Nov. 1830.
29. H.O. 52/8 (Kent).
30. H.O. 52/6 (Cambridge).
31. Rec. Off. Carlisle, Misc. correspondence 1830.
32. H.O. 40/27, pp. 377–8.
33. See A.M. Colson, "The Revolt of the Agricultural Labourers and its Causes, 1812–1831" (University of London M.A. thesis, 1937), pp. 144–60. My thanks to Miss Colson for permission to read and use this thesis.
34. T.S. 11/5035.
35. H.O. 52/9 (Northants).
36. It is true that, in the crisis of May 1832, following Grey's resignation, there was a great deal of agitation in Birmingham and London; there was talk of arming the people and of starting an insurrection, and Place and others called for a run on the banks ("To stop the Duke go for Gold"). But this was largely a middle-class affair, except possibly in Birmingham; and Place, for one, would have nothing to do with the National Union of the Working Classes, discouraged public demonstrations, and admitted that the "revolution" with which he threatened his opponents would be highly "undesirable". See *Life and Struggles of William Lovett*, pp. 78–9; G. Wallas, *The Life of Francis Place 1771–1854* (London, 1918), pp. 278, 289–323; and J.R.M. Butler, *The Passing of the Great Reform Bill* (London, 1914), pp. 377–426.

11

Captain Swing & the Uprising of 1830

The years 1830 and 1831 were among the most convulsive in British history. G.D.H. Cole and Raymond Postgate wrote in *The Common People* that "never since 1688 had Great Britain been so near actual revolution as in 1831"; and the country has probably never been so near to it since. It was the time of the agitation for the great Reform Bill; of the Bristol and Nottingham riots; and the first great strikes and industrial movements in the coal fields and factory towns of the Midlands, north and the west. But none of these movements were as widespread, none were as violent and sustained, and none aroused such panic and vindictive ardour in the Government, Parliament and the Bench as the great country labourers' rising of 1830, which was associated with the "mythical" Captain Swing.

The movement took its name from the swing of the flail of the threshing machine; and it spread, within a space of three months, over more than twenty counties in the Midlands, the south and east of England, stretching from Kent to Cornwall in the south, as far east as Norfolk and Suffolk, and as far north as Yorkshire and Cumberland.

It took various forms: marches in workhouses; wages meetings; assaults on overseers, parsons and landlords; arson; threatening letters; seditious and "inflammatory" handbills and riots over rent, tithe, taxes and enclosure. But most characteristic of all was the destruction of agricultural machinery; particularly of threshing machines, of which several hundred were destroyed between August and December of that year.

The riots grew out of the misery and degradation of the village labourers at the end of the Napoleonic Wars. Long before the wars, the old peasantry had already been disappearing from the Midlands and southern counties and was being rapidly transformed into hired men or rural proletarians, whom a social gulf divided from their employers, whether landlords, farmers or Church of England parsons.

Thus the labourer's new-found "liberty", for which he had traded his old security, left him exposed both to the whim or rapacity of an employer and the growing hazards of the rural economy. The wars, whatever hardships they inflicted, had given the old village a temporary reprieve: for the farmer it was a golden age and even the labourers' wages and employment were protected. But the end of the wars brought a sudden depression and widespread rural distress.

The landlords, after the initial shock, quickly recovered by means of the Corn Laws and by imposing high rents on the farmers. The farmer squeezed by the landlord's rent on the one hand and the Church's tithe on the other, riposted by cutting his labourers' wages or, when work was scarce, putting him on the parish. This had become a regular practice, in many villages, in the winter months.

Moreover, the parish allowance, far from staying at its original "Speenhamland" level, had been progressively reduced to something below half the prevailing wage; and after the disastrous harvest of 1829, thousands of unemployed labourers were drawing an allowance of something like three or four shillings a week. So the fear of another such winter was already a potent stimulus to rebellion.

But further factors were needed to set the movement alight, to generalize it and to drive it across half the counties of England. In part, this stimulus was provided by the outbreak of revolution in Paris in 1830, which served to stoke up the Radical agitation that had already begun over Parliamentary reform, and was already, through pamphlets and press, involving many of the literate craftsmen who often acted as the labourers' spokesmen. More precisely, it was afforded by the introduction of threshing machines—already familiar in Lincoln and Norfolk—in East Kent and in the summer of 1830. On the night August 28, a machine was destroyed by labourers at Lower Hardres near Canterbury. It was followed by others; and by the third week in October almost a hundred machines had been destroyed, mainly in this corner of the county.

Meanwhile, there had been an outbreak of threatening letters (often signed "Swing") and fired hayricks and barns on the borders of Surrey and Kent. It was noted that the villagers frequently gave their moral support to the incendiaries, and from Orpington *The Times* reported that, after a barn had been set ablaze, the labourers stood calmly by, saying "D——n it, let it burn, I wish it was the house."

By early October, arson had spread to East Kent, and a *Times* leader spoke of an "organised system of stack-burning and machine-breaking". Two weeks later the movement had swung to the Maidstone area, and here it took the form of great wages meetings, usually held in broad daylight, where the labourers demanded a minimum daily wage of 2s 3d in winter and 2s 6d in summer.

In early November, as the riots spread westwards into the Kentish and Sussex Weald, new issues were raised. Sometimes it was tithes, sometimes taxes or rents, and the labourers, often in collusion with the local small or "middling" farmers, demanded that the parson reduce his tithe and the landlord his rent so that the farmer could pay his labourer a higher wage. Round Battle and Rye, in East Sussex, the main demand was for better allowances to be paid by the overseers to the poor; and, in the village of Brede, an unpopular overseer was wheeled out of the parish in the parish cart and dumped unceremoniously across its border.

So the movement continued, with increasing momentum, into West Sussex, Hampshire and the counties of the west. In Horsham, then described as "a hotbed of sedition", the marching labourers joined with the farmers and townspeople in packing the vestry meeting and insisting on a reduction in rents and tithes and a rise in wages. The riots reached Hampshire on November 18 and Wiltshire a couple of day later. In both, they barely lasted a week but left a heavier toll of broken machines, forced levies of money and arrested labourers than in any other county. They reached east Dorset on November 23 and south Gloucestershire on November 26 and, after a pause in this area, Worcester, Devon and Cornwall in early December. The most westerly point touched by the movement was the village of Whitney in Hereford, where a "Swing" letter, addressed to a considerable farmer on November 17, urged him to "pull down your Threshing Machine or else Bread or Fire without delay".

Meanwhile, a new focus of rebellion had opened in Berkshire. It began as a wages demonstration by the labourers of Thatcham and developed quickly into a far wider movement, in which threshing machines were destroyed and farmers were held to ransom and compelled to contribute money for food and beer as a reward for "services rendered". One local leader, a bricklayer from Kintbury, near Hungerford, was, when arrested, found in possession of £100, including a couple of IOUs.

The Berkshire movement spread southwards back into Hampshire, westwards into Wiltshire, eastwards into Oxford and Buckinghamshire, and northwards into Bedfordshire and Northampton. Once more, the main targets were the hated threshing machines. But there was an important exception: between Loudwater and West Wycombe, along the Thames, the unemployed paper workers, in some cases with the village labourers' support, destroyed the machinery in half a dozen paper mills. Forty-five prisoners were taken after damage had been done to a value of over £3,000.

A third main centre of rioting was East Anglia, where there had been earlier attacks on machinery in the agrarian riots of 1816 and 1822. Here the movement started at North Walsham, a village in the north eastern corner of Norfolk. It began with the destruction of threshing machines but developed, as it swept southwards towards the Suffolk border, into riots against tithes and assaults on Church of England parsons. In West Suffolk and Essex, the disturbances were generally over wages. In the woodlands of west Norfolk, northern Cambridgeshire, in Lincoln, the Isle of Ely and along the Huntingdonshire border, the emphasis was all on arson; in Lincoln alone, there were over twenty fires in a single month.

"Swing's" influence was felt as far north as Carlisle, where it played a part in local Radical agitation. In early December, after two ricks had been fired, a handbill was posted, offering "£1,000 reward, in the apprehension of Borough-mongers, Stockjobbers, Tax-eaters, Monopolizers, Special Constables, and the Extinguishers of freedom by order of the SWING UNION." There was a brief revival of machine-breaking in Kent and Norfolk in the late summer of 1831; and a final threshing machine was broken at Tadlow, in Cambridgeshire, in September 1832.

But, long before this, the movement had run its course or been broken by the repressive intervention of the military and courts of justice. Wellington's Tory Ministry, with Peel at the Home Office, were at first more concerned about the strikes and discontents in the manufacturing districts, not to mention the events in France, and reacted without much energy; but they attempted to enrol special constables among the farmers (often with little success), appealed to local voluntary bodies to take action, and sent troops into Kent, Sussex and Hampshire. Wellington's Ministry fell and was succeeded by Grey's Whig Government as the riots swept into Wiltshire. On November 23, the day after taking office, Lord Melbourne, the new Home Secretary, issued a proclamation, offering rewards of £500 for bringing rioters and incendiaries to justice, and urged justices to act with greater vigour. A fortnight later, seeing that some magistrates were half-hearted in their efforts to protect threshing machines, Melbourne sternly reminded them that it was "their Duty to maintain and uphold the Rights of Property, of every description, against Violence and Aggression".

Meanwhile, by one means or the other, the prisons had been filled and, in mid-December 1830, there were nearly 2,000 prisoners awaiting trial in more than a score of counties. To set a stern example and encourage the local magistrates to act with greater severity, the

Government set up Special Commissions at Winchester, Salisbury, Reading, Dorchester and Aylesbury to judge those arrested in the major areas of disturbance. In three weeks, they tried 992 cases, at first sentencing 227 men to death (101 in Hampshire alone), though of these only eleven were "left for execution". The remaining thousand prisoners were tried in a further eighty-five courts sitting in thirty counties. When they completed their work, 644 were sentenced to jail and nineteen were hanged, all but three of them for arson.

But the most vindictive act of all was the transportation of 479 men and two women to the Australian colonies for terms varying between seven years and "life", and with virtually no hope of returning to their homes. On no other protest movement of the time—on neither Luddites, nor Chartists, nor trade union pioneers—was such a bitter blow inflicted. It was a measure of the panic that the labourers' action had inspired among the land-owning classes of England, and it has done much to tarnish the reputation of Grey and Melbourne and the Whig "Reform" Government of the 1820s.

What had the labourers' movement achieved? In strictly political terms, they achieved nothing at all. This is hardly surprising as they had set themselves no political goals; least of all had they attempted to start a revolution. Besides, their movement was isolated, confined to the wheat-growing counties or regions of the Midlands, the south and the west and cut off from the manufacturing districts and the Reform Bill agitation of the cities and large towns. They had carried no arms and had behaved with considerable restraint. Their language was violent enough, it is true: there was much talk of "bread or blood" and even of "blood for supper" or "blood for breakfast". But their violence was limited to machine-breaking, rick-burning and strong words: not a single farmer, overseer, landlord or parson was killed or even sustained serious injury at their hands.

Moreover, their organization had been of the most casual and primitive form; they were not members of trade unions, like their Dorset successors of 1834 or of the far wider "Revolt of the Field" of the 1870s. Their object had been to win back some of the lost security of the past, to restore their wages and poor law allowances, and to destroy the machines which threatened to displace their labour and which to them appeared as obnoxious and unlawful as Ship Money had appeared to Sir John Hampden 200 years before; and, like him, they believed that right and justice—and even the law—were on their side.

And, in this last respect at least, they achieved a remarkable success. In many districts, the threshing machine, destroyed or removed in the course of the riots, did not return at all; and, a dozen years later, an observer of the countryside wrote that "in a large part of the

Agricultural Districts of the South, the Threshing Machine cannot be used, owing to the destructive vengeance with which the labourers resisted its introduction". So "Swing", though his methods were the same, did considerably better than "Ludd". And this alone entitles him to be drawn from his present obscurity and raised to an honourable place in the annals of labour history.

References

M.K. Ashby, *Joseph Ashby of Tysoe, 1859–1919* (Cambridge, 1961).
J.P.D. Dunbabin, "The 'Revolt of the Field': the Agricultural Labourers' Movement in the 1870's", *Past & Present* (November, 1963).
Lord Ernle (Rowland Edmund Prothero), *English Farming Past and Present* (1912, frequently reprinted).
J.L. Hammond, *The Village Labourer* (London, 1911, frequently reprinted).
E.J. Hobsbawm and G. Rudé, *Captain Swing* (London, 1969, rev. ed. 1973).

12

European Popular Protest and Ideology on the Eve of the French Revolution

Among the many consequences of the French Revolution was to give a new dimension to popular protest, as to its forms, its content and its ideology; and this was by no means limited to France. This paper will be concerned with European protest of the Old Regime during a period of transition from traditional to more "modern" forms; and it will attempt to show how some of these changes took place and (briefly) what part the Revolution played in the process.

It has often been observed how, after the upheavals of the seventeenth century, the popular movements of the last decades of the Old Regime, particularly those in Western Europe, became relatively muted. Yet, whether violent or muted, they were frequent and varied. For convenience (though this does not present an exhaustive picture), they may be divided into the riots and rebellions of peasants or rural producers, the protests of small consumers, industrial disputes in France and England, and the riots and insurrections that, notably from the early 1760s, became a feature of cities like Paris, London, Naples, Madrid, Geneva, Lyons and Amsterdam.

In rural protest, the striking contrast is between the old-style peasant rebellion, still surviving in the East, and the more sporadic and muted outbreak in the West. In both Russia and the Hapsburg Empire, the demands of war and the developing bureaucratic State, imposed on a society that was still predominantly feudal and medieval, gave a new scope and dimension to traditional peasant rebellion. In Russia, matters came to a head with the succession of Catherine the Great after the murder of her husband, Peter III, popularly believed to be a "liberator" and the peasants' friend. Soon after, Emelyan Pugachev, a Cossack soldier, claimed to be the murdered Tsar who had miraculously escaped his assassins' bullets; and he won considerable support among the

Bashkir people of the Urals and the peasant serfs and indentured servants of the Volga region. He began his crusade in December 1773 and, for over a year, he led a great peasant army through a long series of battles, liberated serfs, and held a large part of the country between the Volga and the Urals before being brought to Moscow in a cage and hanged in chains. The Pugachev rebellion lies in the great tradition of European peasant revolt, including Stenka Razin's earlier challenge in Russia and the great rural uprisings in Germany and Hungary of over a century before.

Revolt in the Hapsburg Empire was also concerned with taxes and feudal obligations that tied the peasant to the soil; above all, it challenged the age-old system of labour service known as the *Robot;* but it was never on quite the scale that it was in Russia. It fell into two stages: the outbreaks that anticipated Joseph II's land reforms and those protesting against their inadequacy or the forms they took. To the first stage belong the rebellions in Silesia in 1767 and in Bohemia, after reform had been promised but appeared to have been obstructed, in 1775. The reforms themselves—the Emancipation Patent (1781) and the Taxation Patent (1789)—were attended by a fresh series of revolts; but when (following the counter-protests of landowners) a great part of this legislation was repealed a year later, the peasants responded by simmering discontent rather than by open rebellion.

In France, this traditional type of peasant outbreak appeared by now to be a thing of the past: since the early 1720s there had been nothing remotely similar to the *furies* that had been a feature of the reigns of Louis XIII and Louis XIV and have been so vividly described, and interpreted from differing points of view, by Roland Mousnier and Boris Porchnev. Now, on the surface at least, the French countryside was relatively calm and where it had earlier been disturbed it was now marked, more typically, by the food riots of the small rural consumers, peasants whose holdings were not large enough to produce grain for the market or even for their family's own needs; but not by the peasants as a whole. The reason for the change (as Edouard Labrousse has shown) was that the more prosperous of the peasantry shared in the agrarian prosperity of the 1730s to 1770s, when the price of grain rose by over 60 per cent while none of the basic grievances of the rural producers—whether large or small—over land, tithes, taxes and feudal services and dues had been solved; so peasant protest, while temporarily muted, still lay near the surface and only needed a general political and economic crisis, like that of the 1780s, to set it ablaze.

In England, as in some other northern countries, the situation was different. England had had no serfdom since the 1550s and, a century later, all traces of feudalism had virtually disappeared. With the agrarian revolution that followed, even the small peasant proprietor—the yeoman—had almost become a figure of the past; and English rural society was already taking on its modern complexion with its division into landowners, tenant farmers and labourers. As society changes so the nature of protest changed with it: the former rebellion of peasants became transformed into the frequent but relatively muted protest of smallholders struggling to protect themselves against the usurpations of landowners and farmers more influential and "improvement"-minded than themselves; against the tolls levied by local authorities and against enclosures scattered over the century (though mainly after the Enclosure Act of 1760). Also turnpikes and gates were pulled down at Bristol in the 1720s and 1750s, around Hereford and Worcester in the 1730s and in Yorkshire's West Riding in 1753. In Norway, a land of small peasant proprietors and small farms where serfdom was unknown, the problem again was different. When the largest peasant movement of the century broke out in 1786, the issues raised were not purely *peasant* issues: in addition to crop failures, they included monopoly buying by wealthy merchants, and, above all, the proliferation of taxes. Besides, the Norwegians were then dependents of the Danes within a United Kingdon of Denmark and Norway; so the peasants were rebelling not only against taxes and monopoly but also against a colonial status that appeared to give all the plums to the Danes. Yet the most remarkable feature of the affair was that the movement was almost entirely peaceful, organized around a petition of grievances which Christian Lofthuus, their leader, presented on the peasants' behalf to the Royal Palace at Copenhagen. This was by no means typical of peasant protest of the time which, whether it took the form of riot or rebellion, was generally attended by violence to property (and, in Russia, where the peasant *jacquerie* survived, by violence to persons as well).

In eighteenth-century Europe, with its predominantly agrarian economy, protest was, typically, rural and continued to be so for some time to come. Only two countries—France and England—had become significantly industrialized (I am excluding purely regional developments as in Saxony, Silesia, Catalonia, Liège and the Urals); so it was as yet only in these two countries that industrial disputes (to use our modern term) had begun to assume a certain importance. In both countries, the old guild system, which had offered the workshop journeyman (daily workers) a certain degree of protection, had either been abolished (as in England) or (as in France) scaled down or had become the sole preserve of the masters and merchants. So journeymen, more and more reduced to the status of proletarians, had begun to set up (illegal) associations of their own: the *compagnonnages* in France and the workers' committees in England. Among other activities, they organized strikes (a term not yet in use) to resist wage-cuts or the employment of "foreigners" as cheap labour—such as Irish in England and Savoyards in France; and they sometimes, though not always, resisted the introduction of new labour-saving machines. But whatever their purpose, strikes were most often, like rural protest, of the direct-action or violent type: peaceful marches and petitions were relatively few and industrial protest tended to turn into riot of which the most common form was the destruction of machines (what Eric Hobsbawm has called "collective bargaining by riot").

Yet strikes were still comparatively infrequent and remained so until the industrial revolution—first in England, later in France—got under way. Far more typical of the times, and far more significant as a form of popular protest, were the protests of the small consumers of town and countryside that generally took the form of riots against the shortage and high price of bread. Even in industrial communities in England and France, such forms of protest probably outnumbered all others and were far more frequent than strikes. There were a number of reasons for this, one of which was that wage-earners, too, were small consumers who, at a time when their own associations were banned, found it more profitable to agitate for cheap bread than for higher wages; besides, when prices were high (as they often were after 1760), bread may have accounted for as much as one half of the poor man's budget. So, at such times, it became a common occurrence for small consumers to band together in villages and market towns, to march on granaries and bakers' shops, to storm markets and destroy or remove their wares and, most typically of all, to impose their own ceiling on the price of grain or flour or bread in what the French called a *taxation populaire*. And this is what happened in the two largest movements of the kind in the pre-Revolutionary years: the English bread-and-grain riots of 1766 and the French *guerre des farines* ("flour-war") of 1775.

City riots, as might be expected, were common to most countries and were more complex and varied. They might take the form of food riots (either overt or disguised), as in Madrid in 1766 and in Paris in 1725, 1740, 1752 and 1775; though in London, due to its location and the effective measures taken to avert them, they were far less common and only began to occur with the outbreak of the wars with France in 1792.

But, unlike industrial disputes or riots in country districts, riots in large or capital cities tended to have political overtones, in which the participants, even if not voicing opinions that were specifically their own, adopted or were touched by the political views of others. Thus, in Paris, there were riots in 1720 stirred by John Law's financial speculations; there were riots in 1720 against recruitment to the Militia in 1743 and 1752 and against the anti-Jansenist stance of the

Archbishop the same year; and, from 1753 onwards, there were repeated outbreaks in support of the aristocratic Parlement in its duels with the crown. Meanwhile, Londoners, in response to Tory influence, rioted against Nonconformist preachers in 1709 and 1715 and protested against the decision to confer British nationality on alien Jews. However, from the mid-1750s, when the elder Pitt was becoming the darling of the crowd, popular rioting became impregnated with the new Radical (or Whig-Radical) ideas emanating from the City of London. There followed the politically more "sophisticated" commotions of the 1760s and 1770s, inspired by the career of John Wilkes; and, in 1780, London was rocked for over a week by the anti-Papist (though covertly Radical) violence stirred up by Lord George Gordon. There was at the time no equivalent in Paris for such displays; and we may sympathise with Sébastian Mercier who, writing in 1783, delcared that such "terrors and alarms" as witnessed in London would be inconceivable in a city as well policed as Paris! But, soon after, as we know, it was Paris's turn and London's radicalism was silenced for a dozen years and revived only under the impact of the revolution in France and the writings of Thomas Paine and his fellow Radicals of the 1790s.

So popular protest in eighteenth-century Europe—whether we speak of rebellious peasants, striking workers, rioting freeholders, small consumers or the *menu peuple* of cities—responded to a variety of issues and causes. Yet their outbreaks, for all their variety, had certain features in common. With few exceptions, they took the form of direct action and violence to property, though not to persons: even the Gordon rioters in London, with all their destructive violence, took no lives. They were also marked by spontaneity and a minimum of organization; yet they were remarkably discriminating in their selection of targets. In short, outside Eastern and East-Central Europe, the general pattern was one of protest in a transitional, "pre-industrial" society in the half-century before the impact of the "dual revolution" (to use Hobsbawm's term)—the social-political revolution in France and the industrial revolution in England.

So much for the forms of protest and the issues involved. But what of the motives that underlay them and the ideology—or *mentalité*—of those taking part? Here only a brief answer will be attempted. As I see it, popular ideology is composed of two elements of which the second, when occasion demands it, becomes superimposed on the first. The first, what I call the "inherent" element, is the traditional body of ideas or attitudes arising within the experience or folk-memory of the common people; and the second, the "derived" element, is that formed by the ideas borrowed from and transmitted by other groups, whether they are read in books, proclaimed from a pulpit or platform or village square, or passed on at street corners, in markets or in workshops: such ideas as those of the *philosophes* like the Rights of Man and the Sovereignty of the People, or more structured systems of ideas and beliefs like Christian and Buddhist theology, or nationalism and socialism in their various forms. This two-stage process does not always arise: it depends on the degree of "sophistication" called for.

In the more elementary forms of protest of which we have cited examples (such as strikes, food riots and largely spontaneous peasant movements), the prevailing concern is for simple "justice"—a "just" wage, a "just" price or a "just" distribution of land; and in such cases there is now need for the "inherent" popular ideology to be supplemented by ideas from outside. But in the case of more structured or organized protest, directed (or partly directed) "from above"—and, notably, in revolutions in which both "leaders" and "followers" take part—the infusion of a "derived" body of ideas becomes a necessity, for there can be no generalized ideology of revolution, uniting both leaders and followers, without it. But how this transmission takes place—in a two-stage process of assimilation and adjustment to popular needs—is a complicated question and one to which space will not allow me to pay adequate attention here.

One important question, however, remains to be answered. What happened to protest of this relatively simple, "pre-industrial" type as the result of the revolution in France and, for that matter, of the industrial revolution that began in England not many years before? (For, like Hobsbawm, I believe that this aspect of the "dual revolution" should also be taken account of.) To put it briefly, the French Revolution gave popular protest (and not exclusively that in Western Europe) a new and deeper political dimension—based, in the first place, on the new concepts of the brotherhood and Rights of Man and the Sovereignty of the People.

Under this impact, the Paris crowd moved left, as did the crowds in many other European cities; though it must be noted that some moved right (for this might also be the result of a "derived" belief), as the crowd in Birmingham did briefly and those in Rome, Naples, and Madrid for some years to come. Moreover, the *menu peuple* began not only to assimilate the political ideas of others but—by that dual process of assimilation and digestion which I touched on just now—to develop political ideas of their own: the most notable example is that of the Parisian *sans-culottes;* but something similar happened, though on a smaller scale, with the craftsmen of London, Sheffield and Leeds. French peasant rebellion, also stirred by the "contagion" of the new ideas, revived in the summer of 1789; but it did not generally continue beyond the summer of 1793 when, with the aid of the Jacobins, the remnants of feudalism on the land were finally uprooted. Food riots also became "politicized" (we have the example of the Law of the Maximum of September 1793); but (contrary to M. Daniel Guérin's view), industrial disputes did not become so before the 1830s. And, finally, a tradition of popular armed rebellion, going back to the Paris *journées* of 1789–95, was established in the streets of cities that did further service, though under different slogans and behind different banners and faces, in the revolutions of the nineteenth century and beyond.

In turn, the industrial revolution, by producing an industrial working class, led to the creation of national trade unions and working-class movements that emerged, almost simultaneously, though strongly marked by their own national traditions, in both France and England in the 1830s. With them, the forms of protest changed further: strikes began to eclipse food riots and industrial workers and "proletarians" came to replace the city "lower orders", *sans-culottes* and *lazzaroni*, as the shock-troops of riot and rebellion. With the passing of the old agrarian economy—earlier in England, later in France and elsewhere—the location of protest also changed and moved from rural districts to the new manufacturing towns. And as the workers adapted to the new industrial society, ideology tended to become more forward-looking and to abandon old Utopias and folk-myths for socialist—or near-socialist—beliefs. So, by now, the break with the past was well on the way to becoming complete.

But, of course, this did not happen overnight: it was a long process of germination and change which, in some countries, took far longer to accomplish than in others; and, even in Western Europe, where the process began, it opened perspectives that reached far beyond the middle of the century that followed. But this is another story that also takes me far beyond the aims with which I started this chapter.

References

R. Forster and J.P. Greene, *Pre-Conditions of Revolution in Early Modern Europe* (Baltimore, 1970).

J. Godechot, *France and the Atlantic Revolution of the Eighteenth Century, 1770–1799* (New York, 1965).

D. Hay, P. Linebaugh, E.P. Thompson *et al.*, *Albion's Fatal Tree: Crime and Society in Eighteenth-Century England* (New York, 1975).

E.J. Hobsbawm, *The Age of Revolution, 1789–1848* (London, 1962).

——— "The Machine Breakers", *Past & Present* 1 (Feb, 1952), pp. 57–70.

——— *Primitive Rebels* (Manchester, 1959).

C.-E. Labrousse, *Aspects de la crise et la dépression de l'économie au milieu du XIXe siècle* (La Roche-sur-Yonne, 1956).

———*Esquisse de mouvement des prix et des revenus en France au dix-huitième siècle* (2 vols., Paris, 1933).

G. Lefebvre, *La Grande Peur de 1789* (Paris, 1932).

—————"Foules révolutionnaires", *Etudes sur la Révolution française* (Paris, 1954), pp. 271–87.

R.B. Rose, "18th-Century Price Riots, the French Revolution and the Jacobin Maximum", *International Review of Social History* 3 (1959), pp. 432–45.

G. Rudé, *The Crowd in History, 1730–1848* (New York, 1964).

————— *Ideology and Popular Protest* (London, 1980).

————— *Paris and London in the Eighteenth Century: Studies in Popular Protest* (London, 1972).

J.H.M. Salmon, "Venal Office and Popular Sedition in Seventeenth-Century France", *Past & Present*, 37 (1967), pp. 21–43.

E.P. Thompson, *The Making of the English Working Class* (London, 1963).

C. Tilly, *The Contentious French* (Cambridge, Mass., 1986).

L. Tilly, "The Food Riot as a Form of Political Conflict in France", *Journal of Interdisciplinary History* 2 (1971), pp. 23–57.

E. Wangermann, *From Joseph II to the Jacobin Trials* (Oxford, 1959).

13

Ideology and Popular Protest

In this chapter, I shall be using the word "protest" to mean a social act (generally a collective act) that seeks to rectify an injustice, to ventilate a grievance of public concern, or to offer a more fundamental challenge to society or its established norms; and the "people" with whom I shall be concerned will be the peasants, wage-earners or *menu peuple* mainly of "pre-industrial" society in England, France and North America. The term "ideology" of course presents a greater problem, as every writer in the social sciences—I am thinking in particular of Marx, Mannheim, Lukács, Clifford Geertz—uses it in his own manner, some (since Marx's *German Ideology*) seeing it as a form of "mystification" or "false reality", others defining it strictly in terms of a structured set of values or political beliefs, others again favouring a more elastic approach in which myths, "attitudes" and what the French call *mentalités* all have their part. As a social historian I, too, lean towards this latter view, preferring an all-embracing concept that takes account of all sets of ideas—whether "sophisticated" and structured or not—that underlie or inform popular protest. (Therefore, in this chapter at least, as I am concerned with action and not silent meditation or passivity, I shall take no account of such expressions of popular ideology as Oscar Lewis's "culture of poverty.")

In my sense of the term, ideology—and, in this case, specifically "popular" ideology—is not a purely internal affair and the sole property of a single class or group. It is a "mix", made up of the fusion of two elements, of which only one is the peculiar property of the "popular" classes and the other is superimposed by a process of transmission and adoption of ideas from outside. Of these, the first is the "inherent", traditional element—a sort of "mother's milk" ideology, based on direct experience, oral tradition or folk-memory and not learned by listening to

sermons or reading books. In this fusion the second element is the set of
ideas and beliefs that are "derived" or borrowed from others, often
taking the form of a more structured system of ideas, such as the Rights
of Man, popular sovereignty, nationalism, socialism, or Marxism-
Leninism. But it is important to emphasize that there is no wall of
Babylon between the two, so that one cannot simply describe the second
as being "superior" or at a higher level than the first. There is in fact a
considerable overlap. For instance, among the "inherent" beliefs of one
generation are many that were originally derived from outside by
another. (In England, for example, the notion of the "Norman Yoke",
which ultimately goes back to the "freedoms" imposed on King John by
his barons in the Magna Carta, had become firmly rooted in popular
culture in the eighteenth and nineteenth centuries.) Again, the second
type, the derived ideology, can only be effectively absorbed, and not
rejected, if the ground has already been well prepared. (The French
revolutionaries found this a problem with the Spanish peasants in 1793.)
Further, the more structured ideas later "derived" by the common
people are often a refined distillation of popular experience and beliefs.
(Karl Marx, for example, drew a great deal of his knowledge of the class
struggle and the factory system from a close observation of the habits
and reactions of the early English working class.)

My two terms must be defined and illustrated more precisely. By
"inherent" belief I mean for one thing, the peasant's belief in his right to
a piece of land, whether owned individually or in common with others: it
is a belief that informs the protests of the Mexican peasant today as it
informed the European peasants in their great rebellions of 1381, 1525,
1773 and 1789. Analogous to the peasant's belief in the common justice
of holding land is the small consumer's belief in his right to buy bread at
a "just" price or the worker's claim to a "just" wage and not simply one
that responds to his employer's whim or to the new-fangled notion of
supply and demand. Similarly, the "freeborn" Englishman demanded
his traditional "liberties" and rioted if he was denied them, and the small
freeholder and townsmen resisted the attempts of "improving"
landlords and farmers, enterprising bourgeois or city authorities to
uproot them or to disrupt their community. Such people tended to
prefer the "devil they knew" and to be "backward" rather than
"forward"-looking in the sense that they were more inclined to demand
the restoration of rights that were threatened or had been lost than to
look forward to change and "reform". But there were others—and not
only among "primitive rebels" or primitive societies—who held
millenarian or chiliastic beliefs, and were therefore more inclined to
stake their fortunes on a sudden change or regeneration such as that
promised by a Second Coming of Christ or the more mundane news of

Louis XVI's decision to summon the Estates General to meet in the summer of 1789.

And now for the "derived" element in popular ideology: the political, philosophical or religious ideas that, at various levels of sophistication, became absorbed in the more specifically *popular* culture. These, in the historical context in which I am speaking, tended to be "forward", rather than "backward"-looking, positing reform rather than restoration, and were more often than not—again in the period of what Robert Palmer calls the "Democratic Revolution"—those transmitted by the up-and-coming *bourgeoisie.* At the more elementary level they might take the form of slogans, such as "Death to revenue officers", "No taxation . . ." or "Vive le Tiers Etat!", which were variously heard in the early stages of the American and French revolutions. Or, at a slightly higher level, they might become part of the everyday vocabulary of the *menu peuple;* already in the spring and early summer of 1789, such expressions as *nation, tiers état, contrat social* and *droits de l'homme* had passed into the common speech of Parisian craftsmen. Knowledge of more structured political manifestoes such as the Declaration of the Rights of Man and Citizen followed soon after. According to my argument, then, these "derived" notions became gradually grafted onto the "inherent" notions and beliefs, more quickly in towns than in villages (for this we can use the testimony of Arthur Young during his travels in France in the summer of 1789), and far more quickly in times of revolution than in times of social or political peace.

One word of caution here. It must not be supposed that the effect of this grafting was simply to add A to B in an elementary arithmetical calculation. It is by no means so easy, as all ideas in the course of transmission and adoption suffer "a sea-change". It was an experience that Martin Luther went through in the 1520s when the German peasants, much to his indignation, "adopted" his ideas to sustain their rebellion against the princes. Luther lived up to his reputation for "earthy" language in his violent denunciation of his luckless followers!

So much for the *theory.* And now let us take three examples to illustrate the process from revolutions and rebellions that involve a distinctive popular element and that are relatively well known to all of us: the American and French revolutions of the eighteenth century and the Lower Canada rebellion of 1837–8. In the first—the American revolution of the 1770s—the dominant ideology adopted and transmitted by the revolutionary *élites,* the planters, lawyers and merchants, was, as Bernard Bailyn and Carolyn Robbins have written, composed of a stock of ideas derived from the writings of Milton, Locke, Shaftesbury and the "Commonwealthmen" which placed considerable emphasis on the "liberties" of the people and the "tyranny" of kings, with George III of England being cast as "tyrant" in the conflict that began in the 1760s.[1] But, more recently, younger scholars—Joseph Ernst among them—have argued that to limit the revolutionary ideology of the people "at the top" to the constitutional issue is to leave out of account the more basic ideology of merchants and mechanics "of the better sort" who were even more preoccupied with the everyday matters which deeply affected their economic interests—the state of domestic manufactures and the imperative necessity of "nonimportation". Such matters, too, they have argued, are reflected in current ideology.[2]

These and other historians have also argued—and none perhaps more insistently than a student of Bailyn's, Pauline Maier—that this dominant ideology (whether limited to the constitutional question or not) was also shared by the common people of the villages and towns—as, for example, the mechanics of Charleston and the "lower orders" of Boston, Philadelphia and New York.[3] Others, however, have gone further and have set out to show that these people not only adopted the prevailing ideas of their leaders but had, in addition, revolutionary notions of their own. Here the first in the field was Jesse Lemisch, with his study of "Jack Tar in the Street", who has shown that the sailors, with their bitter experience of impressment, had quite particular feelings about revenue officers, naval authorities and ports which left their mark not only on the nature of the early riots but on the course of the revolution itself.[4] More recently, a group of young historians, closely associated with Alfred Young of the University of Northern Illinois, have made further explorations into the past of the urban (though also rural) "lower orders". In contributions to Young's "Explorations in the History of American Radicalism", Dirk Hoerder, Gary Nash, Edward Countryman and others have traced the development of a native popular "revolutionary" ideology back through Pope's Day celebrations and urban riots to a period long before the Stamp Act Riots of 1765 in such cities as Boston, New York and Philadelphia.[5] Thus a new dimension—both of popular action and ideology "from below"—is being given to the study of the American Revolution. But whether the records will make it possible to undertake more extensive studies and to look more closely at the process of transmission and evolution of ideas and their effect on action I am not qualified to judge.

The study of the French Revolution, at least, has not been greatly impeded by a shortage of records; and it is hardly surprising that in this field far greater advances have been made than elsewhere. It is comparatively easy, for example, with the knowledge now available, to trace the impact of the ideology of the revolutionary middle class and liberal aristocracy on the common people in the villages and city streets.

That ideology was, as is well known, largely derived from the writings of the *philosophes* of the Enlightenment: above all Rousseau, but also Montesquieu, Mably and a number of others. It is from sources such as these that there emerged such notions as the Social Contract, the Rights of Man and the sovereignty of the People, notions that the French bourgeoisie, on the eve of revolution, accepted with enthusiasm and made their own. Let us see, by stages, how the common people of France—the peasants and urban *menu peuple* (soon to be given the name of *sans-culottes*)—adopted these ideas in turn from the *bourgeoisie* and, in the process, added to them something of their own.

To begin with the year 1775, a year of considerable commotion, when the small consumers of half-a-dozen *généralités* (broadly the same as provinces) on all sides of the capital were engaged in massive food riots, the most extensive of the Old Régime. Yet, though they occurred over a dozen years after the publication of Rousseau's *Emile* and his *Social Contract,* there is no sign at all—among the voluminous *dossiers* relating to the affair—of any "intrusion" of Enlightenment ideas, not even an indication among the poorer peasants of any resentment toward their existing feudal burdens. Their one concern, their one ideological preoccupation, is to impose the "just price". A dozen years later, during the aristocratic revolt which occurred on the very eve of the Revolution, there is still no sign in the countryside of any popular revolutionary psychology; but in the towns there are the first glimmerings of a *prise de conscience,* at least, in the support expressed for the exiled *Parlements*. It is only at the third stage, however—in the summer of 1789 (and even more as the year proceeds)—that crowds in both town and countryside can be seen to be thoroughly impregnated with both the slogans and the vocabulary of the revolutionary *bourgeoisie*. Two years laters, when crowds flock to the Champ de Mars to sign (or "mark") a petition calling for Louis's abdication, many of these newly-named *sans-culottes* are found to be subscribers to the revolutionary press or belong to societies and clubs. By the autumn of 1793, as the Revolution nears its climax, the process has gone further still: by now the *sans-culottes* dominate the Paris Commune, have their own basic organizations and have fairly clearly defined social and political aims of their own.

It is also of interest to see how these ideas were transmitted (though this process is by no means peculiar to the revolution in France). This transmission, in general, falls obviously enough into two parts: the written word and the oral message. The relative importance of the one or the other will naturally depend on the degree of literacy, which was probably higher among Frenchmen in 1789 than among Englishmen in *their* revolution in the 1640s; and, in both cases, it was almost certainly higher among men than among women and among townsmen than among villagers. For such as could read (or could be read to) there was the proliferation of pamphlets, tracts and newspapers that was a feature common to both revolutions. The oral message was probably the more important and the more productive. In the 1640s, its most common channels of transmission were the pulpit, the army and the meetings of the elect. In peasant revolutions, like the one in France in 1789, villages and market squares naturally assume a place of first importance. In cities like Paris, however, where large-scale industry was as yet unknown, it was in the small workshop that the artisan, the independent craftsman and journeyman acquired the slogans and discussed the new revolutionary ideas. In addition, there were the wine shops, markets and bakers' shops, all of which served as a forum for debate and often acted as a launching pad for popular agitation and revolt.

But, as we saw in relation to the German peasants of 1525, the message that came through the channels of transmission was not always the same as the one that went in. As I said before, on such occasions (and they are by no means limited to times of revolution and rebellion), the ideas that are derived and transmitted suffer a sea-change in the process of transmission and assimilation. We find this happening in the French Revolution with words like *tiers état* (Third Estate), "liberty" and "popular sovereignty" to which *menu peuple* or *sans-culottes,* gave an entirely different meaning from that given by their *bourgeois* or Jacobin instructors; but it was always one that best served the political purposes they had in mind—so much so that, before the end of the Revolution (again as we noted before), the common people had acquired a revolutionary programme and ideology of their own. But, of course, a great deal of this depended on the experience they gathered as the Revolution progressed; and, quite apart from the question of surviving records, such a phenomenon—that of the evolution of an independent ideology "from below"—could only happen where it was given time to do so.[6]

In this sense, as in so many others, the French Revolution was unique. It was certainly not an experience shared with the Canadian rebellions of 1837 and 1838 which, in both cases and in both years, were throttled almost as soon as they began. But short-lived as they were, they afford us some opportunity to discern a popular ideology which can be distinguished from that of the leaders. This is particularly the case with the Lower Canadian rebellion which is the better documented of the two; moreover, it has the additional advantage of having been explored at considerable depth by M. Fernand Ouellet of the University of Montreal. M. Ouellet used the court-martial records and the depositions of witnesses to draw up an impressive list of leaders and participants in the two outbreaks that were based respectively on the Richelieu Valley to the north and northwest and the Eastern Townships to the south and southeast of Montreal. The leaders and *élites* among the *Patriotes*, he found, though conscious of the economic crisis from which the rebellion began (and how could they not be?) were more concerned with a *political* and *national* than any economic solution; essentially, they aimed to establish a *nation canadienne* and to take power from the existing *parti bureaucrate* which represented the British "connection". A minority, represented by a radical wing headed by Robert Nelson and Dr. Côté, was in favour of going further: to uproot the old seigneurial and "feudal" system by abolishing the *seigneuries* (whether English-owned or French), the *lots et ventes* (taxes on land-sales), and the tithe paid to the Church as well. But this last demand was strongly resisted by the majority (the lawyers, politicians and merchants of Quebec and Montreal, who played little or no part in the second phase of the rebellion in November 1838) on the grounds that to strike at tithe would be to weaken the Church, which must be defended as a vital element in the *nation canadienne*.

Their followers—the *habitants* of the villages to the north, south and east of Montreal—had, according to Ouellet, other priorities. First on the list were the economic necessities of bread, jobs and land. Next came the national solution which they shared with their leaders; but this, too, tended to be seen as a means to solve their economic problems by removing the foreigner's monopoly and privileged competition. Most significant perhaps was the demand—in some villages at least—to end the *seigneuries* and tithes. It was by no means universal; but had the rebellion lasted longer, is it not likely it would have played a larger part? At any rate, Ouellet supposes that it was the fear of such a fundamental challenge to property "from below" that persuaded many of the leaders either to pull their punches or (like Papineau) to condemn the rebellion even before it began.[7]

One final question remains. What happens to popular ideology once the rebellion or revolution is over or suppressed? Does it disappear so that it has to start all over again? Or does it go underground and re-emerge in a more favourable situation? If we take the most richly documented example of all, the example of France, it would seem amply proven that the second question points to the right answer. In the succession of revolutions that followed the first, the traditions of 1789 and 1793 can clearly be seen to have survived in 1830, 1848 and 1871 (some would add, and with some justice, in May 1968 as well). But the recipients of the message and tradition in these new revolutions are no longer the same as before; they are no longer the *sans-culottes* or *menu peuple* of 1789 or 1793. With the beginnings of an industrial revolution in France there emerge, as the shock-troops of these later revolutions, the *ouvriers* of 1830 and the *prolétaires* of 1848 and 1871. And with the changes in society the message changes as well. Now added to the principles of 1789—the Rights of Man and Popular Sovereignty—come new ideas, forward-looking ideas more closely related to the needs of an emerging industrial working class. In 1848 these are still the somewhat "utopian" (and therefore, in some respects, backward-looking) ideas of Babeuf and Buonarroti, St. Simon, Cabet, Proudhon and Louis Blanc; but during the Paris Commune, in 1871, these "utopian-socialist" ideas are being successfully challenged by the new "scientific-socialist" ideas of Marx and Engels which look solely to the future and draw little comfort from the past. Thus with each generation a new set of derived ideas becomes superimposed on those of the generation before.

So it would seem that there must come a new and permanent shift in the balance of the inherent and derived ideas which, as I have been arguing, are the two main components of the ideology of popular protest—with the balance gradually tilted towards the more formal and structured systems and programmes, and the old backward-looking ideology tending to phase out or to take a back seat.

So it would seem; but, of course, there are set-backs and diversions, as when parties of the extreme Right, far from enriching the store of forward-looking ideas, if given the opportunity, reverse the process and turn the clock back by using the most sophisticated means of communication for backward-looking ends. But this is another story into which I do not propose to venture further here.

Notes

1. Bernard Bailyn, *The Ideological Origins of the American Revolution* (Cambridge, Mass., 1967); Carolyn Robbins, *The Eighteenth-Century Commonwealthman* (Cambridge, Mass., 1961).
2. Joseph Ernst, " 'Ideology' and an Economic Interpretation of the Revolution", in Alfred Young (ed.), *The American Revolution. Explorations in the History of American Radicalism* (DeKalb, 1976), pp. 159–75.
3. Pauline Maier, *From Resistance to Revolution* (New York, 1972).
4. Jesse Lemisch, "Jack Tar in the Street, Merchant Seamen in the Politics of Revolutionary America", *William and Mary Quarterly*, 25 (1968), pp. 371–407.
5. See pieces by Gary B. Nash, Edward Countryman and Dirk Hoerder in Alfred Young (ed.), *Explorations*, pp. 3–36, 37–70, 233–71.
6. For much of the above, see G. Rudé, *The Crowd in the French Revolution* (Oxford, 1959): and Albert Soboul, *The Parisian Sans-Culottes and the French Revolution, 1793–4* (Oxford, 1964).
7. Fernand Ouellet, "Les insurrections de 1837–38: un phénomène social", *Histoire sociale* (Nov. 1968), pp. 54–82.

14

The Germination of a
Revolutionary Ideology among the
Urban *menu peuple* of 1789

At our colloquium at Göttingen I posed the question of the precise moment when the French *menu peuple* of town and countryside moved from a "pre-revolutionary" to a revolutionary state of consciousness.[1] At the time I merely noted the problem while suggesting that it required further examination. This, rather hesitantly I admit, is what I propose to give it here.

This question of the birth or germination of a revolutionary consciousness, or "sensibility", among the common people of France is one that has been broached by a number of writers on the revolution, particularly during the past ten to fifteen years—notably by Robert Mandrou, Michel Vovelle and Jeffrey Kaplow. Mandrou's study, dealing with popular culture in the seventeenth and eighteenth centuries, adds a new dimension to the discussion of the outlook (mentalité) of the urban *menu peuple* during the century and a half preceding the Revolutionary outbreak. The question Mandrou raises is, does there appear from his examination of the "Blue Library" at Troyes, on which his study is focussed, any indication of the emergence among its readers (known to have included many of the "common sort") of a body of "philosophical" ideas or of a critical view of the society of the day? The author, in fact, finds no such sign; and he explains that this so-called "popular" literature, though undoubtedly digested by a wide reading public, was the product of quite different social elements whose intention, far from being to awaken its readers to an understanding of the realities of the social and economic problems of the day, was rather to lull them into a false sense of security or unawareness. In fact, we are here concerned with a "popular" literature only in the sense that it was the common people who read it while its purveyors reflected an ideology that was neither of the middle nor lower class, but of the rulers of the Old

Régime itself. So the author (here following Daniel Mornet) concludes from his material that the popular outlook of the period was still "primitive" and apolitical and that it would be useless to try to locate in it as yet the germs of a "philosophical" or revolutionary body of ideas.[2]

Vovelle's method is different and the questions he asks are more complex. In a recent article, published in England under the French title of "le tournant des mentalités en France en 1750–1789: la sensibilité pré-révolutionnaire",[3] he discusses different aspects of this "pre-revolutionary sensibility" among both the middle and lower classes; and he cites in particular their attitudes to death, to church and religion, to marriage and illegitimacy, and also to crime and Enlightenment literature; and, in the course of his investigation, he notes in particular the changing attitude to these problems among the middle class. But, having noted this change in the outlook of this class, he asks a number of pertinent questions: what part, in fact, did these types of outlook and behaviour play in the transition to the Revolution? And, even more relevant to our present discussion, to what degree did these changes in outlook and behaviour, that Vovelle notes among the eighteenth-century middle class, extend to the lower classes of craftsmen, shopkeepers or labourers? He cites a few examples of this, particularly in a changing popular attitude towards death; but he doubts whether any marked transformation of collective (therefore of popular) "sensibility" came about as the result of the diffusion of ideas and habits (*moeurs*) of a middle-class *élite* formed, in part at least, by reading the classics of the Enlightenment. But changes in popular attitudes, that marked the early days of the Revolution, he would trace back rather to other origins more closely associated with a popular tradition, such as the charivari, the carnival and the *confrérie* (fraternity), which were often marked by the brutal or violent displays that reappear in the Great Fear of 1789, the September Massacres and the food riots of 1789 to 1792. And (he concludes) it is not until after the first years of revolution that the "sensibility" of the bourgeois *élites* will be diffused and become absorbed by the common people. (I shall return to this question of the absorption of others' ideology later in the chapter.)

Let us now turn to Kaplow who had the excellent idea of studying the outlook and behaviour of the Parisian "labouring poor" in the half century before the Revolution. That surely, one might say, is the right way to determine the exact point at which the common people were won over by revolutionary ideas! But to achieve that goal it would have been necessary to have explored the problem far more deeply than the author has attempted; besides—and this does little to advance his aim—he has allowed himself to be bewitched by the unhistorical notion of the "culture of poverty" derived from the sociologist Oscar Lewis. The debt led him to exaggerate the primitiveness and passivity of the Parisian *menu peuple* up to the point of outbreak of the Revolution. This is to ignore the early political lessons, however superficial and rudimentary, that they had learned from the Paris Parlement in the course of its prolonged dispute with the ministers of the Crown from the early fifties onwards. It is also to inflate somewhat the independent role played by the bourgeoisie, important as it undoubtedly was in the education of the people in political ideas. For here, the author appears to be saying, we see the bourgeoisie rushing onto the stage and, like the good fairy in *Cinderella*, transforming the whole scene with a wave of her wand. The bourgeoisie, concludes Kaplow, having made this break-through, "used the labouring poor as their shock troops, and the labouring poor—or at least some of its constituent elements—was in part shaken out of its lethargy and soon began to pursue a program of its own".[4]

My method will be different, I shall examine the various forms of activity of the common people—notably in Paris—in the twenty years before the Revolution in order to attempt to find the moment when their ideas, outlook or "sensibility" became transformed into a revolutionary ideology and consciousness, and I will go on to attempt a comparison (somewhat rapid and superficial, it is true) with popular experience in other towns or cities in France, Britain and America.

Let us begin with the last popular outbreak of the Old Régime: the "flour war" of the summer of 1775 which convulsed the capital itself and a dozen adjoining *généralités* besides. The movement made a big stir at Versailles and Paris and spread widely over the countryside to the north and west of the capital stretching from the Channel to the Loire.[5] There has been no lack of historians and observers (Voltaire prominent among the latter) to explain the incident in terms of a conspiracy hatched by courtiers and clergy with the object of discrediting the physiocratic ideas of Turgot. But, as is by now reasonably well established, the explanation is ill-founded. For, on closer examination, it appears to have been essentially a food riot of small consumers of town and countryside, distinguished by widespread popular price control (*taxation populaire*), which spread by example and word of mouth from market to market and from village to village over a considerable part of northern and central France. What was *new* about it, or was it a largely traditional form of exercise? Or, again, was it a movement whose message betokened the end of an old system and the dawn of a new?

The "flour war", it is true, was new in the sense that it assumed a volume exceeding that of any popular outbreak since the 1720s; remarks were also attributed to some of the rioters in Paris which conveyed an unusual degree of class hostility; and the course and momentum of the whole movement in many respects anticipated the Great Fear that spread through the French countryside in the summer of 1789. Yet, in other respects, the differences between 1775 and 1789 are more striking still; among the rioters of 1775 there was not only no trace of any Enlightenment influence whatever (hardly surprising in itself), but there was also no sign of any particular resentment against royal officials, clergy or landowners. The hostility of the insurgents is still solely directed against hoarders of grain, flour and bread; so the targets as before are the merchant and the baker, and the *curé* and the *seigneur* only become so when their barns and granaries are found to be full of grain. In short, far from being a *peasant* movement in which a degree of peasant consciousness might be looked for, it was a movement of small consumers from towns and villages in which peasants participated alongside the porters and riverside workers who, together with their wives and daughters, thronged the streets of Pontoise, Paris, Meaux and Beaumont-sur-l'Oise, as they had done in earlier years of shortage in 1725, 1740, 1752 and 1768 and would do so again, as shortage continued in 1778, 1784 and 1788.

The bookseller Alexandre Hardy, in his bookshop in the rue de la Parcheminerie in Paris noted half a dozen of these later events in his *Journal*—notably the Toulouse "revolt" of 24 June 1786, when bread sold at five sous a pound and several persons were killed,[6] and the angry popular response to the royal decree of June 1787, which reintroduced freedom of the grain trade, a measure that Hardy deplored "as people [had] not yet forgotten the disturbances provoked by the cost of bread in 1776 (sic!), which were the unfortunate result of a similar policy . . .".[7] But, as we shall see, it was only in 1788, in the middle of the "aristocratic revolt", that Hardy would be able to record that the food riot was beginning to take a "political" turn.

Meanwhile, there had also been strikes in the city, like those of the printers in October 1776 and of the building workers and journeymen carpenters in 1785 and 1786; and, above all, there was the porters' strike in January 1786 which so vividly impressed Marcel Rouff.[8] Daniel Mornet, however, has noted with greater wisdom that strikes of that period were "less important than food riots". Industrialization was still thinly spread and the conflicts it engendered were still comparatively rare, were strictly regional and had limited repercussions.[9] So it is not in such movements that one should look for the early germination of a revolutionary consciousness among the common people. During the Revolution, it is true enough that there were occasions when strikes had political consequences, as in the weeks following the proscription of workers' "coalitions" by the Le Chapelier Law in 1791 and the resistance aroused among workers by the Jacobins' wage cuts of 1794.

But such facts do not justify Daniel Guérin's claim that the strike thereby became converted into a political weapon;[10] for such a development properly belongs to what took place in the silk industry at Lyons in the 1830s; so it is to stretch the bounds of credibility to talk of the emergence of a political strike in France during the still strictly "pre-industrial" period of the 1790s.

A new development, noted by observers of popular attitudes during the half-century before the Revolution, was a growing hostility towards the clergy. This might be largely attributable to the agitation of the Parlement, as in its campaign against the Jesuits in 1727 and its opposition to the Archbishop of Paris over the refusal of the sacrament to Jansenists in 1752. On this latter occasion, the Marquis d'Argenson, a former minister and now a stern critic of government, reported: "Two days ago [it was in May 1752], marketwomen on the Pont Neuf abused the Archbishop saying he deserved to be drowned for wanting to stop them [Jansenists] from receiving the sacraments of the Church."[11] Later in the century, however, the people seem to have developed their own reasons for being critical of the Church or the clergy. Hardy, who commented freely on such matters, noted incidents in the 1780s, in which the behaviour of the parish clergy provoked protests from the common people—as happened at the churches of St. Merri and St. Nicholas-des-Champs in June and December 1783, at St. Séverin in February 1784 and at several other churches in 1786. Yet, on closer inspection, it would seem that popular disapproval might be as readily aroused by an excess of religious zeal on the part of the parishioners as by any general feelings of hostility to the clergy. This appears to have been the case at the church of St. Séverin where the curé proposed to cancel the procession of the Eucharist owing to bad weather but (as Hardy noted in his *Journal*) "was forced to go out and continue with the procession and thus scandalously submit to the dictation of the parish poor". And, five years later, in a somewhat different context, Hardy was astounded to witness the enthusiasm and discipline of the people of the Faubourg St. Marcel who, on the occasion of the inauguration of the new church of St. Geneviève, marched in serried ranks, decked in the robes and bearing the sacred objects of their *confréries;* and he added that the more well-to-do inhabitants of the quarter through which the procession passed wondered what might happen if these humble citizens, marching with such discipline and in such large numbers, chose to turn their demonstration to another purpose.[12]

This fear of the assembled people was nothing new. Both the lawyer Barbier, another chronicler, and d'Argenson himself had drawn attention to it on the occasion of public executions and of the seizure of children from poor families—to be shipped to the colonies, it was believed— more than forty years before. On one occasion, in May 1750, when a score of Parisians of "the meaner sort" gathered outside the Parlement building, Barbier noted that "it was generally agreed . . . that the common people must not be allowed to become aware of their strength, a prospect that causes the government considerable concern"; and d'Argenson, perhaps more given to alarm, more than once warned his readers of the danger of "imminent revolution".[13] Hardy would, of course, have all the greater cause for such premonitions when large-scale popular riots followed the successive "exiles" of the Parlement, in the course of the "aristocratic revolt" of 1787 and 1788. In the first round it was mainly the "crazy young people" of the Law Courts and luxury trades that gathered in the Place Dauphine and on the Pont Neuf in the vicinity of the Courts. But, at the end of August 1788, things took a more serious turn when the *menu peuple* of the Faubourgs, impelled by a sharp rise in the price of bread, began to join the demonstrations; and at 9 p.m. on 24 August we find Hardy noting in his *Journal:* "The common people of the fbg. St. Antoine and the fbg. St. Marcel have come to swell the numbers of the urchins [*polissons*] of the legal quarter and this has steadily increased the disorders."[14]

On 6 August he had reported the arrival of regiments on the outskirts of the capital to ensure public peace (it was said) and "to contain the common people who, the Government feared, were threatening to revolt"; and, on 5 September, he stated more explicitly that troops were brought in "to subdue the inhabitants of the Faubourgs of St. Antoine and St. Marcel and to prevent the outbreak of riots which were expected to follow the rise in the price of bread that the authorities had in mind."[15]

And, in fact, as foreseen, the people rioted; but, even more seriously, under the dual stimulus of food shortages and agitation, they began to be drawn into the political movement; and it was no longer as marionettes manipulated by the Parlement that they were now beginning to challenge their rulers, including the king himself and the princes attending him at Versailles. Hardy, ever sensitive to changes in the popular mood, reported the following exchanges: on 25 November 1788, when the price of the 4-lb loaf rose to 12½ sous, a working housewife shouted in a baker's shop "that it was monstrous to allow the poor to starve in this way, and that they should go and set fire to the four corners of the château at Versailles" and she refused to be silenced;[16] and, on 13 February following, as the 4-lb loaf rose further to 14½ sous, "some people were heard to say [Hardy continued] that the princes had hoarded the grain supply [as in the days of the *pacte de famine!*] the better to overthrow M. Necker whose removal from office they so ardently desired".[17]

So an important stage had been reached in the formation of a sense of consciousness among the common people; in defending their daily bread they were no longer directing their anger against mere bakers and merchants as they had done in 1775, but from now on the target was the Government, represented by the King in his palace at Versailles. It was a stage of development that went far beyond the "culture of poverty" as seen by Kaplow. Nevertheless, it would be premature to read into it the beginnings of a revolutionary ideology; that would come later.

At this point, however, it will be of some interest to attempt a brief comparison between the *menu peuple* of Paris, on the eve of the Revolution, and their counterparts in other cities at a pre- or quasi-revolutionary stage both in France and elsewhere. In England there was, of course, no revolution at this time; yet it is evident that, by 1789, the common people of London at least had reached a far higher degree of political sophistication than those of Paris: to illustrate the point we may cite as examples the events connected with John Wilkes's rise to power in the City and the turbulence and political excitement attending the Gordon Riots of 1780, a popular outbreak that impressed Sébastian Mercier in Paris both by its violence and its discipline. The reason is clear enough: at this stage Londoners still preserved memories of the 1640s; moreover, in the century that followed they still received their political education from the Common Council of the City, a far more radical and "democratic" teacher than its Parisian equivalent, the predominantly aristocratic Parlement. But once the revolutionary bourgeoisie in France came onto the stage the roles would be reversed and it would be the Parisians' turn to surpass the political sophistication of the English.[18]

If the political level of Londoners was higher that that of Parisians before "the age of revolution" began, this was even more the case with the craftsmen and mechanics of the larger towns in North America. To see that this was so one has only to read the recent studies made by a number of young American scholars in the last decade under the influence of Alfred Young of the University of Northern Illinois at De Kalb. These strongly suggest that a rapid political development was taking place among the popular classes in New York, Boston and Philadelphia (towns with a population ranging between 16,000 and 25,000 at this time) during the fifteen or twenty years preceding the outbreak of the revolution and American War. This can be seen in the way these classes turned to their own advantage the great Stamp Act riots of 1765, during which the Bostonians, for example, compelled their middle-class leaders to divert the course taken by their demonstrations in order to pull down the houses of certain of the city's leaders who had enraged the crowd by their imposition of the Stamp Act levy.

It was at Boston, too, that the annual Pope's Day procession, when the Pope was burned in effigy, became "politicized" (as the charivari later became in France) with the substitution for the Pope of Lord North, author of the Intolerable Acts against Boston, as the main target of popular anger. But it was at Philadelphia, a port and industrial city of 25,000 inhabitants, that this popular political awareness reached its pre-revolutionary peak. When Thomas Paine settled there in 1774, he found that the "mechanics" had already had their own political assemblies and organizations for the past two years; alongside the poorer craftsmen and labourers they dominated the recently formed militia and, in 1776, when the old authorities left their posts, it was the craftsmen that entered the breach and took over the direction of municipal affairs;[19] and it was also of them that Governor Morris appears to have been thinking when, after a mass meeting in New York, he declared that "the mob begins to think and to reason".[20]

And what of France's own provincial cities? did the common people, there too have a pre-revolutionary history similar to that of the Parisians? Dijon, Rennes and Grenoble, which like Paris had Parlements of their own, also experienced tumultuous events in 1787 and 1788; yet this does not appear to have been the case with Strasbourg, Bordeaux, Rouen, Nancy and Marseilles unless one takes account of the hundred or more food riots that swept through France between 1774 and 1789.[21] In the weeks preceding the fall of the Bastille their situation is likely to have been similar to that of Nancy where Arthur Young reported on 15 July (when the news of the Paris events of the 14th had not yet arrived) that he had been told: "We are a provincial town; we must await news of what is happening in Paris; yet we must expect the worst from the common people, as they are half famished from the present price of bread and are, in consequence, on the point of riot."[22]

It was only at Lyons, the great centre of the silk industry in the South with its 600 merchant-manufacturers and 6,000 labour-employing *maîtres-ouvriers* that the situation was radically different. "I do not believe," writes Jaurès, "that any other city in France was as violently torn by social conflict in the course of the eighteenth century."[23] In fact, at Lyons, the century was studded with a series of tough battles in which the *maîtres-ouvriers* led their journeymen in struggle against the merchant-manufacturers. But, as Maurice Garden argues, "the workers did not revolt during periods of great economic hardship . . . organized movements could only take place in the rare periods of assured employment and relative prosperity".[24] (This was also true at this time of Paris.) And he cites half a dozen cases of which the most important were those of 1774 and 1786; and he underlines the difference between the two:

> If one wishes [he writes] to distinguish in a few words between these two great wages movements . . . one can say that 1744 marked the refusal of the *artisans* to concede that the merchants had won a virtual monopoly over the silk 'Factory'; whereas in 1786 the *workers* as a whole no longer disputed the ascendancy won by the merchants but united to win better conditions from their rapacious employers. Between these two dates a revolutionary change had taken place in silk workers' consciousness, involving a very different social analysis of working conditions in the industry.

But, he continues, this radical change of attitude applies as much to the merchants as to the craftsmen and their journeymen; and, by now, the employers "are clearly conscious of belonging to a different class from their workers; moreover, by their unity and firm action, they have even succeeded in creating among their former workers the first signs of a class consciousness whose development had been delayed by their ambivalent status within the structure of the 'Factory' ".[25]

This struggle of the two parties on the industrial front became extended to the electoral field when the moment came to nominate delegates to represent their guilds on the Third Estate of the City of Lyons. The first meeting of the silk "Factory" took place in the Cathedral of St. Jean on 26 February 1789, when the *maîtres-ouvriers*, anxious for revenge, proposed the total exclusion of the merchants and their associates from the assembly; and, indeed, at the next day's meeting only *maîtres-ouvriers* were appointed; and, Jaurès noted, among the thirty-four persons elected were "the militants who for the past several years had led the battle against the merchants and their allies within the municipal oligarchy. So the economic struggle was extended to the political".[26]

So, as in no other city in France, at Lyons it was the workers' delegates who were called upon to represent their guild in the assembly of the Third Estate. Yet, for all the significance of the event, nothing of any great moment resulted: the *maîtres-ouvriers*, while conscious of their subordination to the merchants, were quite incapable of demanding reforms that might radically improve their own conditions or those of their journeymen; and, to cite Jaurès again: "There was not a single word or turn of phrase in the grievances they drafted that reflected the particular attitude or needs of these groups."[27] Moreover, this incapability lasted the whole course of the Revolution and survived the Jacobin challenge at Lyons in 1793 as well as its suppression in the Federal revolt that followed and the bloody massacres of the "Thermidorian reaction" of 1795. For, paradoxically, the very class consciousness that had developed in the relations between merchants and workers proved a stumbling block to the effective prosecution at

Lyons of a "bourgeois" revolution like that of 1789; and it was not until
the changed conditions of the early 1830s that the silk-workers were able
to play an independent historical role.

In Paris the situation was quite a different one and neither craftsmen
nor simple wage-earners found themselves at any time in a position
similar to that of the *maîtres-ouvriers* or their journeymen at Lyons; for
(to quote Soboul) "by and large in Paris the workers' outlook was clearly
marked by the petty bourgeois outlook of the crafts, and both drew on
the ideology of the bourgeoisie".[28] And this ideology, whether
"borrowed" or imposed, came to the Paris worker through the impact
and experience of the traditional workshop, where (unlike his Lyons
counterpart) he worked alongside his master, who, under these
conditions, served as a major mouthpiece for the transmission of current
revolutionary ideas. Obviously this proved a great advantage for the
education of the future *sans-culotte*, an education, moreover, that proved
considerably more effective than that provided in earlier political crises
by his former teacher of the Paris Parlement.

But this education could only begin after the campaign for the
elections to the Estates General had been launched in the early months
of 1789. The first great step, of course, was the Royal Government's
invitation to the Estates to meet, followed closely by the publication of
the Abbé Sieyès's famous pamphlet in which the bourgeoisie, as
spokesman for the Third Estate, declared itself ready to assume power
in the name of the nation as a whole. The results of these two
announcements were, as we know, sensational. On the one hand, the
summoning of the Estates aroused in the people the "great hope"
described by Georges Lefebvre: "so strange an event had wakened the
hope, at once dazzling and nebulous, of a new era in which men would
lead happier lives";[29] and Arthur Young, travelling through
Champagne, writes of his encounter (on 12 July) with a young peasant
woman who told him that "something was to be done for the poor by
some of the rich, though she did not know how or by whom, but may
God bring us something better as the taxes and obligations are crushing
us!"[30]

In addition, the notion of the "third estate" began to stir the
imagination of the Parisian *menu peuple* between February and April of
that year: the first sign that I have found of this was in the use of the term
by a Paris craftsman when questioned by the police on 21 April (though,
of course, it may have been in circulation for some weeks before).[31] A
week later, workers of the Faubourg St. Antoine, while rioting against
two local manufacturers who (it was alleged) had complained of the high
level of wages, shouted "Long live the Third Estate!" together with
"Long live the King!" and "Long live M. Necker!";[32] or it might be

used in the more challenging form of a direct question: "es-tu du tiers état?", such as that addressed to Jean Rossignol, a journeyman goldsmith who later became a general of the Republic, when he first came to Paris in the spring or early summer of 1789.[33] But in the mouths of the common people the term took on quite a different meaning from that given to it in January by the Abbè Sieyès. It no longer meant the *nation*, let alone the bourgeoisie; but, having undergone a trans-formation in the course of its adoption by the common people, the "third estate" (usually without capitals) now became the symbol of the people—the common people—in struggle, and they thereby became closely identified with a revolution that they were beginning to claim as their own, and the main enemy of the "tiers état", thus conceived, became the "aristocrats" among whom might readily be counted a wealthy bourgeois like the manufacturer Réveillon for all that he had been elected to represent the Third Estate in the Faubourg St. Antoine. And we find Jean-Nicolas Pepin, porter to a chandler in the Faubourg, when arrested for causing a nuisance on the night of 13 July, explaining his unruly conduct to the police in the following terms:

> that there had been a great throng of people at the "Arquebuse" [musket-range] and that the men assembled there had brought thirty or more companions with them to bring help to the nation against the enemy that wanted to destroy all Parisians, and that the enemy was the nobility.[34]

So the political awakening of the people of Paris took the form of a profound arousal of revolutionary consciousness which extended at least between the months of April and July 1789; and this arousal involved eventually not only the *cadres*—shopkeepers and craftsmen—but also poor uneducated workers like Jean-Nicolas Pepin whose testimony we just cited. The transformation among the peasantry took a different form. Aroused by the "great hope" and the news of the betrayal of the aristocracy at Versailles, the whole village rose in revolt and, for the first time, constituted itself a "class" in order to overcome the obstruction of the landowners, whether noble or bourgeois, and sweep away all feudal survivals.

And what of the common people of the other great cities in France—Bordeaux, Marseilles, Nantes, Rouen, Strasbourg? Did they also take the initiative or did they more simply, as Arthur Young's informants assured him, wait to follow the example of Paris? Jaurès says nothing of this and, since Jaurès wrote, the authors of regional studies do not appear to have broached the question. As for myself, I have not had the occasion to extend my research in the Parisian archives into those in France's provincial towns. So, in this as in so many other questions

touching the seemingly inexhaustible treasure-house of French
Revolutionary studies, there is still work to be done.

Notes

1. G. Rudé, "European Popular Protest and Ideology on the Eve of the French
   Revolution", in the present collection.
2. R. Mandrou, *De la culture populaire aux 17e et 18e siècles* (Paris, 1975).
3. M. Vovelle, "Le tournant des mentalités en France 1750–1789: la sensibilité pré-
   révolutionnaire", in *Social History*, 5 (1977), pp. 605–29.
4. J. Kaplow, *The Names of Kings* (New York, 1972), p. 170.
5. See my articles dealing with the grain riots of 1775 in the *Annales historiques de la
   Révolution française*, 143 (1956) pp. 139–79; and 165 (1961), pp. 305–26; and see E.
   Faure, *La disgrâce de Turgot* (Paris, 1961).
6. S. Hardy, "Mes loisirs, ou journal d'événements tels qu'ils parviennent à ma
   connaissance". Ms. in 8 vols., pp. 11764–89, Bilbiothèque nationale, fonds
   français, S. 6680–7, IV, p. 9.
7. Ibid., p. 123.
8. M. Rouff, "Une grève de gagne-deniers en 1789 à Paris", in *Revue historique*, 165
   (1910), pp. 332–46.
9. D. Mornet, *Les origines intellectuelles de la Révolution française* (Paris, 1933), p. 449.
10. In his *La Lutte de classes sous La Révolution française: bourgeois et bras nus* (Paris,
    1946).
11. *Journal et mémoires du Marquis d'Argenson,* 9 vols. (Paris, 1859), VII, pp. 226–7.
12. Hardy, "Mes loisirs", V. pp. 322–3, 394–5, 410; VI, p. 320; VIII . . .
13. *Journal historique et anecdotique du règne de Louis XV, par E.J.F. Barbier, avocat au
    Parlement de Paris,* 4 vols., (Paris, 1847), III, p. 153, and D'Argenson, *Journal et
    mémoires,* VI, p. 403; VII, pp. 214–15.
14. Hardy, "Mes loisirs", VIII, p. 62.
15. Ibid., pp. 35, 73.
16. Ibid., pp. 154–5.
17. Ibid., p. 250.
18. G. Rudé, *Paris and London in the Eighteenth Century: Studies in Popular Protest*
    (London, 1970), pp. 57–60.
19. Alfred F. Young (ed.), *The American Revolution. Explorations in the History of
    American Radicals* (De Kalb, 1974). See especially G.B. Nash, "Social Change in
    the Growth of Prerevolutionary Urban Radicalism", pp. 5–36; E. Foner, "Tom
    Paine's Republic, Radical Ideology and Social Change", pp. 187–232; and D.
    Horder, "Boston Leaders and Boston Crowds, 1765–1776", pp. 233–72.
20. Cit. Foner, p. 196.
21. Mornet, *Les origines intellectuelles,* pp. 444–8.
22. A. Young, *Travels in France during the Years 1787–1788–1789* (New York, 1969),
    pp. 147–8.
23. J. Jaurès, *Histoire socialiste de la Révolution française* (ed. A. Soboul, 7 vols., [Paris,
    1968–73], I, p. 177).
24. M. Garden, *Lyons et les Lyonnaise au XVIIe siècle* (Paris, 1970), p. 574.
25. Ibid., pp. 580–1.
26. Jaurès, *Histoire socialiste,* I, p. 180.
27. Ibid., p. 181. See also L. Trenard, "La crise sociale lyonnaise à la veille de la
    Révolution", in *Revue d'histoire moderne,* VI (1959), pp. 81–120, esp. 118–19.

28. A. Soboul, commenting on Jaurès' remark concerning the Parisian working-class in Jaurès, *Histoire socialiste*, I, p. 229, n. 26.
29. G. Lefebvre, *Quatre-vingt-neuf* (Paris, 1939), p. 112.
30. Young, *Travels*, p. 144.
31. Archives nationales, Y18762 (21 April 1789).
32. Arch. nat., KK 641, fo. 17.
33. A. Mathiez, *Les grandes journées de la Constituante* (Paris, 1913), pp. 3–5.
34. Interrogation du nommé Pepin, decrété d'être assigné pour être oui, 29 juillet 1789. Ibid.

Part III
Urbanization, Protest and Crime

15

The growth of cities and popular revolt, 1750–1850: with particular reference to Paris

It can hardly be disputed that the older type of European city, in its "pre-industrial" period at least, has appeared as a spawning-ground for popular disturbance. Large capital cities and old industrial centres have clearly been more subject to rioting and revolutionary outbreaks than rural districts or market towns. To prove the point, we have but to cite the example of London in 1640 to 1780; of Paris in 1789 and in the successive revolutions of the nineteenth century; of Lyons in the 1740s, 1780s and 1830s; and of Bristol, Nottingham and Derby in 1831. Popular rebellion has, in fact, appeared to grow out of the size and the structure of cities; and the winding lanes, tall tenements and crowded markets of the Croix Rousse in Lyons, the St Antoine district in Paris, or the Strand and Spitalfields in London have, political factors permitting, been an almost standing invitation for street demonstrations or the erection of barricades.[1]

But what sort of rebellion was it? Was it the more or less spontaneous outbreak of the poorest of the poor, the socially unstable, the scourings of the slum districts or of the "criminals classes"? or was it, more characteristically, the challenge of more "respectable" elements among the lower classes, whether master craftsmen or skilled workers, men of settled occupation and abode? or was it, on occasion, a combination of these two? The question is prompted by the assumption of certain writers in the field of urban history that crime, overcrowding and destitution, following in the wake of rapid city growth, have been the main breeding-ground for social protest, riot and revolution.

In its more conventional and unsophisticated form, the point is made by the late Dr Dorothy George, the distinguished English social historian, who when writing of London in the eighteenth century, attributes, without examination or question, the anti-Catholic Gordon

Riots of 1780 to "the inhabitants of the dangerous districts who were always ready for pillage".[2] Dorothy Marshall has made the even bolder claim that the English eighteenth-century "mob" in general was largely recruited from social dregs, prostitutes, pimps and receivers.[3] A more refined variant of this theme is that promoted by the French historian and sociologist, Louis Chevalier, in his provocative book, *Classes laborieuses et classes dangereuses*.[4] Using a wealth of demographic and literary materials, M. Chevalier illustrates the rapid growth of Paris during the first half of the nineteenth century and graphically relates this growth and its attendant overcrowding and loosening of old social ties to a proliferation of crime, impoverishment and prostitution, and to the emergence of a "new" Paris, resentful, depressed, uprooted and proletarian, as a hostile counter to the "old". These are the "dangerous" classes, easily given to crime and violence, whom he closely identifies with the new urban workers as a whole.

In fact, "classes dangereuses" and "classes laborieuses" become virtually synonymous terms, and Paris appears as sharply divided between two warring camps ever ready to jump at each other's throat. M. Chevalier does not specifically deal with popular disturbance—in fact, he quite deliberately stops short of any such treatment; but he paraphrases with apparent approval Balzac's verdict that "le crime s'emplit de la révolte populaire et se métamorphose en elle"; and, looking back on the Revolution of 1789, he sees it, "à certains égards, comme un règlement de comptes entre ces deux catégories de population: la vielle bourgeoisie et les autres, ceux que l'on désignait aux époques antérieures par ces mots de sauvages, barbares, nomades". Again, the basic conflict of the 1830s and 1840s is presented as "(le) problème d'une population qui tente de se faire une place dans un milieu hostile et qui, n'y parvenant pas, s'abandonne à toutes les haines, à toutes les violences, à toutes les violations".[5] In short, whatever the author's reservations and intentions, the book presents a powerful case for what Mr Charles Tilly has called the "uprooting thesis" of revolution.[6]

M. Chevalier has found a qualified supporter in Professor M. Girard who, in his Sorbonne lectures on the French revolutions of the nineteenth century, writes of Paris as "sick" and unbalanced: "Qu'il y a là un déséquilibre foncier . . . deux peuples différents même d'aspects, aspects démographiques, aspects sociaux enfin, déséquilibre chronique, dangereux pour la vie de la capitale".[7]

"Dangerous", presumably, for the old established order or the old established bourgeoisie. So the implication of the argument, though it is never clearly spelled out, is not only that revolution and social protest derive, like crime, poverty and overcrowding, from rapid urbanization, but that they spring directly from them: in brief, that there is a close concordance between the one set of factors and the other. And the further implication is that this contention is by no means limited to Paris in the early nineteenth century.

So clearly, though we shall be mainly concerned with Paris in this essay, we must set the problem in a wider contest. In the first place, it may be best to put certain questions and to indicate the kinds of sources in which we may hope to find the answers. The first set of questions are similar to those with which M. Chevalier, M. Girard, M. Marcel Reinhard and others have already familiarized their readers—such questions as: how and when did the city's population grow? In which parts of the city did it settle? Was its growth accompanied by a growth of crime, poverty, destitution, suicides or illiteracy? We may follow up with such questions as: when and how did disturbances break out? Of what kind were they: strikes, food riots, rebellions or revolution? In which parts of the city did they occur? And thirdly: who took part in them, and who were their victims? Were those taking part rich, "middling", poor, or very poor? Were they bourgeois, professional men, craftsmen, shopkeepers, skilled workers, labourers, vagrants or unemployed? In which parts of the city did they live, and how were they housed? Were they long-established or recent migrants? Were they literate? Had they a criminal past? And, to do the job thoroughly, we might ask a further set of questions to determine how far the situation had changed since period X and would change further in period Y, and how far the situation in one city differed from that in others. But this would be a long and exacting task, and it will certainly not be attempted here.

Sources will naturally vary according to country and period, and what follows is intended only as a rough-and-ready guide. In the first place, there are the records familiar to the demographer and social historian: the periodic population census (unreliable in the case of France and England before 1801); returns of births and deaths and estimates of immigration; and the statistics and reports of government, parliament, police and charitable institutions relating to poverty, beggary, crime, suicides, literacy and prostitution. To determine the prosperity of districts or social groups, we may need to consult the land tax registers in England or such fiscal and notarial records as have survived in Paris after the fires of 1871. For the frequency and nature of popular disturbances, we must read the press, private correspondence, government, municipal and parliamentary reports and the records of government lawyers, the courts and the police. To determine the composition (or even the motives) of the "crowd", we may rely in part on the eye-witness accounts of journalists, casual observers or police agents; but, to offset their inadequacy and bias we must depend far more on the more "objective" information that emanates from cross-examinations by the police, from prison registers or court proceedings, such as (in England) the printed trials of the Old Bailey and (in France) the records of the Châtelet, the committee of public security during the French Revolution, or of the *gendarmerie* and the Paris prefecture of police. For the great revolutionary occasions, however, we must look to other sources: for lists of the accredited captors of the Bastille; for a return of those charged with taking part in the outbreak of June 1848; and lists of the killed and wounded and of those decorated or receiving monetary compensation or awards for overthrowing Louis XVI in 1792 or Charles X in 1830.[8]

In this short chapter, however, it is not intended to go back to first base: the basic documentary evidence will largely have to be taken as read. I propose, in fact, in depicting the growth of cities and its attendant social evils, to rely almost entirely on the published work of such experts as M. Pouthas, M. Reinhard and M. Chevalier in the case of Paris and of Mr E.A. Wrigley and Dr Dorothy George in the case of London. Equally, for my picture of the popular movements and revolutions of the time, I shall draw mainly on published work and only marginally on new source materials: partly on my own work on the eighteenth and nineteenth centuries and partly on that of others, among them Charles Tilly, David Pinkney and Rémi Gossez.

Let us begin with London in the later eighteenth century: partly because it may be useful to compare it with Paris and partly because some of the basic work has already been done in this field. During the century, the population of the "metropolis"[9] appears, in round figures, to have increased from 575,000 in 1700 to 675,000 in 1750 and to 900,000 in 1801.[10] The population of England and Wales rose, meanwhile, from 5½ million to 6½ and 9 million; so that London retained throughout the century a fairly steady proportion of 10 to 10½ per cent of the national population, compared with 9 per cent in the case of Amsterdam (which, in this respect, came second to it) and a mere 2 to 2½ per cent in the case of Paris.[11] So, relative to the national population, there was no "explosion" in eighteenth-century London—this had happened in the century before[12]—but, both absolutely and relative to the size of the national population, it remained the largest urban settlement in Europe. And it certainly had its full share of crime, violence and prostitution. From the 1750s onwards, magistrates and social workers were as loud in their horrified denunciations of these evils as the police officials and writers cited by M. Chevalier in the case of nineteenth-century Paris; and the printed *Proceedings* of the Old Bailey appear to give them ample confirmation.[13]

In what parts of the city did the population rise or decline? Dr George's figures show us that the increase mainly took place—partly through a fall in mortality, but largely from migration from within and without the city[14]—in the new areas of settlement formed by five parishes lying outside the old "Bills of Mortality" (St Marylebone, St Pancras, Paddington, Chelsea and Kensington) and in the developing "out-parishes" of Surrey and Middlesex. In contrast, the population of several of the older districts (the City, Westminster, Spitalfields) stagnated or declined; this was notably the case with the city of London, whose residential population fell by about 10,000 between 1700 and 1750.[15]

If we now turn to popular disturbances, we shall find two initial points of interest. One is that they certainly increased in scope and violence after the middle of the century, and quite out of proportion to the rise in population. Including industrial disputes, I have counted only four major London outbreaks between 1714 and 1760, compared with a dozen between 1760 and 1795; and the latter include such large-scale manifestations as those associated with John Wilkes, the wave of strikes in 1768, and the Gordon Riots of 1780.[16] The second is that these disturbances were almost exclusively centred in the older areas of declining or stagnant population: the cities of London and Westminster, the Strand, Spitalfields, Finsbury, Whitechapel and the Minories; the exceptions were the expanding parishes of Bermondsey and Southwark and certain of the urban parishes of Middlesex. And, even more significantly, they did not at any time (except briefly in the course of the week-long Gordon Riots) take place in the closely packed centres of crime, gin-swilling and prostitution, such as the shadier alleys and bye-ways of Holborn or the notorious St Giles-in-the-Fields.[17]

And who were the people taking part? Unfortunately, the information is, in this respect, not nearly so rich and so precise as it is in the case of Paris; the police and judicial reports rarely make it possible to determine whether persons arrested had had previous convictions, and there is often a very considerable doubt as to their social class or occupation. However, there are occasions when the evidence is rich enough to enable us to form a shrewd idea of the status, origins and degree of social respectability of a fair proportion of those appearing in the files. This is notably so in the case of the Gordon Riots; and here we find that the 160 persons brought to trial were generally men of settled abode and occupation, they mostly had good personal records (this is amply attested by witnesses at the Old Bailey and Southwark trials), and most frequently they lived in the streets and districts in which the riots took place; and these, though spread widely over the cities of London and Westminster, the Borough and the inner suburbs of Middlesex, barely touched the "dangerous" districts of which mention has been made above.

In the case of the earlier disturbances associated with John Wilkes, the picture is much the same. Looking down the lists of persons arrested and suspected or convicted of taking part in the disturbances, we find the names of London craftsmen, servants and apprentices living in such old-established areas of settled residence and occupation as Southwark, Bermondsey, Finsbury, Shoreditch, Spitalfields, the Strand and the city of London. Once more, the "dangerous" districts and "dangerous" classes played only a marginal role.[18]

The population of Paris,[19] unlike that of London, does not appear to have increased (except, briefly, in 1789) during the last years of the eighteenth century. Certainly, there was no population "explosion", either absolute or relative; in fact, rather the opposite is true, and the population in 1801, after years of revolution as war, had become considerably depleted in comparison with 1789.[20] In this case, statistics are notoriously unreliable as, prior to the census of 1801, there was no settled means of counting heads: sometimes it was done by counting births and deaths, sometimes by baptisms, at other times by households (foyers) or by the distribution of food cards. Official calculations made during the 1760s to 1790s range between 524,186 (the census of 1788–9) and 640–660,000 (Necker's estimate of 1784 and that of the Paris Commune in 1791). The higher appears to be the more realistic, as, to arrive at it, Necker specifically allowed for the inmates of hotels and lodging-houses, the enfants trouvés and étrangers—the whole "floating" population of non-domiciliés which the census generally omitted and which, Necker supposed, would if included have added 100–120,000 to the numbers officially recorded. If Necker's figure for 1784 is accepted, it is likely that the influx of provincials, seasonal workers and vagrants on the eve of the Revolution swelled it to perhaps a maximum of 680–700,000, from which it fell, according to the census of 1801 (which made some, if inadequate allowance for "floaters"), back to 547,756.[21]

But even if the population fell rather than increased during the latter years of the century, there were other factors present that made for that "disequilibrium" which has fascinated both M. Chevalier and Professor Girard. For one thing, there was the large number of provincial-born, which, as various calculations show, may have at any time, as in the case of London, amounted to two in three of the population.[22] M. Chevalier goes further and considers that, even allowing for the heavy fall in population after 1791, the excess of deaths over births and the considerable exodus of émigrés and army recruits were such as to prove that there must have been a considerable immigration into the capital to maintain even the depleted numbers of those years; he estimates this influx to have amounted between 1789 and 1795 to 177,000, or to nearly 30,000 a year.[23] A large proportion of these new arrivals must have been workers, who, with their families, appear already in 1791 to have accounted for half the total population of the city.[24] They accounted for an even greater proportion of the residents in the more congested districts around the central markets, along the docks by Nôtre Dame and the Ile St Louis, and in the streets surrounding the City Hall; it was these areas rather than the outlying *faubourgs* that absorbed the greater part of the navvies, porters, riverside and building workers who formed an increasing part of the city's working population. The overcrowding in these areas is revealed in a survey of 1800 (unfortunately, there is none earlier), according to which the ten sections (or revolutionary districts) with the highest population density were Arcis (near the City Hall), Marché des Innocents and Mauconseil (in the central markets); Oratoire, Lombards, Graviliers, Ponceau and Postes (all in or near the central commercial quarter); and Thermes de Julien and Sainte-Geneviève—the last two alone lying in the *faubourgs* to the south of the river.[25]

Among these workers, many, though settled residents, had rooms in lodging houses and small hotels and therefore, as *non-domiciliés*, were generally excluded from the census: they may have amounted to as many as 50,000 in 1790–1, dropping to 20,000 by 1795.[26] In addition, there were the waves of unemployed countrymen and others whom each upward swing of the economic crisis from the 1770s onwards drove towards the capital, and of whom 22,000 were herded in the *ateliers de charité* at Montmartre and elsewhere in the early months of the Revolution. As early as 1778, no less than 120,000 persons in Paris were said to be in receipt of public relief; similar numbers were recorded in 1790 and 1791; by 1794, with the heavy fall in population, they had dropped to 72,000.[27] And with destitution and overcrowding went crime and prostitution, as is graphically recorded in the daily reports of the police commissioners of the Châtelet in the early months of 1789.[28]

So Paris, both before and during the Revolution, had its slums and destitution, its uprooted, its vagrants, its criminal elements and its "dangerous" districts. How far were these factors directly reflected in the popular movements of the time, and in the nature of their participants and of the districts known to have been the most militant and rebellious?

There was only one popular outbreak of any significance in Paris in the thirty years before the Revolution; and that was the rioting provoked by the high price of bread and flower at the time of Turgot, the so-called *guerre des farines* of 1775. After the markets had been raided, and bakers' shops had been broken into and ransacked and bakers compelled to sell their bread more cheaply, 139 persons were arrested in Paris, including fourteen women. They were mainly porters and labourers; wage-earners alone accounted for nearly three in four of those arrested. They included at least eighteen unemployed. Eighty per cent were provincial-born: but this is not so surprising as the riots swept into Paris from villages beyond and those arrested included several peasants. Two in every three were unable to sign their names to the statement made to the police; 46 per cent of those living in Paris and 37 per cent of the total were inmates of lodging houses or hotels; and 15 per cent had incurred previous convictions, though all but one for relatively minor offences.[29] So here we have a disturbance which, in its Parisian (though not in its provincial) context, appears to conform in several respects to the pattern of rebellion that M. Chevalier and others have had in mind.

But it proves to be an exception, and if we now turn to the next round of riots and rebellions—those of the revolutionary period from 1787 to 1795—we shall find a somewhat different picture. Taking them as a whole, we find that those actively participating in them were a mixed population of tradesmen, workshop masters, independent craftsmen, journeymen, porters, workers in manufacture (though these were remarkably few), city poor, men and women, employed and unemployed; but most of those appearing in the records were of settled abode and occupations; the proportion of provincial-born was not above the average and, among them, only a sprinkling were branded with the "V" of the convicted thief or had been prevously sentenced for any but the most trivial of offences. Yet, within this general pattern, there were of course considerable and significant variations between one type of disturbance and another. There were, as we should expect, more women involved in food riots and fewer in political demonstrations and armed assaults; craftsmen and small masters were more prominent in the more "political" of the *journées,* such as the capture of the Bastille and the assault on the Tuileries; wage-earners and unemployed were more notably present in economic disturbances like food riots (as they had been in 1775); and the proportion of wage-earners involved was significantly higher than at any other time in the Réveillon riots of April 1789, in which the question of wages (exceptionally) played some part.

In sum, the number of those arrested or wounded contain a fair proportion of unemployed and of workers living in lodgings. In the Réveillon riots, for example, two of every thirteen workers arrested, wounded or killed were unemployed and one in four were living in lodgings; and among those arrested in connection with the Champ de Mars petition and "massacre" of July 1791, one in five lived in lodgings and one in six were unemployed. But in neither case does a "criminal element" appear to have played more than a marginal role: in the

Réveillon riots one in eight of those arrested had been previously convicted, though in a single case only on a serious charge; and in the Champ de Mars affair not more than one in forty.[30] Moreover, the percentage of provincial-born was generally not above the two-in-three average for the population as a whole; from police and other records we learn that 31 per cent of the arrested rioters of 1787–8 were provincial-born, 62 per cent of the captors of the Bastille, 66 per cent of the Réveillon rioters, and 72 per cent of both Champ de Mars demonstrators and the insurgents of "Prairial" (May 1795).[31] So newcomers were no more heavily represented among rioters than among the population as a whole; and crime and militancy rarely went together.

This, however, only disposes of a part of the question. The larger problem still remains; were political demonstrations and social protest directly associated with extreme poverty or overcrowding? If we look merely at the records of the participants, the evidence is not conclusive, though it suggests, as in the case of London, that rioters were not recruited in large numbers from the poorest of the poor. But if we turn to the sections from which the rioters were mainly drawn, it looks as though we may have to modify these first impressions. The most consistently "revolutionary" sections in terms of street disturbance (I am not speaking here of militant revolutions by political activists, which is quite another matter) were the three sections of the Faubourg St Antoine—Quinze Vingts, Popincourt and Montreuil; and three of the four sections of the Faubourgs St Marcel and St Jacques—Sainte-Geneviève, Gobelins and Observatoire. All of these but one were sections with a relatively low density of population; the one exception was Sainte-Geneviève which, with a recorded density of 12.5 square metres per inhabitant in 1800, ranked tenth among the forty-eight sections of the capital. But even if the residents of these sections were relatively thinly spread, they included pockets of high population density and enclosed some of the poorest and most depressed districts in the city. When, for example, the Commune distributed 64,000 livres in poor relief in February 1790, the two main recipients were two districts in the Faubourgs St Marcel and St Jacques, followed closely by two districts of the Faubourg St Antoine; and when subsequent distributions were made in 1791 and 1794, the general pattern was much the same.[32]

Moreover, next on the list of militant sections, after those in the three Faubourgs, came a number of sections in the north centre of the city and adjoining the central markets, the docks and commercial quarter. They include Arcis, the densely populated district near the City Hall; Arsenal, lying west of the Bastille; Louvre, Oratoire, Mauconseil and Marché des

Innocents, all adjoining the corn market; and Lombards and Gravilliers in the heart of the commercial quarter. With the exception of Arsenal, they were areas of a highly concentrated population of building workers, market and riverside porters, small shopkeepers; journeymen of sundry trades and domestic servants; and they included the five sections with the highest population density in the capital.[33]

So here, at least, there may be a certain concordance, as in the riots of 1775, between overcrowding and poverty on the one hand and social and political protest on the other. Yet this is only the case if we treat the riots all together; but if we distinguish one type of riot from the other, leave aside the more elementary forms of protest, such as food riots, and confine our attention to the most widespread and significant of these revolts—the three great political *journées* of 1789-93—the picture looks very different. On these essentially *political* occasions, the two great Faubourgs played a part immeasurably more conspicuous than the other areas we have noted. At the siege of the Bastille, the Faubourg St Antoine provided more than two in three of the 600 known civilian captors of the fortress. At the storming of the Tuileries in August 1792, between one third and one half of all the casualties suffered by the assailants were among men drawn from the two faubourgs. Again, in the armed uprising of May-June 1793, which expelled the Girondin leaders from the national convention, it was the Faubourg St Antoine which provided by far the largest number of recruits; St Marcel followed; and of the eight sections enrolling the largest number of contingents only two had a density greater than one of 40 sq. metres per inhabitant.[34] So there is little evidence here to support M. Chevalier's contention that the Revolution was, to any appreciable extent, a "settlement of accounts" between the "nomads" and the old established population of the city.

Yet there remains the awkward fact of the high sums of poor relief paid out in the very faubourgs from which the participants in the great revolutionary "days" were most consistently recruited. How to account for the apparent contradiction? And yet there may be none, as we have no reason to believe that the recipients of relief were the same persons, or lived in the same streets, as those who marched or shouldered arms on the days of riot and rebellion: other evidence indicates, rather, that the contrary was the case. However, the point is of some significance and it has been suggested[35] that even if the most active participants were not themselves overcrowded or living on the brink of destitution, they may have received an additional stimulus for acting as they did by rubbing shoulders with the poverty and hardships of their neighbours.

So we come to M. Chevalier's own chosen field of study—Paris in the first half of the nineteenth century. During these years, Paris did have something of a population "explosion", though it was appreciably smaller than London's and the proportion of Frenchmen living in the capital rose only from 2 per cent in 1801 to 2.9 per cent in 1851.[36] Yet the population grew at a pace that was three times that of the national average,[37] and here, at least, we are reasonably assured that the published figures, though their reliability under the Restoration has been questioned, were not wildly inaccurate. We may tabulate them, in round numbers, as follows:

1801	550,000	1836	866,000
1811	622,000	1841	936,000
1817	714,000	1846	1,053,000
1831	785,000	1851	1,053,000[38]

There is perhaps nothing surprising in the sharp rise occurring up to 1817; by this time Paris had done little more than make up the gaps caused by the Revolution and the wars. So, in so far as we may speak of an "explosion", it was confined to the fifteen years between 1831 and 1846, when the population rose by 268,000, or almost one third, in spite of the loss of 18,000 through the cholera epidemic of the 1830s.[39] Again, as in the late eighteenth century, the rise in numbers was made up almost entirely by migration. These immigrants, according to M. Pouthas, accounted for 88 per cent of the total increase; and M. Chevalier has estimated that there was an annual intake of 22,000 persons between 1831 and 1836, of 16,000 between 1836 and 1841, and 25,000 between 1841 and 1846.[40] Yet the proportion of provincial-born does not seem to have changed greatly since the time of the Revolution: at least not up to 1833, when enquiry revealed that 67 per cent of Parisians had been born outside the limits of the Seine Department.[41]

Who were the new arrivals and in which parts of the city did they settle? M. Chevalier tells us that they were, once more, preponderantly wage-earners and their families. There was no occupational census at this time, and he arrives at his conclusion by the observation of a number of related factors. One was the disproportionate influx of young, unmarried men, particularly between 1817 and 1831, having the result of increasing the ratio of males to females in all but a small number of middle-class districts. Another was the rapid rise in the numbers of those living in lodging houses and hotels: these rose (in round figures) from 23,000 in 1831, to 35,000 in 1836, to 40,000 in 1841, and to 50,000 in 1846, or at a rate that was considerably greater than that of the increase of the population as a whole. A third factor was the continuing concentration of numbers in certain districts—partly through a middle-class migration to more salubrious and hitherto sparsely occupied western districts like the Champs Elysées, the Tuileries and the Chaussée d'Antin; but the greater volume of migrants settled in the already heavily congested areas around the City Hall, the markets and central commercial quarter.[42] This congestion does not appear to have got much worse before 1831, as the census for that year shows that the population density of the two most notoriously congested districts of the revolutionary period—the section (now renamed "quartier") des Arcis and the old Marchés des Innocents—had slightly fallen since thirty years before.[43] But it appears from M. Chevalier's charts that the situation had become substantially worse in the whole of this sector of the city by 1846.[44]

What was new about all this was not so much the demographic factors themselves: these merely repeat, though at an accelerated pace, features that we have already noted during the period of the Revolution. But if we accept M. Chevalier's and M. Girard's arguments—what was new were the social consequences that flowed from them. "Paris est une ville malade", writes M. Girard; and he follows M. Chevalier in claiming that the new migrants became converted, by an almost spontaneous process of generation, from "industrious" into "dangerous" classes.[45] And many contemporaries, cited by these authors,[46] held similar views. They saw the social results of the rapid, lop-sided growth of their city in terms of an alarming increase in crime, prostitution, illiteracy and violence and believed that their properties were in increasing danger from the hordes of invading "nomads". These fears, while no doubt exaggerated and inflated by self-interest, appear to receive some confirmation from the published figures relating to crime, illiteracy and destitution, of which the following is a digest.

Poverty. Wages were uniformly low and, after 1825 when prices rose, real wages declined and continued to do so until the middle of the century.[47] In Paris, in 1828, 167,436 persons drew poor relief in *hôpitaux* and *hospices;* domestic relief was given to 86,413 in 1818, to 200,000 in 1821, and to nearly 300,000 in 1829. In 1830, 227,399 persons were at one time on public relief. In 1836, one third of all Paris deaths occurred in the hospital for the poor, which, in 1847, had 575,000 inmates.[48]

Beggary. In 1829, despite a police ban, there were 1200 beggars on the streets of Paris. In the department of the Seine, the number of beggars arrested, while never above 780 in any year in the decade 1821–30, rose to 910 in 1839, and, between 1840 and 1847, never fell below 847 and rose to 1067 in 1840, to 1158 in 1843, and to 1328 in 1847.[49]

Suicides. The yearly average of suicides, mainly among poor workers, rose from 356 in 1817–26 to 727 in 1839–48.[50]

Illegitimacy. Illegitimate births were 35–38 per cent of all births in

1817–21, 35 per cent in 1827–32 and 31–32 per cent in 1837–46.[51]
Physical degeneration. In 1840, nine of ten army recruits in the ten main industrial districts (including the Seine) were rejected as unfit for service.[52]
Illiteracy. In 1819, only one child in five of those of 5 to 12 was at school. In 1821, 42 per cent of all conscripts were illiterate, as were 3 in 5 of all the adult populations.[53]
Crime. According to Tocqueville, the number of delinquents in proportion to population rose, from 1827 to 1841, from 3 to 17 per cent. The proportion of second offenders in criminal cases rose from 10.8 in 1828 to 23.7 per cent in 1842; and, in 1841, 40 per cent of all persons held in state penitentiaries were second offenders.[54] In the department of the Seine, arrests for larceny (*voleurs*) rose from a yearly average of 159 in 1821–30 to 283 in 1831–40, and to 412 in 1841–7; and the yearly total of all arrests rose from 1340 to 2012 and 3305.[55]

Whether facts such as these justify the alarms of contemporaries or the unrelieved blackness of the picture painted by M. Chevalier, it is not my purpose to judge. Nor will I attempt to circumscribe them with such qualifying factors as the rise in population and the (doubtless) new method of detecting, and therefore of recording crime. But they certainly suggest that there may have been a substantial, though not necessarily disproportionate increase in the volume of beggary, crime and destitution. Once more, the question arises: are these trends reflected in the popular movements of the day? Was it this Paris—the Paris of the destitute, the uprooted, the vagrants, beggars and criminals—that rose to settle accounts with the established and "respectable" classes? or was it, as in the Revolution of 1789, another Paris altogether that manned the barricades and formed the shock-troops of rebellion?

Unfortunately, it is not possible, with the means at my disposal, to give as comprehensive a picture of the Paris of 1815–48 as in the case of the first French Revolution. M. Rémi Gossez's exhaustive study of 1848, which alone is likely to be competent to deal with all the problems involved, has still not appeared; and Mr Charles Tilly's projected enquiry into the political disturbances in nineteenth-century France is still only at its opening stage. However, we have Mr David Pinkney's excellent analysis of the crowd in July 1830; beyond this I shall draw on my own inadequate notes on the events of 1832 and 1848, and supplement these with Mr Tilly's preliminary findings which he has kindly put at my disposal.

Mr Pinkney's picture of the combatants of July 1830 is remarkably similar to that already drawn of the participants in the great revolutionary events of 1789 and 1792. Once more, they bear little resemblance to the "dangerous classes" of M. Chevalier's book. To arrive at his results, Mr Pinkney has drawn mainly on the official list of dead and wounded and of those receiving awards of compensation, either as participants or dependents, for their part in the "Trois Glorieuses". They include the names of 211 dead (a further list of 285 has been lost) and of 1327 wounded or in receipt of compensation. The lists give in each case name, date and place of birth, residence and occupation. In the combined total of 1538, he found 85 professional men, 54 shopkeepers, fewer than 300 labourers and servants (126 labourers, 79 clerks and 52 *garçons*), and nearly 1000 artisans and skilled workers. Within this last group, nearly one in three of the combined total were drawn from the old established crafts: among them 126 carpenters, joiners and cabinetmakers; 118 stonemasons, 94 shoemakers, 57 locksmiths, 31 jewellers, 28 printers, and 27 tailors. While some of these (printers, shoemakers, jewellers and tailors) were represented in almost exact proportion to their numbers in the city, others (notably locksmiths, stonemasons, carpenters and joiners) were heavily over-represented in relation to the total numbers of their crafts. There were 52 women and only 10 students and 19 boys between 8 and 15 years of age; so the legend of the leading role played by *polytechniciens* and *gamins,* as variously propagated by Hugo and Delacroix, proves to be exploded. They were men whose good character was generally attested by witnesses. Once more, as in the Revolution of 1789, the proportion of provincial-born corresponded broadly to estimates for the city population as a whole: 70 per cent among the dead and 71 per cent among the wounded. Many were old soldiers, and more than half appear to have been over 30 years of age.

Mr Pinkney finds little direct evidence that economic motives played more than a minor part in the insurrection. The price of bread and flour had been abnormally high, after two bad harvests, in 1829; but, in July 1830, though the price of bread had again been temporarily increased, the worst of the crisis was over—except for printers, whose livelihood was threatened by the ordinances of St Cloud; and they, though playing an important initiating role, tended to fall into the background as the Revolution developed. So he concluded that the *combattants de juillet* can have had little to do with the "dangerous" classes or "dangerous" districts; that they were largely composed of skilled workers or craftsmen of the traditional trades, were rarely drawn from the uprooted or the poorest of the poor, and could not by any stretch of the imagination be classed among criminal elements or socially dispossessed.[56]

The next round of social disturbances followed remarkably soon after:

there was a crop of industrial disputes, and popular revolt, stimulated by both economic conditions and the circulation of the new socialist and republican ideas, reached almost insurrectionary proportions in the successive outbreaks of June and September 1831, June 1832, April 1834 and May 1839. Here I shall confine myself to the most extensive and the most violent of these: the riots of June 1832, attending the funeral of General Lamarque, who had fallen a victim to the cholera outbreak of that year. According to contemporary reports, the disturbances spread to both sides of the river and ranged over the whole of the central part of Paris before reaching their climax and *finale* in the cloister of St Merri's Church in the central market area. In the ensuing slaughter, 800 were reported dead and wounded; several hundred were arrested, of whom eighty-two were sentenced, among them seven who were condemned to death but subsequently deported. In the judicial records, 230 names appear together with the occupations of a little over a half, the ages and addresses of about one third, and the province of birth of between one third and a quarter. The proportion of craftsmen is not as pronounced as in July 1830 or in the political *journées* of the Revolution of 1789; but the picture bears little resemblance to the proletarian Paris painted by M. Chevalier. Briefly, it is as follows: among 122 whose occupations are given, there are two property-owners; eight students and professional men; four manufacturers and *négociants*; nineteen small tradesmen, street-vendors and shopkeepers (two women among them); three soldiers and policemen; seven clerks and shop assistants; twenty-two labourers, porters and domestic workers; and fifty-seven (a little less than half) craftsmen, skilled workers and independent artisans. The average age was thirty-two, and only about 55 per cent (compared with a possible 67 per cent of the population as a whole) were provincial-born. They came from every part of the city, reflecting the widespread nature of the riots: of seventy whose addresses can be identified, the largest group (twenty-six) lived in the area of the markets, the Louvre, the commercial quarter and the City Hall; seventeen came from south of the river; ten came from the northern part of the city, around the Temple and the northern outer *faubourgs*; fifteen were from the St Antoine district; from around the Place des Vosges, the Rue St Antoine and the eastern *faubourgs* and one came from the old people's home at Bicêtre (but he was no inmate: he worked there as a cleaner).[57]

M. Chevalier has seen the main *dossiers* relating to this affair and concludes, rather more positively than I have done myself, that the largest proportion of those appearing on the lists is formed by skilled craftsmen born in Paris. And he adds that a careful examination of the *dossiers* relating to the insurrection of June 1848 would probably yield a similar result.[58] This seems (if we omit their origins) a likely supposition, but one that will be put fully to the test only when M. Gossez presents his findings. Meanwhile, we can arrive at some provisional conclusions by considering the occupations and origins of the 11,693 persons who were charged with taking part in the affair.[59] Once more, as in July 1830, we find at first sight a remarkable similarity to the trades of those who stormed the Bastille and captured the Tuileries sixty years before—another reminder that Paris, for all its demographic convulsions, remained essentially a city of small workshops and traditional crafts. So, among the largest groups of professions represented on the lists, we count, after 685 labourers of all sorts, 554 stonemasons, 510 joiners, 416 shoemakers, 321 cabinetmakers, 286 tailors, 285 locksmiths, 283 painters, 187 turners, 119 jewellers, and 191 wine merchants (the latter, in particular, highly reminiscent of their role at the capture of the Bastille). It is even possible, though the evidence on this point is not altogether trustworthy, that masters, shopkeepers and independent craftsmen on these lists may have outnumbered the wage-earners by as much as two to one.

But this is not to say that nothing had changed and that this insurrection, which Marx looked on as the first political trial of strength between the modern proletariat and bourgeoisie, was fought out in the same way and by the identical social elements as in 1789. Far from it. For one thing, the wage-earners had, by this time, their own banners, slogans and political clubs, and socialist ideas had spread widely among the skilled workers, at least, since 1830. For another, we know from further evidence that building workers, riverside workers and railwaymen (the latter new arrivals since the 1830s) played a large part in the affair: M. Gossez even describes them as forming "the vanguard of the insurrection".[60] And on the list from which we have quoted there follow, close after the masters and journeymen of the traditional crafts, the names of some 80 railwaymen and 257 *mécaniciens* (many of them from the new railway workshops at La Chapelle). There was, in fact, as Mr Tilly has noted, a significant shift towards modern, even mass-production, industry; and he notes, too, that this time the proportion of provincial-born was above the average: three in four of the arrested and over two in three of the convicted.[61] Another notable feature is that the unemployed workers, whose dispersal from the "national workshops" precipitated the affair, do not figure in large numbers on this list. It reflects, in short, a combination of the old industrial Paris and the new; but it no more reflects M. Chevalier's "dangerous classes" than did the main body of participants in the three earlier revolutions.

Mr Tilly's researches, spreading over a wider field than my own, lend support to this view. They have the advantage of ranging beyond my own terminal point of 1848 and of not focussing, among French cities, exclusively on Paris: thus the problem can be seen in broader perspective and tested over a wider area of experience, Here I shall merely summarize certain of his preliminary conclusions that are particularly relevant to my subject.[62]

(1) That, far from there being any close concordance between periods of peak urban development and periods of popular political protest, rather the opposite appears to be true. In nineteenth-century France as a whole, the peak years of urban expansion and of migration to cities were the later 1850s and the later 1870s, whereas the peak periods of disturbance were 1830–4, 1847–8, 1851 and 1869–71. The growth of Paris was far more remarkable in the years following Louis Napoleon's seizure of power (December 1851) than it was during the comparatively minor "explosion" of 1831–46; and even this followed the Revolution of 1830. It might even be claimed that, as a general rule, migration *followed* rather than *preceded* rebellion or revolution.

(2) That disturbances—and they occurred over a large part of France in 1830, 1848 and 1851—were by no means limited to fast-growing cities. While they occurred, in 1830, in expanding cities like Paris, Nantes, Bordeaux, and Lyons, they occurred equally in slowly-developing cities like Nîmes, Grenoble and Auxerre. Conversely, some fast-growing cities, such as Marseilles, Toulouse and St Etienne, were comparatively untouched by violent conflict at this time.

(3) That political and industrial disturbances were closely related and both tended to occur in old areas of settlement rather than in newly developing manufacturing towns. So Paris was, at least until the 1860s, not only the most "political" but also the most strike-ridden city in France; and it was followed, though at a fair remove, by Rouen and Lyons, also old centres where workers had had time to acquire a longer political history.[63]

(4) Finally, Mr Tilly, like others in this field, notes the continuity in the composition of those taking an active part in disturbances between 1789 and 1848, with its emphasis on the small craftsmen of the old established trades; and he observes: "Cities had their characteristic forms of disturbance: they were indeed training grounds for rebellion, but the training took time and commitment."

In conclusion, is not the basic fallacy of M. Chevalier's prognosis that he confuses individual anti-social behaviour with the collective action of social groups? The two may occur together, as they often did in nineteenth-century Paris (we have but to consult the police files to establish the point) but they arise from different causes, have their own distinctive histories, and there is no necessary connection between the two. We may grant M. Chevalier that Paris, like other cities of this period, had a lopsided growth; that this growth was attended by social evils such as extreme poverty, destitution and beggary, overcrowding and despair; and that these, in turn, among the growing numbers of "uprooted" and socially rejected, bred crime and individual acts of violence. Such elements might also, on occasion, as we have seen, participate in economic protests such as food riots, or even be drawn by hunger to engage in political actions directed against a Bastille, a royal palace or a parliament. But the evidence here presented suggests that such participation was seldom on anything but a minor scale. Nor is this surprising, as the social instability and "uprooting" that were conducive to crime and acts of individual violence were clearly not conducive to any but the most elementary forms of collective action. In fact, as this chapter has amply shown, it was neither these "dangerous" districts nor the newly settled towns or quarters that proved the most fertile breeding-ground for social and political protest, but the old areas of settlement with established customs, such as Westminster, the city of London, Old Paris, Rouen, or Lyons. For, as Mr Tilly reminds us, it "took time" to breed rebellion. It took time not only to breed the social aspirations and political ideas; it took time, too, to build up, through craft and workshop, that *camaraderie* of rebellion that grew out of long association and memories, hopes and hardships shared in common. The whole question needs further study but, paradoxically, was it not rather the *stability* of old social relationships that provided the characteristic seed-bed of rebellion and collective protest, and not the *instability* of mass migration, uprooting and the dissolution of old social ties?

Notes

1. See my unpublished paper, "The 'Pre-Industrial' City and Popular Disturbances", presented to the Annual Meeting of the American Sociological Association, Chicago, August 1965, pp. 2–4.
2. M.D. George, *London Life in the Eighteenth Century* (London, 1951), pp. 118–19.
3. Dorothy Marshall, *Eighteenth-Century England* (London, 1962), pp. 36–7.
4. Louis Chevalier, *Classes laborieuses et classes dangereuses à Paris pendant la première moitié du XIXe siècle* (1958).
5. Ibid., pp. 71, 265, 553.
6. C. Tilly, "Reflections on the Revolution in Paris. An Essay on Recent Historical Writings", *Social Problems*, 12, 1 (1964), p. 108.
7. M. Girard, "Etude comparée des mouvements révolutionnaires en France en 1830, 1848 et 1870–71", *Les Cours de Sorbonne* (n.d.), p. 46.
8. Naturally, such records must be treated with some caution, as they have generally the disadvantage of providing *samples* only of those taking part in the events to which they relate. A rare exception is the list of the so-called *vainqueurs de la Bastille*, complete with names, addresses, occupations and militia units, which is in the Archives Nationales, series T 514 (1). Moreover, there can be no firm guarantee that

those arrested by the police or the military as "ringleaders" or "activists" were, in fact, directly or actively engaged at all. (For a discussion, see my *The Crowd in History* [New York, 1964], pp. 13–14, 210–12.)

9.   The "metropolis" of London is here taken to include the cities of London and Westminster; the Borough (5 parishes of old Southwark); the "out-parishes" of Middlesex and Surrey; and the 5 new parishes of Chelsea, Kensington, Paddington, St. Marylebone and St. Pancras. (See M.D. George, *London Life in the Eighteenth Century,* pp. 329, 409.)

10. For London's population, see E.A. Wrigley, "A Simple Model of London's Importance in Changing English Society and Economy 1650–1750", *Past & Present* (July 1967), pp. 44–5; and M.D. George, *London Life,* pp. 24, 329–30.

11. Ibid. (Wrigley), p. 45.

12. Ibid., pp. 44–5.

13. See my *Wilkes and Liberty. A Social Study of 1763 to 1774* (Oxford, 1962), pp. 10–13.

14. For immigration, see Wrigley, "A Simple Model", pp. 46–9; and for mortality, D.E.C. Eversley, "Mortality in Britain in the Eighteenth Century", in *Actes du colloque international de demographie historique,* P. Harsin and E. Helin (eds), (1965), pp. 351–67. For the large proportion of Londoners born in the provinces (perhaps 2 in 3), see Wrigley, "A Simple Model", p. 49 footnote.

15. George, *London Life in the Eighteenth Century,* pp. 329, 401.

16. In 1714–60, there were the "High Church" riots of 1715–16, the "calico" riots of 1719–20, the anti-Excise riots of 1733, and the anti-Irish riots of 1736. (I have excluded the agitation against the Gin Act of 1736 and against the Jewish naturalization Act of 1753, as neither case led to actual rioting.) In 1760–95, there were the "Wilkite" disturbances of 1763, 1768 (3), 1769, 1771 ("Printer's Case"), 1772 and 1774, the weavers' and coalheavers' industrial riots of 1768–9; the Gordon Riots of 1780, and the riots against the "crimping houses" (centres for army-recruiting) in 1794.

17. The evidence for this, as for the conclusions in the following paragraph, is set out in my *Wilkes and Liberty,* pp. 220–3; and in my "The Gordon Riots. A Study of the Rioters and their Victims", Transactions of the Royal Historical Society, 5th series, vi (1956), pp. 93–114.

18. Unfortunately, in the case of London, it is not possible (as often for Paris), to estimate the proportion of provincial-born among arrested rioters.

19. Paris is here taken to include both inner and outer *faubourgs:* i.e., its limits (the "new" limits of 1785) enclose the Faubourg St. Antoine to the east, the Faubourgs St. Martin and St. Denis to the north, the villages of Passy and Chaillot to the west, and the Faubourgs St. Victor, St. Marcel, St. Jacques and St. Germain to the south. (See A. Demangeon, *Paris. La ville et sa banlieu* [1933], p. 16.) These remained the boundaries of "Paris-Ville" for demographic purposes until 1860.

20. It was estimated in 1795 that, during the past four years, Paris had already contributed more than 150,000 men to France's armies (cited by Chevalier, *Classes laborieuses et classes dangereuses,* p. 264).

21. See M. Reinhard, "Paris pendant la Révolution", *Les Cours de Sorbonne* (Paris, n.d.), pp. 25–24; F. Furet, C. Mazauric, L. Bergeron, "Les sans-culottes et la Révolution français", *Annales (Economies, Sociétés, Civilisations)* (Nov.-Dec. 1963), esp. pp. 1124–5; G. Rudé, "La population ouvrière parisienne de 1789 à 1791", *Annales historiques de la Révolution française* (Jan.-March 1967), esp. pp. 15–21. Yet it is important to note that a considerable proportion of the newcomers were not foot-loose, "uprooted" or forcibly displaced persons. Thus there were normally many thousands of seasonal building workers (from the Limousin and elsewhere) in Paris, as well as migratory craftsmen, such as joiners and cabinetmakers, whose

wanderings were a regular feature of 18th- and early 19th-century France.

22. See Reinhard, "Paris pendant la Révolution", pp. 35–43; J. Ibanès, "La population de la Place des Vosges et de ses environs en 1791", in *Contributions à l'histoire demographique de la Révolution française* (Commission d'histoire economique et sociale de la Révolution, 1962), pp. 71–91. Among persons arrested for participation in the main disturbances of the Revolution for whom such figures are available, the percentage of provincial-born varies between 63 and 72 (see my *The Crowd in the French Revolution* [Oxford, 1959], p. 249).

23. Chevalier, *Classes laborieuses et classes dangereuse,* pp. 263–4.

24. See my "La population ouvrière parisienne", pp. 21–7; and Furet, Mazauric, Bergeron, "Les sans-culottes et la Révolution française", pp. 1118–20.

25. N. Kareiev, *La densité de la population des différentes sections de Paris pendant la Révolution* (1912), pp. 14–15. In descending order of congestion, they are: *Arcis,* 6.9 sq. metres per inhab; *Marché des Innocents,* 7.2; *Oratoire,* 9.0; *Lombards,* 9.2; *Mauconseil,* 10.3; *Gravilliers,* 11.0; *Ponceau,* 11.1; *Postes,* 12.1; *Thermes de Julien,* 12.3; *Sainte-Geneviève,* 12.5.

26. "La population ouvrière parisienne", pp. 17–21.

27. Reinhard, "Paris pendant la Révolution", pp. 112–14.

28. Archives Nationales, series Y: and see M. Rouff, "le personnel des premières emeutes de '89 à Paris", *La Revolution française,* 1vii (1909), pp. 213–31.

29. See G. Rudé, "La taxation populaire de mai 1775 à Paris et dans la région parisienne", *Ann. hist. Rév. franç.* (April-June 1956), pp. 139–79; also *The Crowd in the French Revolution,* p. 249.

30. See *The Crowd in the French Revolution,* pp. 184–90, 246–9. In addition, about 1 in 10 of those taking part in the siege of the Bastille and 1 in 6 of the groceries' rioters of 1792–3 lived in lodgings; but (in the latter case) figures relating to previous convictions are too scrappy to be recorded.

31. Ibid., p. 249.

32. Ibid., pp. 16–17.

33. Ibid., pp. 242–5.

34. Ibid., pp. 58, 106, 123, 242–5.

35. By Mr. Charles Tilly in "Reflections on the Revolution in Paris", p. 108.

36. Charles H. Pouthas, *La population française pendant la preière moitié du XIXe siècle* (1956), p. 143.

37. An increase of 12.28 percent as compared with one of 31.6 per cent (Pouthas, *La population française*).

38. M. Girard, "Etude comparée", p. 29.

39. J. Droz, *Europe Between Revolutions 1815–1848* (London, 1967), p. 21.

40. Pouthas, *La population française,* p. 148; Chevalier, *Classes laborieuses et classes dangereuses,* p. 271.

41. L. Chevalier, *La formation de la population parisienne au XIXe siècle* (1950), pp. 284–5.

42. See Chevalier, *Classes laborieuses et classes dangereuses,* pp. 271–7, 296–308, and charts at end of volume; Pouthas, *La population française,* pp. 157–64; Adeline Daumard, *La bourgeoisie parisienne de 1815 à 1848* (1963), pp. 8–9.

43. The comparative figures are: *Arcis:* 6.9 sq. metres per inhab. in 1800, 7.2 in 1831; *Marches:* 7.2 in 1800, 8.2 in 1831.

44. It will be noted that I am accepting, quite uncritically, M. Chevalier's assumption that high density of population inevitably entails poverty and social misery. I think this is probably the case; but even if it is a debatable point which should not be taken for granted, I am quite deliberately refraining from any discussion as, whether the

assumption is valid or not, it does not affect my main argument in the least.

45. Girard, "Etude comparée . . .", p. 37.

46. Ibid., pp. 37–47; Chevalier, *Classes laborieuses et classes dangereuses,* pp. 451 ff; Droz, *Europe Between Revolutions,* p. 67.

47. Droz, *Europe Between Revolutions,* p. 64.

48. Chevalier, *Classes laborieuses et classes dangereuses,* pp. 443–7; S. Charléty, *La Restauration (1815–1830),* p. 318, and *La Monarchie de Juillet (1830–1848),* p. 216 (vols. 4 and 5, respectively, of E. Lavisse [ed.], *Histoire de France contemporaine depuis la Révolution jusqu'à la paix de 1919* [1921]).

49. Charléty, *La Restauration,* p. 318, Rapports de la Gendarmerie, Seine, 1817–1847, A.N. F7 4159–64.

50. Chevalier, *Classes laborieuses et classes dangereuses,* p. 345.

51. Ibid., p. 383. Here, it will be noted, there was a decline and not an increase.

52. Charléty, *La Monarchie de Juillet,* p. 216.

53. Charléty, *La Restauration,* p. 319.

54. Charléty, *La Monarchie de Juillet,* p. 216.

55. A.N. F7 4159–64.

56. David H. Pinkney, "The Crowd in the French Revolution of 1850", *American Historical Review* (Oct. 1964), pp. 1–17. Unfortunately, Mr. Pinkney's sources have not allowed him to attempt a geographical distribution of the insurgents over the various Paris districts.

57. A.N. BB[18] 1330; BB[21] 378; Arch. Pref. Police, Aa 421 ("1832. Troubles du mois de Juin"). See also Charléty, *La Monarchie de Juillet,* pp. 77–8. I regret that I have not yet had the opportunity to read M. Beveze's essay on this subject for his diploma of the University of Marseilles.

58. Chevalier, *Classes laborieuses et classes dangereuses,* pp. 551–2.

59. *Liste générale en ordre alphabétique des inculpés de juin 1848,* Arch. Nat., F7 2585–6. Where my additions of prisoners differ from those of Mr. Tilly (see note 61 below), I am willing to believe that it is my arithmetic rather than his that is at fault! Such errors in addition, however, do not in any way affect the argument.

60. G. Duveau, *La vie ouvrière en France sous le Second Empire* (1946), pp. 42–3; R. Gossez, "L'organisation ouvrière à Paris sous la Seconde République", in 1848 Revue des révolutions contemporaines, xli (1949), pp. 31–45; and "Diversité des antagonismes sociaux vers le milieu du XIXe siècle", *Revue économique* i (1956), p. 451.

61. Charles Tilly, "A travers le chaos des vivantes cités", in P. Meadows and E.H. Mizruchi (eds), *Urbanism, Urbanisation and Change: Comparative Perspectives* (Reading, Mass., 1969), pp. 379–94.

62. They are from "Urbanisation and Political Disturbances in Nineteenth Century France", unpublished paper presented to the Annual Meeting of the Society for French Historical Studies, Ann Arbor, Michigan, April 1966. I am most grateful to Mr. Tilly for allowing me to quote from this paper. I am also deeply indebted to him for his valuable comments on the first draft of this essay and, in re-drafting it, I have adopted several of the suggestions he put forward.

63. This is in striking contrast to England, where, in 1830, new manufacturing cities and towns like Manchester, Bolton and Blackburn were the main focal points of industrial disputes, whereas old centres of small workshops and crafts, like London and Birmingham, and old chartered towns like Derby, Nottingham and Bristol, continued to be the main centres of political agitation and disturbance. In France, this "divorce" did not occur until after the 1860s.

16

Crime, Criminals and Victims in Early
Nineteenth-Century London

London's population more than doubled in the first half of the
nineteenth century, rising within its Middlesex boundaries from a little
over 800,000 in 1801 to a little under 1,900,000 in 1851—that is, a
growth of 135 per cent in fifty years. The larger metropolitan boroughs
grew in proportion or expanded at a greater pace. Among the first we
may cite St. Marylebone, by then the most extensive, which grew from
63,000 in 1801 to 157,000 in 1851, Shoreditch (from 34,000 to 100,000)
and Bethnal Green (38,000 to 90,000); and among the latter St. Pancras
(31,000 to 167,000), Chelsea (11,000 to 56,000) and Islington, the most
explosively expanding of all, with 10,000 inhabitants in 1801 and
95,000 in 1851. In contrast, the population of the City of London, with
its 102 parishes squeezed "Within the Walls", continued to decline:
falling from 19,327 at the turn of the century to 19,055 fifty years later.[1]
We shall see how this expansion and decline became reflected in the
nature and volume of London's crime.

The main sources used for this enquiry have been:
(1) The printed *Proceedings* of the Middlesex Assizes at the Old Bailey
(1707–1913)—with a focus on the five decimal years from 1810 to
1850;
(2) The London Quarter Sessions rolls for 1810 to 1850 and Newgate
Calendars of Prisoners from 1820 to 1850, both housed in the
London Record Office (now at Clerkenwell), the former including
Calendars of Prisoners from 1846 to 1850; and
(3) The Metropolitan Police Criminal Returns (later cited as MPCR),
1831–92, held by the Library of New Scotland Yard, with focus on
the years 1832, 1840 and 1850.

Such a concentration on court records—particularly on those for the
London Assizes—admittedly has certain disadvantages, of which the

242

most serious is that it pays little attention to everyday crimes like drunkenness, vagrancy and disorderly conduct and neglects even more the numerous crimes committed "within the family"—often violent crimes but such as rarely appear among the cases referred to the higher courts of law. On the other hand, it makes it easier, by its proliferation of case histories, to present a more rounded *social* picture of metropolitan crime by striking a more or less equal balance between both criminals and victims.

I

To begin with the nature of London crime. In the first place, in London as elsewhere, the predominant form of criminal activity was expressed in larceny (or theft), which accounted for 74.9 per cent of all cases heard at assizes in 1810, 79.2 per cent in 1820, 83.5 in 1830, 77.1 per cent in 1840, and falling to 58.8 per cent in 1850—a year, however, in which, by way of compensation, no fewer than 90.5 per cent of all cases heard at quarter sessions related to theft.[2] Larceny, of course, took a variety of forms. Among the most common were larceny "from the person", accounting for 8.8 per cent of all cases in 1810, 17.4 per cent in 1820, 13.9 in 1830, 10.8 in 1840, and 11.75 in 1850; and larceny "by a servant", accounting for 11.1 per cent of all cases of theft in 1810, 8.3 in 1820, 12.7 in 1830, 16.0 in 1840, and rising to the remarkable figure of 30.8 per cent in 1850. We shall return to these figures and their significance for London crime a little later in the chapter.

In contrast with larceny, crimes of violence played a somewhat modest role in the record of metropolitan crime; it was only rarely that, even in combination, they accounted for more than one in eight of all the cases brought for trial at the Old Bailey. Table 16.1 seeks to summarize the incidence of such crimes of violence as a percentage of all crime in London.

Table 16.1: Crimes of violence, 1810–1850 (as a percentage of all crimes tried at the Old Bailey)

	1810	1820	1830	1840	1850
Burglary	7.4	3.1	5.5	4.2	4.2
Robbery	3.5	2.9	0.1	0.4	0.4
Assault	1.7	0.3	0.5	3.7	2.8
Murder/manslaughter	1.3	0.5	1.5	1.5	1.5
Rape	0.8	—	—	—	0.8
Other crimes of violence	0.7	0.5	1.2	1.2	0.8
Totals	15.4	7.3	8.8	11.0	11.5[3]

Of these crimes only assaults appear in the records of London quarter sessions for this period, and they rarely amount to more than 2 per cent of the cases brought to trial at any session; and even among the 77,000 taken into custody by the Metropolitan Police Commissioners in 1831 and the more than 71,000 taken in 1840 and 1850, only five, eight, and six persons respectively were committed for trial for murder, while about ten times that number (still a comparatively modest figure) were committed for burglary and robbery combined.[4]

Yet to the victims of such encounters the experience could be terrifying enough and they might well therefore have been reported—as with modern cases of "mugging" in big cities—more widely than the bare statistics would appear to justify. As, for example, when James Sisson, a failed Hull merchant, assaulted Roger Parker Esq. who was riding home to Hendon along the King's Highway between London and Edgware. It was a real Dick Turpin affair although the assailant carried an unloaded pistol and went on foot. Yet he threatened to shoot his victim and took from him five silver dollars, a half-crown, a florin, and eight sixpennies. There was also the bleak experience of Jane Cox, a laundress of Bethnal Green, who was held up by three men on a snowy December evening on what was conventionally described as "the King's Highway" (but was really Angel Alley, a tough quarter of Bishopsgate Street in the City of London) and violently robbed of the linen she was carrying to the laundry, consisting of two shirts, a tablecloth, two handtowels, and a toilet cloth belonging to Richard Judkins and John Borland. A more recent case concerned Thomas Allerson, a publican, who was assaulted and robbed of his £3 watch and chain in St. James's Square. The "Mob" (as he described them) encircled him and forced him against the iron railings three doors from Lord Castelreagh's house. In these cases the three assailants were sentenced to death. But James Taylor, who robbed Maria Crooks, the wife of a City toll collector, of a silk handkerchief, five yards of printed linen, and a key, and Mary Newman of two yards of printed cotton in quick succession, was more fortunate and was acquitted as there was some doubt about the validity of the evidence.

Another case that was dismissed due to uncertain evidence was that in which Robert Grew and Charles Smith, who frequented "flash" resorts like the Crosskeys Tavern in Bell Lane and Wentworth Street, in the heart of the Whitechapel "Rookeries", hustled John Morgan at the corner of Gunn Street in Spitalfields and snatched the watch from his fob, having first struck him on the back of the head with a bludgeon. William Sharman Wilson, who lived on the Old Kent Road, was also robbed with violence when he missed his last bus home from Hampton Court. Near Twickenham, he fell in with Charles Dunneclift, a labourer formerly in the service of the Queen Dowager, who, after drinking with him in a pub at Teddington, robbed him of 3½ gns. By this time the victim was drunk and later failed to give a coherent account of what had happened in court. And, finally, there was the unusual case of Edward Oxford, a barman of West Place, West Square, who was charged with treason and attempted murder when, in June 1840, he fired a loaded pistol at Queen Victoria as she drove with Prince Albert in Constitution Hill on her way to the Palace. The motive appears to have been political, as he belonged to a rightwing Tory group that was aiming to take power. The court gave the case its careful attention: the trial took up forty-four pages of the Old Bailey's printed *Proceedings;* yet it ended in the prisoner being found guilty but insane and ordered to be detained at Her Majesty's pleasure.[5]

But, as we have seen, such cases of violence were comparatively rare. Far more typical of London's early nineteenth-century crime was the rich variety of larceny that played so large a part in the Old Bailey's *Proceedings.* One case concerns John Robson, a carpenter lodging in Rosemary Lane, who stole a whole set of carpenter's tools from a first-floor warehouse in Botolph Lane where Jesse Tupp, a journeyman carpenter, had left them, as he believed, for safe keeping. The haul included two saws (12s.), four planes (12s. 6d.), a screwdriver (9d.), a pair of pincers (18d.), a square (18d.) four chisels (2s. 6d.), an oil stone (3s.), and a Mallet (4d.), to a total of 34s. 9d.

A more exotic story involved a merchant, Jacques-Alexandre Carrol, and a farmer, Alex-André Vitemont, who were convicted of illegally importing 200 black slaves into Mauritius, "an island governed by the United Kingdom". Another somewhat unusual incident raised the possibility of "sacrilege". According to the law, it was sacrilege to steal three yards of baize (4s.), three gallons of wine (20s.), 24 bottles (2s.), a box (5s.), 6lb candles (3s.), and a looking glass (7s.) from the vestry of a Church of England chapel, as Thomas Newby did at Stepney in 1820. But when, in September 1830, Philip Phillips, of Rosemary Lane, stole a gown worth £2 and two sets of robes (£24) belonging to the Revd Andrew Reed, a minister of the Congregational Church in Cannon Street, he was found guilty of larceny but "not sacrilegiously", as there had been no injury done to the Established Church.[6]

Among common crimes in London were stealing pint pots in public houses and stripping lead from buildings. In the night of 25–6 August 1830, Andrew Mann, William Lemon and Peter Gray stole 300 lb. of lead (26s.) fixed to J.H. Tritton's dwelling house at 46 Mortimer Street, St Marylebone, for which they were transported to Australia for seven years; and, in August 1850, a sweep and three sailors removed 630 lb. metal piping and a pump (together valued at £15) from the docks at

Poplar. Meanwhile, in April 1810, Daniel George had taken three pewter pots from three separate pubs in Marylebone High Street; and Henry William Miles, proprietor of *The Volunteer* in Upper Baker Street, which became famous a century later for its swearing parrot, had been robbed of a bill of exchange for £53. 9s. 6d.

Another common crime, though calling for particular skills, was the forgery of banknotes or bills of exchange and passing them on to unsuspecting tradesmen with a view to defrauding them, or the Government, or the Bank of England. This combined activity of forgery and fraud accounted for 0.77 per cent of all cases heard at Assizes in 1810, 5.7 per cent in 1820, 1.3 in 1830, 3.0 in 1840, and rising to a peak of 7.7 per cent in 1850. Sometimes defendants charged with this offence followed one another in rapid succession in court; at other times the court tried twenty or more cases at a single sitting—as when twenty-one defendants pleaded guilty of having in their possession a quantity of Bank of England notes, well knowing that they were forged, and were transported for fourteen years. But when George Stewart, an engraver, and twenty-five others were committed on the same charge a few months later, the prosecutor surprised the court at a certain stage of the proceedings by refusing to present further evidence; so the case was dropped.[7]

London being a great centre of communications, it is not surprising that common crimes included larceny on coaches and buses (though not yet on trains) and on river craft and ships from overseas that docked in the Thames. In April 1820 William McDonald was sentenced to seven years' transportation for stealing a coach glass, the property of Lynch White, a livery stable keeper; it appears to have been taken on an evening coach ride to Covent Garden Theatre. On this occasion, one of the prisoner's accomplices (he escaped arrest) asked rudely as the constable came up to seize his prisoners "What does that b-l-dy b-g-r want?" When James Carter, of Lisson Grove, Paddington, arrived at Castle Street, City Road, by the Paddington stage, he was drunk, missed his step, and fell on the footpath where he was robbed of his watch before he could be put back on a bus to the Barbican. In December 1840, John Wells, a pawnbroker, and his wife Jane, of Upper Phillimore Place, Kensington, were also robbed on a bus—in this case of £16. 1s. in notes and coin; they had picked up the bus near a bank in Piccadilly and went on to Bond Street and Sloane Street before alighting, and were robbed on the way. In September 1830, Edward Tierney, a cabin boy on the *Boston Cutter,* stole eight waistcoats (£8), five coats (£20), and four pairs of trousers (£4), the property of Charles David Gass, the ship's master, as the vessel lay in London Dock. Unfortunately for him the young thief fancied himself in his new fine clothes and displayed them nightly at the

Three Crowns hostelry, which led to his arrest and conviction.

And, finally, in this category, a tale of crime and adventure on the high seas: in this case on the *Wales*, a Chinaman sailing from Ceylon to London in the spring and summer of 1850. The victim, here described as a "poor lady", Caroline Pereira, a native of Ceylon who had spent twelve years in the service of the Governor, Sir Edward Barnes, caught the ship at Madras and enrolled on board as a nursemaid to the Darwood family; she also entrusted her jewellery, four pairs of eardrops, and ten brooches, valued at £405. 6s. and £99 respectively, to Patrick Smith, a musician, and his wife Sarah, who were masquerading as "Lord" and "Lady" Smith, to smuggle ashore; but they refused to hand it back on arrival. The two Smiths were found not guilty, probably because their credibility appeared greater than the "poor lady's"; and, to add further spice to the tale, their alleged victim was later charged at the Old Bailey with having stolen the same goods on the high seas from her new employers, the Darwoods.[8]

But for crimes most characteristic of London in the early nineteenth century we have to return to the all-pervading crime of larceny, and specifically to that part of it labelled in the court records as either "larceny by a servant" or "larceny from the person"—in short, to "inside jobs" committed by servants, lodgers, shopmen, clerks, and to larceny by pickpockets and prostitutes. Between them, as we saw before, these two forms of larceny amounted to 20 to 25 per cent, or even more, of all the larcenies tried at assizes between 1810 and 1850. Thus in 1810, 11.7 per cent of larceny was committed by a "servant" (a term that might apply to any employee living in the victim's house or working in his shop or other business) and 8.2 per cent was taken "from the person"; in 1820, "servants" accounted for 8.3 per cent and "personal" theft for 17.4; in 1830, for 12.7 and 13.9; in 1840 for 16 and 10.8 per cent; and, in 1850, when 30.8 per cent of all larceny was committed by "servants" and 11.8 per cent represented theft "from the person", they reached a combined total of over two in five.

Most commonly the "inside jobs" were performed by servants or lodgers, who gained access to the house and its contents by spending a short term of employment there, or by renting a room for a few shillings a week, before choosing a favourable moment for removing sheets, clothing, and furniture to deposit at the pawnbroker's down the street. Thus, in 1810, James Harvard, a servant, took two sheets (14s.), two tablecoths (12s.), one apron (1s.), two shifts (5s.), and a petticoat (2s.) down from the clothes-line where they were hanging to dry, the property of his employers, Rees Griffiths, an oil man, and his wife Amelia, of Paddington Street, St Marylebone. Elizabeth Scott, in June of the same year, came to lodge in William Kenny's house in Whitecross

Street, in the City of London, for 4s. 6d. a week; but she left after four nights, taking with her a quilt (2s. 6d.) and two sheets (3s.). Another lodger, Maria Smith, a widow, took a room with Emma Vickerman, a single woman, living in Daniel Lynn's house in Tash Street, Gray's Inn Lane. After three nights she broke the padlock to her victim's room and took away a scarf (£2), two shawls (50s.), a bonnet (£5), and three petticoats (15s.). Oddly enough, the defendant thought it useful to justify her precipitate departure by citing the "immoral conduct" of her victim, alleged to have brought in a man to keep her company at night.

Sometimes the "inside job" was performed by an employee in a shop, an office, or warehouse. Henry Walker who, in November 1850, pocketed £25. 4s. 2d. in toll money, worked for Abraham Redon, a tollgate collector at Cambridge Heath; he told the court that he and three others had borrowed the money to pay for beer. John Summerford, a records clerk at the Admiralty, also found opportunities for removing packets of sugar and books from the garrets adjoining his office; and it was said that he had, over a period of two years, been removing these packets in 28 lb. bundles wrapped in handkerchiefs which he sold outside at 4d. a pound. A somewhat similar case was that of Charles John Preece and Thomas Evans, customs officers employed as weighers in a tobacco warehouse in the London docks, who, in 1830, stole 6lb. 12oz. of tobacco (5s.), the property of HM the King.[9]

At other times the offender might breach the defences of house or shop by stealth or by enlisting the help of accomplices from "inside". Robert Anderson, who stole a watch (£3), a seal (2s.), and a bed-book (1s.) from a coal merchant's house in Golding Street, Westminster, had walked into the victim's shop next door to ask the price of charcoal and later, when the shop closed, had walked through into the parlour adjoining where the watch, as was common practice, was hanging over the fireplace by a nail. Similarly, Thomas Stevens, a jeweller, who stole 12 yards of woollen cloth from Henry James Brooke's counting house in St. Stephen Coleman Street, had the task made easier for him by having been provided with a key to the house. And John Barnes, a former footman to the Marquess of Bath at 6 Grosvenor Square, found it less exacting to rob the premises of 61 silver plates (valued at £400) because he was familiar with the house and its inmates. He told the court frankly that "the plate was kept in a strong stone closet in the pantry; the pantry door opens with a secret spring and bolt". "Was he in the house when the larceny was committed?" "Oh yes, he was *below*." (The whole story, in fact, is an excellent account of "Upstairs-Downstairs" living in a late-Georgian household in St. George's Hanover Square.[10]

Larceny "from the person" in London at this time took two principal forms. One was the robbery of sleeping or drunken sailors or strangers to town by prostitutes, sometimes working in groups of two or three (at times with a pimp thrown in), in the courts and alleys of Westminster, St. Giles in the Fields, or in the dockland of Whitechapel or Stepney (one such report speaks of "the great many women about Whitechapel"). A few examples will suffice. In December 1810, John Tagny, a tailor of Chandos Street, after spending the night in a coffee shop, fell in with Margaret Graham in New Road Court and accompanied her to Vine Street to drink gin—the usual refreshment offered—and bed; she was later accused of stealing his watch (£3), but he was too drunk, as often happened in such cases, to sustain his charge. In September 1820, John Ellis Salmon, a cabinet-maker from Manchester Square, wandered into High Street, St. Giles at midnight, where (he alleged) three women accosted him, all of whom lived together in Maynard Street. According to his story, he gave each one 1s. to buy gin, admonished one on "her situation", and took another to her room where he was robbed of his watch and seal. But he, too, failed to convince the court of his credibility and the case was dismissed. A third case concerns Timothy Hall, a higgler from Wisbech, who drank gin with two women whom he met at a theatre door in Whitechapel, went up to a room where he gave them each 2s. 6d., but subsequently lost his watch, valued at 10s. This time the charge stuck and the two women were transported for life. In a fourth case, John Johnson, a sea captain from Norfolk and master of the *Lively,* was robbed by two women and a man he met in Rosemary Lane, Whitechapel; the stolen purse (he was robbed of) contained £33. 9s. A woman and a man, Hannah Brown and Cornelius Quinlan, were found guilty of the crime and were sent to Australia for fourteen years.[11]

And so we come to the most characteristic of all London crimes of the day, as immortalized by Dickens in his picture of the Artful Dodger and his young band of purse-snatchers. The picking of pockets had, by this time, in fact, become almost a professional art and one that was punished with great severity. Occasionally the pickpocket operated on his own, though then he could only hope for smaller pickings and ran a greater risk of being caught. In July 1810, William Russell and Joseph Willis, both 19 years old, each stalked his own particular prey—Charles Green, a superannuated warrant officer in the first case, and William Youard, a carrier, in the second—across Westminster Bridge, where their victims stopped to watch the "rowing match" that was going by between four and five that afternoon. In January 1820, William Brett (18) and William Woodcock (19) followed an unnamed gentleman along the Strand to Charing Cross, where Brett stole his handkerchief and passed it on to his companion. In December of that year, another unknown victim was stalked by a veritable Faginite trio, two older boys of seventeen and eighteen and a smaller, but nimble-fingered apprentice—down the

Strand and Fleet Street and up to Serjeant's Inn. They "picked the gentleman's pocket", reported a police witness, "within four yards of the Inn Gate which lies in the County". Another police witness, who watched pickpockets at work in the City at the height of the agitation attending Queen Caroline's visit to London (see below), described one operation as follows: "I saw the prisoners and a larger boy; they were acting under his directions . . . they did it awkwardly, and then the other seemed to reprimand them." Another skilful operation was performed by three older thieves, a carpenter, a French polisher, and a woman, all in their early or middle twenties. The woman first accosted their victim off the Haymarket while the others stood by. Then PC Murrell watched the three of them follow their prey down Panton and Oxendon Streets before Sarah Dean, the woman, stole his £10 watch from his coat and passed it down the line to each of her male companions.[12]

To the pickpockets the greatest boon was a crowd. So the mayoral procession on Lord Mayor's Day (9 November) and the inaugural mayoral drive to the Guildhall three months later provided favourable occasions for picking pockets; and Henry Norwood, a 16-year old weaver, was seen robbing an unknown gentleman of his handkerchief as he walked "among other suspected pickpockets mingling with a crowd in Strand and Chancery Lane waiting to see the Lord Mayor's carriage". Further opportunities were provided by the elections held at the Guildhall to return the City's four Members to Parliament. In 1820 the elections lasted from 8 to 14 March. Three men were robbed of their handkerchiefs on 7, 10 and 14 March; but Edward Stanfield, a painter of Mortimer Street, Cavendish Square, did worse; for as he went to see his banker in Henrietta Street, Covent Garden, on the 13th—he remembered "It was the time of the election"—he was pushed into the crowd by three young men, who stole his watch. The Middlesex election followed at Brentford Butts on 17 March; and here, too, there were pickings: Robert Balls, a grocer of Brentford, who "attended Mr. Whitbread to his carriage", was robbed of a £5 watch and his chain and seal. His thief, William Farmer, a bead-blower, who claimed he had gone to Brentford "to meet my friends who are freeholders", was sentenced to transportation for life at the Old Bailey on 2 May of that year.[13]

But the greatest godsend of all to the pickpockets operating in the streets of Westminster and the city of London was the prolonged visit to the capital of Queen Caroline, the "injured Queen" who had been rejected by her husband, George IV. Her cause was espoused by radical aldermen and a large part of the City's merchants and shopkeepers who fêted and adopted her rather as their forbears of half a century before had fêted and huzzaed for John Wilkes. So when the Queen arrived from the

Continent in early June 1820, she was greeted by an outburst of popular enthusiasm that continued intermittently until her death and funeral in London over a year later.[14] Inevitably, too, it was a period when the pickpocket came into his own.

On 6 June, the very day of the "injured" Queen's return, Henry Cato, who was up in town for the day from Stafford, was robbed of a pocket book and a bill of exchange for £90 as he waited in Audley Street to see the Queen. On 3 July, Nicholas Dechemont, of Frith Street, Soho, lost a £10 watch, two seals, and a ring as he waited in Oxford Street to watch the City professions return from presenting the Queen with an Address. On the 24th, Joseph Fernie, an accountant of Leadenhall Street, was stripped of his watch and seal as he watched the Weavers' Committee march along Bishopsgate Street with music and flags flying, and it was about this time that Samuel Furze also lost a watch as he saw the Queen climb into her carriage before a large crowd at her temporary residence (a mere "cottage") in Portman Street.

One victim gave an interesting account of the pickpockets' behaviour and composition at this time. He was John Middleton, a gentleman, who on 15 August, was robbed of a book, a purse, a watch and chain (£30), and seven £1 notes as he stood in the Strand watching the City procession on its way to present an Address to the Queen. He later told the court that his passage was barred by "a crowd of persons along the Strand", twenty or more, who were "what they called *ramping* [robbing] every gentleman who came along; they moved in a phalanx, keeping a little ahead of the Sheriff's carriage". And he added: "There were 25 or 26 of them, all young and generally genteelly dressed".

Later in August, when Caroline moved into a more stately home in Brandenburg House, the crowds grew larger and the pickpockets more insistent. On the 22nd, James Stoner, a tailor of Skinner Street, was standing (as he thought) "clear of the mob" in King Street, St. James's Square, but he was robbed of his watch, a ribbon, and key (value £3. 10s. 2d.) by ten young men who dashed across the road to grab them. The next day, Richard Peters came from Duke Street, Lambeth, to see the Queen ride past the Horse Guards; he was robbed as he stood there of his watch and a seal (valued at £9 in all), by Peregrine Wood (it was said); yet, when arrested, the prisoner cried out indignantly: "Me got your watch! Search me! (Presumably they did and found no watch as he was acquitted at the Old Bailey soon after.) On the 24th, James Sherriff came up from Aylesbury, where he was Keeper of the Gaol, to watch the Queen pass through St. James's Square; as a precaution he tucked his watch-seals under his waistcoat, but a seal and a chain were stolen all the same. On the 28th, Richard Chapman, a cabinet-maker of Ashley Street, was robbed of his watch, seals, and a ring as he stood opposite Caxton

House, by two young men who were in the "mob" around the Queen's carriage; and similar scenes were enacted on Westminster Bridge and in St. James's the next day. On one of these occasions Constable Yates saw the prisoner, John Thompson, "very active in the mob" and found six handkerchiefs on him after he "attempted a dozen people's pockets". Not surprisingly, he was sent to Australia for life. In another encounter a pocket book and a £5 note were taken from John Dean, of Swallow Street, as he stood in St. James's Square while the Clerkenwell Address was being presented to the Queen; and, on 31 August, John Jones, a milkman of Tower Street, lost his watch and chain and two seals as he stood waiting to see the Queen drive down Parliament Street. It was a busy day for the police. An officer reported that "about 40 thieves surrounded us; they attempted to take every gentleman's watch who came along".

Further processions and Addresses followed during September and October, though at a slackened pace; and the activities of pickpockets are recorded in the Old Bailey *Proceedings* for 11, 13, and 25 September and 2 and 25 October.[15]

After Queen Caroline's death and funeral procession in August 1821 there followed an inevitably sharp decline in the exuberant Addresses of City merchants and the activities of the pickpockets that attended them. So there was quite a lull, but the succession of Queen Victoria in the late 1830s did not fail to draw the crowds again. We find examples for the following dates and occasions in 1840: the Queen's drive to the House of Lords on 16 January, when Peter Howard of Lambeth was robbed (of a mere handkerchief) in Parliament Street; a royal visit to the theatre in St. James's, Piccadilly, on the evening of 28 February; and the "Night of Illumination" on 25 May following Victoria's marriage to Albert. But it is perhaps worth recording that the heyday of pocket-picking was already past—partly due, maybe, to better policing, but probably more to the change in men's fashions which, by phasing out the "fob" from the frontal waistline of breeches after 1829, left the gentleman's bejewelled watch—worn as much as an ornament as a time-keeper—less easily exposed to the attentions of the nimble thief; moreover, as the waistcoat lengthened in the 1830s, the watch began to be worn in a waistcoat pocket. So it is hardly a coincidence that, whereas in Queen Caroline's day the pickpocket might get away with a £5, an £8 or a £10 watch, in the early Victorian age he would more likely have to settle for a cheap handkerchief, worth 2s. to 5s. 6d. at most, removed from the tail of a frock-coat or a long jacket (still persisting until 1850).[16]

II

A little over 4,500 prisoners were tried at the Middlesex Assizes within our ten-year sample between 1810 and 1850. They included an unusually high proportion of women: 23.9 per cent in 1810, 16.8 per cent in 1820, 21.2 in 1830, 21.7 in 1840 and 18.2 per cent in 1850, with an overall percentage for the half-century of 22.3. The proportion of women taken into custody by the Metropolitan Police between 1832 and 1850 was considerably higher, being 35.7 per cent in 1832, 33 per cent in 1840, and 33.5 per cent in 1850; but it fell back to 25 per cent of those committed for trial. Of the 4,500 prisoners committed to assizes about three in four of both sexes were found guilty and may therefore be said to be "criminals".[17]

The social and occupational distribution of the Old Bailey prisoners is presented in the tables that follow:

Table 16.2: Prisoners at London Assizes 1810–1850 in main social groups as percentages of all indictments ★

Social Group	1810	1820	1830	1840	1850
Labourers and servants	32.5	54.5	65.5	67.0	63.5
Craftsmen	2.5	5.0	2.1	2.5	1.8
Shopkeepers, petty tradesmen	1.9	4.3	4.0	3.7	7.5
Clerks	—	—	0.7	1.1	3.0
Soldiers, sailors	2.6	5.1	2.4	3.0	—
Women +	23.9	16.8	21.2	21.7	18.2
Miscellaneous	1.1	3.8	2.1	—	4.0
Unknown	35.5	10.5	2.0	1.0	2.0
	100.0	100.0	100.0	100.0	100.0

★OB *Proceedings*, 1810–50; London RO, Newgate Calendars, 1820–50 (OB/CB, registers, vols. 4, 9, 17, 18).
+ These include women of all social groups.

The above Table requires little explanation: we should expect the large majority of prisoners—or "criminals"—to come from the labouring and working population, while shopkeepers and other small property-owners would be likely to play a minor role. Table 16.3, however, is perhaps noteworthy for the comparatively small part played by industrial workers, who, among our occupational groups, trail behind workers in building, consumer trades, clothing, domestic service, and both luxury and foreign trade. In fact, the numbers here listed (including smiths, braziers, founders and others from the petty

Table 16.3: Occupational groups indicted

	No. of indictments	Percent of all indictments
Labourers (inc. 72 servants)	1,108	26.8
Women (not included in other groups)	538	13.0
Building trades: bricklayers, carpenters, cabinet-makers, painters, plasterers, plumbers, sawyers, stonemasons	203	4.9
Consumer trades: inc. food, drink, barbers, sweeps	171	4.1
Clothing: drapers, hatters, shoemakers, spinners, tailors, 20 weavers	167	4.0
Domestic service: inc. 14 coachmen, gardeners, 24 grooms, porters, 71 servants	160	3.9
Luxury trades: bookbinders, booksellers, goldsmiths, jewellers, prostitutes, watch and clockmakers	157	3.8
Foreign trade: sailors, mariners	93	2.2
"Industrial": 35 smiths, 20 weavers, brass founders, braziers, turners, a dozen small crafts, 3 clothing workers	90	2.2
Inland transport: bargemen, 14 coachmen, 24 grooms, saddlers, harness makers, watermen, only 1 railwayman (a porter)	79	1.9
Banking, business: clerks, errand boys	67	1.6
Petty commerce: dealers, hawkers	57	1.4
Occupations of prisoners unknown*	1,244	30.1

*The large number of "unknowns" (as in Table 16.2) are largely due to the absence of Newgate Calendars for 1810 and gaps in 1820.

productive crafts) may well be an over- rather than an understatement. This bears out the point that, in nineteenth-century London, crime, as befits a great commercial and administrative city, was far more *commercial* than *industrial*.

Let us turn then from the general to the particular in the hope of finding a further answer to the question: what sort of Londoners committed crimes or were indicted to answer charges at the Old Bailey assizes? A few prisoners achieved notoriety or fame, including two men whose names appear in consecutive months in the *Proceedings* for 1820. One was Arthur Thistlewood, the Cato Street conspirator, whose trial, along with that of his eleven companions, began at the Court of Justice in April 1820, lasted for sixty-five days and took up sixty-two pages of the printed *Proceedings*. These men were charged, with the aid of a Government informer who had entered their ranks, with conspiring to blow up Lord Liverpool's cabinet. Thistlewood and five others were hanged, their heads severed and their bodies left to hang in chains—the last survival of a barbarous medieval custom—and a further five were transported to Australia, where the youngest man, John Strange, rose to become Chief Constable at Bathurst, in New South Wales, and was pardoned after serving twenty-two years of exile.[18]

The other prisoner, whose life is recorded in the *Australian Dictionary of Biography,* was the Danish adventurer, Jorgen Jorgenson, who early in his career, when enlisted on the British side in the Anglo-Dutch war against Napoleon, sailed to Iceland in command of a privateer, arrested the Danish governor, and proclaimed the island's independence with himself as Head of State, a position that he held for a bare nine weeks. His adventures in the next twelve years had no such glamour, ending in his arrest in London in May 1820 for larceny in Sarah Stourbridge's house in Warren Street, Fitzroy Square. The lodger, who had boasted of being a "gentleman" and of his friendship with Lord Castlereagh, one night decamped carrying with him his bed (40s.), a bolster (5s.), two blankets (4s.), and a quilt (2s.) which he pledged with a pawnbroker along the Tottenham Court Road. He was sentenced to transportation for seven years: but, after a number of visits to Newgate, he only arrived in Australia, now with a life sentence, in 1826. He settled in Van Diemen's Land (today's Tasmania), became a constable and an explorer, secured a pardon and wrote histories and travelogues; but he remained the immoderate drinker that he had always been and, in January 1841, died at Hobart of "inflammation of the lungs".[19]

We should perhaps also add a third prisoner of some notoriety, who in 1850 appeared for trial at the Old Bailey where he was charged with an attempt to assassinate the Queen. He was Robert Pate, of 27 Duke Street, a "well dressed" gentleman and former officer in the 10th Hussars. Slightly crazy, he had already accused his cook of trying to poison him. On this occasion, he appears to have felt slighted—perhaps in relation to his pension?—and sought revenge, or redress, by swishing his cane at the Queen as she drove in Royal procession through St. James's. It was a trivial gesture, but it caused alarm; and Pate was transported to Australia for a seven-year term.[20]

None of the other prisoners in our sample made as great an impression as these three; but some of them attract our attention for a variety of qualities, both good and bad, that they displayed in court or when arrested by the police and brought to Bow Street. Some for their cheek, their ready repartee, or willingness to argue or answer back. John Porter, a 21-year old labourer, for example, who, when arrested for stealing 3¾ yeards of silk, thought it "a hard thing to be imprisoned for nothing"; and James Swayne, sentenced to be transported for seven

years for stealing 6lb. lead and a brass cock from a building, found it hard
to accept the verdict: "It is a d-d hard thing you can't let a man get his
living". Michael Roach, a young tailor, who had stolen two coats and
twelve pairs of trousers from a dwelling house and was told he would be
transported for fifteen years as he had been previously convicted of a
felony, objected: "but that is no reason why I should be guilty of this".
And George Humphries, who was charged with stealing thirty-two
yards of the best blue woollen cloth from a draper's shop in Henrietta
Street, Covent Garden, objected to the terms of the charge: "The cloth
has grown", he protested in court, "it has got four yards bigger since I
came from Bow Street".[21]

Other prisoners quite stoically accepted their fate or even welcomed a
sentence of transportation. William Patterson Flanaghan, a 36-year old
printer who was sentenced to be transported for seven years for stealing
from a public house, welcomed the verdict and insisted that he "sought
for transportation"—possibly because he had fallen on hard times: he.
told the court that in his former job as a printer he had earned 104 gns. a
year. There was also Andrew Daniels, 27, a labourer who, in June 1850,
was sentenced to a second term of transportation (the first was imposed
in December 1845) for stealing a silver watch in Pimlico. On being
arrested, he is reputed to have told the police: "I stole it and sold it, and
hope I shall be transported for it". It was a hope he shared with many an
Irish labourer at this time, in the hideous aftermath of the Great Famine
of 1845.[22]

Some prisoners were scrupulously polite in dealing with their victims,
showed due contrition in court or, despite their recent fall from grace,
enjoyed a generally good reputation among their victims or employers.
John William German, a bootmaker, wrote to his victim, Jesse Clarkson,
a hairdresser of Wandsworth, after he had robbed him of four tea-cloths:
"You will no doubt feel shocked to find I have been your enemy instead
of your friend; my respects to the cook". Charles Evans, an errand boy,
who had stolen from his employer, James Swallow, a purse, a ring, and 3
gns. from his housekeeper, told the court that sentenced him: "I humbly
beg leave to state that when I engaged in this transaction I had no idea of
the extent of criminality attached to it"; and he assured the court of his
"sincere contrition". And James Webber, 20, who had been Samuel
Scott's servant for twelve months before he burgled his house for forty-
nine silver spoons, heard his employer tell the court that "he never
found the prisoner dishonest and had trusted him with all he had". The
defendant was sentenced to death but he was recommended to mercy on
the grounds of his good charater and the belief that he had been "misled
by evil men".[23]

Sometimes women took the lead in a criminal enterprise, as when

Mary Wood (18) and Jim Regan (15) robbed John Brigg's six-year old daughter of 4s. 6d., the change from the 5s. piece that her father had given her to buy a loaf of bread. As the two robbers ran away from the scene of their crime, it was Wood who was heard to give her companion the warning: "Don't split or we shall be booked". In another case involving larceny, Susan Harris (16) stole 6lb. of bacon worth 4s. from a cheesemonger's shop in Fitzroy Square. She had two accomplices, William Jones (15) and William Harrison (14); but at their trial George Anthony, a witness, told the court: "I had every reason to believe that the boys are the dupes of the female prisoner; I have seen her about".[24]

Some prisoners, far from being courteous, good-tempered, or amusing, were bloody-minded and violent in both words and deeds. Joseph Skelton, was charged with murder when he lost his temper in a thoroughfare in Covent Garden. His dust-cart was held up by a coalheaver in Chandos Street; so, wild with fury, he drove his horse onto the pavement, crushing his victim who died soon after. Alexander Lovell, who stole three straw hats from Catharine Wallis's shop in Holborn, uttered blood-curdling threats to his woman victim: "B-r you, I'll stick a knife in your b-y guts!" And when William Murray and John Crawley broke into a house of Gray's Inn Lane and stole two curtains and a tea-tray, Crawley threatened the female lodger in the following terms: "You b-y whore, if you make a noise, I will cut your throat!"[25]

Occasionally in these records we come near to a criminal underworld. John Glynn, a 24-year-old labourer, was charged with "receiving 3lb. of soap, the property of Daniel Cooper, a corn chandler of Eyre Street Hill, of Field Lane, which had originally been stolen by three boys who had sold it to the prisoner for 5d. The incident seems insignificant enough, involving a quite derisory sum; but Constable G 127 told the court that the prisoner "belonged to a notorious gang of thieves and had been several times previously convicted", and he was transported for ten years for what on the face of it seemed a trivial offence. Another case, which involved the burglary of the dwelling house of a watchmaker of Drury Lane by four women and a man, who stole 25 watches, 75 pencil cases, and 20 seals (a £49 haul in all), was an "inside" job, as one of the prisoners, Mrs Ann Mason, lodged in the house and it appears that the bureau had been left open. An interesting feature of the story is the suggested part in the exploit played by a Mr. Schooley, a professional lock-picker and safe-cracker. The real smell of a criminal *milieu* penetrates even more strongly in the strange case of John Nash and John Hurley of Rosemary Lane, charged with taking £22. 4s. from the poor boxes at St. Bartholomew's Hospital in West Smithfield. Both men had been previously convicted and Nash had planned the recent operation while a prisoner in Cold Bath Fields a few months before. He was also a body-snatcher by occupation and a professional informer and *agent provocateur*. But, in their own way, they had deserved well of the medical profession by disinterring corpses for the Faculty of Medicine at Bart's. So when they were sentenced to death for burglary (the usual sentence at this time), the prosecutor and jury recommended the unsavoury pair to mercy.[26]

III

So we come to the victims of London crime, once more based on our 10-year sample from the Old Bailey assizes and here presented in their main social categories in the table that follows:

Table 16.4: Victims of crime in Middlesex, 1810–1850 (as a percentage of OB crimes)*

Social Category	1810	1820	1830	1840	1850	Mean 1810–50
Gentry	2.1	4.8	1.6	3.2	3.5	3.0
Shopkeepers (also merchants, manufacturers, farmers)	48.0	42.8	48.4	50.2	50.2	47.9
Householders	2.0	2.4	5.3	4.0	3.7	3.5
Clerks	2.0	—	1.6	1.6	0.8	1.2
Labourers	7.5	7.3	6.6	6.4	3.8	6.3
Craftsmen	6.5	3.0	4.5	3.4	2.1	3.9
Women	7.5	8.8	9.4	9.0	13.4	9.6
Occupations unknown	18.6	12.7	15.8	15.5	17.8	16.1
Miscellaneous	5.8	18.2	6.8	6.7	4.7	—
	100.0	100.0	100.0	100.0	100.0	

*OB *Proceedings*, 1810–50 (author's calculations). Neither the QS records nor the MPCR after 1831 have been of use in this matter.

But, of course, behind these sombre figures lay a rich variety of victims, far richer in London, as we might expect, than in any other part of the country. Among persons of distinction there was Queen Victoria herself, who, as mentioned before, was on one occasion threatened with a pistol and in another by the swish of a cane. There was also the Tsar of Russia, though in his case there was no suspicion of any personal danger—only the embezzlement of two certificates in a Sinking Fund bearing his name and converted by a certain Edward Nairne "to an unknown use". An aristocratic house was robbed of a £10 note by one Pleasant Neil, who had access to the Marquess of Donegal's town residence at 67 Eaton Place through the favours he enjoyed with a housemaid. In our sample there are at least two Knights among the victims—Sir Frederick Beilby Watson, who was robbed of ten forks, six medals worth £22, two candlesticks, a penrack, and two pistols by his hairdresser, Henry John Manbridge; and Sir Robert Burdett, one of four gentlemen-distillers of Vauxhall, who lost a five-gallon cask of brandy (£6. 5s.). The victims also included bankers and other heads or directors of business firms. Among the banks was the Commercial Bank of London, on which a false order for £10 was drawn by John Avan Broom, a 17-year-old clerk; while a larger amount—a bill of exchange for £100—was drawn by a drunken Naval captain on Sir John William Lubbock Bart's, a City banking house. The London Dock Company was robbed of a fishing rod by one of its employees, and the New River Co. of £5. 14s. by one of its labourers. The St. Katharine Dock Co. thought it had lost 44 lb. of lead, but it was found in a privy branded with the Company's mark; while the Chartered Gas, Light and Coke Co. lost 2½ lb. of brass but failed to secure a prosecution as its charter was not produced in court. And, in inland transport, the Grand National Junction Canal Company and three of London's Railway companies suffered losses through larceny, forgery and embezzlement.[27]

There were distinguished foreigners among the victims, or at least some that bore distinguished-sounding foreign names. Two of these were Amédée Frédéric Armand Davenes and his brother Auguste-Nicolas Davenes, partners in a provision-dealer's in Turnmill Street that specialized in the sale of pigeons; the brothers were robbed of twenty-one dead pigeons, worth 12s. 3d., by two of their carmen. There was also Louis Henri Godineau, of the Union Hall at 33 Salisbury Square, who was robbed of his £15 watch by a prostitute, well-known to the police, who took him up to her room one night in a notorious "house of ill-fame" at the Temple. Among other such victims were Count Henri d'Avigdor, whose house at Acton was burgled one night of various goods amounting in all to a value of £4. 6s.; and Elizabeth, Margravine of Brandenburg–Anspach–Baireuth, who was robbed of two chimney pieces (£30), a pestle and mortar (7s.), and twelve books (6s.), removed from her Pavilion at Hammersmith by three men who lived on a barge. An unusual-sounding victim was "Sheik Betchoo", who in July 1850 was robbed in a city brothel of two whistles (8s.), two handkerchiefs (3s.), and 1s, in cash. And, for good measure, among the overseas visitors to London there was Colonel Robert Anstruther of the Canadian Army, whose residence in Monmouth Road, Bayswater, was burgled of a snuff box and other objects, worth £16, by a plumber and a bricklayer who had been drinking in a neighbouring beer-house.[28]

Among victims of the "middling" sort, we have already amply

attested the dominating presence of shopkeepers; publicans, too, on a smaller scale were in evidence. The London publican had two occupational hazards, of which one was a rather heavier liability than the other. The lesser evil was the frequent removal of beer-mugs, then commonly referred to as pint beer-pots; and the larger was the passing of "dud" coins or banknotes. Every Old Bailey session at this time witnesses at least ten or a dozen such cases; half a dozen of them often followed each other in rapid succession. Such was the case of Susannah Bennet, widow and licensee of the *George Tavern* at Snow Hill, who was passed a bad half-crown in 1840 but was astute enough to have the two defendants put in jail for twelve months; and of landlord Russell Poole, of the *Rose and Crown* in Bartholomew Close, in the Inner City, who was also passed a false half-crown; he, too, brought his two assailants to justice.[29]

Many victims, as we have seen, were poor, either as wage-earning labourers or as part-time workers living on a depressed wage or allowance among the city poor. Some tried to hide it by investing in relatively expensive clothes. For example, when Richard Markson's lodging-house in Liquor-Pond Street, St. Andrew's Holborn, was burgled in January 1830, Richard Yates, a labourer, was the principal victim. Yet his wardrobe, part of which was stolen, betrayed a man of relatively expensive tastes; it included a pair of trousers, worth 14s., a waistcoat (9s.), and two shirts (18s.), in addition to 17s. 6d. in cash. But this is probably an exceptional case; and it was certainly not true of the hats stolen by a gang of pickpockets in a Chelsea street in January 1820. A Chelsea pensioner, who was one of their victims, reported that the thieves were all wearing others' hats; and he added (ruefully, no doubt): "The hats all appeared to belong to poor people." Joseph James Castle, a carver of Bethnal Green, who was robbed of his watch in November 1840, earned no more than 6d. an hour and slept in his employer's workshop in Fleet Street. Thomas Cox, of Union Gardens, Kingsland Road, drove a cart for his wife who took in laundry. In October 1820 five pelisses (£2) were taken from his house. When he caught up with the thief in the *White Horse* in Fursby Street, he asked him, "How d'you come to rob a poor man like me?" He received no reply to the question; whereas when Thomas Stephen Watson, who let apartments in Alie Street, Whitechapel, was robbed of a watch and chain by "a well-dressed lady" who had come to look for a room, he asked her "how she could rob such poor people as us"; and "she said she did not give that a thought". But sometimes prisoner and victim were in the same boat: when Benjamin Gitkins, a stonemason, who worked on a job in Mecklenburgh Square, put down his tools (nine chisels and a hammer) to go to lunch and had them stolen, he asked the culprit, "what could induce him to rob a poor man like me?"; and the thief replied simply, "it was through poverty that he did it". Similarly, when John Wheeler, a carpenter, working at 10 New Street, in the City, was robbed of two planes (5s.), an oil-stone (2s.), and a square (18d.), the offender, a brickmaker, told him " he was in great distress". When Robert Harman, a bargeman, stole a coat (10s.), a pair of pants (5s.), two waistcoats (3s.), and 2s. 6d in cash from a barge on the Thames at Millbank, it turned out that the principal victim was James Andrew, "a poor boy", who begged the thief not to take away the two quarter loaves he was taking home to his mother. And when John Coles and his wife, drapers though described as "very poor", were robbed of five caps, three yards of ribbon and four handkerchiefs by a visiting nurse, the wife was seized for the rent while the husband went to the watch house to see the prisoner wearing one of their caps![30]

On the other side of the barrier dividing criminals from victims were those victims—and there were many employers among them—who were extremely reluctant to prosecute: it is evident enough that, except in the case of serious crime, few employers would be willing to send a good workman to jail. Such a workman was William Kirby, a butcher, who took 3¾lb. beef and ¾lb. suet from his master's shop in Goodge Street, Tottenham Court Road. The master butcher's wife, who ran the business, held the prisoner in high regard and at first refused to prosecute; but when, persuaded by the police, she agreed to do so, she gave him an excellent character. So the prisoner was recommended to mercy by both victim and jury and escaped with a month in jail.[31]

IV

There are three further questions that need to be answered. The first relates to the classification of the main types of crime that have been discussed in this chapter. Traditionally, it has been common to divide crime into the two major categories of crimes against property and crimes against the person. Does such a division still have any practical value? I think not and, in its place, I have argued elsewhere—and will not repeat the arguments here—that, whether in the metropolitan or provincial context, it is more relevant today to classify crime under the three heads of (1) *acquisitive* crime, or crimes committed strictly in pursuit of material gain; (2) *survival* crime, in which the criminal's main concern has been to feed or clothe or shelter himself and his family at a time of unemployment or trade decline; and (3) *protest* crime, or crimes committed in attempting to redress injustice or social ills.[32] In the case of early nineteenth-century London, there seems little doubt that, while protest—measured in terms of arrests and committals—played a minor role, crimes for "survival" were far more in evidence than any others.[33]

The second question concerns the growing volume of crime in urban society. Is the commonly held opinion correct that crime tends to increase in proportion to urban growth and most rapidly in cities in the course of rapid expansion? In the case of London the proposition has a certain validity: in all its most rapidly expanding boroughs (St. Pancras, Paddington, Islington, Chelsea, Bethnal Green and Kensington) we find a steady increase in the volume of crime betwen 1800 and 1840; but while the population continued to grow, the volume of crime fell noticeably between 1840 and 1850—presumably because more favourable economic factors (and, possibly, the impact of the "new" police after 1830?) had begun to play a counteracting role. Most remarkable, however, was the experience of the City of London "within the Walls". Its population, as we noted before, marginally declined between 1800 and 1850, but its volume of crime (though falling, as elsewhere, between 1840 and 1850) far surpassed that of St. Marylebone, the largest and most "criminal" of London's boroughs, in each one of the five decennial years.[34] These two examples—the example of the year 1850 in general and that of the City of London in particular—are reminders that while the rule of a continuous rise in crime in relation to urban growth has a certain validity, it is not a golden rule as the intervention of other factors may serve to negate it.[35]

Finally, can one reasonably speak at this time of a London "criminal class" or of specifically "criminal" districts? Patrick Colquhoun, stipendiary magistrate and founder of the Thames Police Office before the turn of the century, certainly believed that one could. In his *Treatise* on the London police of his day, Colquhoun claimed that in the 1790s no fewer than 115,000 persons, or one-eighth of the city's population, were regularly engaged in criminal pursuits: half of them prostitutes or "lewd and immoral women"; with 8,506 cheats, swindlers and gamblers; 8,000 "thieves, pilferers and embezzlers"; 4,000 receivers of stolen goods; 3,000 coiners; while 2,500 others preyed on docks and arsenals in the guise of "Lumpers, Lightermen and Riggers"; and a mere 2,000 were conventional "Professional Thieves, Burglars, Highway Robbers, Pick-Pockets, and River Pirates".[36] Yet Colquhoun appears to have allowed his Gaelic imagination or middle-class prejudices to run away with him. For this certainly is not the picture presented by the Old Bailey's *Proceedings* of half a dozen or a dozen years later; besides, the author's own account, when stripped of its lurid trimmings, showed that by the time he wrote the more violent types of London crime were already on the wane and that his figures were largely inflated by a rising tide of "economic" crimes and crimes against poverty.

More revealing perhaps are the suggestions of a London underworld of crime made on an earlier page. We then heard mention of a "Mr. Schooley", a professional lock-picker and safe-cracker, and we also became briefly acquainted with the unsavoury John Nash and John Hurley, sentenced to death for burglary and robbing the poor boxes at St. Bartholomew's Hospital, of whom one at least was a professional police informer and an *agent provocateur* (see p. 258 above). And we might add the case of John Grettis, unemployed, who was sentenced to transportation in 1820 for assaulting Edward Kelly, a toll-collector at Kilburn, under arms and with intent to rob, and being in the company of a gang of hoodlums, one of whom had already been executed and a second sentenced to be transported (yet the prisoner does not appear to have been very bright: he missed taking his victim's purse which contained £320 in cash.)[37] Such men were no doubt "professionals" and maybe, too, among those frequenters of London's "Rookeries" and flash-houses of which Tobias—following Dickens and Mayhew—gives so lurid and dramatic a picture.[38] Yet, according to the records of the Old Bailey at least, they do not appear to have amounted to very much; and the notorious parish of St. Giles in the Fields, so fashionable in the annals of metropolitan crime, appears to have been past its prime as a generator of criminal violence by the 1830s, or even before.[39]

What of vagrants who, for some, appear to have been an even richer source of "professionals" or hardened practitioners of crime? Here the Old Bailey *Proceedings,* and even the records of quarter sessions, are of little use; for vagrants, when rounded up, were most often brought before petty courts of justice, or, after 1831 in London, summarily discharged or convicted by a magistrate of the Metropolitan Police. The vagrants certainly presented a problem because of their numbers, though these tended to diminish as the years went by: thus, 9,325 were taken into custody in 1832, 4,437 in 1840, and only 2,700 in 1850; and, in each of these years the magistrate summarily discharged rather less than half and sentenced the rest to varying terms of detention. These terms, however, do not suggest that the prisoners were taken very seriously by the police as they amounted most often to two to six weeks or a few days in jail and very rarely indeed (there were two such cases in 1840) were they committed even to quarter sessions for trial.[40]

So, after this last brief survey, we may conclude that, even in London, for all its reputation as a centre of professional crime and "dangerous districts", the case for the existence of a definable "criminal class" has not been made. There were, no doubt, a minority of hardened criminals and isolated gangs of "professionals", and perhaps even more "professionals" working on their own account; but, properly speaking, in this half-century at least, they were not in sufficient numbers to constitute a "criminal class".

Notes

1. *Victoria County History, Middlesex* (7 vols., 1911–82), II, p. 112. The Kent and Surrey portions of the metropolis are excluded from these figures.
2. O.B. Proceedings, 1810–50; London QS Calendars of Prisoners for 1850.
3. The reader is once more reminded that the absence from this record of unreported crimes of violence "within the family"—involving, in particular, wives and husbands—undoubtedly distorts the picture. Yet it would be difficult, without considerable further investigation, to make suitable allowance for the omission.
4. London QS Calendars of Prisoners, 1850: MPCR, 1831–2, 1840, 1850.
5. *Proceedings*, 1840, pp. 464–1510; 1850, no. 1112.
6. Ibid., 1820, no. 275; 1830, nos. 1258, 1954.
7. Ibid., 1810, nos. 249, 367, 493; 1830, nos. 504, 1060, 1209, 1954.
8. Ibid., 1820, p. 420; 1830, no. 1013; 1840, no. 504; 1850, pp. 148–63.
9. Ibid., 1820, nos. 240, 294, 432; 1830, nos 804–8; 1850, nos. 1, 842, 2096.
10. Ibid., 1840, mo. 1226.
11. Ibid., 1810, nos. 231, 370; 1820, no. 774; 1830, mo. 932; 1840, no. 1426.
12. Ibid., 1810, nos. 331, 612; 1820, nos. 302, 344, 1083; 1850, no. 1098.
13. Ibid., 1820, nos. 354, 380, 388, 396–8, 430, 461, 474, 496.
14. See John Stevenson, "The Queen Caroline Affair" in *London in the Age of Reform*, ed. J. Stevenson (Oxford, 1977), pp. 117–48.
15. *Proceedings*, 1820, nos. 396, 489, 625, 772, 925, 946–1955, 1081–3, 1130, 1134, 1154, 1164, 1182, 1196, 1217–8, 1243, 1262.
16. Ibid., 1840, pp. 464–510 and nos. 550, 1040, 1590. See also, for changing fashions, C. Willett and Phillis Cunnington, *Handbook of English Costume in the Eighteenth Century* and *Handbook of English Costume in the Nineteenth Century* (Boston, 1969, 1970), passim.
17. *Proceedings*, 1810–50; MPCR, 1832–50.
18. *Proceedings*, 1820, pp. 215–77; G. Rudé, *Protest and Punishment* (Oxford, 1978), pp. 194–5.
19. *Proceedings*, 1820, no. 701; *Australian Dictionary of Biography*, II 1788–1850, pp. 26–8.
20. *Proceedings*, 1850, no. 1300.
21. Ibid., 1820, nos. 310, 469; 1850, no. 164.
22. Ibid., 1820, no. 913; 1850, no. 1636.
23. Ibid., 1810, no. 604; 1820, 2602; 1850, no. 110.
24. Ibid., 1840, no. 2602; 1850, no. 110.
25. Ibid., 1810, no. 604; 1820, no. 2602; 1850, no. 110.
26. Ibid., 1830, no. 448; 1840, nos. 700, 1046.
27. Ibid., 1810, no. 187; 1830, no. 1024; 1840, nos. 312, 314, 322, 238, 330, 348, 390, 550, 570, 580, 789; 1850, nos. 688, 1140, 1300, 1312, 1406, 1420, 1452. There was also among these notable victims the case of *The Times*, which, in 1810, prosecuted 19 defendants on a conspiracy charge. Judgement was respited (see *Proceedings*, 1810, nos. 472–3).
28. Ibid., 1820, no. 1024; 1830, nos. 330, 379; 1840, nos. 1572, 1756; 1850, no. 2098.
29. Ibid., 1840, nos. 1154, 1594.
30. Ibid., 1810, nos. 374, 390, 483; 1820, nos. 510, 1970; 1830, no. 1672.

31. Ibid., 1850, no. 1160.
32. See my *Criminal and Victim. Crime and Society in Early Nineteenth-Century England* (Oxford, 1985), pp. 78–88.
33. In addition to the objective evidence, see the numerous declarations made by prisoners at the Old Bailey professing economic hardship, interspersed throughout this period but reaching a peak in 1830. (For details, see *Criminal and Victim*, pp. 81–5.)
34. *Proceedings*, 1810–50; *Victoria County History*. Middlesex, ii, pp. 112–19.
35. It must be conceded, however, that the City's continued commercial expansion could not fail to attract criminals from outside as well as from within its walls. Yet a study of the *Proceedings* for the period does not suggest that the numbers of "outsiders" came near to surpassing that of the "insiders"; so the case here being argued for the City's quite peculiar criminal record appears valid enough.
36. P. Colquhoun, *A Treatise on the Police of the Metropolis* (London, 1796).
37. *Proceedings*, 1820, no. 470.
38. J.J. Tobias, *Crime and Industrial Society in the Nineteenth-Century* (London, 1967), pp. 97–121.
39. In terms of the number of inhabitants per crime in its most "criminal" year—in this case 1830—my calculations place it 38th on a list of 42 major Middlesex parishes (see my *Criminal and Victim*, p. 134).
40. MPCR, 1832, pp. 8–9, 18–19; 1840, pp. 6–8, 12–14, 18, 26; 1850, pp. 20–1.

Index

Page numbers in italics indicate central discussion of the item.

Acton, Lord, 88-9, 120
agricultural labourers, 2, 10-15, 54, 69, 150, 168-70, 183-8
American Revolution, 27, 72-3, 76, 147, 199-200, 211-12
aristocracy, aristocrats, 31-4, 78, 80-104, 109, *124-34*, 137, 141, 157-9, 201, 208, 215
artisans (English/British), 148-61, 167-8, 171-3
   see also sans-culottes
Aulard, Alphonse, 87-100, 109
Australia, Australians, 5, 15-17, 35-6, 56, 64, 69-70, 150, 170, 187

Babeuf, Graccus, 138, 204
Bailyn, Bernard, 199-200
Bastille, siege of, 30, 58, 84, 107, 110, 131, 145
Belgian Revolution of 1830, 13, 72, 130, 149, 168
Birmingham, 150-2, 156, 171, 194
Bonaparte, Louis-Napoleon III, 47-8, 147, 237
Bonaparte, Napoleon I, 80-3, 90, 133, 147
bourgeoisie, 18-23, 31-4, 76-8, 85, 93, 100, 109, 125, 130, 139-40, 144, 201, 207, 211, 214-15
"bourgeois revolution", 33-4, 51, 76-8, 80, 95, 100-1, 103-4, 109, 139
Briggs, Asa, 60, 62-3
Brinton, Crane, 61, 72-5
Bristol, 174-6, 178-80
British Marxist Historians, 1, 3-4, 23-4, 35-6, 51-4
   see also Dobb, Maurice; Hill, Christopher; Hobsbawm, Eric; Morton, A.L.; Thompson, Dorothy; Thompson, E.P.
Burke, Edmund, 6, 57, 80-1, 107, 115

Canada, Canadians, 5, 15-16, 199, 202-3
"Captain Swing", 1, 11-16, 54, 69-70, 168-70, *183-8*
Carlyle, Thomas, 84, 117
Catholicism, Catholics, 22-3, 25, 209
Chartists, 11, 15, 64, 148-9, 157-61
Chevalier, Louis, 222-38

Christianity *see* Catholicism,
    Catholics; Protestantism,
    Protestants; religion
Church *see* Catholicism, Catholics;
    Methodism, Methodists;
    Protestantism, Protestants;
    religion
class and class struggle, 4, 9, 12-14,
    17, 20, 24-6, 30-5, 53, 56,
    148-61, 215, 261-4
  class consciousness, 24-6, 53,
    189-217
Cobb, Richard, 4-5, 59-60, 66-8, 141
Cobban, Alfred, 35, 57, 60, 103, 127
Cobbett, William, 151-3, 173-5,
    178-9
"common people", 1, 3-4, 8-27, 32,
    50-4, 75-7, 139, 148-61, 198,
    200-2
  see also peasants; *sans-culottes*
Comninel, George, 33-5
conservative and conservative
    historians, 2, 6, 9-10, 15, 18,
    20, 28-9, 80-104, 115-22
Countryman, Edward, 200
crime, criminals, 6-7, 9-18, 83,
    221-41, *242-65*
  "protest crimes", 16-17, 261-3
Croker, John Wilson, 118
crowd, crowds ("mobs"), 2, *5-14*,
    17-27, *57-71*, 107-13, 150-61,
    168-80, 221-2
  see also riots

Danton, Georges Jacques, 82, 88-9,
    92, 94, 117-18
democracy, democrats, 80, 82,
    84-104, *135-47*, 199, 211
  see also Parliament (British)/
    parliamentary suffrage
Dobb, Maurice, 51

Engels, Friedrich, 24, 28, 30, *43-50*,
    54, 57, 93, 144, 148, 204
England, English, 1-7, 10-17, 21-2,
    26-7, 32, 34, 43-5, 51-4, 61-4,
    148-88, 190-5

English Revolution, 21, 27, 51-2,
    72-3, 136-7, 201
Europe, Europeans, 1, 6, 27-8, 30,
    48-9, 189-95

feudalism, 45, 85-6, *124-34*, 140
  see also "transition from
    feudalism to capitalism"
France, 1, 3-11, 18-20, 26-7, 30-4,
    46-8, 50-1, 57-61, *80-147*, 157,
    190-5, 200-2, *205-16*
freemasons, 89
French Revolution of 1789, 1, 3-11,
    18-20, 26-7, 30-4, 50-1, 57-61,
    73-9, *80-147*, 189, 194, 200-3,
    205-16, 228
French Revolution of 1830, 13, 27,
    54, 73-4, 146-7, 149, 158, 168,
    203, 233-5
French Revolution of 1848, 27,
    46-7, 83-4, 86-7, 135, 147,
    203-4, 235-7
Furet, F., 103

George, Dorothy, 7, 221, 224-5
Germany, 45, 72
Gordon Riots, 5, 7, 22, 61-2, 193,
    211, 225
Gramsci, Antonio, 23-5, 36
"Great Fear", 18, 50-1, 59, 98, 112
Guérin, Daniel, 100-1, 103-4,
    195, 209

Hammond, John and Barbara, 13,
    150
Hapsburg Empire, 190
Hegel, G.W.F., 50
Hill, Christopher, x, 3, 51-2, 54, 77,
    136
Hilton, Rodney, 3
history, historians, historiography,
    1-123
history from below, history from the
    bottom up, *1-36*, *50-4*, *57-71*,
    92, 96-100, 107-13
Hobsbawm, Eric, x, 1, 3-4, 12-16,
    23, 31, 52-4, 60-1, 63, 66, 69,

193-4

ideology, ideologies, 2, 10, *17-27*, 50, 54, 56-7, 71, 77, *193-5*, *197-217*
industry and Industrial Revolution, 11, 13, 27, 29, 34-5, 43-4, 53, 149, 167-8
intellectuals, 20, *23-6*
Ireland, Irish, 149, 150, 158-60, 169

Jacobins, Jacobinism, 7, 31, 82-104, 115-22, 135-47, 202, 212-15
Jaurès, Jean, 92-6, 212-13, 215

Kaplow, Jeffrey, 206-7, 211
Kiernan, V.G., 3
Krantz, Fred, x, 13-15

labour and trades unions, 15, 20, 53-4, 150-2, 159-60, 170-2
Labrousse, C.-E., 19, 75, 95-6, 190
landlords (English), 149-50, 184-8
Latin America, 27, 50, 53
law and justice, 15-17, 54, 61-2, 170, 186-8, 242ff.
Lefebvre, Georges, 3-4, 18, 30-1, 34, 50-5, 57-61, 94, 96-104, *106-13*, 137, 214
Le Bon, Gustave, 65, 111
Lemisch, Jesse, 200
Lenin, V.I., 3, 10, 20, 24, 56, 75, 103, 158
liberals and liberal historians, 6, 15, 29, 33, *80-104*, 115-22, 136, 138, 157
literacy, 201-2
London, 1, 3, 5-11, 17-22, 32-3, 36, 46, 57, 59, 62-3, 151-2, 158-60, 174-5, 192-5, 211, 221-6, *242-65*
"lower orders" *see* "common people"
Luddites (machine-breakers), 14-15, 53-4, 64, 150-1, 160, 171-3, 188
    see also "Captain Swing"

Lukács, George, 23-4, 197
Luther, Martin, 45, 77, 144, 199
Lyons, 212-14

Manchester, 43, 68, 151-2, 171-2
Mandrou, Robert, 205
Marx, Karl, 3, 4, 24, 28, 30, 33, *43-50*, 56-7, 70, 92-3, 100, 135, 197-8, 204
Marxism and historical materialism, 4, 23-5, 28-30, *32-5*, *43-54*, 56, 59, 92, 100, 103-4, 198
Mathiez, Albert, 57, 94-104, 108
"menu peuple" see "common people"; *sans-culottes*
Methodism, Methodists, 156-8
Michelet, Jules, 6, 57, 83-4, 86-8, 91-104, 107-9, 117
middle classes, 17-22, 32, 63, 80, 91, 157-61, 174-80, 199-201, 211
    see also bourgeoisie, Third Estate
monarch, monarchy (French), 78, 80-106, 125-7, 133, 137, 144, 214
Moore, Barrington, Jr., 8, 99, 141, 147
Morton, A.L., 51-2, 63-4
motivation (of crowds), 2, 7, 10, 16-23, 61, 64, 70-1, 77-8, 109
Münzer, Thomas, 45

Napoleonic Wars, 28, 138, 167, 183
    see also, Bonaparte, Napoleon I
Norway, 2, 191

Paine, Tom, 193, 212
Palmer, R.R., 102-3, 139, 199
Paris, 3, 5-7, 9-10, 17-21, 46-9, 57-61, 78, 96, *107-13*, 140-7, 192-5, 202, 206-12, 214-15, *221-41*
    Paris Commune (1871), 46, 48-9, 86, 147, 203-4
parlements (French), 77-8, 83, 128, 133, 144, 207, 209-12, 214
Parliament (British), 8, 148-61, 170, 173-80, 184, 186

parliamentary suffrage, 148-61
peasants, 10, 18, 26, 45, 47-8, 50-1,
    59, 76-8, 85, 97-8, 103, 109,
    112, 124-34, 140, 147, 189-92,
    208
    Peasant War (Germany), 45, 49,
        199
    see also "Great Fear"
philosophes, 77-8, 83, 85, 88, 144,
    194, 201
property, 127-33, 136
Protestantism, Protestants (incl.
    Puritanism, 45, 51-4, 156-7
    see also Methodism, Methodists
Pugachev Rebellion, 189-90

Radicals (English), 149-56, 170-80,
    184, 193
Reform movement, 148-61, 173-80,
    184
religion, 45, 50-4, 99, 156-7, 194,
    198, 209
    see also Catholicism, Catholics;
        Protestantism, Protestants
        revolution, 48-9, *72-9,*
        80-104, 148-63
    see also American Revolution;
        Belgian Revolution;
        "bourgeois revolution";
        English Revolution; French
        Revolution; Paris
        Commune; Russian
        Revolution
rights and liberties, 13, 20-2, 31,
    77, 88, 125-6, 132, *135-47,*
    194, 198-9, 201-2, 204
    see also democracy, democrats;
        Parliament (British)/
        parliamentary suffrage
riots, 5, 7-14, 17-21, 26, 58-9, 67,
    110, 142, 150-3, 168-73,
    176-80, 183-8, 192-5, 198,
    200, 228
    enclosure riots, 191
    food riots, 9, 21, 59, 110, 142,
        190, 192, 194-5, 207-8, 210
    see also crowd, crowds

Robespierre, Maximilien, 30-1, 57,
    80, 91-2, 94, 101, 115-22, 138,
    146
Rousseau, Jean Jacques, 144, 201
    see also philosophes
Russia (pre-1917), 189-90
Russian Revolution (Bolshevik),
    73-6, 92, 101, 143

sans-culottes, 5, 9, 11, 19-21, 27, 31,
    51, 57-61, 77, 80-5, 91-3,
    96-100, *107-13, 138-47,* 194,
    201-3, *205-16*
Saville, John, 3
Smelser, N.J., 23, 73-4
Soboul, Albert, 4-5, 30, 34, 51,
    59-60, 77, 98-100, 103-4
socialism, socialists, 9, 24-5, 29, 36,
    49, 92, 138, 151, 157, 198,
    204
sociology and social science, 23, 29,
    58, 65-9, 73-9, 111
Stretton, Hugh, x, 28
strikes, 167-73, 191-2, 208

Taine, Hippolyte, 6, 9, 17-18, 86-9,
    91, 93, 107, 110-11, 127
Third Estate, 93ff., 130, 139-40,
    144, 202, 213-15
    see also bourgeoisie; middle
        classes; *sans-culottes*
Thompson, Dorothy, x, 3
Thompson, E.P., 3, 15-16, 23, 26,
    35, 52-4, 65, 171
Thompson, J.M., 121-2
Tilly, Charles, 12, 65, *73-9,* 222,
    224, 236-8
tithes, 185-6, 203
Tocqueville, Alexis de, 28, 84-5,
    88, 93-104
"transition from feudalism to
    capitalism", 3-4, 12, 27, 34-5,
    51, 100, 103
transportation (mode of
    punishment), 15-16, 70, 187,
    242ff.

urbanization and cities, 43-4,
    107-13, 189, *221-64*

Vovelle, Michel, 205-6

Wellington, Duke of, 152-5, 160,
    175, 177, 186
Wilkes, John and "Wilkes and
    Liberty", 1, 6, 11, 19-23,

62-4, 151, 211, 225-6
working-class (proletariat), 9, 25,
    43-4, 49, 53, 58, 149-61,
    171-3, 195, 204
    see also "common people";
    sans-culottes

Young, Alfred, 200, 211